Steven Gaines has  h Boys over the las p columnist of the *N* is news-breaking jou r- tainment articles h s, including *New Yo* or which he was American correspondent), and *Playgirl*. His other books include *The Love You Make: An Insider's Story of the Beatles* (with Peter Brown), *Marjoe*, the biography of evangelist Marjoe Gortner, *Me, Alice*, the biography of rock star Alice Cooper, and the novels *Discotheque*, *Another Runner in the Night* and the best-selling *The Club*. He lives in Greenwich Village, New York.

By the same author

The Love You Make: An Insider's Story of the Beatles
  (with Peter Brown)
Marjoe
Me, Alice

Fiction

Discotheque
Another Runner in the Night
The Club

STEVEN GAINES

Heroes and Villains

The True Story of the Beach Boys

GRAFTON BOOKS

A Division of the Collins Publishing Group

LONDON GLASGOW
TORONTO SYDNEY AUCKLAND

Grafton Books
A Division of the Collins Publishing Group
8 Grafton Street, London W1X 3LA

Published by Grafton Books 1988

First published in Great Britain by
Macmillan London Ltd 1986

ISBN 0-586-07464-3

Acknowledgements
'California Girls.' Lyrics and music by Brian Wilson, © 1965 & 1970, Irving
Music, Inc. (BMI). All rights reserved. International copyright secured.

'Fun, Fun, Fun.' Lyrics and music by Brian Wilson and Mike Love, © 1964,
Irving Music, Inc. (BMI). All rights reserved. International copyright
secured.

'God Only Knows.' Lyrics by Brian Wilson and Tony Asher, music by Brian
Wilson, © 1966, Irving Music, Inc. (BMI). All rights reserved. International
copyright secured.

'Heroes and Villains.' Lyrics and music by Brian Wilson and Van Dyke
Parks, © 1967, Irving Music, Inc. (BMI). All rights reserved. International
copyright secured.

'I Get Around.' Lyrics and music by Brian Wilson, © 1964, Irving Music,
Inc. (BMI). All rights reserved. International copyright secured.

'In My Room.' Lyrics and music by Brian Wilson and Gary Usher, © 1964,
Irving Music, Inc. (BMI). All rights reserved. International copyright
secured.

'Surfin' USA.' Copyright © 1958 and 1963 by ARC MUSIC
CORPORATION. Reprinted by permission. All rights reserved.

Printed and bound in Great Britain by
Collins, Glasgow

Set in Times

For Mom and Dad

Introduction

I was with Brian Wilson the first time he surfed.

It was Father's Day, June 20, 1976, a glorious summer Sunday on Trancas Beach, Malibu, half a mile from the Wilson clan's rented summer home. Standing by the edge of the ocean, Brian Wilson was a wondrous vision. Six feet three inches tall, weighing an imposing 240 pounds, he was dressed in a soft forest-green terry-cloth robe that flapped about his bare legs in the brisk June winds. His almost perfectly round belly – like a soft pink volleyball – swelled out from under the robe and was exposed to the chill late afternoon air. The wind blew his black hair away from a bearded, handsome, cherubic face. There was something mystical and childlike about him; he radiated an aura, a magnetic presence that drew people to him. He turned and looked out to the ocean, and the distance in his eyes made the expanse of the Pacific seem small.

But those eyes. Those cold blue eyes were terrified. Brian Wilson was somewhere else, struggling hard to be in touch with what was happening on the beach, but from the other side of a psychic glass wall. Brian Wilson is schizophrenic. As the producer–composer of the Beach Boys, Brian, along with his brothers Dennis and Carl Wilson, cousin Mike Love, and friend Al Jardine, had proselytized the legendary California good life around the world for fifteen years, but for twelve of those years Brian had been on a reclusive psychological odyssey.

That Sunday in June was not only Father's Day, it was also Brian's thirty-fourth birthday and an unofficial celebration of his rebirth. Only eight months before, with the aid of Los Angeles therapist Eugene Landy, Brian had gotten out of bed in his $500,000 Bel Air home for the first time in four years and begun a daily routine of jogging, athletics, and sporadic trips to the recording studio.

Brian was on the beach that day, along with a few family members and his therapist, to film a segment of an upcoming NBC-TV special on the Beach Boys, 'The Beach Boys: It's OK.' The show was part of the general excitement about Brian's recent steps back to reality. Produced by 'Saturday Night Live' producer Lorne Michaels, the special was a celebration of Brian's rebirth. I was invited to the beach that day as a journalist writing a story about Brian for *New West* magazine.

To photograph Brian Wilson surfing was Lorne Michael's *ne plus ultra* irony: Brian Wilson had never surfed. Although the Beach Boys had sold an estimated eighty million records – twenty million of them with surfing as a major theme – and Brian had splashed around in the water with his brothers for publicity photos, he had never mounted a surfboard before. Indeed, photographing Brian in the surf was almost a cruel joke, because Brian had a deep, abiding fear of the water, and in his childlike manner he would warble in a thin voice, 'The ocean *scares* me!' Nevertheless, that day Brian would face the Pacific.

The segment of the show opened with Brian lying in the bed to which he had retreated for so many years, a four-poster adorned with a headboard of carved angels. He was a huge, whale-shaped figure under the blankets, with only his large bearded face visible, and those small, scared eyes blinking expectantly. Into the room, dressed in policemen's uniforms, strode two 'Saturday Night Live' regulars, John Belushi and Dan Aykroyd. Belushi and Aykroyd presented Brian with a warrant for his arrest, charging him with never having surfed. They marched him down the curving staircase of the house, and brought him to the beach in a patrol car with a surfboard attached to the roof.

Now, with the cameras trained upon a terrified and wooden-looking Brian, the surfboard tucked under his arm, Belushi ordered, 'Let's go, Wilson, here's your wave.'

With his bathrobe still wrapped around him, Brian bolted into the water, the waves crashing around his corpulent body. For a fraction of a second he mounted the board on his huge belly, but the ocean quickly pulled him under, baptizing him. 'I felt the power of the sea,' he later told me. 'It was cold and I felt the sea begin to grasp me.' His wet terry robe clung to him as he regained his balance. With a stunned and questioning look, he turned toward the cameras, hoping his ordeal was over. But the people on the beach only laughed and cheered and shook hands, paying no attention to Brian at all, and the cameras rolled on. So Brian, ever the trouper, turned bravely back into the surf, his robe falling away from him as he played farther into the icy water after his drifting surfboard. When he finally emerged from the water, his wife, Marilyn, shielded him from ungracious photographers as she toweled and dried her shivering husband.

From that day on, my fascination with Brian Wilson and the Beach Boys grew to a passion. That summer I made three trips to California and spent nearly a month following the Beach Boys around, interviewing all of them at some length, including Dennis Wilson, Carl Wilson, Alan Jardine, and Mike Love. Mike Love not only consented to an interview, but even invited me to his apartment in Marine Del Rey for a lecture and meditation session. I also interviewed Beach Boys' mother Audree Wilson, and was invited into Brian's home by his wife,

Marilyn Wilson, for a long and candid interview.

During those same weeks I spent several days and evenings with Brian's therapist, Dr Eugene Landy, in direct interview. Dr Landy invited me and my tape recorder to remain with him in his office during a therapy session with Brian Wilson. Thanks to Dr Landy, I was also allowed to interview Brian extensively and observe him in his private life, which included going bowling with him at Pico Lanes, jogging in Rancho Park, and attending with him various public events for the taping of the NBC-TV shows. The time I spent alone with Brian was the most exciting and valuable of all, and I am deeply grateful for this personal access. Brian is rawly honest and revealing, a child-man, terribly vulnerable to journalists and strangers, alternately frightened and eager to please. At the beginning of our first interview, he stopped after just two sentences. 'I don't know why,' he told me. 'I'm just thinking of ending the interview here and letting you write the story.' But he didn't stop there. He stayed for that interview and several more, all of which are included in this book.

Although in the preparation of *Heroes and Villains* I have depended heavily on those initial interviews and tapes with Brian Wilson and the Beach Boys and their families, over a hundred new interviews were conducted exclusively for this book. To my great regret, several sources with firsthand knowledge of the Beach Boys' personal and business lives refused to be identified, and would only agree to be interviewed anonymously. To these people I am indebted for their insight and for their massive contributions to this text. However, for this reason I must also caution the reader that a character's inclusion or exclusion in a scene or event does not necessarily indicate that that person has contributed to this book.

Fortunately, I am able to thank Brian Wilson's wife for nearly sixteen years, Marilyn Rovell Wilson, for her time and trust in me and her tremendous help with this book, which included many hours of interviews, as well as her endorsement of me to other participants. My thanks also to her sister, Diane Rovell, who worked and lived with the Beach Boys at Marilyn's side, as well as to their mother and father, May and Irving Rovell. Their exhaustive interviews and kindnesses – including May's delicious chicken soup – are greatly appreciated.

I am especially grateful to Karen Lamm, for sharing her life with Dennis Wilson in over twenty-five hours of interviews, including access to personal diaries she scrupulously kept over the last fifteen years; Carol Bloome, Dennis Wilson's first wife, for her long and candid interview; Barbara Charren Wilson, Dennis's second wife, for her exclusive interview and trust in me during the preparation of this book; Chris Kable, Dennis Wilson's personal assistant and dear friend, whose outspoken support has sustained me through many troubled times; Annie Hinsche Wilson, Carl Wilson's former wife of fourteen years, for her interview; Jerry Schilling, Carl's personal manager, for his interview; and Robert L. Levine, Dennis Wilson's personal and business manager, whose insights and information greatly enhanced the preparation of this book.

Rick Nelson, Brian Wilson's personal business manager, was instrumental in my gathering substantial information for this book, as was Janet Lent-Coóp Nelson, former president of Brother Enterprises and Brian Wilson's co-business manager.

Stanley Love, brother of Mike and Stephen Love, also helped to inform this book substantially, as did his grandmother, Edith Clardy Love, and his father, Milton Love.

I am indebted to Eva Easton and David Leaf, for their

support and kindness, and for putting up with my early morning phone calls. Without their help, and David's 1978 book on the Beach Boys, this book would have been a greater struggle. And to Peter Reum, whose Beach Boys archive is the finest in existence, and who supplied many of the exclusive photographs used in this book.

I would also like to thank, for their varied assistance and/or interviews, many patient people, some of whom indulged me with two and three interviews, including Fred Vail, Van Dyke Parks, David Anderle, Gary Usher, Eddie Merado, David Marks, Nik Venet, Rich Sloane, Chuck Kaye, Tom Murphy, Curt Boetcher, Bob Merlis, Chris Clark, Steve Goldberg, Michael Moss, Coleen McGovern, Bill Oster, Bruce Morgan, Dorinda Morgan, Joel Moss, Carol Thompson, Joe Saraceno, Bud Cort, Ida Smith Kennedy, Bob Kennedy, Catherine Pace, Stephen Kalenich, Fred Morgan, Ben Edmonds, Gil Lindner, Maggie Montalbano, Michelle Meyers, Joanne Marks, Diane 'Croxey' Adams, Rick Henn, Jeff Bolonski, George Hormel, Jr, Alice Fiondella, Mike Klenfner, Tony Martell, David Oppenheim, Chip Rachlin, Gail Buchalter, Andy Goldmark, Brenda Lewis, Michael Vosse, John Hanlon, Connie Pappas Hillman, David Elliot, Stephen W. Despar, Tony Asher, Nick Grillo, Stanley Shapiro, John Vincent, Gregg Jakobson, Ginger Blake Schackney, Tandyn Almer, James Reiley, Rene Pappas, Christine McVie, Richard Duryea, Rusty Ford, Peter Marshall, Keith Devoe, Brad Elliot, Steven Korthof, Charles Wilson, Jeanne Wilson Torbet, Rocky Pamplin, and Nancy Rosenthal.

My thanks to my attorney and friend, David Hollander, and to Bruce Roberts and his family, who gave me shelter and comfort during my long sojourns in Los Angeles, as did E. J. Oshins and Stephen Poe. My gratitude also to Bernie Berkowitz.

Finally, I would like to thank my agent, John Hawkins; my editor, Michaela Hamilton, for her encouragement and guidance; my wonderful publisher, Elaine Koster, for her faith in me; and Joseph Olshan, who put up with this all over again.

Steven Gaines
Wainscott, New York
1986

One

1

It was a surfer's dream. It was just after dawn on Santa
Monica Beach, December 4, 1983, a magnificent clear
and cool winter Sunday morning, the kind of day when
the Pacific is cold but the surf is up and the waves sweep
to the beach in perfect breakers and no intrepid surfer
can see the ocean without a sigh. But on this day Dennis
Wilson, a surfer since he was ten years old, hardly noticed
the Pacific at all.

It was the morning of Dennis Wilson's thirty-ninth
birthday. Dressed in green army pants, T-shirt, and flimsy
jacket, he had just sleepily hitchhiked his way from a
friend's house to the Santa Monica Bay Inn, a beachfront
motel. Here his estranged nineteen-year-old wife, Shawn
Love Wilson, lived with their fifteen-month-old son,
Gage, in a $125-a-week kitchenette. Dennis intended to
pay them a surprise visit, but it was he who was in for the
surprise; he was about to find his wife asleep in bed – fully
clothed – with two men.

The Bay Inn, as it is called, is a large three-story motel
with a hundred units. Facing the beach, with a breathtaking view of the Pacific, it boasts a raised swimming-pool
area fenced against the ocean winds by clear fiberglass.
Located just two blocks south of the carny-like Santa
Monica Pier, and not far north of the drug-ridden, artists'
beach community of Venice, the Bay Inn, with its reasonable rates, drew a transient crowd of young residents,
attracted as much to the area's drug activities as to the

15

year-round beauty of Santa Monica Beach. The strip of motels and hotels, from the Sheraton on Wilshire Boulevard all the way south to Pico, was part of what the local hotel people called the Ho Chi Minh Trail, which ran all the way from Florida, fed by Interstate 10. If you were poor or drunk or drugged and hitchhiking across America looking for the Pacific, Ocean Boulevard in Santa Monica is where you'd come out.

It was not exactly where you would expect to find Dennis Wilson, a man known for his expensive taste and style, his Rodeo Drive wardrobes, his Ferraris and Rolls-Royces and his six-figure income. The drummer and middle brother of the Beach Boys, Dennis Wilson had for two decades been the personification of American virility and derring-do. It was Dennis who embodied the spirit of the Beach Boys to tens of millions of teenagers around the world; he was the epitome of the surfer playboy.

Over the years he had, much to his own pleasure, developed a reputation as one of California's most notorious symbols of wanton lust and overindulgence, the rock-and-roll James Dean of a generation raised on free love and fast cars. Mischievous and fun-loving, he was the group's sex symbol. A ruggedly good-looking man, he had been muscular and tanned year-round from surfing and working on his boat. His thick, brown, sun-crested hair, parted down the middle, framed a strong, bearded face. His blue eyes twinkled coyly, and his quick smile was not so much crooked as it was a devilish sneer. Men felt instant comradeship with him; women found him irresistible.

Dennis's ineluctable appeal had its spoils. From the time he was twelve years old, he bragged, girls were lining up to sleep with him, and he turned down not a single one. Indeed, Dennis was as addicted to women as he was

16

to his other vices. He was obsessed with sex. Getting laid was a major preoccupation with him. He called himself 'The Wood,' because he was always hard and ready. Although he had been married five times previously and was father to five children, throughout all his marriages he had countless affairs – daily – including one with Patti Reagan, the president's daughter. He had recently ended a turbulent, three-year liaison with Christine McVie, the singer–composer of the English rock band Fleetwood Mac. His best-known – and most publicized – marriage was to the beautiful blonde actress Karen Lamm, whom he married not once, but twice. It was a marriage straight out of the pages of *People* magazine. Together they were the perfect gleaming vision of a California couple, young, rich, and famous, whizzing down the coast highway in one of their matching Ferrari convertibles.

But if Dennis was every teenage Walter Mitty's fantasy of the California playboy surfer, the Dennis Wilson who hitchhiked to his beloved beach on his thirty-ninth birthday was not the same young stud revered around the world as the essence of the California myth. He could have easily been mistaken for a man a decade older. Instead of the muscled and tanned athlete familiar to his fans, he was pudgy and overweight, bloated with edema from drink and drugs. What had once been the brine and vigor of sailing and the outdoors was now the gray of heroin and cocaine. His bearded face was lined, his eyes puffy and bloodshot. He spoke in a roaring, rasping voice, worsened by several operations to remove polyps from his vocal cords and the consumption of at least two packs of Lark or unfiltered Camel cigarettes a day. Over the years, in various alcoholic accidents, he had cut or broken almost every appendage of his body, and everything ached. And if you looked carefully, in his eyes you could

17

see a deeper damage than that self-inflicted by drugs or booze. Dennis was being *eaten away*.

His recent marriage to Shawn Love had only worsened his problems. Shawn was a round-faced, doe-eyed, blonde teenager with a shag haircut and a pug nose. In a Byzantine twist, Shawn was the illegitimate daughter of Dennis's first cousin, the Beach Boys' Mike Love. She had been conceived in a one-night liaison with then secretary Shannon Harris and subsequently born out of wedlock. Her mother had sued Mike Love for paternity in Santa Monica Superior Court two decades ago. Shawn reportedly won an award of $300 a year in child support and the right to use the name Love when she turned eighteen. Her father shunned her for most of her life, and she and her mother appear to remain very bitter toward him.

To make this volatile situation even more explosive, Dennis Wilson and Mike Love despised each other. Since they were children, there had been a hostile and open rivalry between Mike and Dennis that even led to public fisticuffs. Eventually, a mutual restraining order was obtained in court to keep them apart. Mike, it was said, resented Dennis's image as the group's sex symbol; he considered Dennis a child, overindulged and uncontrollable, yet adored by all the Beach Boys fans and always forgiven by an indulgent family. Mike, by contrast, was a hardworking, competitive man, a devout vegetarian and Transcendental Meditator who never drank or smoked. Dennis, naughty child that he was, goaded and provoked Mike at every turn. Once, on the Beach Boys' private plane, Dennis raced over to a small compartment where Mike was meditating, ripped open the curtain, and vomited in front of him. On another occasion, onstage at the Greek Theater in Los Angeles, Dennis flicked off

18

Mike's omnipresent cap to uncover his balding pate in full view of the audience. Dennis also enjoyed taking various young women into the meditation room in the Beach Boys' privately owned recording studios and making love to them on the floor. Later, when Mike arrived to meditate, the room was often fragrant with spent passions.

Indeed, for Dennis to have married Mike's illegimate daughter could be seen as nothing but the most bitter spite work. Yet few would deny that Dennis sincerely fell in love with and felt sorry for Shawn. She was only fifteen when she first started living with him in a small house on Wavecrest Avenue in Venice Beach. Dennis swore at first that the relationship was not sexual – that he was just helping straighten out a mixed-up kid by putting her up in a room in his large house – but soon they were sleeping together, and not long after she was pregnant. Dennis called two female friends to ask where Shawn could have an abortion, but reportedly she refused, and Gage was born on September 3, 1982. Dennis married her nearly a year later, on July 28, 1983.

From the start it was obvious that Dennis and Shawn had come from two different worlds and would have a hard time getting along. Shawn was used to scraping along with very little money, and she guarded every penny. Dennis, on the other hand, was famous for his prodigious spending. When she tried to instill her frugality in him, violent arguments ensued. One of the couple's close friends described the marriage as 'one big fight.' Screaming and punching matches were not unusual. The past November, one argument culminated with Shawn driving her silver BMW automobile right into the front door of their rented Trancas Beach house. On the wall of the house, scrawled in crayon, were the phrases 'No love' and 'No respect.' Dennis would often call his friends or

19

manager and complain, 'What am I doing with her? She's such a kid.' They had filed for divorce in November, not even four months married.

During the short time they were officially husband and wife, Dennis continued to see other women on the sly, but he remained sexually faithful to Shawn, as he saw it, by only allowing himself to get blow jobs, and thus avoiding the possibility of contracting a venereal disease. Such loosely defined fidelity did not work both ways in Dennis's chauvinistic rule book. The thought of Shawn with another man was something his fragile ego could little deal with, and of late Shawn had been friendly with a young man in his early twenties named Brant,[1] of whom Dennis highly disapproved and was violently jealous. Yet through all the torment of the relationship, and even with their divorce impending, Dennis could not bring himself to stay away from her. Their infant son, Gage, kept him coming back over and over again. Dennis loved and adored this towheaded, precocious little tot, whom he had come to visit that early December morning at the Santa Monica Bay Inn.

As he made his way up to room 353 of the motel's north wing, Dennis did not stop at the front office to phone ahead, because the management had already thrown him off the premises on several occasions; and anyway, most of the time when he called the room, Shawn wouldn't take his calls, and then he was left arguing with the operator. Already the switchboard had logged dozens of pleading phone calls to Shawn, which she had refused to answer. Yet Dennis needed to see Gage with an uncontrollable passion. Gage seemed the only constant in his life, the only living thing he could hold on to. Of course, Gage could hardly talk; but with him there was

[1] Not his real name.

20

no hurt, just simple, uncomplicated love. In a way very few people understood, Dennis needed the baby more than anyone in the world needed him.

Dennis would replay over and over again for friends the scene that greeted him that morning in Shawn's room. According to Dennis, when he entered the room, he found Shawn asleep on the bed with two young men – one of them her steady boyfriend, the other a relative stranger to Dennis. All three were fully clothed, and it appeared they had innocently fallen asleep together. Shawn's boyfriend, Dennis claimed, was a 'heavy' drug user, and Dennis had complained many times to friends and business associates that Shawn was involved in the use of hard drugs. Gage, with his golden-white hair and angel's face, an active and inquisitive infant, was wandering around the room unattended.

'*What the fuck is going on here*?' Dennis rasped, rousing the threesome from sleep. When he screamed with his hoarse throat, it was like a great lion's roar. '*What are you, fucking crazy*?' he shouted to Shawn.

Before the occupants of the bed could compose an explanation, Dennis went berserk, and began ripping apart the motel room. He turned over furniture and punched holes in the door and walls. While all four screamed at the top of their lungs – Shawn with an incessant chorus of 'Get out! Get out!' – a tug-of-war ensued over Gage. Dennis reportedly threatened to have Gage legally taken away from Shawn because she was consorting with drug users. The frightened child shrieked hysterically while Dennis threatened to call the police and have them all arrested for possession of narcotics. Then Dennis suddenly snatched Gage away from Shawn and raced out of the room with him.

With the child howling and squirming in his arms,

Dennis flew down the three flights of steps, past the pool area, and out of the motel onto Ocean Park Avenue. Darting in and out of traffic, he ran pell-mell across the broad palm-lined boulevard, and took shelter in a cool, dark bar called Chez Jay's. Located almost directly across the street from the Bay Inn, at 1657 Ocean Park Avenue, Chez Jay's was one of Dennis's favourite hangouts. A small and quiet bar, its interior was lighted mainly by multicolored Christmas lights strung along the ceiling down the center of the room. The owners and employees all knew and liked Dennis, and Alice Fiondella, Jay's mother, who owned a small hotel next door, was there that morning with the clean-up crew when he came in. Dennis, who was frantic and near tears, told Alice he needed a taxi to take Gage to a friend's house. Alice called one for him while he tried to calm Gage. After a while he laid the infant down on a maroon Naugahyde banquette beneath a red-and-white-checkered tablecloth. It was cool in the dark bar. Dennis took off his jacket and wrapped it around his tiny son, who shortly fell asleep.

While Dennis waited for a taxi, he sat in the booth next to Gage and nursed his vodka and orange juice, which he often carried with him in a pint bottle. Ironically, this morning's events were no special trial for him. In fact, they seemed like just another thread in the incredible tapestry of his life. As he sat at the table, the past few months fell heavily on him, and he began to weep.

2

Since early November, when his household possessions were cleared out of a rented beach house in Trancas and put into storage, Dennis had had no real place to live, no special place to stay, and probably not more than ten dollars in his pocket at any one time, if that. It was impossible for him to have any money because he had virtually no control over his spending. He was nearly half a million dollars in debt, and the stories of his squandering were legion. Each friend had a favorite: Dennis orders a Rolls-Royce over the telephone and destroys it in a drunken traffic accident the same night; Dennis picks up the $600 restaurant tab of five virtual strangers; Dennis allows anyone who takes his fancy to move in with him, rent and telephone free – including, at one point, the entire Charles Manson family; Dennis pours a bottle of honey all over a table in a restaurant and then tips the waiter $100 to clean it up. 'If he had a thousand dollars in his pocket,' one of his ex-wives said, 'he'd spend it.' There was no way to impress Dennis with the stupidity of his largesse, even as he teetered on the edge of bankruptcy. He had borrowed so much money from his mother that even she was turning him down. 'It's hard to imagine,' Stephen Love, Dennis's cousin and one-time Beach Boys manager, told a reporter, 'that anyone could just blow so much money, but Dennis did. He was totally unrestrained and undisciplined; he was foolishly, self-destructively generous.'

His personal and business manager, Bob Levine, who had handled his finances since 1978, tried his best to rein Dennis in, but it was like trying to tame a bucking bronco.

Levine, along with others, had begged him to stop spending and drinking, promising to guide him back to financial solvency if only he cleaned up his act. Levine diligently set up an extensive fiscal plan for Dennis, with a timetable and an arrangement for him to pay off his enormous debt, which included two years of back taxes and interest, numerous personal loans, unpaid insurance policies, and various child-support payments. But it was no use. Every time Dennis promised to control himself, the promise would be broken an hour later.

By that autumn, 1983, his drinking problem was threatening his health. He had tremors from the moment he woke up, and recently, in Malibu, where he had a charge at the local supermarket, he had had to go out into the parking lot and drink two cans of beer before he could stop shaking enough to sign his name to the charge slip. He had had dozens of alcoholic accidents, including one in which he dropped a glass bottle of Sparklett's water that sliced open his foot so deeply the tendons had to be sewn together; subsequently, all his toes moved in tandem. Dennis's driver's license had long since been revoked. All his friends assumed he had stopped driving because of his constant drunkenness, and Dennis let them think it; but the real cause was the alcoholic seizures and blackouts he had begun to suffer over the past year. That summer, while driving on Malibu Coast Highway with Gage in the car, he had blacked out, wrecking the car and nearly killing his son. After that, he swore never to drive again. But even the seizures and near-fatal accidents didn't seem to slow him down.

There was something so eminently likable about Dennis that it was hard to be angry with him for long; he was a puppy who would not listen. But by now, the rest of the Beach Boys were exasperated with his behavior. Since

24

they were a family unit first and a band second, they were especially close. As Dennis once put it in his inimitable way, 'We've done everything together. Shit, eat, fart, cry, laugh. Everything.' But as much as they cared for him, he was twice as incorrigible, and there was growing concern he would drag the band down with him into scandal. The situation had come to a head in front of a sold-out crowd at the Universal Amphitheater in June 1979, when Dennis mumbled something into the microphone about 'cocaine and Quaaludes.' In a backstage squabble with Mike Love about the comment, Dennis was kicked in the balls. When the group returned to the stage, Dennis lost his temper, knocked his drums off the risers, and leaped across the stage at Mike Love in full view of the audience. He was officially thrown out of the group – fired by telegram until he 'obtain[ed] medical attention for [his] present condition' – to which Dennis replied that no one could stop him from showing up. He arrived uninvited at a concert in San Diego, and the security guards held him outside as he forlornly watched the Beach Boys drive into the stadium in a long caravan of limousines. Dennis eventually talked his way inside, but he was barred from going up on the stage.

When he was reinstated as a member of the touring group in the summer of 1981, the official dictum was that Dennis absolutely could not appear drunk onstage. To help him as least be sober for the shows, a team of bodyguard–baby-sitters was hired to keep him from hitting the bottle for at least two hours before the show, at a reported cost of $600 a day. 'They were there to lock him in his room,' said Levine, 'beat him up if they had to, and physically restrain him.' But Dennis always found a way to sneak the booze, usually aided by one of his alcoholic friends – the 'loadies,' they were derisively nicknamed – who were always around for the ride. One night Dennis simply turned to his 'bodyguard – baby-sitters' and said,

'Enough. I'm smart enough to hire you guys and I'm smart enough to fire you.' Bob Levine took them off the job the next day.

Everybody who cared about Dennis had tried at one time or another to get him to go for professional help. He tried Alcoholics Anonymous but wouldn't go to regular meetings. He went to a few private therapists, including Don Juhl, who also worked with David Kennedy, Jr, but he always gave up after a few visits. Dr Margaret Patterson, who had cured rock guitarist Eric Clapton of his heroin addiction, agreed to treat him, but Dennis never made an appointment. In one instance the other Beach Boys asked Dennis to come to a meeting with them in Dallas, where there was a program for athletes with drug and drinking problems. He brought Gage with him to the meeting and, holding the baby in his arms, he told them, 'I appreciate what you guys are trying to do for me, but I have to do this myself. I will not talk about my personal life with a stranger.'

The rest of the group, in a gesture of support, rented a private jet plane at a cost of $5,000 and put it at Dennis's disposal to take him off to whichever center he chose to enter, but he never got on the plane. The group also flew Dennis and Shawn to New York, all expenses paid, and put him in the Parker Meridian Hotel in anticipation of his entering a clinic, but he never left the hotel. To make detoxifying even more attractive, they offered to pay him one-fifth of the touring money – even though he wasn't on tour with them – as long as he was in a clinic. Since the Beach Boys were commanding $50,000 a show, plus a percentage of the profits over that, it was a very attractive offer, but one that Dennis didn't take. Dennis would shake his head and smile sadly. 'I really want to clean up my act, I really do,' he'd say with that gorgeous earnestness, 'and I'm going to do it this time.' But 'this time' never seemed to come.

With all this support and concern, and with so much at stake, Dennis still couldn't find the strength in himself to detox. There was a part of him so tormented, so helplessly frightened and childlike, that he could not be reached. He always had an excuse for himself, but the most recent – and heartfelt – excuse was that he didn't want to leave Gage, especially alone with Shawn. According to Bob Levine, 'Shawn was an extreme detriment to these programs.' That autumn, Dennis had tried to convince Shawn to let him take the baby with him to a detoxification center outside of Phoenix, Arizona, called Cottonwood. Levine had made arrangements for the baby to stay in a nearby home with round-the-clock nurses who would bring the little boy to visit Dennis every day. 'Shawn put up a big stink about it, but then you could see her attempts [to stop it] were waning, she was going to let it happen, and then all of a sudden she got fired up again.'

At one point, Dennis took Gage to the Los Angeles International Airport without Shawn's knowledge. When Shawn learned where Dennis had gone, she rushed to the airport and tried to get Gage back. A screaming fight over the child was conducted in the public terminal during which Shawn nearly bit off Dennis's thumb; the trip for rehabilitation was put off. The following month Dennis actually managed to get to Cottonwood for several weeks. 'But he's the type who can't be alone,' Levine said, 'So he kept calling Shawn . . . she threw roadblock after roadblock.' Shawn reportedly encouraged him to return to Los Angeles, but Dennis didn't even have the money for a plane ticket, and frantic to return, he convinced one of his 'well-meaning' loadie friends in Venice to send him the fare.

When the lease was up at his Trancas house in November 1983, no substitute place was found for him to live. Levine says this was 'basically by his own choosing,' because Dennis had promised to enter a detox center. When he finished detoxification, it was decided, Dennis would be found a new house along with his new beginning. But that day never came, and by the morning of his thirty-ninth birthday, Dennis had grown resigned to drifting with no home, no money, and no transportation.

3

When a taxi arrived at Chez Jay's to pick him up that morning, Alice Fiondella thought she had seen the last of him. But over an hour later he was back again, the cab driver at his side. Dennis was frantic. He had been all over the area looking for shelter, but no one seemed to be at home or willing to take him in. 'They had driven everywhere,' Alice said. 'The driver took him all over. The baby had messed in the backseat, and there was no money to pay the fare.' The cab driver, who felt sorry for Dennis, shook his head sadly, and Alice agreed to pay the fare. Dennis finally managed to reach one of his closest cronies, Chris Clark, on the phone. Chris told him to wait in the bar until he could borrow a car to come get him. Dennis sat in a booth, rocking Gage in his arms, while he waited for Chris to arrive.

Dennis's 'Little Buddy' Chris Clark was a Sancho Panza with whom Dennis could tilt at his alcoholic windmills. He was a pudgy, good-natured, loyal fellow, age thirty-two, who was struggling with his own alcoholic problems. For the most part unemployed, he had been friendly with Dennis for the past several years in Venice Beach. Chris Clark adored and looked up to 'Denny' as a kid looks up to a big brother. In awe of Dennis's sexual prowess, his fame, and his capacity for alcohol, Chris was ready twenty-four hours a day to gallivant with him. At night they would often sit out on the beach together, getting drunk, staring up at the stars. 'You know what, Little Buddy?' Dennis would tell Chris, pointing to the black sky littered with sequined stars. 'I've been there and back again.'

When Chris arrived at Chez Jay's shortly before noon, he was alarmed to find Dennis in tears. 'It just tore me up,' Dennis told Chris. 'Shawn was in bed with *two* guys,' he said, although, when pressed, Dennis admitted they were dressed and the situation did not seem of a sexual nature. Dennis thanked Alice and told her to call his business manager to get the taxi fare back. Then he and Chris went out of the dark bar onto the sunny boulevard and walked to the car Chris had borrowed. While Dennis was putting Gage in the backseat, he noticed that the 1982 Silver BMW he had bought for Shawn for $17,500 was parked in the lot next to Chez Jay's. Originally there were two BMWs, twins, but Dennis's had been stolen in a parking lot during a concert. The sight of the BMW seemed to enrage him. Poking around in the backseat of the borrowed car, he found a baseball bat. Before Chris could stop him, he raced to the BMW and smashed out the front windows. Chris yelled, 'Whoa! Dennis, stop!,' but at the same time he loved seeing him do it. Not surprisingly, nobody passing by on the street interrupted him at work with the baseball bat. When he was through, he seemed somehow relieved. 'Now she won't be able to come after Gage,' he told Chris, and ordered him to drive off.

After dropping Gage with friends in Venice who would look after him, Dennis spent the rest of his birthday cruising around with Chris in the borrowed car. At

29

sundown, they drove to a palatial log-cabin-style house at 14400 Sunset Boulevard that had once belonged to humorist Will Rogers. Dennis had rented this house in the late sixties while he was divorcing his first wife and money was pouring in. It was a period of wild abandon for Dennis, but it was also in this house that he had lived with Charles Manson and the Family. It was an era of orgies and drugs, a time in his life he once said 'destroyed' him. Yet he liked to return there; it was a way of revising some of his past glories, despite its associations, and it was with this idea that he directed his friend Chris Clark to drive there.

The beautiful, heavily landscaped house on Sunset Boulevard was then occupied by George Hormel, Jr, the fifty-six-year-old heir to the Hormel meat-packing fortune. Hormel had bought the house from its owner in 1968 for less than $500,000, and it was now worth nearly $3 million. The owner of a popular recording studio, Village Recorders, Hormel had been acquainted with Dennis for several years through the music business. They had first met many years before at Village Recorders, and then a few years later when Dennis brought Christine McVie over to show her the house. Hormel had grown fond of Dennis. 'He was just a big puppy,' he said. 'Scratch him once behind the ears and he would follow you anywhere.' Another year or so had gone by when, just that autumn, Dennis popped by unannounced and asked Hormel if he would work with him producing some tracks for an album. Dennis was very drunk and stoned, but after listening to the tracks Hormel agreed to work with him – 'If you're straight,' he admonished.

Dennis became a frequent visitor to the house, sleeping there when he had no other place to stay, and Hormel had become one of the latest of a long list of people whom Dennis had come to depend upon for support. During that November and December, he and Dennis had exchanged nearly $5,000. 'He had accumulated four or five thousand dollars' worth of debt for dope and I don't know what else – I didn't ask – and I gave him the money. I made sure that it was to get people off his tail and not to buy more drugs.' But by early December Hormel wouldn't give Dennis any more cash. 'He wasn't getting it out of me. I was supporting him only as long as he was straight.'

In the month and a half that Dennis stayed at Hormel's, they had long conversations about Dennis's addictions, and for a time Hormel believed Dennis was actually going to stop. Frequently they would stay up most of the night, talking into the early morning about Dennis's troubles. Hormel remembers that most of the conversations revolved around Dennis's personal problems with women and his family, and particularly his desire to end his alcohol and drug habits. Many times the conversations ended with Hormel convinced that Dennis was resolved to stop drinking. It was clear he couldn't go on as he was, Dennis's health had been deteriorating, and his epileptic-like seizures had increased. Hormal saw 'several' of them during December. Dennis would suddenly fall to the floor, his eyes rolling back, and churn convulsively. 'I witnessed a couple of really scary seizures,' Hormel said. 'He didn't remember a thing when he came to, but he knew something had happened.' The next day another episode in the drama of his life would send him off-center and he would need another drink.

Hormel wasn't surprised to find Dennis ringing the bell at the gate that December night. Hormel's son John was there, along with several friends and musicians with whom Hormel worked. When Dennis bashfully admitted it was his birthday, everyone made a big fuss over him, and they all went to the kitchen and baked a cake to celebrate.

31

That evening Dennis vacillated between bravado and sunken depression. At age thirty-nine, he saw the Big Forty and middle age coming up, and he knew he was getting too old to be a Beach Boy. But as soon as Dennis found himself becoming maudlin, he would catch himself and mask his mood with drunken gregariousness. He told several funny stories, acting them out dramatically in his big, rasping voice, and at one point Chris Clark said to him. 'You know, your problem is you're just mad you never made it as an actor. That's why you have to act everything out.'

Dennis grinned at him and said, 'How did you know that?'

They all sang 'Happy Birthday' and Dennis became a little boy for a moment, embarrassed and pleased and flustered when he blew out the candles. Later in the evening, they went to the billiard room and played pool. Dennis suggested they make the ante a thousand dollars a game, and everyone agreed, because it was play money anyway.

By the small hours of the morning, Dennis was blitzed on every accommodation of the household. George Hormel couldn't stand to see him that way, but instead of asking him to leave on his birthday, Hormel just locked himself in his study. In a few minutes Dennis was banging on the door, asking to be let in, and the inevitable conversation followed: he loved Shawn, but she was using drugs; he had to dry out, but he was just so lonely; he loved her, he hated her, he couldn't live without her; she was destroying him every minute they spent together.

He stayed at Hormel's house that night and on and off for the rest of December, sleeping off his binges or just hanging out there during the day. It surprised Hormel that Dennis seemed to have not one penny, but he took it for granted this lack of funds was part of the pressure

Dennis's family and management were putting on him to detoxify. As the weeks passed, Dennis drank less, readying himself for another go at a detoxification clinic. But when Hormel returned home one night around the twentieth of December, he found Dennis on a wild drunken binge. Getting blotto seemed to make sense to Dennis. 'Everybody goes on a last binge,' he said, and then poured nearly an entire bottle of wine into the mixing console of Hormel's home studio. Hormel was exasperated. Ultimately the truth hit home: if you gave Dennis shelter, you became part of the problem. Unable in good conscience to give him a home and booze to drink, Hormel had to ask him to leave, and by Christmas, Dennis was homeless again.

4

The impending holidays loomed like some nightmare for Dennis. Without a home, without a cent in his pocket, he felt lost and adrift. He crashed in cheap motels along the Ho Chi Minh Trail or at the apartments of friends. He made several attempts to go to Alcoholics Anonymous, and the Beach Boys' manager, Tom Hulett, in a gesture of support, accompanied Dennis to one meeting. But outside the meeting, the two argued about money, and Hulett reportedly took a large roll of bills out of his pocket and offered Dennis fifteen dollars. Dennis was so insulted by the paltry amount, he refused to take it, and Hulett reportedly threw the money on the ground. Other reports say that the next day Hulett broke down and gave Dennis a hundred dollars; but the money quickly went for more booze and drugs. At this point Dennis was on the edge; he would either clean himself up and pull out of the nose dive, or else.

Dennis was finally able to steel himself for the ride to a detoxification ward two days before Christmas. He said it didn't make much difference to him to be in a detox ward of a hospital on Christmas; he had no other place to go, and perhaps it was the best Christmas present he could give himself. On Friday morning, December 23, Bob Levine drove Dennis to St John's Hospital and Health Center in Santa Monica, only a mile from the Santa Monica Bay Inn.

He was checked into the detox unit by Dr Joseph Takamine, who headed the twenty-one-day detox program. According to Dr Takamine, Dennis was serious about the program and determined to stick it through this time. His blood test on admittance showed a .28 alcohol level and traces of cocaine. Dennis told the doctor he had been drinking about a fifth of vodka a day and using what he called 'a little coke.' The doctor prescribed 100 mg of Librium every two hours 'so he could come down slowly and maybe start the program in five days.' Takamine and Dennis talked extensively on Saturday, and the doctor told him their discussions would resume on Monday morning when the doctor returned to the hospital following a one-day Christmas break.

All Christmas Eve day Dennis suffered tormenting physical and psychological withdrawal symptoms cloaked by the 100 mg doses of Librium. Itching to walk out, he spent the day obsessively making phone calls to friends, all of whom encouraged him to stick it out, promising to visit or call him whenever they were allowed. He reportedly called his brother Carl, vacationing in Colorado, several times, his mother, Audree, and his brother Brian, but could not reach them. Only Bob Levine came by to see him that day. 'I brought him some presents, some

34

necessities, toiletries, cigarettes, things to make the guy feel respectable. He was trying again. And then the siren called.'

The 'siren' was Shawn. Dennis had placed dozens of phone calls to Shawn at the Bay Inn. She refused most of them until Christmas Eve, when she told Dennis that she and Gage were being thrown out of the Bay Inn for nonpayment of rent. The manager said he had been given the runaround about payment for too long. Dennis would say Shawn would take care of the bill, Shawn would say Dennis would be by later to pay it. The physical damage Dennis had caused to the room was also a factor. Dennis became determined to leave the hospital and see Shawn and Gage.

Shortly after Shawn's phone call, Dennis's friends Steve Goldberg and Denice Graves visited him in his room and encouraged him to stay, promising him that Shawn and Gage would be all right. But by 3:30 Dennis was on the phone to his 'Little Buddy' Chris Clark, telling him he was about to walk out of the hospital. He asked Chris to pick him up and take him out for a drink.

Chris Clark was disgusted. He had no idea what to say to keep Dennis in the detox ward, so he hurried over to the hospital and offered to stay with him overnight. Dennis calmed down somewhat, and Chris slept on the floor next to Dennis's bed, talking him through the night. On Christmas morning, about 8:30 A.M., the hospital staff insisted that Chris leave. 'If I leave, he's not going to stay,' Chris warned the nurses in the hallway outside of Dennis's room. But they insisted Dennis could not go through the therapy with a friend. Chris reluctantly went back inside the room to say good-bye.

Immediately after Chris Clark left, Dennis called Steve Goldberg at least six times, demanding to be picked up at the hospital. Goldberg refused to be an accomplice in this self-destructive act. By noon, Dennis had walked out himself. From St John's, he hitchhiked his way to his friend Nick's liquor store in Venice, where he begged a bottle and some cash. Then he went to Shawn's mother's house on Twelfth Street in Santa Monica, where Shawn and Gage were paying a Christmas visit. Reportedly, everything there was copacetic. 'He said he was really lonely and that he wanted to be with us on Christmas,' Shawn said. After an hour, he left to hitchhike his way to the nearest bar.

Later Christmas night, John Hanlon, a recording engineer and one of Dennis's longtime friends, received a panicky phone call from one of Dennis's loadie friends who said that Dennis was making a commotion at a club called At My Place in Santa Monica. Would Hanlon come by and help get him out of there? Hanlon, twenty-seven, loved Dennis. Dennis had given him his first break as an engineer at the Beach Boys' Brothers studios and had comforted him through many difficult personal times. He knew in what condition he would probably find Dennis, but went to get him nevertheless. Dennis was in the worst shape Hanlon had ever seen him. 'He was a total drunk,' Hanlon said, 'disrupting business, yelling at patrons, screaming at the barmaids, trying to get up on stage, making a general mess of things.' Hanlon managed to coax Dennis out of the club and drove him back to the Santa Monica Bay Inn, although Dennis kept insisting he be driven to George Hormel's house. 'I didn't know where to take him. I made a phone call to George, who said, 'It's not a good time right now because I'm with family.' Dennis was sitting in my car throwing booze all over and he was making a mess and I was getting real uptight. I said, 'Look, I called Geordie for you, and there's nothing else I can do. I can't deal with this anymore, you've got to help yourself.'

Dennis said, 'Nobody loves me, John. Nobody.'

'That's not true, Dennis,' Hanlon told him softly, helping him out of the car. 'Everybody loves you, man. Too many people love you, that's your problem.'

'I don't want to live another couple of weeks,' Dennis said.

'That's stupid talk,' Hanlon answered.

Dennis shouted, '*I'm not leaving. You're taking me over to Geordie's!*' He began to break the antennae off the car's hood and then tried to tear the door off the hinges. Hanlon screamed at him to stop. Seeing his words had no effect, he jumped behind the wheel and sped off, leaving Dennis standing on the street. Dennis stumbled across the road to Chez Jay's, and at about midnight he set out for the Santa Monica Bay Inn.

When he arrived unannounced at Shawn's room, she was there with her male friend. Dennis later told Chris Clark, Bob Levine, and others that he demanded to use the telephone and Shawn's friend wouldn't let him in. A shoving match quickly escalated into a fistfight. Now came out of the craziest moments of the past few weeks: Dennis decided not to fight back. He simply made fists at his side to withstand the pain. He was so doped from his hospital treatment, he felt very little of the serious damage being done to him by the repeated blows. Dennis said, 'I just stood there and let him hit me. I didn't do a thing.'

Severely beaten, he stumbled out of the motel room and walked down to Ocean Boulevard. He called Chris Clark from a phone booth and convinced him and Steve Goldberg to come get him in Goldberg's pickup truck. His friends found him bleeding from bruises on his face, with scrapes on his forehead and one black eye, holding his ribs, drunk and sick. They took him back to St John's, the hospital he had walked out of several hours earlier. On the way there, his complexion gray, Dennis told Chris

Clark about letting Shawn's boyfriend hit him. Chris couldn't help but laugh. 'That's the most destructive thing you've ever done,' Chris told him.

But Dennis was in no shape to laugh. 'I just want to go down there and kick his ass,' he kept repeating.. 'I'm gonna call the cops. Close the place down. Bust everyone.' That was Dennis's ultimate revenge, to call the police. But he could not bring himself to do it. Dennis had stopped hitting back.

Inside the hospital Chris Clark got Dr Michael Gales on the phone and tried to convince him to readmit Dennis to the program. But Gales said he couldn't. 'He's just too much trouble,' Dr Gales reportedly told Clark.

'He might die, you know,' Chris Clark said earnestly. 'He just stood there and got the shit beat out of him.'

'He may have to die,' the doctor allegedly replied.

Chris Clark knew another doctor, Christopher Bador, at the Daniel Freeman Marina Hospital, who worked with drug and alcohol abusers, and called him to get Dennis admitted. Dr Bador reportedly suggested that, in order to restrain Dennis, the police lock him up, but Chris couldn't bring himself to call the police on his friend. By now it was 2:00 A.M. on December 26.

Dennis was eventually admitted to the Marina Hospital that morning, and again Chris Clark convinced the hospital staff that he would have to spend the night with Dennis in order for him to stay in the hospital. Chris slept on the floor until Dennis went off into a fitful sleep. But in the morning came the same hospital rules: Dennis had to see this through alone, and despite his repeated warnings that if Dennis was left alone he'd walk out, Chris Clark was made to leave the hospital.

It wasn't forty-five minutes later that Dennis started calling him. 'Where am I going to meet you, Little

Buddy?' he asked. Chris was adamant this time; he would not see Dennis anymore if he walked out of the hospital. Next Dennis called Steve Goldberg to pick him up, and Goldberg also refused. And sometime within the next hour, Dennis walked out yet again.

He wound up at another favorite haunt in Venice – Hinanos, a dark bar with sawdust on the floor, at the end of Washington Boulevard near the beach. There he got steadily drunk until 1:00 P.M., when again he called and asked Steve Goldberg to pick him up. Goldberg was busy tinkering with his van, and anyway, Hinanos was only a few blocks from where Goldberg lived. 'Why don't you just walk over here?' he said. But Dennis was cantankerous and stubborn. He called Goldberg several more times that afternoon as he got drunker, demanding money and a lift. When it became clear that Goldberg wouldn't budge, Dennis got angry, ending the phone call with the word *termination*.

Said Goldberg, 'I don't know if he was referring to the conversation, our friendship, or his life.'

5

Later that afternoon, Dennis got in touch with a sometime girl friend of his called Crystal, who had just returned from her Christmas vacation, and she arranged to pick him up. Born Coleen McGovern in Wisconsin, she claimed she was nicknamed 'Crystal' when she worked as a Playboy bunny at the Lake Geneva Playboy Club. Dark-haired and pretty, she was full of the same kind of fidgety nervous energy as Dennis. At the time she lived in a furnished two-bedroom apartment in the Fox Hills apartment complex in Culver City with a female roommate and two pet birds. She had only recently taken a position of prominence in Dennis's life, as a last resort for comfort, shelter, and a beer.

She first met Dennis the Thanksgiving of 1981 at a party in Venice across the alley from a rented house where Dennis was living. Dennis was shyly sitting outside on the steps, drinking, and she asked him to come in and have a plate of food. 'I asked someone who he was, and when I found out I said, "Oh, OK, forget about him." I didn't want to have anything to do with him at first. Too heavy for me.' Yet in the coming weeks she kept running into him, and eventually they struck up a friendship. 'We just hit it off, but I still kept my distance. He had Shawn and I had this boyfriend, so I didn't want to mess things up.' But as time passed and his marriage to Shawn dissolved, his relationship with Crystal blossomed into a romance of convenience, and Dennis spent many nights at her apartment in Fox Hills. Crystal picked him up at Hinanos and took him to a pay phone at the Fox Hills shopping mall.

Realizing that all of his pals were burned out on his broken promises, aborted detox attempts, and drunken scenes, Dennis phoned an old friend from better times, Bill Oster. Oster, forty-four, was a moustachioed, weathered outdoorsman who owned a fifty-two-foot yawl, the *Emerald*. The *Emerald* was kept in a berth at the Villa Del Mar, a three-story white-stucco apartment building and 'rudder and racquet' club at 13999 Marquesa Way, Marina Del Rey, where Dennis had once berthed his favorite possession, the sixty-two-foot, sleek sailing boat he called the *Harmony*. The last time Oster had seen Dennis was fourteen months earlier, backstage at the Greek Theater, where the Beach Boys were performing. Oster was surprised to hear from him after so long, but unpredictability was part of Dennis's charm, so when

Oster heard his voice on the phone, now hoarser and scratchier than ever, he took it in stride. 'Pick me up at the Fox Hills Mall,' Dennis ordered him, without saying hello.

Just like Dennis, Oster thought. 'After all these months, he couldn't even ask, just kind of demanded.'

Oster first met Dennis in 1978, just as Dennis's second marriage to Karen Lamm was breaking up and he was beginning to miss many tour dates. Dennis was living full-time on the boat, and he and Oster became close friends. Living on his boat was one of the best times for Dennis. He keenly loved the *Harmony*, with its flashy, hand-carved teak fittings and a beautiful carved golden teak pelican on the prow. Purchased years before in Japan, it had once been sunk and submerged, and Dennis had painstakingly refurbished it to its original beauty. But Dennis loved the *Harmony* not so much for its physical beauty as for the total freedom it represented. Only the open sea was fierce and strong and unrelenting enough to be his full-time companion. The *Harmony* became Dennis's chief means of escape; over the past few years it was only on the *Harmony* that he was not in pain. He sailed up and down the coast, or to Catalina or to Hawaii, but mostly he just kept it berthed at the Villa Del Mar so he could stay close to his beloved ocean. Oster had gone on several trips with Dennis on the *Harmony*, and once, sailing up from San Diego, Dennis discovered a huge school of porpoises swimming and playing next to the boat. Exhilarated by the beautiful mammals, Dennis wrapped one hand in the mastings and hung over the side of the boat in the ocean breeze, serenading the dolphins with his harmonica as they popped up and down like corks in the rush of the wind and waves.

But by the summer of 1981, the always-erratic installment payments to American City Bank hadn't been made

41

in several months, and one day, while Dennis was walking down the long wooden boat slip, he discovered a city marshal on board. Dennis didn't tell the marshal who he was. Instead, he got on to Oster's boat across the dock and stood there, his heart breaking, as the marshal posted repossession signs, locked the door, and chained the *Harmony* to the dock. For a while, a marshal's representative lived on the *Harmony* until it was auctioned off for $53,000 – half its worth. It tore Dennis up so much to lose his boat that Oster offered him the *Emerald* to live on, and Dennis stayed there for a while, greeted with the empty slip of the *Harmony* when he got up each morning. The slip remained empty to that very day.

The Fox Hills Mall was a large shopping mall near the end of the Marina Freeway, about a mile from where Crystal lived. Around 7:30 P.M. on Tuesday, December 27, Oster and his fiancée, Brenda, found Dennis, dressed in army fatigues and T-shirt, waiting for him near a pay phone with Crystal at his side. He looked pretty beaten up; there was dried blood on his ear, and he had scabs on his nose and forehead. His ribs ached terribly, he said. It seemed to Oster that Dennis always had quite a few drinks in him, but the first thing he asked for was to be driven to a liquor store. Oster tried to dissuade him, but Dennis complained about the pain in his ribs and said the liquor would be good for him. Oster relented. On the way to the dock, they stopped at Marina Liquors, where Dennis bought a bottle of the house-brand vodka, Delray.

When Brenda and Dennis arrived at the *Emerald*, Dennis began drinking in earnest. None of the others drank, hoping to slow him down. They stayed up talking until midnight, trading stories about old times. Oster told Dennis, 'It wasn't six months ago that I said to Brenda, "I hope the next time we see Dennis it's not at his funeral."'

42

Dennis looked Oster in the eye and said, 'Don't you worry about that.'

Later, Oster told Dennis that by ironic coincidence the *Harmony*, after it had been repossessed and purchased at auction, had been berthed by its new owner just the second dock down from where they sat. The boat had been for sale about six months ago for $180,000, but now, Oster heard, it could be bought for $115,000. Dennis thought the price was inflated – the boat needed a lot of work – but he would love to have it back. About midnight, Oster and Brenda went into the forecabin and fell asleep.

In the middle of the night Dennis woke up and talked with Crystal about getting the *Harmony* back; he decided that was what he wanted more than anything just then. He told Crystal he intended to call Bob Levine in the morning and promise to present himself at any rehabilitation clinic the Beach Boys named, if they would only help finance buying the *Harmony* back. This time, he swore, he was going to stop drinking. It was just that it was so damn *lonely* in those places and the shakes were so bad. Dennis talked about a crazy scheme of having Gage live with Crystal in an apartment near the detox clinic so he could see them on visiting days. 'He wanted to be able to take someone with him that he loved and to be with them through this whole thing,' Crystal said. 'He knew he needed it, and he wanted to do it for his son and for the band.' Most important to him, Dennis knew that in his impending divorce from Shawn there would probably be a custody battle for Gage, and he needed to be sober to prove he was a fit parent.

Never needing much sleep, Dennis got up at 9:00 A.M. and looked around for his bottle of Delray vodka. The night before, Crystal had hidden it behind the trash bin in the galley so Dennis wouldn't find it, but he complained and moaned and searched all over the boat until he discovered it. 'He knew we were going to make it difficult for him,' Oster said, 'but he also knew that we most likely wouldn't pour it down the drain on him because we did have some concern that if we completely dried him out he would have a seizure.'

Oster and the women had coffee while Dennis fixed himself the first screwdriver of the day. Then the women went out for a shower in the dock facilities. By the time they got back to the *Emerald*, Dennis was excited and flying high. He said he had called Bob Levine to say he wanted the boat back, *had* to have the boat back, and that he was determined to sober up. He and Levine discussed a thirty-day detoxification program in New Mexico, and the possibility of his going back to Cotton-wood in Phoenix.

'He made me a deal,' Dennis said of Bob Levine. 'Thirty days' detox and he'll buy the boat back for me!' He hugged Crystal and asked, 'Do you want to live on the boat with me?'

Crystal, taken by surprise, said, 'What about Gage?' And Dennis said, 'No problem, no problem. Gage too.' This time, he swore over and over again, he would complete the program. He knew how important it was – Gage was at stake – and he sat around the floor of Oster's boat for the rest of the morning, talking about detoxing and pulling his life together and how much he loved Gage.

Oster suggested that he and Dennis put together a new rowing rig that Oster had purchased but never used. This project caught Dennis's attention for a while, and the two men assembled the small boat and went rowing around the marina. Dennis wanted to row across the marina to Aggy's Chris Craft, a large boat sales and repair shop whose owner he knew. When Dennis owned the *Harmony*, he loved to hang out at Aggy's and frequently offered to buy the place from him.

'How much do you want for it?' he bellowed at Aggy that morning. 'How much? Just tell me how much and it's yours!'

'A million dollars,' Aggy said, smiling.

And Dennis said, 'Just call up my business manager and he'll send it to you!' They soon left Aggy's and by noon were back at the *Emerald*.

This time the bottle had been hidden better. Dennis went through an elaborate search until he found it. He fixed himself another drink, and they all settled down to have lunch. Brenda made turkey sandwiches from Christmas leftovers, and Dennis talked again of getting the *Harmony* back. After lunch, Dennis spilled his drink all over his pants. Oster loaned him a pair of cutoff jeans that were slightly too baggy for him. Dennis rinsed out his stained pants and laid them on the deck in the sun to dry.

Suddenly, Dennis said he was going swimming.

'You're crazy,' Oster said to him, and Crystal chimed in with, 'Dennis, it's too cold!' But Dennis went up on deck, and in another moment there was the sound of a splash as he jumped into the water. Oster decided he should go up on the deck to watch him. He found Dennis swimming around in the murky water of the empty berth once filled by the *Harmony*. The water was thirteen feet deep and hovering at an icy fifty-eight degrees. The most hardy swimmer would have needed a wet suit, but Dennis just took a few deep breaths of air and then disappeared below the surface for what seemed like a long time. Oster grew worried, but in another moment he heard Dennis surface on the far side of the dock, laughing at having tricked him. Oster again tried to cajole Dennis out of the water, but Dennis only swam back over to the spot where the *Harmony* had been berthed, and began diving in earnest. On each trip to the bottom, he found another piece of *Harmony*, sometimes only a small piece of junk, pieces of metal fittings and battery parts, and an old rotted piece of rope.

After about twenty minutes, he got out of the water to have another turkey sandwich. Inside the boat, as he started to eat his sandwich, he got the shivers. They put a towel on the floor for him so he could sit in front of the heater, but his teeth wouldn't stop chattering. He sat there sipping vodka and orange juice, trying to warm up, and whenever his back was turned Oster would try to water down his drink. When Dennis caught on to what Oster was doing, he complained loudly and, sitting there on the floor, practically finished off the fifth. The whole time, he was talking about the 'big box' he had seen on the floor of the marina where the *Harmony* had been docked. 'I betcha it's a treasure chest. I know it is! It's a treasure chest with a bag of silver dollars.' He entertained Oster, Brenda, and Crystal with the story of a submerged treasure, some of it a bag filled with silver dollars he had allegedly thrown overboard himself. None of them really wanted Dennis to go back in the water, but Dennis was intent on finding it. Oster complied by going to get a line of rope so Dennis could take it down with him and tie it to the 'big box' he had seen.

But meanwhile, Dennis, annoyed that the bottle had run out, had wandered off to find more booze. He walked a few berths down to the houseboat on which Lathiel Morris lived. Dennis seemed very excited, according to Morris. 'I'm getting my boat back,' he bragged. Morris had his pretty sixteen-year-old granddaughter on board, and Dennis smiled and flirted with her. Dennis talked about his impending divorce from Shawn, and Morris asked how many times he had been married. Dennis told him six. 'I'm lonesome,' Dennis told Morris. 'I'm lonesome all the time.'

And Morris said, 'Ahhh, baloney,' gesturing toward Crystal across the way on Oster's boat.

Soon Oster went out looking for Dennis and caught up with him talking to yet another boat owner he knew from the marina, asking if there was any vodka to spare. Just as the man was about to hand over a half-filled bottle of vodka, Oster signaled frantically behind Dennis's back not to give it to him. The boat owner caught on right away and said, 'Wait a minute, Dennis!' He whisked the bottle back into the galley. A moment later he brought the same bottle back with much less vodka in it. Dennis thanked him and took it back to the *Emerald*. Then he swigged it right down, not even mixing it with his usual orange juice.

Almost immediately Dennis insisted on diving again. Despite everyone's protestations, he jumped back in at the outward end of the dock and dived under the surface once or twice before disappearing for what seemed like a long time. Eventually, he surfaced close to the dock and handed Oster a rectangular object about the size of a book, coated in mud. Dennis held on to the side of the dock with both hands while Oster rubbed off some of the muck. It was a wedding picture of Dennis and Karen Lamm in a sterling-silver frame that rock manager–producer James Guercio had given to them the first time they got married. Dennis had thrown it overboard in a fit of anger during their divorce. The glass was shattered, but in the faded, water-bleached photo Dennis was still tanned and handsome and young, and Karen was laughing, her baby-blue eyes sparkling, and they were such a perfect couple, it took your breath away.

Oster called to his girl friend. 'Brenda, come over here and see this,' and then Dennis went back down again, down into the dark waters of the marina.

*If there wasn't the Beach Boys and there
wasn't music, I would not even know them. I
would not even talk to them. But through
the music I fell in love with my brothers. –*
Dennis Wilson

Two

1

'Hey, Dennis! Play it again!' Murry Wilson roared from his bed. A great big bear of a man under the sheets, Murry loved bed. For Murry, bed was like a throne for a potentate. He would lie there for hours in the mornings, reading the papers, talking on the phone, watching TV, the bedsheets pulled halfway up his huge, rotund belly.

He was a big man, with a meaty face and a double chin. His thick brown hair was carefully combed back from a high forehead, and his half-framed mock tortoiseshell glasses sat across the bridge of his small, wide nose. His left eye – which he had lost in a freak industrial accident when he was twenty-five – had been replaced by a glass prosthetic eye that he kept in a container on the dresser at night. Even in bed he smoked his omnipresent pipe. It jutted out from between his teeth, the bowl blackened and charred by the double kitchen matches he used to continuously light it. The smoke filled the room with a pungent sweetness that his family and friends associated with him; occasionally an ember would billow from the bowl and land on his chest, singeing the gray hair.

'Hey, Dennis!' Murry bellowed again in his deep, sonorous voice, like the giant's voice in 'Jack and the Beanstalk.' 'Put it on again!'

Murry had just listened, for the tenth time that morning, to 'Two Step Side Step,' a composition he had written a few years before. By occupation Murry owned the ABLE machine shop – Always Better Lasting Equipment – a small company that imported lathes and drills from England. But in his heart he considered himself a songwriter. He had been writing songs since he was a teenager, and after many years of dogged pursuit, one or two of his songs had actually been recorded. But, according to his wife, Audree, his songs 'just died. They never did anything.' Yet Murry's love for music was still his abiding passion. The very sound of music soothed him; he would close his eyes and tilt his head back, losing himself in the melody and chord changes, which seemed to transport him someplace joyous and peaceful. He especially liked to hear one of his own compositions playing on the hi-fi as he lay in the small, dark bedroom of his modest Hawthorne, Los Angeles, bungalow. 'Dennis!' His voice boomed through the house. 'Put it on again!'

In the modern pink kitchen at the rear of the house, Murry's thirteen-year-old middle son, Dennis, sat stubbornly at the dinette table, his face knotted in pure resentment. He was a thin, wiry adolescent, athletically built, his sun-bleached, blond hair electric-razored into a flattop crew cut. He remained at the table, purposely ignoring his father. Dennis and his father were the family antagonists – although Murry was often at odds with all three of his sons. In many ways, Dennis and Murry were the most alike. Fiercely loyal and devoted to each other, they were totally unable to express their feelings. Instead, they seemed to be locked into some terrible competitive duel. On the surface it appeared to be a typical generation gap of the late fifties, with Murry's tough, Depression mentality and hard-work ethics pitted against Dennis's casual, California teen sensibility; but the passions

49

between this father and son went well beyond any ordinary generation gap.

Audree Wilson gingerly turned the bacon strips in a frying pan at the stove. A pleasant and cheerful young housewife, she was in the pressure spot of mediating the daily turmoil between her husband and three sons. Looking anxiously at Dennis, she said to him, 'Go ahead, Dennis, put it on for him.' Slightly plump, with blond hair and a warm smile, Audree made the kitchen her domain and salvation. Food was a major preoccupation in the Wilson household – for everyone but Dennis – and the kitchen was the center of household activity. It was also by far the most modern room in the simply appointed bungalow. Facing the rear of the house, with a small garden beyond, the kitchen had been remodeled by Murry on several occasions. It now sported new cabinets and appliances, including a dishwasher and a two-door refrigerator, making it look like the kitchen of a much larger, more expensive house, like the set from a suburban TV sitcom.

Dennis looked at his mother and groaned. 'Oh, Ma, do I have to?' he asked. He went to the small monophonic record player in the music room and put the stylus back to the beginning of the spinning 78 disc. Dennis thought all this music-writing stuff was stupid. Just one listen and you could tell Murry 'couldn't write a fucking good tune'; that he was a 'frustrated piece of shit writer.' Murry couldn't even play an instrument.

But Murry could pick out chords on the piano, and despite Dennis's critical opinion of him, many people thought he wrote beautiful melodies. His musical ideas did seem a bit corny, if not downright anachronistic. Murry first took song writing seriously as a teenager when he entered one of his compositions in a New York radio contest that was aired in Los Angeles. Over the years his

50

songs were turned down hundreds of times, and on occasion he was cheated outright by unethical publishers, as when he wrote the lyrics to an obscure single for which he claimed he was never paid. But the small group of Murry's tunes that were published and recorded gave him supreme pleasure. One of Murry's favorites was Jimmy Haskell singing Murry's 'Hide My Tears' on Palace Records; another was the 'Fiesta Day Polka.'

Perhaps Murry's all-time favorite was the record on the phonograph in the family room, 'Two Step Side Step,' which was recorded by a group called the Bachelors on Palace Records. It was an upbeat, hillbilly tune that Lawrence Welk, then at the height of his fame, once played on live radio. There was even sheet music for it, and Murry was so certain the song would sweep the nation he invented a little side-stepping dance that went with it. But the cha-cha and the merengue were the big popular dances at the time, and 'Two Step Side Step' was hardly noticed. When the record ended this time, Murry called out to Dennis once more, 'Play it again! Play it again,' and Dennis, a little more resentfully, put the needle back to the start.

2

Murry had something of a hyperactive personality. He had a commanding voice and spoke so forcefully that he was at once galvanizing and irritating. His speech cadence had all the energy of a tough football coach cussing out his team. Five feet ten inches tall, balding, overweight, he had the air of a desperate salesman. Actually, 'Murry was a very good salesman,' one of his neighbors, Joanne

Marks, remembered. 'The only trouble was he oversold everything and then ruined it.' Said another neighbor, Ida Kennedy, 'He was a loudmouth.'

Yet at heart, Murry was nothing more than the average American who believed in the American Dream and achievement through hard work. Although raised as a Lutheran, he wasn't a frequent churchgoer; but he was a religious man who believed in God and heaven and hell, and he worked hard for his living. He was born Murry Gage Wilson on July 2, 1917, in Hutchinson, Kansas, on the Arkansas River, smack-dab in the middle of the middlemost state. The son of William Coral Wilson and Edith Sthole, he was third oldest of four brothers and four sisters. His father, nicknamed 'Bud,' was a land enthusiast – not that he ever had enough money to buy any. A plumber by trade, like his father before him, Murry's father traveled first to Montana, then to Texas, looking for a new homestead for the family, before finally moving to Escondido, California, along with the tens of thousands of other dustbowl families in search of the California dream. In Escondido, Bud Wilson played semi-professional baseball before the lure of better employment brought him and his large family to Los Angeles in 1922. They rented a big farmhouse at 9722 South Figueroa on the corner of Ninety-eighth Street.

'He was very strict and struggled hard to feed eight kids during the Depression,' remembered Bud's youngest son, Charles. 'I don't know how he survived.' While Bud took whatever plumbing work he could find, including long stints in the desert helping to build the Los Angeles aqueduct, his wife, Edith, worked a steam press, ironing clothes for a garment manufacturer. Most of the family's clothing was handmade by Edith, a formidable figure five feet eight inches and weighing over two hundred pounds. 'Nobody got sassy with her,' said Charles.

Nor with Bud. He was a hard drinker with an explosive temper who often wreaked havoc on his large family, beating the kids and his wife. 'He was an ornery son of a bitch,' remembered one of his sons-in-law. 'He punched around and beat up his wife and kids – until the kids were big enough to beat him up back.' On one occasion, Bud beat Charles so badly for breaking his eyeglasses that the entire family was up in arms against him. Another time he punched Murry so sadistically that Murry finally hauled off and smacked him back. There was so much bitterness that after Edith Wilson passed away, Murry and his younger sister Emily never saw their father again, although he lived to be ninety-two. Emily hated her father in particular for the way he treated her mother. But the other children had fonder memories of Bud Wilson, including the nightly family sing-songs around the old upright piano Bud and Edith had saved up to buy second-hand. Often the younger kids would fall asleep listening to their parents singing in the living room.

Murry was an active, curious child, always into some mischief, but good-natured, with a soft side. He was so sensitive that he would cry if someone was mean to him. He met Audree Korthof at Washington High School in Los Angeles. Born in Minneapolis, Minnesota, Audree came to California in 1928 with her mother and father, Betty and Carl Korthof, when she was ten years old. Her family settled in downtown Los Angeles, where her grandfather and father were both bakers. Eventually her father opened his own bakeshop, the Mary Jane Bakery, in central Los Angeles. Audree was a pretty girl, already a bit overweight, but cheerful and warm. Murry fell for her instantly. They had in common a great love of music. Audree belonged to the school glee club, and had a beautiful singing voice, an attribute that was of no small importance to Murry Wilson.

They were married on March 26, 1938, and moved to a small apartment at 8012 South Harvard Boulevard, where they were living when Audree gave birth to their first son, Brian Douglas Wilson, on June 20, 1942, at Centinela Hospital in Inglewood. 'When Brian was born, I was one of those young, frightened fathers,' Murry Wilson once said, 'but I just fell in love with him, and in three weeks he cooed back at me.' Their second son, Dennis Carl, was born December 4, 1944, and a third son, Carl Dean, was born on December 21, 1946.

Three months after Dennis's birth, the family moved to the south bay community of Hawthorne. With a hard-earned and harder-saved $2,300 down payment, they bought a small, neat, two-bedroom house at 3701 West 119th Street on the corner of Kornblum Avenue. Located just three blocks north of the Hawthorne Airport, where light planes would land and take off, the community was a barren tract, with no trees for shade. There weren't even any sidewalks; the front lawns just tapered off into the street, where the newly dug sewer lines had been put in. Because the house had only two bedrooms, all three boys slept in the same twelve-by-ten-foot room, with one small window overlooking Kornblum Avenue.

The Wilsons were hardly out of place in Hawthorne, the 'City of Good Neighbors.' It was one of the many new and burgeoning communities of young marrieds and new families that had sprung up throughout the south bay area just after the war. Twelve miles southeast of central Los Angeles, the small community didn't have electrical power until 1910 or even a police department until 1922. Nearly half of the population was on relief during the thirties and the working-class residents almost all declared bankruptcy; almost three thousand parcels of property were sold off for delinquent taxes, some at one dollar each. The community was virtually saved in 1939 by the

Northrop Aircraft Company, which opened offices there and brought with it dozens of contractors and twenty thousand jobs.

By the time the Wilsons arrived in Hawthorne, during the postwar urban sprawl, it was still a predominantly white, working-class community. Flat, bleak, hot, it comprised seemingly endless patches of development homes laid end to end, street after street – row after row of duplicate tract houses, available for under $10,000 each. It was a community of Mah-Jongg and checkers, Foster Freeze, supermarkets, churches, Little League, and cookouts on Sundays. It was the essence of heartland Los Angeles, and if there was anything unusual about Hawthorne, it was that it was the most benignly typical Los Angeles suburb you could find.

Murry worked as a clerk for the Southern California Gas Company, and later at the Goodyear Tire and Rubber Company. One day at the plant, when he was working near a high-power machine that conditioned rubber with acid, one of the swabs of acid flew across the room and hit him in the face. It splintered his glasses and completely burned out his left eye. Murry spent two weeks in the hospital, followed by long months despairing at home. He was fitted with a glass eye, but the scarred socket was too sensitive at first for him to be able to wear it, and Murry sported an eyepatch for a time. 'When I was twenty-five, I thought the world owed me a living,' Murry said. 'When I lost my eye, I tried harder, drove harder, and did the work of two men in the company and got more raises.' After leaving Goodyear he worked for Air Research Industries, and then for his brothers, who were in the machinery business. After some time he borrowed money against his home to open ABLE Machinery in Southgate. Murry was especially proud of the fact that his company imported the Binns and Berry's

55

lathe. According to Murry, the business 'succeeded against millionaire dealers. Now you figure it out. Guts.' But in truth, the business wasn't all that successful. According to Dennis, Murry never brought home more than $15,000 a year, although in those days that might have meant he was doing much better than most of his struggling neighbors.

3

All three Wilson boys went to nearby York Elementary School, and later to Hawthorne High School, on the corner of El Segundo and Inglewood. Hawthorne High was a large school of two thousand students, a compound of long, low, turquoise buildings built of cinder blocks and Quonset huts, bounded on one end by railroad tracks, the town swimming pool, and a large athletic field. Since the city of Hawthorne was just a few miles from the Los Angeles International Airport, jet planes passed over the school at regular intervals, like spaceships gleaming in the hot afternoon sun. The Wilson brothers were fair-to-middling students at best; Dennis being the worst and Carl a chronic hookey player.

Brian was the best-looking of the Wilson sons, a handsome youngster with a sweet smile, gorgeous hazel-blue eyes, and dark hair. By his teens he had grown into a gangling, six-foot three-inch smirking teenager with a crew cut. He was a gentle soul, a polite and caring young man, always eager to please and to be accepted by his peers. Around Hawthorne High he was considered a 'regular guy.' He loved sports, cars, junk food (meals and snacks were a major event for him, and only his youthful metabolism kept him slim) – and girls. The girls didn't take him very seriously, though, despite his appealing, dreamlike qualities. But perhaps he was a trifle too romantic for the other teens at Hawthorne High. For years he worshipped a girl named Carol Mountain from afar. He was crazy about her and talked to his friends about her all the time, but she wouldn't give him a second look.

Like many teenagers in Hawthorne, where a small-town mentality pervaded, Brian was remarkably unsophisticated. He was a fun-loving, immature kid, a real 'locker-room cutup.' He developed a penchant that he would never outgrow for practical jokes, along with a huge, deep laugh: 'Har! Har! Har!' His sophomoric pranks were fairly typical. Once, on the way to school in his beat-up two-tone '57 Chevy, he stopped his car at a light. To the astonishment of the driver behind him, he threw up what seemed like a river of milk by hiding the carton next to his mouth. During some horseplay in the school locker room, he once pretended to be knocked unconscious by a wet, knotted towel. While he lay on the floor of the shower, refusing to get up, one of the other guys urinated on him, which brought him to his feet quickly enough. Some of his other pranks were less inspired, such as cursing at the passengers of other automobiles and then hiding on the floor of his car; wrapping toilet paper around his head like a bandage while visiting a friend in hospital; and introducing his mother to friends by saying they thought she was over-weight and needed to diet. Even Murry was not exempt from his pranks. He once filled Murry's favorite pipe with grass from the lawn and laughed till tears rolled down his cheeks when Murry tried to light it.

But pranks on Murry were rare events indeed. As the oldest son, Brian had the gravest responsibility to please his father, and wholeheartedly tried to live up to Murry's expectations of him – never an easy task. Murry was impossibly hard on Brian, with rarely a kind word. One close neighborhood observer said, 'Brian had a tremendous capacity for love, and he wasn't able to express it around his family. He got no love from his father, and his mother was always balanced between them. Murry would say, "Audree, if you love me, you will see my point, and don't give in." Audree was always being put in the middle. If she agreed with the kids, then she deserted Murry, and he'd throw a tantrum and there'd be hell to pay. If she agreed with Murry, then the kids lost their mother *and* their father.'

Brian played left field for the Little League 'Seven Up' baseball team. Murry was always at the sidelines, coaching and complaining about Brian's performance. Later, in high school, Brian played center field for the varsity baseball team and quarterback for the Cougars, the school football team. A dead shot at practice, Brian would clench up and fumble balls as soon as he was in a game. And Murry never let him forget it. As Brian recalled: 'I had him come to my football games, and I'd say, "What did you think of me?" and he'd say, "You sloughed off! You're lazy!" I used to catch it from him all the time over that stuff. "Don't slough off, get in there and fight!"'

Although Brian got along with almost everybody, the one person he didn't get along with was his middle brother, Dennis. 'We were very competitive because Brian was the oldest and the most important,' Dennis said. 'I spent more time with Carl because I could beat Carl up.' Indeed, Dennis not only swatted Carl around unmercifully, calling him a 'pussy' at every turn; he also had trouble getting along with most other people.

Dennis looked the least like the Wilsons, with his blond hair and slim, athletic body. 'I felt guilty because I wasn't fat,' Dennis said. 'I felt out of place. I couldn't stay at the

58

dinner table, I'd have to run out.' And yet, Dennis was the most like his father. Strong-willed, arrogant, fearless, with no sense of physical danger, he was filled with nervous energy. Even when he was too small to go out alone, he would spend hours standing by the screen door, staring out into the street and the world beyond. Athletics became a natural release for him, and the beach held a special lure. When Dennis was old enough, Murry bought him a blue nine-foot two-inch surfboard. Although he never mastered surfing completely, he had such perfect co-ordination that he could wiggle each toe independently and entertained the girls on the beach by picking up dimes with his toes. On weekends, when the family would drive toward the beach, Dennis would stand up in the backseat of the car, waiting breathlessly until the ocean appeared over the last rise.

A typical middle child, without the authority of his older brother or the sympathy of the baby of the family, Dennis never got enough attention. So he developed some specific ways of attracting it. 'My brothers both had a bed-wetting problem, until they were thirteen or fourteen,' Dennis said. 'I hated those motherfuckers for that – they got all the attention. You know what I'd fucking do? I'd pee in their fucking beds in the middle of the night, once in a while, just so they'd get into trouble. I was the wild boy in the family.'

By the time he was a young teen, Dennis was smoking cigarettes, the pack rolled up in the sleeve of his dirty white T-shirt. Anytime something was wrong in the neighborhood – broken windows or air let out of car tires – Dennis was likely to have had something to do with it. The neighbors called him 'Dennis the Menace.' Ida Kennedy, who lived a few doors down from the Wilsons, could not keep Dennis from climbing the telephone pole in her backyard until she put him in charge of keeping the other children off of it, a duty he performed with relish. Once, he tried to purchase a gallon of gasoline at Lindner's Grocery Store. Gil Lindner quickly discovered that Dennis intended to concoct a bomb to throw down the sewage ravine and blow it up. When he was a little older, Dennis arrived at a neighbor's house crying real tears, carrying a Mason jar filled with ashes. 'It's Brian,' he told the neighbors. 'He was trying to light the gas heater and it exploded.'

Murry was not exempt from Dennis's mischief either. 'I was very proud of my dad's glass eye,' Dennis said. 'It was the only one on the block. When I was very young, I took it off the dresser while he was asleep and took it to school for "show and tell." I was very proud of it. Of course, when my dad woke up, he couldn't leave the house without it, and he was pretty pissed off.'

As Dennis got older, his pranks got him into more trouble. When he was fourteen he hot-wired Murry's car and drove it around the neighborhood with friends, stripping all the gears. On a nearby street he offered a little girl a nickel to get into the car with him. It was a joke to Dennis, but not to the little girl's parents, who called the police and had Dennis hauled off to the local station.

'I grew up beating up every guy in sight,' Dennis said. 'I was the fighter. I was always slugging away. I'd be set off like that [snap], I'd go, "Oh, yeeeah?" I walked around with a chip on my shoulder. I was happy but I wasn't.'

Carl, a pudgy, square-faced little boy with a chip-toothed grin, looked the most like his father. The baby of the family, he was by far the most spoiled – although none of the Wilson children was spared the rod. While his bad case of adolescent acne cleared up as he grew older, his weight problem only got worse. He was terribly self-conscious about it, even as an adult. Dennis taunted him with the nickname 'Porky.' Carl was a quiet, fairly withdrawn boy who idolized his brother Brian. Said Audree, 'Carl . . . was always sitting, watching the parade go by, very calm.' His mother's favorite, Carl was able to develop a more sensitive side that Murry would not allow Brian. He was not exactly a momma's boy – the Wilson kids were much too tough for that appellation – but he developed a closeness and empathy with Audree that Brian would always resent.

Carl has sweet memories of his childhood. 'We'd all sleep in the same room,' Carl remembered, 'and after we went to bed, Brian would sit there trying to make us laugh. First, my mother would come in and warn us. If our father came in, then it was curtains. So we'd be trying not to laugh, covering our mouths, hiding under the sheets, and Brian would keep cracking us up.' They would often fall asleep harmonizing with each other, often on a hymn called 'Come Down, Come Down from the Ivory Tower.' But Carl still remembered Murry with the same respectful awe as his brothers. 'When my dad walked through the house, it would shake,' he said. 'It sounded like a giant.'

The Wilson house on the corner of 119th Street and Kornblum was a vortex of neighborhood activity. With three growing boys, each with his own group of friends, there were always bikes lying on the lawn, a game of catch, or touch football in the yard, often with Murry at the helm, coaching, directing, putting in his two cents. On Saturdays the boys would have to go down to Murry's shop in east LA and help him clean the machines, a chore they all dreaded. Murry saw himself as the perfect all-around dad; as far as he was concerned, he and the boys were buddy-buddy, and nothing was wrong. In fact, he bragged to friends that he had told his sons all about sex one night, 'eyeball to eyeball,' all in bed together, kind of like a pajama party. Some nights, Murry would invite the boys into his bedroom and make them massage his back to relax his muscles.

To the outside world, the Wilson boys seemed to be well-behaved children who toed the line for a strict father. But something more was going on behind the doors of the Wilson household. In a neighborhood of simple values, where a good swift crack for a misbehaving child was thought to be a good thing, a disciplinarian father was not out of the ordinary. But Murry's discipline went beyond any swift crack. Twenty years later, when it would become a national issue, it would be called child abuse.

4

'My father resented the fucking kids to death,' was Dennis's explanation for it. 'The motherfucker hated us, or he would have loved the shit out of us. It's that fucking simple. That asshole beat the shit out of us.' Then Dennis grinned sardonically. 'He just had a very unique way of expressing himself physically with his kids,' he said. 'Instead of saying, "Son, you shouldn't shoot a beebee gun at the streetlight," he'd go *boooom*!!! I got the blunt end of the broom. *Crack*! One minute late! Just one minute late! *Boom*! And that's it. Brian and Carl would hide in the bathroom, "Oh, God! He's getting it!" Later they'd ask, "Did it hurt, Dennis?"'

Murry's father beat him; Murry beat his children. Audree watched helplessly from the sidelines, according to Dennis frightened of Murry herself. 'Ohh, please, Murry, no, don't do that.'

According to Audree, 'He was a taskmaster. He really

was. He was tough. And I used to think he was too tough. But, it was a very hard job for him having three teenage boys. He used to call them "young stallions."'

'Denny did [get] some pretty hard spankings . . .' Audree said. 'Dennis reminds me very much of his father. Sometimes I think, I don't believe this, it's like Murry revisited. Dennis got the worst of it. Because he was more aggressive. But what constitutes a beating, I don't know.'

Indeed, if beating the boys had been all Murry did, it would have been one thing. But Murry had red-faced, screaming, roaring tantrums. On many occasions his punishments went beyond simple beatings into the realm of the sadistic. Dennis spoke of Murry beating him up in the bathtub so he couldn't break anything by kicking. Once, to humiliate a preteen Brian, Murry reportedly forced him to defecate on a newspaper or plate in front of the family. (This story has many versions. Another popular one is that Brian and his brothers served up a portion of rubber 'doggie-do' to Murry on a plate, which was taken as a good-natured prank. Both versions of the story are sworn to.) Another time, Murry reportedly tied Brian to a tree for punishment, and once, when he caught Brian masturbating, he made him go without dinner for two nights. Dennis was summarily punched, kicked, and beaten with a two-by-four. At a family Christmas gathering, when Murry noticed Dennis sneaking drinks, he actually picked him up and tossed him across the room, where Dennis crashed against the wall and collapsed in a pile on the floor. Once, Dennis refused to eat the tomatoes on his plate. Thereafter, Murry forced him to eat one every time they were served until he vomited at the sight of them. Throughout his adult life, Dennis was never able to eat another raw tomato. In another incident, Dennis remembered, 'I almost burned the house down a couple of times. I was four or five or six, and I was playing with

63

matches on the curtain, the little balls of lint . . . and they'd go *fooom*. The punishment for that was he burned my hands with the matches. He was brutal.' Murry also used his prosthetic eye – which he could pop out to reveal the gnarled and scarred socket – to punish the boys. At the dinner table, he would sometimes roll the glass eyeball next to his plate while winking the empty socket at them. While the socket frightened and horrified Brian and Carl, it fascinated and amused Dennis, with his macabre sense of humor.[1]

In some ways, Brian got the worst of it, if not in terms of physical punishment, then in terms of psychological torment. Brian was a nervous wreck as a teenager, and the slightest challenge made him extremely anxious; he had to take a tranquilizer to go through with his driver's test. Brian found it next to impossible to satisfy Murry. He claimed the only reason he got B's and A's in school was so he could come home and say, 'Hey, look, Dad,' but the grades were never good enough. Indeed, Murry seemed to have a special way of attacking Brian. In later years, a project called the High Risk Consortium, comprising fifteen major research centers around the world, was formed to study schizophrenic children. As reported in the *New York Times*, the findings of the consortium indicated that 'specifically, when showing disapproval . . . parents tended to attack the child himself rather than to criticize things he had done; they habitually told the child what the child's feelings and thought were rather than listening to what the child had to say . . .' Said Dr Michael

---

[1] In 1971, when some of Murry's bizarre punishments came to public light for the first time in a *Rolling Stone* article by Tom Nolan, Murry vehemently denied them. Reportedly, Murry phoned Brian and accused him of spreading vicious rumors, particularly about defecating on a plate. Brian was supposed to have responded, 'Let's tell them that I shit in your ear and you hit me in the head with a plate.'

J. Goldstein, the director of a study at the University of California at Los Angeles, 'The parents of these kids engaged in character assassinations. Instead of criticizing what the child had done, they would make a personal attack, saying, "You're no good," which damages the child's self-esteem.' Brian once described Murry's criticism of him after school football games in this way. 'It bothered me because it made me feel like I was goofing up, that I was inferior. It made me feel worthless.'

When Brian was only six or seven years old, the family noticed that he had a peculiar way of turning his head to listen. According to Audree, Dennis and Carl had frequent ear infections, but not Brian. A doctor suggested that all three boys should have their tonsils out. Audree related, 'The doctor said that Brian's tonsil on the right side was so huge that if we had his tonsils taken out . . . that [it] would stop blocking . . . his eustachian tube – he said after three months he should be okay. But it wasn't okay. They say it's a nerve deafness . . . it could be congenital or it could have been caused by an injury. We had a neighbor who he got into a fight with one time. He hit him really hard on his ear . . .'

What is really important is that Brian believed that Murry was responsible – a belief that he was only able to admit much later in his adult life. In Brian's mind, his deafness was possibly the result of Murry smacking him on the side of the head when he was only two years old.[2] Incredibly, this hearing defect – only 6 per cent of normal hearing in his right ear – meant that Brian, who was to become one of the great innovative producers of modern

[2] This story has been embellished with time until some witnesses, including Brian's high-school music teacher, Fred Morgan, claim they saw Murry hit Brian in the head with a baseball bat at Little League. If this is the case, it is unlikely it caused Brian's nerve damage, which occurred before he was old enough to play baseball.

music, would never hear stereo. The irony of this loss would plague him for life.

'My dad was an asshole,' Dennis said, 'and he treated us like shit, and his punishments were sick. But you played a tune for him and he was a marshmallow. This mean motherfucker would cry with bliss, like the lion in *The Wizard of Oz*, when he heard the music.'

5

If music can soothe the savage breast, the Wilson children learned to make music at an early age.

Brian's musical accomplishments were prodigious, embellished by family pride and media legend over the years. At the age of eleven months, Brian allegedly was able to hum the entire 'Marine Corps Hymn.' Murry would sing 'do, do, do, do, do, do' and Brian would repeat the sequence of notes exactly. According to his proud daddy, before he was a year old he was able to say 'Mi-sez-zip-py.' Brian said his earliest musical memory was of listening to 'Rhapsody in Blue' at his grandmother's house when he was two. This Gershwin piece, he said, became his 'general life theme.' When the boys were still toddlers, Murry did an extensive renovation on the garage and built a music room with a Hammond organ where he and Audree would harmonize at night, just as his own mother and father had.

'Brian took six weeks of accordion lessons when he was very young on a little, almost toy accordion,' Audree said. 'He excelled, he just flew through it, but we couldn't afford to buy the big accordion.'

Brian started to sing at age three. He was able to pick out chords and 'he'd sing right on key,' according to

Audree. Later, Brian joined the church choir, where he was asked to be a soloist, and would often sing for school functions. One Christmas he and three other students dressed up as clowns and did a satire on 'Jingle Bells' that Brian wrote. He had a pure and beautiful alto voice, almost like a *castrato*, and the children in school laughed and made fun of him, calling him a sissy. Dennis remembered Brian running home from school in tears. 'It broke my heart to see him emotionally involved in the music at such an early age and have his friends laugh at him.' He learned to sing in a deeper voice, saving the falsetto he was developing for when he was alone.

Fascinated by harmonies, Brian would come home from school and go directly to the music room. 'There was many years of his life when he did nothing but play piano,' Carl said. The Four Freshmen became something of an obsession for him. 'Months at a time. Days on end. He'd listen to Four Freshmen records.' He would sit next to the hi-fi, his head cocked, carefully picking out the different harmonies and studying how they wove into the melody line.

'When Brian was fourteen, the Four Freshmen were playing someplace in Hollywood,' Audree said. 'We couldn't afford to take [everyone] – we didn't have very much money – so Murry took Brian this Sunday night just in the hopes he could meet them because he was so thrilled with their music. He was already writing vocal arrangements, even though he hadn't had any musical training. Years later, when they were the Beach Boys, the Four Freshmen remembered meeting Murry and Brian.'

For his sixteenth birthday Murry and Audree gave Brian a Wollensak tape recorder. For the first time he could record the harmonies himself. First he taught Audree the simplest part and sang harmony with her into the tape recorder. Then he would play it back and he and

Audree would sing live to it, creating four parts. Later he would expand the parts to include Murry, with the bass line, and eventually Carl.

While Brian was into classical music, Gershwin, and harmonies, Carl was into rock-and-roll, particularly Chuck Berry and Little Richard, whom he listened to on the radio. 'Carl was the second one to show interest,' Audree said. When Carl was three years old, 'he was really into the cowboy music and Spade Coolie. He would stand with his foot on a stool pretending he was playing the violin. Carl was twelve when he decided he wanted to play the guitar, so we bought him an inexpensive one, and he took a few lessons from a neighbor. One day he came home and he was playing an old standard, and one of the chords was way off, and I was appalled. And Brian said, "How can you let him take lessons when he's learning wrong chords?" Well, that didn't last long; Carl began to play on his own and he loved it.'

Dennis was the last to participate – reluctantly; he stubbornly refused to join in on the family sing-alongs. But he started playing the piano on his own when he was fourteen. He never had any formal musical training, but he played well enough to hack out a mean boogie-woogie.

On Friday nights the whole family would go down to ABLE Machinery and pick up Murry in his 1950 'Henry J,' which Dennis thought was 'the ugliest car in the world.' 'My dad would take us out to dinner and we used to write tunes,' Dennis said. 'The three of us would sing three-part harmony every Friday night in the backseat.'

6

Every Christmas, the Wilson family would attend elaborate holiday parties at the home of Murry's younger sister, Emily 'Glee' Love. Glee and her husband, Milton Love, lived with their five children in a large, imposing home on the corner of Mt Vernon and Fairway, in the Baldwin Hills section of Los Angeles. The house was not a mansion, but in contrast to brother Murry's Hawthorne bungalow, it was quite impressive: a five-thousand-square-foot Mediterranean villa on three levels, situated atop a sloping lot. At Christmas, the house would accommodate as many as sixty family members and friends. After a huge traditional feast of turkey and hams and puddings, which Glee would spend all week preparing, there might be a small musicale in which the family members would perform. Sometimes the guests would put on their winter coats and go out into the chill Los Angeles night air to stroll from house to house, singing carols for the neighbors.

'Glee would teach us the carols, and we'd harmonize,' Brian remembered. Often, when the caroling was over, Brian and his eldest cousin, Michael, would go off by themselves to a quiet room and sing their own harmonies, usually to 'Happy, happy birthday, baby . . .' 'Mike would add a few little bass lines, and I used to recognize that he had a great bass voice,' Brian said. 'I started teaching him Four Freshmen parts . . .'

Michael Edward Love, born March 15, 1941, was fifteen months older than Brian. Tall and skinny, with reddish-blond hair that began irrevocably to thin from the time he was a teenager, he had piercing, cold blue eyes.

The oldest child, with two brothers and two sisters, Michael was looked up to by his siblings and was the favorite of his grandmother, Edith. A bright, quick-witted young man, he inherited the Wilson family's musical interests. When he was only four years old, he sang 'That Old Black Magic' in perfect pitch, remembering the lyrics from beginning to end. For one of the musical shows at his mother's Christmas galas, he wrote a song called 'The Old Soldier,' which so impressed Murry that he felt compelled to write new lyrics for it. Brian dutifully performed the number at the next family gathering, wearing his first set of long pants, and, according to Murry, 'He brought the house down.'

Michael was never very interested in school. He started out with fair grades, but he got bored easily and his marks fell as he went into high school. The teachers complained that he disrupted classes with his wisecracks and that he would read his own books under the desk when he was supposed to be studying. At Dorsey High, where he graduated in 1958, he was an extremely well-liked student who distinguished himself as a cross-country runner. Much was expected of Mike, and his mother was quite demanding of him. He was expected to baby-sit for his brothers and sisters whenever needed, and once when he forgot to close the lower casement windows so his siblings wouldn't fall out, Glee threatened to throw him out of the house and took all of his clothing and put it on the front porch.

All kinds of achievement in music, arts, and athletics were encouraged in the Love household. Any music lessons the children wanted were supplied. Mike's younger sisters, Maureen and Stephanie, were talented harpists and singers; younger brothers were both outstanding athletes, Stanley an exceptional basketball player and brother Stephen a surfer, as well as a promising

70

student. Maureen was the first female student-body president at Western High School, and Stephen was student-body president at Morningside High.

The children's interest in music was inherited from their mother, Glee, who loved music as much as her brother Murry did. Glee had a beautiful, clear soprano voice, and would sing along to the recordings of opera stars she played. As the hi-fi blared away, she would study the librettos and learn the words to the popular operas. A supporter of local LA opera, she attended all the new productions. Milt would go along with her bravely, but he didn't care for opera very much. Though proud of their mother's pretty voice and impressed with her interest, the children too found opera stuffy, and much preferred listening to rock-and-roll. However, rock-and-roll had to be played *very quietly* in the Love household, and sometimes at night the boys would sneak a transistor radio – a new invention – under the covers to listen to their favorite tunes. In fact, when Brian slept over, he and Mike would often fall asleep outside in the family's Nash Rambler, listening to the radio.

As a young girl at George Washington High School, Glee was considered one of the prettiest in school. She was in all the school plays (where her future sister-in-law, Audree, was in the chorus), and starred in a production of *The Red Mill* in her senior year. She was just a pretty girl of fifteen when she was introduced to Milton Love, seventeen, also a student at George Washington High School, where he graduated in 1935. They dated for three years and, despite the objections of her parents, ran away and got married in Ventura, California.

Milton Love's family was of English–Irish descent. Grandpa Edward Love was born near Shreveport, Louisiana, and came to Los Angeles with his family in 1905. They were so poor they pitched a tent on Huntington

Beach and lived there until Edward could find a job and rent a house on Thirty-first Street in downtown Los Angeles. There Edward met a neighbor, Edith Clardy, who was born in Glendora, California, on an orange ranch. They were married on January 4, 1917. Edward went to night school and later into the sheet-metal business. When their two sons, Milt and Stanley, were old enough, they joined their father in the growing family-run concern, the Love Sheet Metal Company. Theirs was a fortuitous situation; Los Angeles in the forties and fifties was experiencing an unprecedented building surge. The Love Sheet Metal Company got many of the major fabrication contracts to install new stainless-steel kitchens for hospitals and schools. They made a great deal of money, and in the late forties Milt and Glee moved to their handsome View Park home.

But by the end of the fifties, things started to change drastically for the Love family. First their golden boy, Mike, didn't seem to have much direction in his life. 'I was in the oil business for a while,' Mike said. 'Gas and oil, check the tires.' He worked the night shift at a Standard Oil station at Washington and La Brea. He hated it, particularly after he was held up at gunpoint. During the days, he was an apprentice at his father's sheet-metal factory. It was around then that he found out that his high-school sweetheart, Francine St Martin, was pregnant. He wanted to take her to Tijuana for an abortion, but his mother wouldn't hear of it, and they married soon after. The wedding was a small affair at Franny's mother's house. A daughter, Melinda, was born in 1959. Although the Loves liked Franny, the family couldn't help feeling that perhaps Mike had ruined his life. The young couple took a small apartment on Eighth Avenue in Inglewood.

In the late fifties the recession began to hit the building industry hard, and the sheet-metal fabricating business, particularly that part of it where Milton Love and his brother were making most of their money, was soon wiped out. 'It happened before we realized it,' Milton said. 'There was much more money owed out than coming in.' They struggled to keep the business together for a few years, but in 1959 it was clear the bottom had fallen out. The bankruptcy laws were stringent at the time, and not only was it considered the utmost shame to have to declare bankruptcy, it cleaned the Loves out financially. Everything they owned was gone in a year: the house on the corner, the cars, all of it. For the children, especially the younger ones, it was a great trauma. The family moved to a much smaller, three-bedroom house, at 10212 Sixth Avenue in Inglewood. 'It was two miles from Hollywood Park racetrack,' remembered Stanley Love, 'two miles from Morningside High School, where I attended, as did my brother Stephen, and three miles from Hawthorne, where the Wilson family lived.' On Wednesday nights Brian and Mike and Maureen would walk home together from the Angela Mesa Presbyterian Church Sing Night, singing, 'In the Still of the Night' at fever pitch.

When Mike was twenty, Brian nineteen, Dennis sixteen, and Carl fourteen, they were asked to sing at an evening talent show at Hawthorne High School. Although Brian had already graduated from Hawthorne High the year before and was now attending El Camino Junior College, hoping to become a psychologist, he thought it would be fun to go back to the old school and perform. For some reason, Carl didn't want to do it and Audree insisted. To coax Carl along, Brian named the impromptu group Carl and the Passions. They intended to sing only for this one high-school assembly. Dennis suggested they write a song about the surfing craze, and Mike came up with a 'bob-bob-dit-dop' scat for the middle. The act was great fun, but nobody took it very seriously.

*You know, few families are together
spiritually and emotionally over a piece
of art.* – Dennis Wilson

Three

1

'It was a dreary afternoon in 1961,' Dorinda Morgan
wrote years later. 'My husband Hite and I were in our
office on Melrose Avenue in Hollywood. We were just
about ready to call it a day when Alan Jardine came in.'
The Morgans were old-time Los Angeles music publishers, Alan Jardine an aspiring folk singer.

At the time, the Morgans owned Guild Music, a small,
storefront recording and publishing firm located in a one-
story building just across the street from KHJ Studios in
the old Capitol Building. A large plate-glass window faced
the street, with a sign that read STEREO MASTERS. The front
part of the store was the office. In the rear was a small
monophonic recording and mastering facility. Through
the doors of this small store had passed scores of beginning groups, singers, and songwriters auditioning for Hite
and Dorinda Morgan. Kindhearted, open, and encouraging, the Morgans had seen practically everything the
business had to offer during their long careers in music
publishing, which they had begun in New York with
offices in Tin Pan Alley before they moved to Los Angeles
in the late forties.

Alan Jardine was one of the many hopefuls who came
to the Morgans' offices. Nineteen years old, only five feet
four inches tall, with blue eyes and brown hair, he had a

74

ready smile that showed slightly buck teeth. Immaculately clean and neat, Alan had an elflike quality that made him 'cute.' A second-year student at El Camino College, he was a sedate, conservative folk-song aficionado. He had first called the Morgans for an appointment several months earlier to arrange an audition with a group of friends, doing a song about the Rio Grande. The Morgans were unimpressed. 'Professional, but not original,' Dorinda Morgan said. 'We turned them down. They were imitators, not innovators.'

A few months later, Alan Jardine was back with a new folk group called the Pendletones. One of the boys innocently explained that they had named the group after the manufacturer of the wide-striped shirts that were fashionable at the time, hoping they might get free clothing that way. The Morgans thought it was a silly, but cute name, and didn't bother to tell the boys they had already auditioned another group using it.

'The tallest boy in this group said, "Mrs Morgan, I bet you don't remember me,"' Dorinda Morgan said. 'He was right.' But Brian Wilson certainly knew who the Morgans were; they had known his father since the early 1950s. Not only had they published several of his songs, including 'Two Step Side Step,' but Murry had brought Brian to the Morgans' home several years earlier to audition to record a song called 'Chapel of Love' (not the Dixie Cups hit of 1964) when they were looking for a 'young voice.' Brian, twelve or thirteen years old at the time, was rejected. Over the years the Morgans had become social friends of the Wilsons, and the two couples dined together occasionally. It was Murry who had originally recommended the Morgans to Alan Jardine, when Al asked him how to get started in the music business. Murry gave Al the Morgans' phone number, then called Hite Morgan himself and said, 'See if you can do anything for him.'

Alan had known Brian from Hawthorne High, where both boys had been on the football team and in rival singing groups. But they had only recently become friendly and started singing together. Born Alan Charles Jardine on September 3, 1942, in Lima, Ohio, he was the second child of Charles Jardine and Virginia Louise Loxley. His mother was a housewife, his father a plant photographer for the Lima Locomotive Company. The Jardines lived outside of Lima on Rural Route #5, where Alan's grandfather first taught him to play clarinet. When Charles Jardine moved to California to manage a blue-printing plant for the Scott Railroad Company, Alan wound up at Hawthorne High, where he joined a folk group called the Islanders. He had been singing and harmonizing with various groups ever since.

During the summer of 1961 Alan had run into Brian Wilson on the El Camino campus. Alan had once suggested nonchalantly to Brian that they form a singing group. 'I said, "Let's do it, let's get together."' They met the next day in the nurse's room in the college medical center. Alan brought along 'a football player, a deep bass singer who couldn't carry a tune,' he said. 'So Brian said, "Hey, my little brother Carl can sing." And I said, "*Him*?" I remembered him from high school, when he was about three feet tall . . . twelve years old. And Brian said, "He's young but he's really talented and so is my cousin Mike . . ."' Alan gave it a shot and came over to the Wilson's house to harmonize. Eventually the boys called themselves the Pendletones.

The Pendletones intended to audition for the Morgans with some old favorites that Alan had dug up, but the Morgans told them that they needed original music to get recorded. 'You've got to have an angle,' Mrs Morgan told them. 'Something to set you apart from the others.' Suddenly, the boy with the blond crew cut and the devilish

76

twinkle in his blue eyes piped up, 'Have you heard about the new surfing craze?' The other kids in the group looked at Dennis as if they wanted to shoot him.

'I honestly have not,' Mr Morgan said. 'What's that?' Dennis described the floating slab of wood the size and shape of an ironing board, on which you stood while being hurled toward the shore by a wave. 'It's the biggest thing happening at the beach,' Dennis assured the Morgans. 'Everybody's got a surfboard. They even give surf reports every morning on the radio.'

The boys pointed out that there were already scores of musical surfing groups throughout southern California. Every beach community along the coast had a surfing band with a local following, and many of the kids in the groups were avid surfers themselves. The better groups, like the Surftones, had already broken through and recorded on small labels. The boys confessed they had recently started writing a song called 'Surfin',' and the Morgans agreed to hear it when it was finished. Dorinda Morgan in particular liked the idea – she told the boys to write down all the surfing phrases they knew, add them to the lyrics, and polish the melody. She sent them home to work on it. If she liked what she heard when they came back, they could record it.

Audree and Murry were not at home. They had gone off to Mexico City for a long weekend with a business associate of Murry's, Barry Haven, who was visiting from England with his wife. Before leaving, Audree had stocked up on coldcuts for the boys, and had left some money in case they wanted to eat out. The boys took the food money and rented instruments to work on the song about surfing for the Morgans.

2

It was quite remarkable that the Morgans had never even heard about surfing; it was already one of the biggest recreational crazes ever to hit California. Hollywood had begun to exploit the California beach scene in 1959, with Columbia Pictures's release of the first 'beach' picture, *Gidget*, which included an early surf song, 'Lonely Surfer.' Based on the real-life adventure of a petite surfer girl named Kathy Kohner, nicknamed 'Gidget,' shorthand for 'girl-midget,' the story came from a best-seller written by Gidget's father, Frederick Kohner. This vanilla classic of the innocent teenager in a bikini, tempted with sex, love, and the ultimate virginal romance, was high teen fantasy. It immortalized Sandra Dee as Gidget, and included James Darren and Cliff Robertson in the co-starring roles. But most important, it romanticized surfers and surfing for the first time; the Boy on the Board was on his way to becoming a sturdy part of California folklore.

Yet what was happening along the beaches was no plastic Hollywood product – it sprang out of the real California postwar life-style. The baby boom's millions of first-generation Angelinos were coming into adolescence; the first modern generation of southern Californians was developing its own culture. For most young natives – whose life was literally bordered by the Pacific – surfing was more than just a sport. It was a part of their natural environment. Surfing was almost addictive; it had a hypnotic effect. Many said surfing was like sex – it felt good every time you did it. The surfing craze had spread as far inland as San Bernardino and up and down the coast in a crowded arc from Malibu to Redondo Beach, where there were already about two hundred well-known surfing beaches. By 1961, when the boys first told the Morgans about surfing, there were already an estimated thirty thousand regular surfers on the beaches each weekend; by 1968 there would be one million.

The California surfing craze came as no surprise to the people of Australia, where, since 1954, there were so many surfers that surfboards were registered like automobiles. The Polynesian 'sport of kings' had been discovered by westerners when Captain James Cook visited the Hawaiian Islands in 1778. But surfing wasn't popular in America until the 1920s, when the Hawaiian surfing champion, Duke Hahanamoku, who had broken the hundred-meter freestyle record in the Olympics in Stockholm in 1912, gave a surfing demonstration in Atlantic City. It wasn't until the fifties that the sport reached mass public interest among the war babies coming of age along the California coastline.

The surf music being produced at the time was supposed to duplicate the feeling of surfing. It was a musical brew specific to beach and surf that was best appreciated live, but it had become big radio business too – KFWB, called 'Color Radio,' was the 'surfer's choice.' There were dancing clubs and 'surf groups' all over the south bay area – the Chantays, the Pyramids, the Rumblers, the Challengers, and the Marquettes, whose most popular number, the 'Surfer's Stomp,' had its own dance that was supposed to simulate the movements of riding a board. The best-known group was Dick Dale and the Deltones, who used to pack the Rendezvous Ballroom in Balboa every weekend. Born in Beirut but raised in California, Dale was nicknamed 'The Pied Piper of Balboa,' and at Friday-night dances at the Rendezvous the Deltones would draw four thousand kids. Dale claimed he invented his staccato guitar style to simulate riding a wave. The

Deltones' repertoire included 'Miserlou,' 'Surfing Drums,' 'Death of a Gremmie,' and the famous 'Let's Go Tripping' and 'Surf Beat.' Although Dale was a popular live performer, his songs never recorded well. His tunes were raunchy, chord-throbbing instrumentals that all sounded as if they were recorded live including the hoots and holler of surfers.

The surfing culture had already developed its own etiquette, dress code, and language: 'outside' meant 'in the fast-breaking waves'; the 'boneyard' was the area between the breaking waves and the beach; 'cutting back,' 'climbing,' and 'dropping' meant 'hotdogging,' or making moves that the better surfers made; trunks were called 'baggies'; to 'hang ten' meant to run up to the end of the board and hang your toes over the end (boards are now usually too small for this to be possible). Using bits and pieces of this slang, Brian and Mike Love sat down in the music room of the Wilson bungalow and wrote a version of a song called 'Surfin'.'

They had the song completed when Audree and Murry returned home from Mexico with Barry Haven and his wife. The two couples walked in the door to find the den full of equipment, including amplifiers and microphones. 'We saw all this stuff,' Audree said. 'They had used all of the grocery money. They had borrowed some from Mike Love, and they rented the mikes and the bass. I'm not sure about the drums – I think they bought them.'

Murry's face turned deep red as he exploded in full fury. How dare they spend all the grocery money on equipment!

The boys knew how to diffuse Murry's anger immediately. They rushed to the instruments, warmed up the amps, and started to play. Murry grew calmer with each note. 'His attitude changed pretty fast after he heard the song,' Barry Haven said. 'Oh, they had the teen beat and all that, but also some pretty melodies and chords that really made you feel like relaxay-vooing.'

The boys had something there, Murry decided. And of course, he wouldn't mind giving them a few pointers.

3

The Morgans liked the surfing song and booked time for the boys at a small, privately owned studio in Beverly Hills called Keen Studios. During the rehearsals and preparation of the song, there were major blowouts with Dennis, and by the time of the recording date, Brian and the others had decided he wasn't good enough to play with them. Audree finally insisted the boys let Dennis stay in the group. However, on the night of the session the boys arrived with another drummer, whom Brian had heard play in a country-western band at a club called the Shed House. Dennis put on a brave face, standing on the sidelines when the replacement drummer set up. Brian and Mike teased Dennis, while Carl tried to act as mediator. Dennis glowered in the background at the boys started to warm up.

'This other drummer was a hillbilly Gene Krupa,' Dorinda Morgan said, 'a real hotshot. I let them do one set with him and I said, "No way, this guy has got to go." We paid him and sent him home.' Dennis took over on drums – but not that night. According to Carl's version of the session, 'I played basic chords on the guitar, Al thrummed bass, Brian took off his jacket, laid it across the drum, and beat it with his hand, while we all sang into one microphone.' Although Carl remembered that there was a drum, Brian probably only played the top of a

81

plastic trash-can cover. In most future sessions Dennis was the official drummer, but he never learned to hold his drumsticks in the 'approved' manner. As he was to admit years later, 'I'm not an artist; I'm a clubber.'

The finished song was no knockout. Produced by Hite Morgan, with assistance from studio engineer Dino Lappas, it took all of an hour to record. Nasal, whining, and childlike, the two-minute-and-ten-second song was hardly a hint of what would become the Beach Boys' warm layers of bell-like harmonies. But it was certainly an authentic-sounding surf song, and different. When the track was finished, the boys were surprised to learn that the Morgans insisted the 'B' side of the single be a composition by their own son, Bruce, who was nineteen at the time. Bruce had been writing songs since he was eleven, and the Morgans felt his one-minute-and-forty-three-second 'Luau' was right for the other side. Grudgingly, the boys laid down the track.

A standard songwriter's contract dated September 15, 1961, was signed between Guild Music Publishing and Michael Love and Brian Wilson for the song 'Surfin'.' They were to receive 28.5 per cent of the wholesale royalty on sheet music, and 50 per cent of the publishing, as well as six cents a copy – a typical low-end contract. The Morgans also agreed to get the boys into the musicians' union.

When the session was over, the Morgans took the boys out to one of the nearby chain restaurants. After wolfing down burgers and fries, the boys politely thanked the Morgans and left, ditching Dennis, who was driven home by the Morgans. Over apple pie à la mode, Dennis pretended not to mind that the others had left him behind. 'I really want to be a screenwriter,' he confided to Hite and Dorinda, 'or maybe write short stories.' He admitted that he was earning pocket money by sweeping out a local laundromat for a dollar a day and didn't have high expectations for his brothers' musical career.

4

Although record sales had tripled in the last half of the fifties, from $60 million to $205 million (and would triple again to an astounding $600 million by 1965), the Los Angeles music business in the late fifties and early sixties was a far cry from the multimillion-dollar industry it would soon become. The centers of musical growth were still Manhattan, where the Brill Building saw the height of songwriting activity; Detroit, where Berry Gordy had started Motown; and Nashville, the home of the country-music sound. The major record companies in existence – Capitol, RCA Victor, MGM, Decca, Mercury, and Columbia – were only signing 'star' quality singers; that meant mostly white, middle-class Americans, with a big-band sound. The airwaves were full of such artists as Connie Francis, Percy Faith, Bert Kaempfert, and Brenda Lee. The teen market, which consisted of a host of young vocalists like Fabian, Shelley Fabares, Del Shannon, and Frankie Avalon, was considered a passing phase. Only Elvis Presley had crossed over to an adult audience in a big way. Gimmick records were quite popular: Sheb Wooley's 'Purple People Eater,' David Seville's Chipmunk songs, and Chubby Checker's twist records, to which Jackie Kennedy was dancing at the Peppermint Lounge in New York – were all on the hit parade.

In the west it seemed the only way to be discovered was by small, independently owned companies, who could take the time and effort – but often did not have the money – to seek out unknown groups and record them.

The problems of distribution were much tougher for independent labels. Their only route was to wholesale the record to 'one-stops' – large clearing houses with warehouses full of every possible record. The records would then be distributed nationally to the thousands of 'Mom and Pop' record stores all over the country. Since accounting malpractices were common, many of the 'indies' worked on a 'two-record payment system,' in which they took it for granted that the Mom and Pop stores would cheat them on the revenues from a hit record. The only way a new group could collect its just royalties was to have a second hit and then withhold the second record from the one-stops until the Mom and Pop stores paid up. The most cutthroat part of this struggle was that often the major record companies would quickly cover hit records put out by the independent labels – that is, record a duplicate version of the song with one of their own stars. Under this system, the original artists would remain relatively unknown.

Yet hitting it big held a special lure for an independent label. There was a gold fever mentality. Los Angeles in the late fifties and early sixties had hundreds of independents, publishers, and mastering companies all over Hollywood in hot little offices on back streets. Some, like the Guild Music Company, listened keenly to whatever might be the next big thing to come along. 'Surfin',' the Morgans hoped, was that next big thing.

The Morgans knew Joe Saraceno, the artists-and-repertoire man at a small label called Candix Records. They played 'Surfin'' for Saraceno, and he in turn called Russ Regen,[1] a one-time recording artist who worked at Buckeye Record Distributors, which distributed Candix,

---

[1] Russ Regen went on to an illustrious career in the music business, and eventually became president of 20th Century records.

among many others. Saraceno played 'Surfin'' over the phone to him. Regen thought the boys sounded like another local group, Jan and Dean, who already had a hit with a single called 'Linda.' He thought 'Surfin'' had a shot, but the name of the group – at that point Saraceno was calling them the Surfers – just wasn't right: 'There's already a group on Hi-Fi Records called the Surfers.' Laughingly, Regen added, 'Why don't you call them the Lifeguards or the Beach Bums . . . something to do with the beach? I got it! Why don't you name them the Beach Boys?'

The newly christened group was released on a small subsidiary called X Records on December 8, 1961.[2] Hopeful and excited, the boys waited for reaction. Meanwhile, the Morgans got to work. Along with Saraceno and several others connected with the deal, they started calling programmers at local radio stations. The Morgans knew Bill Angel, the record librarian at KFWB – the station that gave surfing reports and was on the air twenty-four hours a day. KFWB claimed to have introduced the 'Surfer's Stomp,' Connie Francis's 'When the Boy in Your Arms,' and Frank Sinatra's 'Pocketful of Miracles' in the Los Angeles area. Bill Angel listened to 'Surfin',' liked it, and decided to play it. At the same time, a disc jockey named Sam Riddle introduced the song on KDAY.

A few days later, the boys were cruising around Hawthorne in Brian's 1957 Ford listening to the radio when the disc jockey announced a contest. Three songs would be played, and the one that drew the most phone calls would be added to the playlist. One of the three songs was 'Surfin'.'

The boys went berserk in the car. 'Nothing will ever

[2] 'Surfin''/'Luau' was first on the X label. The name of the label was changed to Candix reportedly because of the threat of legal action by an RCA subsidiary with the same name.

85

top the expression on Brian's face,' Dennis said. 'Ever
. . . *That* is the all-time moment.' Carl got so excited he
celebrated by drinking as many milkshakes as he could
before throwing up. Dennis ran up and down the street
screaming, 'Listen! We're on the radio.'

On December 29 'Surfin'' officially debuted on the
KFWB playlist at number 33. 'So this record was out and
going strong and we booked them at the Rendezvous
Ballroom,' Dorinda said. They took the boys to a small
tailor shop in Glendale and bought them cheap gold
jackets to wear for the performance. The boys didn't get
paid to play, but the Morgans thought it was good
exposure; Dick Dale was headlining, and the Challengers
and the Surfaris were also on the bill. But the inexperi-
enced Beach Boys could hardly hold the crowd's attention. They were only allowed to play during the
intermission, and the audience quickly grew restless and
bored before the Beach Boys even finished their two
songs. The performance was clearly a bomb. Although
they were all disappointed, the group seemed undaunted –
except for Brian. 'He was really humiliated,' Dorinda
Morgan remembered. But in Brian's humiliation, a spark
of competitive determination was lit.

On New Year's Eve that same year the group appeared
for a second time, at a Richie Valens Memorial dance.
They were paid what seemed like a shockingly large sum
at the time – $300. By January 13, 1962, 'Surfin'' on the
Candix label was number 118 in *Billboard*. Thrilled with
their success, the boys signed contracts to publish and
record several more surfing songs with the Morgans. On
February 8, 1962, the Morgans recorded four more songs
with the group at Keen Studio: 'Surfer Girl,' 'Surfin'
Safari,' 'Judy,' and 'Karate.' Before the session, Murry
insisted the boys record one or two of his own songs.
When they refused, Murry considered it an insurrection,

but Brian held firm. No Murry Wilson compositions were to be recorded by the Beach Boys that night.

Meanwhile, 'Surfin'' ate its way slowly up the charts, each week the song's progress seeming more incredible. The excitement at the Wilson household grew into a frenzy. From 118 'Surfin'' went to 112, the first week of February to 105, the next 101, the next 93, and then 90. By March 24, 'Surfin'' had sold fifty thousand copies and reached number 75 in the *Billboard* charts. The Wilsons were in heaven.

Murry was so pleased with the Morgans for their overnight magic that he practically gave the group to them in a grand, sweeping gesture that he would soon regret. On newly printed Beach Boy stationery ('Teenage Dances, Recording Artists, Television and Radio and Stage Appearances, Brian Wilson leader, M. Wilson Manager') that he had quickly printed up, Murry sent the Morgans an unsolicited letter of 'Intent and Agreement,' dated March 29, 1962. It said (in part) that the Morgans would be expected to 'perform the duties of producing, recording and promotion, any or all songs written. It is also hoped that you will obtain major recording contracts, to distribute the group's releases and that as producers can made decisions pertaining to the leasing of the Beach Boys tapes, masters and songs . . . and will protect the rights of the Beach Boys in matters of contracts.'[3]

According to Dorinda Morgan, 'Murry was so ecstatic he just handed them to us on a silver platter.'

---

[3] Murry added a paragraph that read, 'It is understood that Brian Wilson, leader of the Beach Boys, may hire or fire anyone of the Beach Boys from time to time at his discretion, to keep the group together or to improve same . . .' This, presumably, to keep Dennis in line.

5

Now that 'Surfin'' was a hit, Mike Love didn't want to keep working at his father's sheet-metal factory, and told him so.

'Well, what if this doesn't work out?' Milton asked him.

Mike shrugged. 'So if it doesn't, I'll be back scraping shit off metal.'

The success of 'Surfin'' caused a change in Brian that no one expected. To say that it went to his head is no understatement – even his hair changed one day when he arrived home with bleached-blond locks. He said he felt his 'public' needed to see his hair the sun-bleached color of the surfers he wrote about. When Audree saw it, she howled, 'Oh, my God!' and took him right into the bathroom to see how much of it she could wash out. She finally made him dye it back to its original color, and it wound up with a greenish tinge.

Brian was suddenly very much aware that he was a *star*, of sorts, and his public – the people in the neighborhood – received kind but condescending treatment. Brian started getting 'pushy,' according to the Morgans. A competitive streak a mile wide suddenly emerged in him. It wasn't so much that he wanted to further his own self-esteem – he seemed to want to beat out the other surfing groups. He kept asking the Morgans what kinds of awards and accolades the group could win. 'What do you care?' Dorinda Morgan said. 'Here's this kid – a month ago he didn't have anything and now he's Paul Anka. He got so "up the neck," my husband and I started to get a little fed up with him.'

Murry, of course, had his own characteristic reaction to

the success of 'Surfin'.' Having a national hit, even at number 75, was a feat of which any family would have been proud. But when Murry Wilson heard the record 'Surfin',' he hated it. It was amateurish – bush-league. Everything was wrong with the record; it was put down live and had all been done in one take on one track. It was mixed terribly, with a disappearing bass line and buried vocals.

Brian's heart sank like a stone. 'My father was critical of the first thing we did,' he remembered.

'It's crude,' Murry Wilson said. 'It's rude. Well look, you don't hear the guitar, you don't hear this, what is going on here? Listen, I'm going to have to take over as producer.'

'Which he did,' Brian said. 'He took over as producer.'

One of Murry's first ideas was, of course, to have the group record and sing some of his *own* songs. Good old-fashioned songs, with his boys' pipe-organ harmony. Suddenly Brian found himself with Murry as a songwriting partner, ready to live out his own aspirations through his sons.

*Oh man, he fought for his kids, he got them
a contract at Capitol. –* Audree Wilson

Four

1

Diagonally across from the Wilsons' house on 119th Street
lived the family of Benny Jones. Mr Jones knew that the
Wilson children were local celebrities, and he mentioned
them to his sister's son, Gary Usher. A handsome, lanky
twenty-four-year-old, Gary Usher had a small claim in the
music business – he had recorded two singles on the small,
independent Titan label when he first moved to California
from Massachusetts after high school. While nothing had
happened to the obscure songs, Usher had a cursory
knowledge of the Los Angeles recording scene and more
than a passing interest in it. By day he worked as a teller
at the City National Bank in Los Angeles, and at night he
took courses at El Camino Junior College. In Hawthorne
he lived with his grandmother, but spent much of his time
at his Uncle Benny's house, where he could see Carl and
Dennis racing up and down the street on their bicycles.

One Sunday in January 1962, just as 'Surfin'' was
hitting the *Billboard* charts at 118, Gary Usher heard the
Wilson family practicing in their converted garage. With
his Uncle Benny's encouragement, he followed the music
across the street and sheepishly introduced himself. Usher
said, 'Maybe I inflated my two credits more than they
were worth,' but he must have seemed very expert to
Brian. The five-year age gap – Brian was only nineteen at
the time – seemed to melt in their mutual interest, and

90

the young men took to each other instantly. 'What happened in those days was something I've never experienced since. There was a spirit going down between us. It was actually magical. There was a freshness, a naïveté.'

That evening Usher played guitar and bass while Brian picked out some melodies with him on the organ. Within twenty minutes they had written their first song together, 'The Lonely Sea,' which would later appear on a Beach Boys' album and in the surf movie *The Girls on the Beach*. Brian and Usher became inseparable friends. During the next several months they wrote over thirty songs together, twelve of which would be recorded, among them several Beach Boys classics.

The alliance with Gary Usher would mark the first of many times that Brian looked outside of his immediate family for a collaborator. Although he continued to write music with his cousin Mike, for the rest of his career he would generally be aided by a New Best Friend – an adjunct personality for which Brian had a strong need. In part, these friendships happened because Brian didn't think of himself as a competent lyricist. But in his own peculiar way, Brian fell in love with his song writing collaborators – he would develop an intense, psychological bond. 'We became almost platonic lovers,' Usher said. 'Brian isn't gay, and neither am I, but there was a really deep attraction.'

While they were making a demonstration tape of their first song, Usher was introduced to Brian's whimsical side. For 'The Lonely Sea,' Brian wanted to record the actual sound of the ocean as background, and since they had no means of overdubbing sound effects, he insisted on lugging his huge, forty-pound monophonic tape recorder to Manhattan Beach to record the surf live. Because the recorder was electrically powered, Brian brought a hundred-foot extension cord with him to the beach. 'I'll never forget walking up to somebody's house at one o'clock in the morning and asking if I could plug in a line . . .' Usher said.

A few days later, Brain had an idea for a song in the tradition of New York song writers Jerry Goffin and Carole King, whose smash hit 'Locomotion' had been recorded by their maid, rechristened 'Little Eva.' Brian's West Coast version was called 'Revolution' – but since the Wilsons had no maid, Brian decided they should go out and look for one. Brian told Usher, 'Oh, you just go down to the black part of the city and get a singer. Let's go in the car.'

Usher said, 'Shit, we'll get killed for sure. You don't walk up to some black girl and proposition her to sing.' But Brian insisted it would be safe. Shoeless, in bleached chinos and T-shirts, the two of them drove to Watts in Usher's car. They parked the car on a busy street, and Brian blithely walked up to the first stranger he saw and asked, 'Do you know a girl who sings?'

'It turned out a lot of guys knew girls who sang,' Usher said. 'I can remember knocking on a guy's door at five o'clock in the afternoon and saying, 'Does your daughter sing?' We actually found a girl singer and we tried her out, but she was bad. Even so, that led us to another singer, and she was good.' This girl's name was Betty Willis, but they credited the record to Rachel and the Revolvers for commercial purposes. The song was later released on Dot records, backed with another tune Brian and Usher wrote together called 'Number One.' It was one of Brian's first productions outside of the Beach Boys.

Some of Brian's ideas went beyond the whimsical. As Usher describes this side of Brian, 'He was sensitive to the point of being unbalanced. He was esoteric and very eccentric. If it was two in the morning and Brian had an urge for a milkshake, he couldn't go to bed unless he had a milkshake. If he wanted to play Ping-Pong at eleven-thirty at night, he'd knock on the neighbors' door and get them out of bed to play Ping-Pong.' One night, in the music room, they got into a discussion about parallel dimensions and of the possibility of life existing on another time plane. In the middle of the conversation Brian was suddenly petrified. He insisted that a being from another dimension had appeared outside the window. For Brian this was no joke – he became so frightened that he scared Usher, who fled the Wilson house.

Gary Usher's greatest musical contribution was that he helped Brian inaugurate a new Beach Boys specialty – the automotive song. Cars were not merely a teenage obsession in California in the sixties – they were a necessity. Usher owned his own car, a 1961 248 white Chevrolet that he had bought with money he earned at the bank. His dream was to own a 409 Chevrolet, one of the fastest cars on the market. Brian and Gary were driving on Western Boulevard, headed for an auto-supply store, when Usher started talking about saving up for his dream car. 'Save my pennies, save my dimes,' Usher said, and Brian started to hum a tune. 'I need more horses,' Usher said of his 248 Chevy. 'This dog's not going quick enough.' Suddenly Brian said. 'That's it! We gotta write a song about the hottest car on the road.' That night they wrote '409,' which added to Brian's growing stockpile of tunes.

Brian often discussed his problems at home with Usher, but his fierce loyalty to Murry prevented him from completely opening up. The Wilsons' was a household where everyone's emotions – except Murry's – were kept inside, and there was really no one for Brian to confide in. Brian had only one place where he could retreat from the tension that pervaded his life – the music room, where he

93

now slept. 'Brian was always saying that his room was his whole world,' Usher said. One day they decided to write a song about it called 'In My Room.' Although Usher wrote the lyrics, they were all based on Brian's sentiment. 'In My Room' not only turned out to be one of the most hauntingly beautiful of Brian's early compositions, but also one of the most telling – and one of the most prophetic.

> There's a place where I can go,
> to tell my troubles to,
> In my room, in my room . . .

Of course, Murry was at once suspicious and jealous of Usher. He was alarmed to see that Usher and Brian took to each other so quickly, and he was wary of Usher's influence on Brian. Usher not only ran with what Murry presumed was a fast Hollywood crowd, but he would frequently take Brian with him into Hollywood and introduce him to the other people he had met in the record business. Usher's greatest crime, however, was that he was an outsider collaborating musically with Brian. When Murry learned how many songs Brian and Usher were writing together, he practically insisted that Brian write songs with him. Usher once attended one of these father–son songwriting sessions. It began with Murry saying, 'Let's write a song about yellow roses.'

Usher couldn't believe what he was hearing. 'That's really old-fashioned,' Usher told Murry, not realizing what he was daring.

'It is *not* old-fashioned . . .' Murry began to sputter.

'Oh, come on, Brian,' Usher said. 'You don't have to write with him. He's doing Lawrence Welk stuff, let's do Goffin and King.'

Murry flew into a rage and threw Usher out of the house.

Usher was upset. He could hear Murry screaming at Brian all the way down the street as he walked back to his Uncle Benny's house. 'Walking into the Wilsons' house was like walking into twelve soap operas in one day. You never knew what was going to happen. It was always some scene . . .' Indeed, Usher walked into the house one day to find Murry lying on the floor in his bedroom, beating his fists with rage. The next time Usher came over, Brian apologized profusely for his father's behavior.

Before long, Usher decided he wanted a fair share of the publishing ownership for the songs he and Brian wrote together. He suggested a fifty-fifty deal. Brian said he'd have to talk to Murry about it, and any further discussion was put off for several weeks. Then Brian apologetically gave Usher the verdict. Murry wouldn't hear of any deals. Brian wasn't twenty-one and couldn't enter a deal on his own. Brian said Murry thought Usher was trying to drive a wedge between him and his brothers. Murry believed Usher was only thinking of his own concerns and not thinking about what was best for the brothers – which would be to have their own publishing company.

And so Murry formed his own publishing company, Sea of Tunes, to handle Brian's songs. If Usher was going to write songs with Brian, Murry would split the publishing three ways: Usher would receive one-third of the profits, Brian one-third, and Murry one-third for administering the growing catalog. The proposed split in itself was not particularly unfair – often the publisher gets 50 per cent in return for a cash advance – only there was no cash advance and the publisher is not often your father. 'When the deal was made,' Usher said, 'if I wanted my money, I had to sign a contract,' which limited his royalties as a writer. Moreover, Murry wrote the contracts so that he owned controlling interest in Sea of Tunes, giving him an enormous influence over the Beach Boys' career.

2

Murry's bedroom – more specifically, Murry's bed – soon became command central for the Beach Boys' activities. Murry's next move was to take over the boys' personal appearances; he began to manage them, with Audree doing the bookkeeping. However, in the beginning there wasn't very much bookkeeping. It was Murry's idea that exposure was more important than salary. According to Audree, 'My husband used to say they did forty freebies . . . we used to drive to San Bernardino, to Fresno, to many other cities [and give free concerts] . . . it was actually a smart move . . .' The station manager of KMEN in San Bernardino remembers that Murry 'literally begged' him to let the Beach Boys play a teenage fashion show in a local department store, and that they looked and played very badly.

'The DJs were all putting on their own dances at the time,' Audree said. 'They called and asked [for the Beach Boys to perform for nothing], and we'd say yes. At that time, my husband and I were doing everything . . . wild days . . .' So wild, in fact, that some of Murry's practices verged on payola, which included giving gifts of cheap necklaces to radio-station managers, encouraging them to play the boys' recordings.

His approach with the people at the boys' record company and distributor was more direct. Murry would attend meetings with the record-company people without the Morgans' knowledge, and they hated it. 'He was very aggressive, very pushy,' Dorinda Morgan said. 'He was a born high-pressure salesman. It put almost everybody off. So he sold and then he unsold.'

Murry's relations with Candix grew worse when the royalty check came in for 'Surfin'' and turned out to be less then $1,000. 'He always said they really got cheated,' Audree said, 'because that record went to number seventy-five in the nation, it was a big hit on the West Coast. At that point Hite was their publisher, and Brian said to his dad, "Would you please help us? . . ."' Murry took the difference out of his own pocket so each of the boys would earn an even $200. Murry became even more suspicious and unhappy when he learned that Candix Records was reportedly having financial troubles. They had spent so much money pressing copies of 'Surfin'' that the company funds were depleted before they could get their money back from the slow-paying distributor. In the interim, Hite Morgan tried to make arrangements with Era Records to pick up the distribution of the boys' records. Allegedly that gave Murry the right to terminate the contracts and go elsewhere.

Although only months before, he had signed an exclusive management contract for the boys with the Morgans, Murry booked time at Western Studio without telling them. On a Sunday, with a talented engineer named Chuck Britz at the controls, Murry had the boys rerecord several of the songs owned by the Morgans – 'Surfin' Safari,' which Brian had written with Mike Love; Brian's solo compositions, 'Judy' and 'The Surfer Moon'; and the Gary Usher collaboration, '409.'

Murry set out with these demos under his arm and made the rounds of the record companies one by one. Dot, Decca, and Liberty passed.[1] It seemed that with the current popularity of white solo singers, the major record companies weren't interested in a vocal group. They were

[1] Audree remembers that these demos were done with Hite Morgan's knowledge, and that both Murry and Hite 'cooled their heels at Decca and at Dot and someplace else.' Dorinda Morgan disputes this.

on automatic pilot, so blithely indifferent to discovering new talent, that if the switchboard of a recording company got a call from someone who had a new group, the operators were instructed to say they weren't signing anybody for six months. Murry and his sons were lost.

Murry had a different tactic for approaching Capitol Records, the next company on his list. Some years before, Murry had submitted a few of his own songs to Capitol's country-western A&R man, Ken Nelson, who had passed on them. But Murry thought Nelson might like the Beach Boys' old-fashioned harmonies and called his office several times asking for an appointment. Nelson was much too busy to hear Murry's sons' songs and was hardly the right man at Capitol to champion a surfing group. Instead, he referred Murry to a colleague in pop A&R who could relate to the idea of a surfing group a little better.

Twenty-one-year-old Nikolas Venet was Capitol's youngest executive and probably the only one to have a surfboard on the top of his car, which in his case wasn't a car at all, but a Leland Land-Rover jeep. A first-generation Greek-American born in Baltimore, Venet had moved to Los Angeles in the late fifties and started working for a jukebox company. Savvy, glib, and charming, Venet was considered Capitol's 'street connection,' and was by the older men esteemed because he was in touch with the 'youth market.' Venet already had an impressive track record. At the age of nineteen he had produced several hits for the Lettermen, including 'When I Fall in Love,' 'The Way You Look Tonight,' and the number 1 hit song 'Tom Dooley.' Ken Nelson's secretary called Venet's office and asked him to please see Murry because he was driving Nelson crazy.

Venet's connection to the Lettermen made him the perfect contact for Murry, who called him shortly before Venet was to take a two-week vacation in Baja, California. Murry waited impatiently until Venet got back and then went to see him in his twelfth-floor office in the famous circular Capitol Building in Hollywood. Murry blustered and raved, making his usual indelible impression on Venet. After telling Venet at length how wonderful his sons were, he finally put the demo of 'Surfin' Safari' on a turntable in the office.

'Before eight bars had spun around, I knew it was a hit record,' Venet said. 'I wasn't one to hide my feelings. I got all excited, and of course [Murry] got all excited, because he wasn't one to hide his feelings either. I knew the song was going to change West Coast music.' Venet promised he would recommend that Voyle Gilmour, a Capitol executive, purchase the masters, and Murry asked for a three-hundred-dollar advance per song.

The story of what happened next differs according to who tells it. Murry's version, which is firmly part of the Beach Boys legend, has it that Murry, Brian, and Gary Usher waited in a nearby coffee shop for only an hour before going back to hear Voyle Gilmour's decision. According to Venet and Usher, Gilmour was busy, and it took a few days for Venet to pressure Gilmour into making an offer. Gilmour said $300 for the masters was too much money, and suggested offering Murry $100. Venet wouldn't hear of it. 'Voyle, you gotta give them three hundred dollars,' Venet said. 'It would cost that much to make it here.' Venet eventually went over Gilmour's head to chief executive Lee Gilette and was able to pay Murry his asking price.

In the days when record albums sold for $2 each, $300 for the outright purchase of a master, plus 2.5 per cent royalties, wasn't as poor an offer as it sounds. At the next meeting, Murry accepted the offer. According to Usher, when Venet asked about buying the publishing rights, he quickly said, 'It's already taken.' Venet paused for a moment, as if this might queer the deal. Usher had his heart in his mouth until Venet finally said, 'Okay,' and called the contract department to draw up an agreement.

In the elevator, going down from Venet's office, Murry cornered Usher, putting his bright red face up close to his, and said in his most menacing tone, 'You do that one more time and you're finished!'

'He made mincemeat, he decimated me in front of Brian on the way down,' Usher said. Ironically, not turning the publishing rights over to Capitol was one of the best things that could have happened to Murry. Within a few years, those rights would be worth millions of dollars.

3

Meanwhile, the Morgans got wind of the impending Capitol release of the rerecorded tracks they already owned. 'We found out through the grapevine,' Dorinda Morgan said. 'We were a little angry, but we weren't surprised; this is a dog-eat-dog business, and you're not surprised at anything. They started to make it – it was very simple.'

To soften hard feelings, as a sort of farewell present, a few members of the Wilson family showed up at the Morgans' studio and put some vocals on prerecorded instrumental tracks of two songs written by their son Bruce. Alan and Carl were on the tracks, but not Dennis or Mike Love. Even Audree sang along. The tracks were attributed to a group the Morgans called Kenny and the Kadets.

Hite and Dorinda Morgan discussed what to do about Murry's recutting the songs they clearly owned and selling them to Capitol. With the signed contracts and management agreement, they had enough ammunition to win a lawsuit, but neither of them could bear the thought. Murry was too overpowering to drag through a suit; if he wanted his boys that badly, he should have them. In the long run, in terms of aggravation, the Morgans thought they were better rid of him. Hite Morgan's farewell statement to Murry was 'Rots of ruck to you!'

'Can you imagine that?' Audree said. 'That's what the man said. "Lots of luck to you." '

'That statement cost him two million seven hundred thousand dollars,' Murry gloated. 'Two million seven hundred thousand dollars.'

Hite and Dorinda Morgan had some legal recourse, however. The Morgans sued Capitol for the use of the songs they owned. The suit was resolved, after many years, with a reported cash settlement to the Morgans of $80,000. The Morgans' small part in the Beach Boys' history was over.

Now came a strange twist of fate. Just as the Capitol contracts were about to be signed, Al Jardine left the group. He was discouraged by the small amount of money they had made through Candix. 'I made the decision I didn't really want to put a big investment into the group, and at the same time I wanted to finish dental school . . . so there was David Marks for a year . . .'

David Marks was a bratty fourteen-year-old neighborhood kid who lived across the street from the Wilsons. David and his mother and father, Joanne and Elmer Marks, were from a small town south of Newcastle, Pennsylvania. They had moved to California when David was seven. After renting for a time, the Markses bought a house at 11901 Almertons Place in Inglewood. David met Dennis Wilson the day they moved in. He was eight, Dennis was ten. Dennis Wilson, as usual, was up to no

101

good. The Marks's home was just on the other side of the sewage lines that divided Hawthorne and Inglewood, and according to neighborhood status, it was better to live on the Hawthorne side. While the Markses were moving in, Dennis was busy throwing bags of garbage across the street to the Inglewood side. David Marks threw it right back, and he and Dennis became fast friends. David would often play with the Wilson boys at their house, and Murry used to love to roughhouse with the kids. David remembers Murry getting him into a headhold and giving him a 'noogie,' a hard pinch in the back of the neck. 'They hurt like hell,' David said.

The Wilsons' offer to David to become a replacement for Alan Jardine wasn't given much thought; that he played rudimentary guitar was enough of a qualification. The boys and Murry showed up at the Marks's house one night while David was watching 'Bonanza' and asked him to join the group. David was thrilled, but his parents weren't sure it would be a good thing for him. There was school to think about, and the group traveled constantly on 'personal appearances.' The Wilsons and David spent an hour cajoling and begging, until Joanne and Elmer finally consented.

'So when they signed their first contract with Capitol,' Audree said, 'David was one of the original Beach Boys. He was at our house all the time. David was so young – I always liked him and felt sorry for him. He was a pain in the neck, he really was, he drove everybody crazy. Brian would not allow him to sing on the records, because he *couldn't* sing . . .'

And now, with a new lineup, a contract from one of the majors, and complete control, Murry set out to make his boys *stars*.

4

At the time, Brian was deeply in love with a girl he knew from school called Judy Bowles. She was pretty, with azure eyes and reddish-brown hair that she wore in the bangs and French roll that were fashionable at the time. She dressed like a proper lady, in skirts and white blouses. Judy was Brian's first 'true love.' In Hawthorne, and in Brian's simplistic, romantic conception of things, the girl you pinned and went steady with, the girl you made love to, was the girl you were going to marry. There was never any doubt in Brian's mind that Judy Bowles would be the mother of his children and his partner for life. She became the inspiration for many of his early songs, including 'Judy.' When Brian started to attend El Camino College, he proposed and gave Judy an engagement ring.

Brian and Judy frequently double-dated with Gary Usher and his fifteen-year-old girl friend, Bonnie Deleplain. Brian, Gary, and the girls would spend evenings driving around Hawthorne and Inglewood, visiting the Fosters' Freeze or buying a couple of six-packs. A typical date included a drive-in movie and a visit to the neighborhood haunt, the 'Which Stand, where Brian would order his usual vanilla Coke and fries drenched in ketchup. 'I can distinctly remember being half drunk with Brian and singing "Sherry" in the car at the top of our lungs with the windows rolled up,' Usher said.

Usher and Brian's major concern at the time was birth control. The only available method was condoms. Buying them would have been a near-impossible hassle; hiding them in the house from Murry was unthinkable. Instead, they practiced the birth control of the fifties – 'pulling out.' 'I'm surprised she didn't get pregnant,' Usher said.

Brian's need for privacy with Judy instigated his decision to move out of the Wilson home for the first time when he was twenty years old. Life at the Wilsons' hadn't changed much, even though 'Surfin'' was a hit. Dennis and Carl were both under eighteen and treated like children. Murry still made them go to the shop on Saturdays and clean the lathes. Brian's purchase of a red-and-cream-colored 1960 Impala gave him more mobility, but he remained very much under Murry's thumb, and the pressure was unrelenting. Brian would sit in the music room composing, and if Murry heard a chord change he didn't like, he would come barreling out of his bedroom to criticize Brian's work. 'I remember one incident,' Audree said. 'Brian was in the music room writing and Murry was in the bedroom watching television, and Murry came rushing down and criticized Brian's rhythm. Brian was furious, just furious. He said, "Fuck you!" which was horrible. I said, "Brian!" And Carl was there too and he said, "Brian!" Murry never got over that. He used to bring it up all the time. I was supposed to go over and hit Brian with a board, or clobber him or do something horrible.' The arguments became more frequent as Brian's creative ego expanded, and soon it became untenable for him to live at home.

Brian met his first roommate while playing at a Sigma Chi fraternity party at the University of Southern California. Murry had booked the date for them while 'Surfin'' was still on the charts. Bob Norberg was a twenty-three-year-old USC alumnus, a part-time salesman of copying machines who also taught swimming, and on the side had toyed with a career in music. At the same fraternity party, during the Beach Boys' intermission, he performed with his girl friend, Cheryl Pomeroy. The friendship that developed between Brian and Norberg echoed Gary

Usher's friendship. For a time, Norberg was to become Brian's New Best Friend.

Soon after the fraternity party, Brian brought Norberg home and introduced him to the family. Norberg passed muster at the Wilson household as an 'okay guy,' although Murry was still suspicious of outsiders. But Norberg didn't seem to be one of those 'Hollywood phonies' Murry hated so much, and finally Brian was given tacit permission to move out. 'He was ready to be on his own a bit more, get more independence,' Norberg said.

Brian moved into Norberg's hundred-and-fifty-dollar-a-month, one-bedroom apartment at the Crenshaw Park Apartments at 10800 Crenshaw Boulevard in Inglewood, not far from where the Wilsons lived. It was furnished cheaply – wall-to-wall carpeting littered with Norberg's barbells and surfboards, and two mattresses on which Brian and Norberg slept. There was a huge, antique mirror that Norberg had bought to work out dance steps for his act with Cheryl.

Norberg had a good understanding of electronics, and he pieced together a crude recording system with a quarter-inch, seven ips monophonic Wollensak tape recorder, along with a second tape deck, hooked together with kits for pre-amps and amplifiers. This system enabled Brian to record overdubs for the first time, and the process would become integral to all Beach Boys recordings. Brian even began to record guitars this way, sometimes detuning them to create a clashing sound. Many of the rudimentary Beach Boys sounds were developed in that apartment on Crenshaw. Norberg played guitar, and Brian bass, using Dennis's drumsticks and a 'block,' with a TV-dinner aluminum container for a cymbal sound – all recorded over and over many times.

Before long, Brian wrote a song for Norberg and his girl friend Cheryl called 'The Surfer Moon.' Again, Brian wanted realistic sound effects on the record, so he and Norberg dragged the Wollensak outdoors at night to record the sound of real crickets. Murry took the demo of 'The Surfer Moon,' backed with a song Norberg had written called 'Humpty Dumpty,' and sold it to Safari Records. Curiously, Bob Norberg's name appears on the credits as Bob Norman. Norberg says he was 'swayed' into it because Murry claimed Norman was a more commercial-sounding name; others said it was because Murry thought the name Norberg sounded too Jewish. The record was a flop, but marked the second time Brian composed and produced outside of the Beach Boys.

Norberg later recorded his own song, '1204,' which was arranged by Murry, for Tower Records, but his recording career was short-lived, as was his New Best Friend status with Brian. Norberg had started to fly planes privately, and he wanted to do it full-time. Within a few years he was hired by TWA and has worked for them ever since.

5

On June 4, 1962, Capitol released its first Beach Boys single, '409,' backed by 'Surfin' Safari.' Initially there was some discussion at Capitol about what song to put out first. Although 'Surfin' Safari' was a likely follow-up to their first hit, Nik Venet was concerned that the surfing theme would confine sales to the West Coast and decided to put it on the 'B' side of the single, releasing the automotive song '409' first. But when '409' didn't attract much airplay in its first few weeks of release, Capitol changed tactics and started to push 'Surfin' Safari' instead.

'That record was a hit in a matter of hours,' Nik Venet said. 'Eight hours after it was in the field, we were getting isolated reports from places like Phoenix, Arizona. The biggest order Capitol had from a single market all year was from New York City – where there was no surfing. It sold approximately nine hundred thousand records, but not enough for a gold.' The record appeared first on the national *Billboard* charts on August 11 at number 85. Throughout the summer and into the fall, it made a slow but steady ascent up five or ten positions each week. From the thirteenth through the twenty-seventh of October, it clung to its best position, number 14.

In the interim, Capitol rushed the Beach Boys into the studios, and in one twelve-hour session they recorded an entire album of songs, *Surfin' Safari*. It was an adolescent mish-mash – including a hymn to root beer, 'Chug a Lug' – produced by Nik Venet (except for '409' and 'Surfin',' which were the masters Murry had produced). For the album cover, Venet snuck the boys away from Murry and out to Malibu, where for $50 they rented a truck from a local beach contractor named Calypso Joe. Photographer George German airbrushed Calypso Joe's name from the door, and Venet and the boys decorated it with palm fronds. Dennis proudly held a surfboard. The album didn't do as well as the singles, however. Over the next three months it straggled up the charts to number 32 – a fair but unspectacular showing. But it was good enough for Capitol's enthusiasm about the Beach Boys to continue.

'409' got massive airplay in Los Angeles, particularly at KFWB, the city's most popular rock station, which was known as 'Channel 98.' KFWB's most popular disc jockey was Roger Christian, a short, handsome young man with wavy hair who worked the night shift. One night Christian was on the air discussing what the lyrics to '409' meant. 'A 327 was really better,' he later recalled. '. . . But the 409 was the big number they were pushing back then.

Everybody who got one thought it was just the biggest thing around . . . So I was playing the record, and I said it was a good song about a bad car.' Christian went on at length to discuss some of the technical details of the 409 that he thought were deficient.

In his bedroom in Hawthorne, Murry Wilson was listening to Roger Christian's erudite explanation of positraction and four-barrel carburetors, and decided *this* was the man to write more car lyrics with Brian. And it would be a good way to get Gary Usher out of the picture. He picked up the phone and called KFWB, announcing that he was the father of the Beach Boys, and demanded to be put through to Roger Christian.

'Say, you're really into cars,' he told Christian.

'We got to talking,' said Christian, 'and he asked me if I wrote songs. I said I'd written a couple of things.'

Murry suggested he try writing with his son Brian and arranged for the two of them to meet. Often Brian would go over to KFWB when Christian got off from the nine-to-midnight shift, and go out and have hot-fudge sundaes with him at a place called Otto's. 'We'd be writing lyrics . . . and all of a sudden we'd realize we wrote fifteen songs.' Christian would come up with a lyric and Brian would produce a melody instantly. Over the course of their collaboration they wrote more than fifty songs, sixteen of which would appear as Beach Boys records. Now Roger Christian was Brian's New Best Friend.

Gary Usher was crushed by Brian's new friendship. 'When Roger Christian really came in heavy, frankly, I felt a little hurt,' Gary Usher said. 'Roger was Brian's new love . . . love in the sense of attention, and I wasn't . . . I no longer enjoyed Brian's company. It was a great relationship and it slowly drifted apart for no reason . . .'

The *coup de grâe* that Gary Usher received from Murry began with a violent family argument that caused Dennis to move out. Murry had promised some business friends from Europe that Dennis would make them a hand-carved cigar box. At sixteen, Dennis greatly resented being forced into fulfilling this promise. One Saturday afternoon Murry came out to the garage, where Dennis was working, and examined the cigar box. 'It's not good enough,' he said, tossing it down on the workbench in disgust. 'It's lousy.' One word led to another and suddenly Dennis punched Murry in the face. It was the first time that Dennis had actually lifted a hand to Murry, and the incident turned into an all-out brawl. The racket that came out of the garage could be heard all over the neighborhood. David Marks and his father rushed across the street to help separate the two. 'They would have killed each other,' David remembered.

Murry banished Dennis from the house, and for several days he slept in the backseat of his friend Louie Marado's car. After a week or so, Dennis caught a bad cold and Audree insisted he come back to live with them. But Murry was still angry, and shortly after Dennis felt better, he moved back to Louie Marado's car. One morning Gary Usher ran into him – he looked exhausted and unwashed. Dennis told Usher what had happened, and Usher, who had recently rented his own apartment on Eucalyptus Avenue, invited Dennis to stay there. Dennis happily accept the invitation. Usher remembered that Dennis's first activity was to line up some girls. 'Dennis had an incredible knack for picking up girls,' Usher said, 'as well as a strange drive. Often he would have twelve girls in a week.'

'When Murry found out [that Dennis was my room-mate],' Usher said, 'I might as well have been dead.' Under Murry's orders, Usher was pushed out of the Beach Boys' professional circle forever. To seal his fate, Capitol next released one of Usher's collaborations with

Brian titled '10 Little Indians,' a lame vocal rendition of the famous nursery rhyme, backed with another Usher song, 'County Fair.' Both of these songs were unqualified failures and the only real out-and-out flops of the Beach Boys' early career.

6

Capitalizing on the success of 'Surfin' Safari,' the Beach Boys launched into their first professional tour in the summer of 1962. The forty-day midwestern trek marked the beginning of the prolonged road trips that would characterize the rest of their career. With Mike Love and Brian the oldest at twenty-one and twenty respectively, Dennis seventeen, Carl fifteen, and David Marks fourteen, they were too young to go out on the road alone. Much to the boys' relief, Murry had no time to go with them, since he was still running ABLE Machinery. Instead, he hired a professional road manager, John Hamilton, who had once road-managed the Ventures.

'The first tour, we went out in a station wagon,' Mike Love said, 'and we got so crazy in that station wagon it was ridiculous. There were five of us and the driver, and we all lugged our own instruments. We'd drive sometimes five hundred miles to the next date . . . Fargo, North Dakota, and then to Minneapolis, Minnesota, and then over to northern Michigan . . . we drove like eight hundred miles from one place to the next. We set up our own equipment and played on existing PA systems, which were really horrible.'

Dennis remembered that they 'played at halls for men who were all over sixty. It went down all right. When you're playing, you think it's fantastic. I don't know whether the people liked it, because they'd never seen anything like it before. They all walked out, all twelve of them. But we kept on playing and we got ten dollars between us.'

For Mike, the first impact of the group's success came one night at a concert in Hatfield, Minnesota, shortly after 'Surfin' Safari' had come out. 'It was literally a barn, converted into a dance hall, and there was a stage that was so narrow . . . A drunk sat down on my foot.' The boys had just finished their second set and had gone outside through the employees' door to get some fresh air. They were stunned at what they saw. There was a line of cars, pairs of headlights stretching a mile and a half into the distance, waiting to pull into the club's parking lot to see them. 'So,' said Mike, 'I knew something was happening.'

Those first road tours were fondly remembered by the boys as a wonderland of sex and freedom during which they indulged in as much debauchery as any teenager might dream about. At one hotel Dennis painted his penis green, hung it out of his fly, and went downstairs to the lobby for a Coke. In another hotel they paraded around naked in front of their window. 'There were a bunch of old ladies sitting around in the street in front of the hotel, and we were scratching our nuts from the second floor and jumping up and down in front of an air-conditioner. From the street they saw five guys jumping up and down and they didn't know why.'

The boys had lots of petty quarrels on the road, especially Dennis and Mike, who got into an occasional fistfight. 'Dennis usually instigated stuff,' David remembered. 'Once we went into the bathroom and peed in these squirt guns and put soap in them. Al Jardine was sitting on a couch reading *Reader's Digest*, and Dennis and I came in and squirted him. Al just levitated three

111

feet off the chair.' (This was a tour when Al and David were on the road together.)

Naturally, girls were a major preoccupation on the road. 'On my fifteenth birthday we played an amusement park in West Virginia,' David Marks said. 'A multimillionaire owned the park. He was a fun-loving guy who wore khakis and drove a jeep. After we played the show, he took us in his yacht club, which was a converted underground speakeasy. He got me some scotch and took me upstairs with some twenty-one-year-old whore that was sitting on the chair. I remember washing my cock off in a pan with soap and water – I don't know why – and she said, 'Don't come in the pan, now.''

When David left the room. Dennis was waiting in the hallway to go next. 'Was it nice and warm in there?' Dennis asked with a dirty smirk on his face.

'Oh yeah,' David answered naïvely, 'I think the heat was on.'

Carl also lost his virginity to a hooker on one of their early tours. More sensitive and serious than his brothers, he found the experience depressing. When Dennis congratulated him afterward, he shook his head sadly and said, 'She didn't even care.'

John Hamilton's employment ended when David Marks got the clap on the road and told his dad, who told his mother. She went straight over to Murry's house and complained. Murry fired Hamilton and went on the road himself for one week, determined the boys would be as decorous as a group of nuns. He made them absolutely miserable, trying at first to be reasonable. He lectured the boys, 'Now, this is a business we've involved in, and you have to act right. You can't just smile when you feel like it; you *have* to smile onstage, it's part of the performance.' At times they would be in the middle of a show and Murry would come running up the aisle screaming,

'Treble up! Treble up!' But he couldn't stop them from having egg fights in hotel rooms, and he quickly turned into a tyrannical taskmaster.

'One time Murry was sitting in the backseat,' David remembered, 'and I just leaned up and farted in his face. Murry turned around and said, 'Well, that's OK, Dave, now just don't show me any disrespect, that's all.' Murry would regularly call Joanne Marks to complain about David. 'He doesn't smile onstage and he doesn't carry his own amp,' Murry would tell her. 'He takes girls to the motel . . .'

When Murry decided that he wasn't cut out for the road, David Marks's father, Elmer, was elected for the job. 'It was just him and the boys,' Joanne Marks said. 'He hadn't been working – he was ill with a back problem – and Murry said "OK, you can be the road manager. Go with the boys and watch them . . ."' Murry then suggested that perhaps Audree should go on the road with Elmer Marks to help keep an eye on the youngsters. 'Audree didn't really want to go,' Joanne said, 'and there was no sense in her going. When everyone was away, Murry asked me to dinner. He thought he was going to strike up a relationship with me,' she said. Joanne Marks refused the dinner invitation, but the next Saturday morning she looked out the back door of her house and saw Murry crossing the street. Frightened, she locked the door before he could get there and refused to let him into the house. Joanne felt it was 'punishment' when Murry subsequently fired Elmer. David Marks claimed he never saw a penny from the road because Murry always said all the money went toward expenses. This was just the beginning of many quarrels between the Marks family and Murry. Said David Marks, 'Murry talked to me like he was dealing with a man, and I was just a kid, just out of the dirt with my cars and trucks – and all of a sudden here I was copping whores and drinking whiskey.'

If everybody had an ocean
across the USA
Then everybody'd be surfin'
like Californiyay!
  – 'Surfin' USA'

Five

1

By mid-October of 1962, 'Surfin' Safari' had hit number
14 on the national record charts, and in Los Angeles,
where the Beach Boys were local celebrities, it was
number 1. His boys were riding high, and Murry booked
them at one of the hottest clubs on Sunset Boulevard,
Pandora's Box. Sunset Boulevard was undergoing a trans-
formation. Once a more expensive preserve of nightclubs
and restaurants, it was now becoming the mecca of teen
nightlife in Los Angeles. The area between Highland
Avenue and Doheny Drive was turning into a turbulent
strip, populated by swarms of teenagers and college
students cruising up and down the street in expensive
cars. The exclusive restaurants and chic beauty salons
were being replaced by scores of trendy clothing boutiques, coffee-houses, and teen discos. Pandora's Box was
one of the better-known teen clubs, a tiny place built on
a small triangular island in the middle of the strip. No
liquor was served, and the oversized handscripted menus
boasted cappuccino, iced tea, and hot chocolate – which
is what Ginger Blake and her cousins, the Rovell sisters,
were drinking the night the Beach Boys took the stage.

Ginger Blake and the Rovell sisters were friends of Gary Usher. Although Usher had been relegated to a bench position on the Wilsons' team, he still kept in touch with Brian at the apartment Wilson shared with Bob Norberg. Usher was busy promoting his own career with appearances at high-school proms and record hops, many of them emceed by Brian's new collaborator, Roger Christian. It was at one of these hops that Usher met Ginger Blake, a teenage singer promoting 'Dry Tears,' which she had recorded on the Titan label. Ginger Blake was an adorable, petite Jewish girl whose real name was Sandra Glantz, and Gary started dating her although she was only fifteen. It turned out that Ginger had three cousins around her own age who also sang semiprofessionally – Diane, sixteen; Marilyn, fourteen; and Barbara Rovell, thirteen. One day Ginger invited Usher over to the Rovells' house on Sierra Bonita Drive to meet her cousins. Usher boasted to the young girls about his association with the Beach Boys, and the next weekend, when they were appearing at Pandora's Box, he invited Ginger and her cousins to see them.

The Rovell sisters were what the decidedly anti-Semitic Hawthorne crowd considered 'Fairfax Jews' – they had grown up in the ethnic stronghold south of Fairfax Avenue in LA. The three sisters looked remarkably alike, with beautiful dark skin and large brown eyes. All three had deep, distinctively froggy voices. Barbara was cute and quiet. Marilyn was the charmer; easy to laugh, vicacious, and bright, she was the leader, her moody elder sister, Diane, the follower.

The first night at Pandora's Box, only Ginger and Diane went to see the Beach Boys, and they instantly fell in love. 'They were these darling little surfer boys in their Pendleton shirts,' Ginger said. She was so taken with them that the next night she came back with her cousin Marilyn in tow. The Beach Boys ran through their set while Brian smiled down at the sweet, suntanned young girls sitting at stageside. Between songs, Brian asked Marilyn if he could have a sip of her hot chocolate, and as he handed it back, he spilled it all over her. But she didn't mind at all. 'He was so gorgeous,' Marilyn said. 'He had a perfect nose and he was very good-looking.'

Later, backstage in the crowded, dimly lighted dressing area, Ginger and Marilyn chatted with the boys and were introduced to Murry and Audree, who attended every show. Murry was very stern with the boys after the show, criticizing their performances, berating them for mistakes. 'You can't sit there and tune your instruments,' he told them. 'You have to play.' Then he turned to the girls and said, 'You know, girls, I'm only doing this for their own good.' Then he made a little wisecrack and softened up for a moment before abruptly becoming stern again.

The girls came back every night of the Beach Boys' week-long engagement, and on the last night Brian invited them out to visit his parents' house in Hawthorne. Marilyn enthusiastically agreed to come. But it wasn't Brian Wilson, who seemed much too old and sophisticated, that Marilyn had her eye on – it was his chunky, fifteen-year-old brother, Carl. 'You know, when you're young,' Marilyn said, 'everyone chooses to have a crush on someone, and I chose Carl.' Diane says she chose Dennis for herself, and set out to pursue him; but most observers at the time distinctly remember that Diane had a crush on Brian.

Marilyn was infatuated with Carl only for a few days, but a strong bond formed between them that would last a lifetime. 'One time we both ran to the park . . . I kind of chased him,' Marilyn said, 'and we fell all over each other and were cracking up . . . I remember I wanted to kiss

116

him and I don't think he had kissed a girl yet, and we just kind of looked at each other and laughed.' When they got back to the house, flushed and out of breath, Audree gave them a suspicious look. 'Then we just got to be friends with him and Dennis,' Marilyn said, 'and we went over to their house a few times. Then Brian moved out of the house and moved into the apartment with Bob Norberg.'

One night Marilyn and Diane brought the boys back to the house on Sierra Bonita Drive to meet their parents, May and Irving Rovell. Irving was a tall, reserved man with an aristocratic Jewish nose and a large moustache; May a short, round-faced, warm, Jewish mother. The Rovells and their three daughters had come to Los Angeles in 1955 from Chicago, where Irving owned a hand laundry. In Chicago the family had lived in a damp basement apartment, and every winter the girls used to come down with chronic tonsillitis. When the children's health could no longer withstand another bleak Chicago winter, Irving's mother loaned him $6,000 and they loaded up their old Buick, setting out for Los Angeles. Shortly after they arrived, they purchased a two-bedroom house with white stucco walls on Sierra Bonita Drive for $16,000, an unheard-of-sum in those days. To make ends meet, Irving held down two jobs, one at the Lockheed Precision Factory, as a sheet-metal worker, and the other a weekend position as a clothing salesman.

With their first savings, May and Irving bought an upright piano for the small living room. May was the musical one in the family, having studied piano as a young girl. She could listen to a song just once on the radio and pick out all the chords. All three of her daughters had strong, harmonious voices and loved to sing. May entered them in various talent contests, including the 'Yeakles

117

Amateur Hour,' which was broadcast on a local television station throughout the night. May sat up with the girls until three in the morning for their chance to sing 'Sugar in the Morning.' Their heart's desire was to sing professionally.

For Brian Wilson, the warm, loving Rovell household was an exotic change from the tension-charged atmosphere in Hawthorne. The Rovells were so giving and generous that he was not only fascinated with them but found their house a refuge. The Rovells, particularly Irving, enjoyed Brian a great deal; used to living in a house with four women, Irving took to Brian at once. 'Brian made him laugh,' Marilyn said. 'I never saw my father laugh so much. And my mother loved him.'

Brian quickly became a fixture at the Rovell's house. May's unfailing generosity and open kitchen – no matter how tight her budget – enthralled him. It was literally impossible to enter the Rovell's house, no matter what time of the day or night, and not have May prepare a meal for you. If Brian was hungry at three in the morning, May would organize a feast without hesitating. The Rovells opened their home not only to Brian, but to his brothers and all their friends and business associates. They entertained what seemed like every Los Angeles disc jockey and session musician in the business. Since many recording studios were located near their house, May was not surprised to get a phone call at 5:00 A.M. alerting her that the boys and their friends would be over at 7:00 A.M., when she would happily prepare breakfast for fourteen. Although May's food budget was only $30 a week, the boys left so much money lying around, some of which fell into the cracks of the sofa, that she started a fund from lost cash and added treats to the revolving menu. Often the street in front of the Rovells' house would be filled with teenagers drag-racing their automobiles, while Carl and Brian were in the backyard testing a new amplifier. Suddenly the small, happy home on Sierra Bonita Drive became the center of the Beach Boys' social scene. Everyone was allowed to sleep over if the hour grew late. David Marks remembers, 'I would go over there and get drunk and pass out on the couch. I would kind of open one eye and Marilyn's little sister Barbara would be covering me up.'

One discordant moment so stung Irving Rovell that the incident remained with him for years. Of all the Beach Boys' entourage, only Dennis was seldom a visitor to the Rovell household. On one of his rare appearances, he was bragging to Irving about how much money the Beach Boys were making and how little it meant to him. To illustrate his point, he took out a dollar bill and tore it up. Irving, who worked seven days a week at two jobs, was heartsick. After Dennis left, he saved the pieces of the dollar bill and taped them together. He keeps the dollar in his wallet to this day.

By now Carl and Dennis were objects of great resentment at Hawthorne High School. Dennis had already been suspended for throwing a screwdriver at another boy in his shop class. Soon after he turned sixteen, he was expelled. The way Dennis told it, 'There was this tall guy . . . who had ten all-day suckers – you call them lollipops. I didn't have a nickel to buy one, so I took one of his. He said, "Meet me in the boys' bathroom." We had this fight and I didn't mean to hit him in the head – he had braces on his teeth – but I did.' Dennis went to school with his father the next day, and the school administrators suggested that perhaps Dennis would be better off out of school. Dennis spent his nonworking hours speeding around in his newly acquired XKE automobile. Carl, who was still under sixteen, was required by law to stay in school. But he hadn't been attending many classes, and with his newfound celebrity he received either inordinate attention or cruel and derisive teasing. It was mutually decided by the school and his parents that he would leave Hawthorne High and attend the Hollywood Professional School, along with David Marks. It wasn't long before Marilyn and Diane Rovell joined them there.

'We were both at Fairfax High at the time,' Marilyn said, 'when Carl and David found out about Hollywood Professional School.' It let out at 12:30, and some of the younger Hollywood stars went there – along with a lot of kids who couldn't handle regular school. Every morning Diane and Marilyn would walk to the corner of La Brea and Hollywood. Carl and David Marks would pick them up and take them to school.

On Thanksgiving of 1962, May Rovell prepared a giant spread for her extended family. Brian, Carl, and Dennis showed up for dinner, along with several friends. It is still fondly remembered as one of their happiest meals together. After dinner and a good deal of wine, they all started to tell their favorite jokes, each one getting more risqué. May and Irving, who never cursed, couldn't help roaring with laughter. When it came time for May to tell a joke, she couldn't bear to curse, and instead she came up with a new word, 'fick.' This convulsed everyone at the table even more – they begged her to say the real word. But May held firm. She did make a promise, though; when the girls' recording career got under way, and they had a hit record, she would say the word the real way.

Brian was determined to promote the Rovells. By now he had enough clout with Capitol and Nik Venet to record

120

and release practically any single he wanted. When Marilyn, Diane, and Ginger came up with the idea for an all-girl version of a surfing group, called the Honeys (surfing terminology for 'female surfers'), Brian brought up the idea to Nik Venet. At first Venet wanted just Ginger to join the Beach Boys as a Beach Girl, but when Brian insisted that all the girls be included, Capitol agreed to pay for studio time and give it a try. Brian and the girls chose to record an old Stephen Foster favorite, 'Way Down Upon the Swanee River,' and turning it into a surfing tune called 'Surfing Down the Swanee River.' Another surfing tune, 'Shoot the Curl,' composed by Sandra Glantz and Diane, would go on the 'B' side. Produced by Brian and Nik Venent and released on Capitol later that winter, the record never made it onto the charts. Two more Honeys singles followed and met the same fate as the first. Finally, Brian suggested to Venet that the Honeys record an entire album, but Nik rejected the idea gently. May continued to say 'fick,' but the girls' desire to become recording stars remained very much alive.

In January 1963 Brian moved into a three-bedroom apartment with friends in Inglewood, but went back there less and less. He soon became a regular overnight guest on the Rovells' living-room sofa, and after a few months, it appeared he had permanently moved in. May was doing his laundry, and often his brothers' laundry as well. Brian reveled in his relationship with May, and they frequently spent late nights having intimate conversations about his life. After a month or two of sleeping on the sofa, Brian moved into a small rear bedroom, furnished with two little dressers and twin beds, which Marilyn shared with her younger sister, Barbara. The two girls slept in one bed together and Brian slept in the other. This arrangement didn't seem to raise any eyebrows at the Rovell household, although May and Irving were particularly moral and conservative. May seemed to have wisely decided that whatever was going to happen, it would be better happening in her home than in the backseat of an automobile. Anyway, Diane was considered to be Brian's girl, and she wasn't in the room. Some visitors at the Rovells' remember that May and Irving were extremely encouraging over Brian's relationship with their daughters and would have liked to have him as a son-in-law.

'One day,' Marilyn remembers, 'I spent the afternoon with Brian together, alone. And then we wound up spending days together. I was crazy about him but I was so young . . . Once he came into my life I was immediately . . . fascinated.' Marilyn admits, 'I did have a little bit of sexual fantasy. One time I saw him in his underwear, and I went, "Wow."'

But Brian was still engaged to Judy Bowles, whom Marilyn saw when Brian took Marilyn to the studio for a recording session. Marilyn remembers Judy as being sweet and naïve, and that she and Brian fought all the time. Brian would often complain to Gary Usher that Judy wanted to break off with him, and several times Gary had to comfort a weeping, distraught Brian after a turbulent argument with Judy.

'I do know he really cared for her,' Marilyn said, 'and I never ever tried to take Brian away from Judy . . . no one did . . . it just happened. He came into the room one night and said, "That's it. I can't deal with her anymore. Our relationship is never going to work."'

'All of a sudden,' said Marilyn, 'before you knew it, Brian and I were kissing, out of nowhere. I don't even know how it happened.'

For a short time, no one in the family knew about Brian

and Marilyn's budding romance – not even Diane. It was often unclear to outsiders exactly which sister Brian loved best. He seemed to have crushes on all the girls, including Barbara. Brian later wrote one of his most telling songs about this era, the title a phrase uttered to him by Diane, 'Don't Hurt My Little Sister' – perhaps referring to Barbara. But there was no curtailing Brian's ambiguous romantic interests in the sisters. Diane and Marilyn found themselves caught up in a benign competition that would last for many years.

2

In March 1963 the Beach Boys broke through to national prominence and success with a force that staggered everyone at Capitol. 'Surfin' USA,' Brian's most recent single, written in collaboration with Mike Love, was one of his cleverest ideas to date. The song not only avoided alienating the vast sections of the country where there was no surfing, but united a nation of teenagers in the California dream. Its lyric, beginning 'If everybody had an ocean,' brought the entire nation to California shores. Ironically, this first giant hit did not even have an original melody. The tune derived from a Chuck Berry song called 'Sweet Little Sixteen,' combined with the idea of Chubby Checker's lyrical theme from 'Twistin' USA,' in which the names of many US cities are mentioned.[1] Brian and Michael wrote a vibrant arrangement for the song, with a

---

[1] Naturally, Chuck Berry's music publishers, Arc Music, sued for this uncredited use of his melody. The case was settled out of court by Capitol, which gave Berry an undisclosed sum and writer's credit on the song.

heavy surf-guitar sound and an instrumental break. 'Surfin' USA' spent seventeen weeks on the national charts, topping out at the number 3 position. It was an unqualified smash hit, in which the Beach Boys came into their own with their characteristic harmonies, falsettos, and production style.

The flip side of 'Surfin' USA,' 'Shut Down,' was a short catchy automotive song about a drag race between a Corvette Sting Ray and a 413 Dodge. It featured Mike Love's nasal vocals and was the first song released from Brian's collaborations with Roger Christian. 'Shut Down' hit the charts for thirteen weeks and climbed as high as number 23. In response to the two hits, Capitol rushed Brian and the boys into the studio and quickly released an album late in March, also entitled *Surfin' USA*. This album was undistinguished except for the hit singles – it included five instrumentals – but nevertheless *Surfin' USA* spent seventy-eight weeks on the charts, hitting the number 2 position by the Fourth of July weekend.

Capitol took notice of the Beach Boys now, but not in the way Brian or Murry had expected. The company was indeed impressed with the group's success, but primarily as a sales vehicle for what they considered fad-oriented teen music, rather than as an emerging, creative sound in the music business. Capitol shifted into an unprecedented, intensive release schedule of Beach Boys songs that was to continue unabated for the next three years, in an attempt to milk Brian and the group before their popularity died. The ferocity of the scheduling, and the enormous amount of material Brian was asked to produce, would have depleted a lesser composer and producer. 'There was a compulsion involved [in pouring out singles],' Brian said later. 'We did it out of compulsive drive. You see so many pressures happening at once, and you grit your teeth . . .' As Brian saw it, he was 'in a state of creative panic . . .' To complicate matters, Brian refused to record any more songs at Capitol's cavernous studios, which he claimed were giving a hollow ring to his productions. At the time, it was unheard of for an act to take its sessions elsewhere, since all recording artists were summarily charged for their studio time. But Brian put his foot down and Murry was sent up to Capitol to work it out. Finally Brian was allowed to record where he wanted – with Chuck Britz as engineer at Western's number 3 studio.

The next single, 'Surfer Girl,' clearly showed the difference the new studio made. 'Surfer Girl' was the first Beach Boys ballad, intended to broaden the group's appeal. It was one of the original tunes Murry had first brought to Capitol. Rerecorded for this release, it was a sweet, dreamy tune about a little surfer girl that 'made my heart come all undone,' written about Judy Bowles. This was also the first Beach Boys tune that Brian recorded without the other members of the group, using studio technicians and his friends on the vocals. Yet the finished song sounded just like the group – which certainly gave all the other members pause; Brian could do it without them, without Capitol, and certainly without Murry. Significantly, it was also the last Beach Boys single about surfing. Brian was moving on. 'Surfer Girl' hurtled up the charts to the number 7 position, while the flip side, another automotive song, called 'Little Deuce Coupe,' managed eleven weeks on the charts, hitting number 15 at its best.

Less than a month later, another Capitol album appeared, *Surfer Girl*, which stayed on the charts for well over a year, hitting the number 7 position. This album's most notable inclusion was Brian's moody – and unexpected – 'In My Room.' The rest of the cuts were forgettable mediocre songs about surf and cars, with titles like 'Catch a Wave' and 'Surfer's Rule.' And yet, just two months later, Capitol sent a fourth LP, entitled *Little Deuce Coupe*, out on the market. Although it was unashamedly stuffed with four reissued songs ('Little Deuce Coupe,' '409,' 'Our Car Club,' and 'Shut Down'), it rode the charts for a staggering forty-six weeks, hitting number 4 on the *Billboard* listing. The *Little Deuce Coupe* album contained Brian's most crystalline teenage effort yet, 'Be True to Your School.' An anthem for high schoolers, the song was recorded with the aid of fifteen sidemen (borrowed from top producer Phil Spector) and rerecorded as a single with an opening chorus of cheerleaders sung by the Rovell sisters, billed as the Honeys. 'Be True to Your School' spent twelve weeks on the charts, hitting the number 6 position. To polish off this remarkable year, on December 9 Capitol released a Beach Boys Christmas single, 'Little St Nick,' backed with a lovely version of 'The Lord's Prayer.'

Ironically, the first number 1 single that Brian ever wrote was given away to another California group. Jan and Dean had already had several hit songs, dating back to their 1958 debut single, 'Jennie Lee.' After a few flop records they had returned to school, but had been drawn into the music industry again when a single, 'Linda,' reached 28 on the national charts. The singing duo, whose vocals many people mistook for those of the Beach Boys, met the group at a concert early in their career, when the Beach Boys were the opening act. After the Beach Boys sang their two or three hit songs, Jan and Dean took the stage and sang theirs. When the audience wanted more, they asked the Beach Boys to come back on stage on the spot and play their few songs over again, to which Jan and Dean jammed. They added some highs and lows to

126

Brian's precision parts, and sang 'Surfin'' and 'Surfin' Safari' with them.

Soon afterward, Jan and Dean, under the guidance of their manager, Lou Adler, decided to do a surfing album and capitalize on the success of 'Linda.' At Adler's suggestion, they called the album *Jan and Dean Take Linda Surfing*. Jan and Dean told Brian they wanted to record 'Surfin'' and 'Surfin' Safari' for their album, and asked if he and the guys would do backup. Thrilled that Jan and Dean would think to cover his songs, Brian rounded up the group and brought them into the studio, where they graciously sang the same arrangement they had sung on stage. Brian further obliged Jan and Dean by showing them the rudimentary studio techniques of doubling parts he was developing. After the session was over, Brian played some of his new tunes, and Jan and Dean picked out songs to record as though choosing breakfast cereal from a supermarket shelf. One of the songs, which they eventually co-wrote, was called 'Surf City.' It was about a mythical kingdom – California – where there were 'two girls for every boy.' Brian agreed to sing at the recording session of 'Surf City.' By midsummer of 1963 it was number 1 on the national charts.

Brian was thrilled, Murry infuriated. Murry felt, with some justification, that Brian had given away the group's first number 1 single to competitors. Murry called Jan and Dean 'pirates,' and when Jan heard how enraged Murry was, he arrived at a Beach Boys session at Western Studios dressed in elaborate pirate's costume, complete with eye patch. Murry was not amused; from now on, all of Brian's hit songs would be kept in the family.

3

Meanwhile, back on the twelfth floor of the Capitol Tower, Venet had his hands full with Murry and the boys. Capitol wasn't too pleased about the financial settlement it had had to make with Hite and Dorinda Morgan, and because of it regarded Murry's business practices as forever suspect. Murry had recently borrowed from the company $17,000 against the Beach Boys' next advance, to buy a piece of equipment for ABLE Machinery, which he was still running part-time. It was anybody's guess whether the Beach Boys would ever see that money again. Capitol soon learned that Murry had his own conception of what show business was like, and strong ideas about the Beach Boys' promotion. The trouble started in December 1963, a few weeks after they signed new Capitol contracts. Murry arrived at Venet's office with all the boys in tow and a photographer, saying they wanted to take a picture of the contract signing. Venet was not enthusiastic. 'Nobody takes pictures of kids signing contracts,' Venet told him. 'That's union stuff.' But Murry blustered on about what a good idea it was. Finally all the boys were huddled into a conference room and a photograph was taken of them holding a piece of paper. 'The pictures always looked like something you would see at the A&P,' Venet said. Another of Murry's promotional ideas was to print five thousand buttons that said, 'I know Brian's Dad.' Murry was an admirer of the Kingston Trio – a group produced by Voyle Gilmour – and of their 'clean' image. He immediately found out where they bought their short-sleeved striped shirts and bought a dozen for the Beach Boys, and several dozen more to give away to disc jockeys. These were the shirts the Beach Boys wore in their earliest Capitol publicity pictures.

Venet was often forced to spend hours listening to Murry's own songs, and he had to pay attention, because somewhere in the conversation Murry would slip in what Brian's next single would be or when it might be available. Venet was reluctant to give Murry trouble – though it happened all the time; Murry soon discovered that it was easy to go over Venet's head within the company. Venet claims he once looked out of his office window and saw Murry with the 'president of the company,' whom he had 'cornered in the parking lot.' Venet rushed down to the lot to create a diversion, getting Murry away from the executive by pretending he had new photographs of the boys to show him.

On another occasion Murry stormed into Venet's office, insisting the legal department fire Mike Love on the grounds that he breached the morals clause in his contract. (It seems he said the word *fuck* several times backstage.) 'There were reporters present,' Murry told Venet, 'as well as disc jockeys. If the disc jockeys heard him use the word *fuck*, they might take the Beach Boys off the air.'

Venet said, 'Fuck, you're kidding,' and Murry stormed around the office biting on his pipe.

'One of the major problems I had with Brian and Murry,' Venet said, 'was that Brian would often look at me and say, "Why is this man sitting where my father usually sits?" or "Why does this man tell me things my father tries to tell me?" Brian would confuse things he felt about me with disloyalty to his father. There was a constant struggle with disloyalty, and Murry – I must tell you – played it to the hilt.'

129

Murry remembered the situation very differently. As he saw it, the boys didn't really know what they were doing in the studio, and it was Murry's expertise that saved them. He would browbeat Brian mercilessly, telling him all his songs were rotten. In 1971, Murry told *Rolling Stone*, 'Truthfully – I'm not beating myself on the back, but knowing them as a father, I knew their voices, right? And I'm musical, my wife is, we *knew* how to sing on key and when they were flat and sharp and how they should sound good in *song*. I'd *surge* on the power to keep the level of their musical tone the same. Or if they were singing a phrase weak, when Mike was singing "She's fine, that 409," we'd surge on the part. [I did this] Without their knowledge at first.' However, 'surging' the volume and speeding up the recording to make the boys sound younger, along with putting echo on, was virtually the extent of Murry's production expertise. In desperation, Chuck Britz rigged up a fake control panel for Murry to fiddle with during recording sessions.

Anything was bound to happen in the studio, where family fights ensued with no more restraint than in the living room in Hawthorne. Venet says he witnessed instances when Murry hauled off and smacked the boys, particularly Dennis, who once jumped out from behind his drum set to tackle Murry but was held back by his brothers. On another occasion Dennis actually took a swing at Murry, who stepped aside and let Dennis punch the wall instead. Chuck Britz put a picture frame around the broken plaster to commemorate the event. 'If you run out of dialogue with your manager or attorney, you walk out,' Venet said. 'But we had a father-and-son relationship here, and Murry would not let them separate. When you disagreed with Murry, it wasn't a manager you were talking to, it was your father.' Yet the group was hot, and

Capitol was willing to put up with a lot from Murry to keep those teen songs coming in. 'I would tell Voyle Gilmour, "That man is a maniac," and Voyle would say, "Don't talk like that where anybody can hear you."'

Venet remembers the last time he was in the studio with the Beach Boys. Earlier that day Brian had dropped by his office and said, 'Please don't invite my father to the session tonight. We don't want him at the studio.' Later on, Dennis called him and said that the boys had had a huge blowup with Murry that morning and didn't want him around. 'If my father shows up tonight, I'm going to freak out. I'm going to punch him in the mouth and I'm going to punch you in the mouth. I want that session closed and I don't want my father in that studio.'

Venet was more than happy to comply, but later in the afternoon he got a phone call from Murry. Murry told Venet that he and the boys had 'patched it up' and that it was all right for him to attend the session. 'What time is it?' Murry asked.

'Well, Mr Wilson, it's starting at seven, but are you sure – '

'Yes, yes,' Murry told him. 'it's all patched up. I won't be staying. I'm only going to drop in.'

That night Venet and the engineer, Peter Abbott, were sitting in the booth while the boys were doing vocals in the studio on the other side of a huge glass window. The door opened, and Venet could see Murry's figure, pipe in mouth, reflected in the window. 'I turned around and the music stopped and everything stopped,' Venet said. 'Murry was standing there doing the championship hand-clasp above his head.' Murry proceeded to loosen his tie and take off his jacket, sitting down between Venet and the engineer. All hell broke loose. Accusations flew from both sides, and in another five minutes the session was

131

canceled. In the long run, however, the kids took Murry's side. Venet stopped producing, remaining merely the liaison at Capitol, coordinator between the company and the group.

4

By now the Beach Boys had become a major concert attraction, and the complications of booking tours grew to be too much for Murry. Although he once swore he would never do it, Murry signed the boys up with the William Morris Agency. Comedian Milton Berle's young son, Marshall Berle, was their responsible agent. Ira Okun, who was head of the concert department, remembers, 'Those early days were not difficult because they seemed to catch on all over the country. On the first major tour that I booked for them, they did major business. It was incredible, we didn't believe the numbers they did. We were booking them a guarantee against a percentage, and they were taking in triple and quadruple the money . . . that's how hot they were.'

But Brian clearly hated being out on the road. Before one performance in northern California, he drank an entire bottle of wine to give himself the courage to go on. He complained about his hearing problem, and that the amplification of the stage speakers created a painful buzzing sound. As the Beach Boys' touring schedule grew heavier, they were out on the road for weeks and then months at a time – there was little time for Brian to compose and meet Capitol's heavy production schedule. Day by day Brian grew more resentful about being forced to go on the road. Promoter Irving Granz remembered,

'The William Morris Agency had booked them on a big tour and Brian Wilson . . . refused to go because there was a two- or three-day drive before they came to Oklahoma City, which is where the tour began. Ira Okun, the agent, asked me to fill in dates or cities before the first one so they could play their way through. He said, "Just book them, no matter what. Just get them in there." Because they had all the money in for the tour, and the rest would have been profit, I thought there was nothing to lose and booked them at a college – the University of Arizona at Tucson – which thought they were a folk act, because I'd booked folk groups there before . . . The ceiling fell down from the vibrations of the guitar – they'd never had anything like that before.'

Eventually, Brian began to miss so many dates that Murry invited Alan Jardine back into the group. Jardine had since married a pretty young girl named Lynda, and was back studying at El Camino Junior College. Since the group was obviously in a good financial position, Jardine agreed to go out on the road with them. Both Alan Jardine and David Marks toured with the group, but not for long. Having Jardine back was just what Murry was waiting for, as a way of getting rid of David Marks. David made that easy. Hurt because Jardine was suddenly playing on sessions, and cocky because the young girls in the audience liked him so much, Marks said to Murry, 'You'd be happy if I quit, wouldn't you?' When Murry remained sullenly silent, David said, 'Okay, I quit. Happy now?'

'You heard him!' Murry bellowed. 'He quit! You heard him, he's out!'

Although the rest of the group tried to get both Murry and David to reconsider, David stuck to his word. Within a few months he had formed his own group, David Marks

133

and the Marksmen, one of the first groups to sign with the newly formed A&M Records. When Murry heard this, he started a campaign against Marks among the local disc jockeys, telling them not to play any of his records. David Marks's new group lasted only a year, after which he joined Casey Kasem's group, Band Without a Name. Later came a stint as a session musician with the Turtles, and soon after that, an early retirement. According to Marks, he spent several years, 'lying on my back on LSD in Venice.' Eventually, he went to the Berkley School of Music in Boston, and later to the New England Conservatory of Music. As of this writing, David Marks is reliving his past glories and living off his royalties from the early Beach Boys albums – an estimated $300,000.

The rubber band had stretched as far as it
would go. – Brian Wilson

Six

1

January 1964 greeted the Beach Boys with exciting news.
They were about to embark on their first foreign tour, a
week-long trip to Australia, with a stop for a concert in
Hawaii on the way back. The bad news – Murry insisted
on going along.

Naturally the boys did not want Murry on this trip, but
they had little choice. Murry wanted to oversee the
business and practical end of the tour, and he intended to
curtail one of the boys' expanding extracurricular interests
– girls – as well. With the Beach Boys' newfound fame
came the spoils of teenage groupies, a bonus that particularly distressed Murry. He was not only morally opposed
to the boys' sexual adventures, but saw them as a potential
route to easy scandal. A competition was raging between
Dennis and Michael as to who could have the most
beautiful girl on his arm, and Michael seemed to be
winning. This was one contest Murry was determined to
end.

The tour had hardly gotten under way in Sydney when
Murry invoked some of his most stringent rules about the
road. There was to be absolutely no fraternization with
members of the opposite sex, and anyone caught cussing
or drinking in public was to be fined – not a $100 fine as
had been established in the past – but $1,000, which

Murry would subtract from the touring proceeds. Murry even sat in the hotel hallways outside the boys' rooms to make sure they couldn't sneak a girl up the back stairs. At one concert, Murry slapped Dennis's face for cursing in front of some fans. Dennis was so shocked and mortified, he burst into tears and ran away. These incidents, compounded by Murry's constant criticism and badgering, were finally too much for them to bear. By the end of the tour, the boys agreed that in the near future Murry would have to get the ax. 'There was too much tension in the family,' said Carl. 'It was difficult separating the family thing from the group thing.'

The cataclysmic moment occurred in Brian's exclusive domain – the studios. Earlier in the year Murry had canceled a session for one of Brian's new songs called 'Fun, Fun, Fun' because he 'wasn't happy with the material.' In fact, 'Fun, Fun, Fun' was one of Brian Wilson's best songs. It was written in a car while he and Mike Love were discussing Dennis's obsession with young girls. Dennis had told Mike about the girl who borrowed her father's Thunderbird, allegedly to go to the library, when in reality she was going to meet Dennis at his apartment. Brian and Mike liked the idea so much, they easily turned it into a classic of teenage rebellion. The lyric, 'She'll have fun, fun, fun till her daddy takes her T-bird away' was soon to become a catchphrase in American culture – but not for Murry, who thought the song was 'weak' and called Chuck Britz at Western Studios to cancel the session. When Brian found out, he angrily rescheduled the recording date and called Murry to give him hell.

Several months later, while 'Fun, Fun, Fun' was sitting near the top of the chart at number 5, Brian and the group went back into Western's number 3 studio to record a clever follow-up, titled 'I Get Around.' This catchy, fast-paced song was by far the best-crafted, best-produced tune of Brian's career to date. With its soaring vocals and breezy lyrics about a group of guys who cruise around in their cars, who have 'never been beat,' and who 'never miss yet with the girls we meet,' 'I Get Around' was soon to become the most identifiable Beach Boys song Brian had written. But that April, sitting in the control room while they were recording it, Murry would not stop criticizing the song and Brian's production techniques. Murry rambled on about what a loser Brian was, how poor the music was, and how only Murry had the real talent in the family. At one point he insisted that Brian end the session because something was wrong with the bass line. Murry kept poking Brian with his finger as he challenged him.

'You don't know what you're talking about, Dad,' Brian finally told him.

Murry flew off the handle. 'Don't you ever speak to me that way!' he screamed at Brian. 'I *made* you and the Beach Boys! Hear me? You'd be *nothing* without me!'

Brian tore off his headset, rushed over to where Murry was sitting, tore him out of his chair, and physically threw him up against the wall, ripping his shirt. 'Get out of here!' Brian screamed. 'You're *fired*! Do you understand? You're *fired*!' For a moment there was an agonized silence in the control booth. Then Murry adjusted his clothing and left.

In retrospect, Audree defends Murry's fanaticism about the boys. 'He did about seven jobs, without experience, just native intelligence. Always do better, always be stronger, always be honest. They heard that so much . . . The boys just weren't happy, they really weren't. At that time they were having growing pains, and they thought they really knew . . . Murry wasn't happy either, he was miserable most of the time . . . so it was just a natural thing . . . It happened right after they came home from their first trip to Australia where they had lots of strife and problems . . . and they fired him. I know he was devastated. The funny part was he said he wouldn't work for them anymore anyway, he said he couldn't stand it. But it really crushed him. He went to bed for about five weeks – he really did, just totally stayed in bed.'

Shortly afterward, Brian and the boys hired an accounting firm, Cumming and Currant, in Torrance – the same people who did Murry's taxes – to oversee their finances. But Murry was far from finished. He still held sway over the boys' activities, and let Brian know exactly what he thought of each decision that the group made. A few months after he recovered from the shock of being fired, Murry was ready to get even.

2

That same winter of 1964, a cruel fate awaited Brian Wilson – the Beatles. First in Liverpool, then throughout Great Britain, the Beatles had swept the population into frenzied ecstasy. With their long hair, collarless jackets, and simplistic love songs, the Beatles seemed as gimmicky as the Beach Boys with their surf and automobile songs. Yet the Beatles' music was much more widely received than that of the Beach Boys; Brian immediately perceived the group as a threat. Worse, he was distressed to discover that his own record company, Capitol, was about to launch for the Beatles one of the biggest publicity blitzes ever attempted in the recording industry.

'The Beatles Are Coming' – a promotional campaign including posters, bumper stickers, hundreds of radio spots and clever 'talking head' commercials – made it seem as though the Beatles were arriving in every city across America. The airwaves were full of the Beatles, as were newspapers and TV news reports. Their widespread publicity certainly made Murry's 'I Know Brian's Dad' buttons seem pathetic. As an extra little jab to Brian's fragile ego, both groups began with the letters *Bea*, and they were listed right next to each other on every company roster and in every record-store rack. Even Carl Wilson had a picture of the Beatles on his wall. ('He's a traitor,' was Murry's comment.)

The day before Brian's latest masterpiece of abandon, 'Fun, Fun, Fun,' first appeared on the *Billboard* record charts at number 116, the Beatles appeared on 'The Ed Sullivan Show.' Now began a blatant competition for consumer dollars. Already the Beatles' new single, 'I Want to Hold Your Hand,' had far surpassed 'Fun, Fun, Fun' by leaping onto the charts at number 45. The single sold half a million copies in ten days, obliterating the record previously held by the Beach Boys for 'Surfin' USA.'

To Brian's ego, the Beatles' challenge represented a fight to the death. 'When I hear really fabulous material by other groups, I feel as small as the dot over the *i* in "nit,"' Brian told a journalist at the time. 'Then I just have to create a new song to bring me up on top . . . That's probably my most compelling motive for writing new songs – the urge to overcome an inferiority feeling . . . I've never written one note or word of music simply because it will make money . . . and I do my best work when I am trying to top other songwriters and music makers.'

Even Phil Spector remembered, 'When "Fun, Fun, Fun," came out, [Brian] wasn't interested in the money, but wanted a top-ten record. He wanted to know how the song would do against the Beatles and if KFWB would play it.'

During the coming year in the studio, Brian turned out a prodigious amount of hit songs, one after another, with an album every three months, and numerous singles. Indeed, Brian rose to the Beatles' challenge so admirably throughout the summer and fall of 1964 that the Beach Boys had seven singles on the charts at one time. For a brief period, the Beach Boys were clearly the most important and popular group in America. 'Fun, Fun, Fun' leaped its way up the charts to 69, then made a huge jump to 27, and finally, four weeks later, to its peak at number 5 in *Billboard* on March 21. Not a bad position, but Brian couldn't break into the top four because those positions were being held by the Beatles. It wasn't until July 4 of that year that Brian was able to overtake the Beatles, with the Beach Boys' first number 1 single, 'I Get Around.'

The success of 'I Get Around' was quickly followed by the release of an album, *All Summer Long*, which shot up to number 4 on the album charts. By the end of August, 'When I Grow Up,' another single, was released, and that fall, it too would be at the top of the charts, reaching number 9 by October 17.

This enormous recording popularity spurred a national public-appearance schedule that was staggering. The group was getting $20,000 a night, plus percentages, selling out wherever they appeared. As *Billboard* reported, 'The Capitol artists have never been able to make extensive [public-appearance] tours in the past because one or more of the group were still in school.

Last June, Carl Wilson, the youngest member of the group, was the last Beach Boy to graduate.' In September 1964, they began to tour heavily, hopscotching across America traveling to Buffalo, Syracuse, Boston, Hartford, Salt Lake City, Boise, Miami, Montgomery, Nashville, Providence, and Oklahoma City, all topped by the Beach Boys' first appearance on 'The Ed Sullivan Show' on September 17 – which, for them, certainly signified their 'arrival.' Their last date on this tour was in Worcester, Massachusetts, where the group quite literally brought down the house – the *Worcester Telegram* reported that 'officials termed it the most damage done to the auditorium in thirty-one years.' Finally, in October, the Beach Boys' touring party set out for its most exciting journey yet – a twenty-three-day performance and promotional tour of Europe. The best part about it: no Murry.

3

The Beach Boys' first major European tour was well documented by a middle-aged, goateed hipster named Earl Leaf. Leaf, a former photographer for *National Geographic*, a world traveler, and a Hollywood sharpie, in the early sixties was the editor and chief writer of an in-house Capitol publication called *Teen Scene*. A glossy magazine with flattering pictures of Capitol recording artists, *Teen Scene* was used to tout the company's popular singers. Leaf's column, 'My Fair and Frantic Hollywood,' gave him the best access of any journalist to the Beach Boys in their early years, and he became the primary

141

source of much of the early information and many of the photographs available on the group.

Aside from Earl Leaf and the new road manager, Doc Rice, there were eight members of the Beach Boys' touring party. An interesting coincidence occurred on the way to England. The group was grounded at Shannon Airport in Ireland for several hours while waiting for the weather to clear at Heathrow. Also stranded in the VIP lounge with the Beach Boys was Brian Epstein, the Beatles impresario, who at this point was nearly as famous as his wards. Brian Wilson was eager to meet and speak to Epstein, and his primary concern was finding out when the Beatles would next be arriving in America. Epstein assured Brian that he was safe for almost a whole year; the Beatles couldn't make it back there until the next American swing of their world tour – in August 1965.

Perhaps the greatest reassurance to Brian's competitive spirit was the frenzied, enthusiastic reception the Beach Boys received in England. Their music, perceived as the encapsulation of the American dream, was in some ways more popular in England than in the United States. Heathrow was filled with young girls waiting for them despite the wet, cold weather, and an even larger crowd had assembled at their hotel, the London Hilton. The trip to England was a purely promotional eight-day whirlwind of interviews, TV shows, and press conferences to plug 'I Get Around.' Capitol's parent company, Great Britain's EMI, held a high-powered reception at the headquarters, causing such a sensation in the building that all work came to a halt. In the Beach Boys' first English appearance, for the BBC, they gave a short performance at the Playhouse Theater, followed by a spot on the '*Top Gear*' television program on October 24.

In Paris, where the boys were terrified of the French

audiences, they learned they had sold out the prestigious Olympia theater after only a few radio advertisements. They headlined a show there, singing for an hour and a half and thoroughly captivating their listeners. From Paris they went on to Sweden, Rome, Berlin, Munich, Frankfurt, and Copenhagen, stopping at each place for just a few TV and radio appearances to promote their new songs.

Earl Leaf had some hotly disputed memories about the tour. About Mike Love, Leaf said, 'He was awfully wild . . . girlwise, he'd fuck anybody . . .' Then Leaf reconsidered. 'Dennis was the worst. Dennis was an animal.' Leaf claimed that Mike was naïvely taken in by professional women in Paris, where they 'pumped' him with champagne at 'about four thousand francs a bottle' until about 4:00 A.M., closing time, when the young women disappeared into the night and left Mike with the bar bill. Leaf also claimed a girl took money from Mike in London, promising to have sex with him and never showing up.

In Munich, Mike and Don Rice had just left a club on their way back to their hotel when, in the parking lot, they saw a young woman being dragged into a Mercedes 300 SL. Mike intervened, only to find himself staring down the muzzle of a Luger pistol. 'Three hours in the clink, a bruised hand and a $250 fine taught Mike a lesson,' Leaf wrote in *Teen Scene*. Later, Leaf claimed that Mike hadn't gone to the aid of a damsel in distress at all. Instead, 'He went and found a girl and started feelin' her up and her pimp came and got a gun and held him until the police came. He spent the night in jail.'

'Earl's a lecherous old man,' Mike contended in response. 'He's just jealous. Anything Earl Leaf says must be sifted through a sieve. He elaborates in his senility.' Mike claimed he only had trouble once on that tour, in Germany. 'I was going to go to this girl's house for a drink. I found her outside with some other fellow in a Mercedes. I was pretty drunk. I had on these black gloves. I smashed his window in. The only minor problem was, he had a gun. That was in my wild youth. I don't do that, anymore. I never did make a habit of it.'

But of all the Beach Boys, perhaps Brian's behavior could be considered the most notable on this trip. In Copenhagen, the three Wilson brothers were walking through a red-light district called the Nieu Haven when Brian got an inspiration to write a song. He dashed into the nearest restaurant, a 'dance hall–opium den–chop-suey joint,' according to Leaf, where he ordered a meal and tried to take possession of the piano from the piano player. A struggle ensued between the restaurant's keyboardist and Brian over the piano stool, and Brian ran from the restaurant just before the bouncer could throw him out. He raced back to the Royal Hotel and spent the night locked away at a piano in the hotel café, composing 'Kiss Me Baby' (which would appear as the flip side of 'Help Me, Rhonda' the following year) into the early hours of the morning. Equally childish but less trouble-some was his sudden impulse to kiss a statue in the Palais de Chaillot in Paris. He climbed a huge column and began to kiss the statue on the mouth when Alan Jardine yelled, 'Cheese it, the police,' and scared Brian into coming down. Another peculiar moment occurred in a Munich beer hall. The boys were getting pleasantly drunk when Brian, who was particularly smashed, started talking about Audree. 'She's such a wonderful woman,' Brian kept saying. Then he suddenly started crying uncontrollably. 'Isn't she wonderful?' he kept asking his brothers, sobbing. 'Isn't mother a wonderful woman?' Finally, they took Brian back to the hotel and put him to bed.

Al Jardine, characteristically, remained separate from the rest of the group, spending his early mornings touring the various cities, visiting museums and shops. He also spent hours on the phone with his wife, Lynda, and reportedly ran up several thousand dollars' worth of phone bills.

4

In the autumn of 1964 Brian finally moved out of the Rovells' house to his own one-bedroom apartment at 7235 Hollywood Boulevard. It was in a large, anonymous building and Brian was lonely there. From the day he moved in, he was constantly on the phone with Marilyn. 'Please come over,' he'd say, 'I can't stand it. I can't stand to be without you . . . please come over.'

Marilyn would say, 'Oh Brian, it's too *cold* to go out,' and he would keep her on the phone for two hours. Then Marilyn would catch a few hours' sleep before the phone rang again. It would be Brian begging her to come by. When she turned fifteen and a half, she was of legal age to drive a motor scooter, and Brian bought her one. Now there was no excuse for her not to come over. 'It was freezing out, and I would bundle up – I mean gloves, hats, you name it – and at two in the morning I would get on my little motor scooter. I would say that his apartment was about two miles away and I would go and be with him.'

The nighttime visits soon extended into protracted mornings, until Marilyn finally wound up spending the entire day with him, accompanying him from appointment to appointment. 'Somehow he felt really comfortable with me, and we were the best of friends. I was in awe, he was so different. I would do everything for him just out of caring. So I had started falling in love with him. I knew he really liked me and I knew that he cared for me, but I didn't think he was in love with me.'

Everything changed one day in November when the group was about to leave for their second trip to Australia, where their popularity had reached the same proportions it had in England. Marilyn and the other girl friends and wives went to Los Angeles International Airport to say good-bye. While waiting in the lounge for the group to board the plane, Marilyn and Brian sat next to each other – but didn't hold hands. 'I'm sure Brian hadn't told everybody that he was in love with me. I think the rest of the guys knew that we had started sleeping together. I was very young . . .'

While waiting for final boarding to be called, Mike Love turned to Brian and said, 'Hey, Brian, we're really going to have a blast [in Australia] . . . we're just going to have a ball, you and me.'

Marilyn sat there listening to them talk about all the conquests they would have in Australia, growing more annoyed by the minute. Finally she remarked pointedly, 'I hope you guys enjoy yourselves, because I'm going to have a good time too.'

For the first time Brian seemed to snap to attention. According to Marilyn, his mouth dropped open in surprise. 'What did you say?' he asked her.

'I said that I was going to have a good time while you're gone, too.'

A few hours later a telegram for Marilyn arrived at the Rovells' house that amazed them all. Brian had it sent from the plane, insisting the pilot wire it. The telegram

146

read, PLEASE WAIT FOR MY CALL. I LOVE YOU. BRIAN.

'I just couldn't believe it,' Marilyn said. 'I almost fainted. It was just unreal.'

Early the following morning, Marilyn was awakened by the telephone. It was Brian in Australia. 'That was the most painful trip I have ever taken on an airplane in my life,' he told her. 'Just to think of losing you, all of a sudden it was like a arrow shooting straight through my heart . . . all of a sudden I realized how much I love you.'

'Oh Brian,' Marilyn said, swooning.

'We've got to get married,' he said. 'We've got to make plans when I get back.'

Marilyn said she would have to discuss it with her parents. After all, she was only fifteen years old. But Brian insisted, and throughout the entire Australian tour the phone would ring day and night with long-distance calls from Brian, proposing marriage. At the time, Marilyn was working at a doughnut shop trying to earn back the money that her father had loaned her to buy costumes for the Honeys, and sometimes May Rovell would speak to Brian on the phone. Brian begged May to arrange for the wedding, but May refused. 'I'm not going to arrange your wedding, honey,' May told him. 'You do it yourself when you get back.' And then she added, 'You better take it easy with these long-distance phone calls, Brian. I can imagine what this phone bill is going to be like!'

When Brian returned to Los Angeles, he was as certain as ever that he wanted to marry Marilyn, although his family had some reservations about her age. There was also the problem that Marilyn was Jewish. According to Ginger Blake, 'Murry was not too happy about it at first. But then he got to know May. Can anybody not like May?'[1]

---

[1] Some sources say that the Wilson family, as well as Brian's friends,

The very day that Brian returned from Australia, he insisted on marrying Marilyn, *right then*. 'When I say that day,' Ginger says, 'I mean that day.' Because California law required that the couple wait, they decided to fly to Las Vegas and be married there by a justice of the peace. Brian called his friend Lou Adler, manager of Jan and Dean, and said, 'I want to marry Marilyn. We've got to set everything up.'

'Don't worry about it,' Adler said. 'You get Marilyn and I'll get the room together.'

Marilyn, May, Diane, and Ginger rushed out to the airport with Brian and caught the next flight to Vegas. Lou Adler arranged accommodations for them at the Sands Hotel. May, Diane, and Ginger had a large room, while Brian and Marilyn had the bridal suite, which Adler had filled with flowers and champagne.

The next stop was the marriage-license bureau, where officials asked for Marilyn and Brian's birth certificates. Marilyn had hers, but it never occurred to Brian to bring one. Brian produced his driver's license with his picture on it, but it wasn't good enough. He held up the license to the clerk and said, 'Can't you tell that's me? That's me and this is the date I was born.' Then he looked at the license carefully and said, 'Yeah, that's me. Look!' But it wasn't acceptable, and everybody rushed outside to a pay telephone booth, where Brian called home. Murry and Audree weren't home at the time, but Carl and Dennis were. Brian asked them to find his birth certificate and get on the next plane with it. After a lot of hemming and

---

were strongly against Brian's involvement with a Jewish girl, and it took them years to appreciate Marilyn and her family.

hawing, they said they couldn't find it.[2] Brian got so upset he kicked the phone booth and smashed the glass. Marilyn stood nearby crying.

That night they went back to the hotel. Marilyn cried herself to sleep in the bridal suite, while Diane and Ginger drove around Vegas in a rented car. The next morning they all returned to Los Angeles, where Brian found his birth certificate. At this point May took over and found a judge at the city courthouse. Brian and Marilyn were married in a municipal ceremony on December 7, 1964.

The personal lives of the other Beach Boys were also changed with their newfound fame and fortune. Mike had left his wife and children and filed for divorce, settling on a reported $200-a-month support payment for the children. Carl and Dennis had moved to their own apartments in the same complex in Inglewood. Dennis had fallen in love, but he wisely hid his new relationship completely from Murry. Coincidentally, the girl he loved, like Marilyn, was Jewish, but she was regarded as a pleasant change from his previous girl friend, a Mexican biker with a tattoo on one arm.

Dennis met his new love at the Carolina Pines, a hamburger-and-fries hangout on Highland and Sunset. Dennis liked to go there late at night after work in the studio, and word always spread quickly that a Beach Boy was present. There wasn't a girl in the place who didn't want to meet Dennis, and he shortly picked up one named Ellen Brown, who happily went back to his apartment with him. By this time Dennis had moved to a relatively

---

[2] There is some dispute over whether or not Carl and Dennis willfully withheld Brian's birth certificate so he wouldn't be able to marry Marilyn. Audree claims this is not so, but many familiar with the situation at the time claim that the two brothers, knowing Brian's sudden whims, wanted to give him more of a chance to think about it.

expensive apartment building on Hollywood and Sycamore that had its own swimming pool. After spending a
few days with Dennis, Ellen Brown called her girl friend,
Carol Freedman, who had also been in the Carolina Pines
that night, and asked her to visit. It was the last time
Ellen Brown would see Dennis.

Carol Freedman was sixteen, already married, and the
mother of a one-year-old named Scott. Born November
10, 1946, in Michigan, she had moved to the Los Angeles
area with her parents when she was an infant, and had
grown up in Hollywood. Carol was pleased to be invited
to Dennis Wilson's apartment and was impressed with the
apartment building and pool. But she was confused by
Dennis. 'I couldn't figure out what he was doing,' she
said. 'He was hugging Ellen Brown and holding two
fingers up behind her and mouthing "Two o'clock."'
Carol was quite shocked when, at two o'clock in the
morning, Dennis showed up at her parents' house in West
Hollywood. Her parents weren't too happy with this
nocturnal visit either. But Dennis was so charming, Carol
said, 'that even when you were angry he could make you
laugh.' He smiled and they had to smile.

Dennis came back the next day because he wanted to
meet Scott. 'He literally fell in love with Scotty,' Carol
said. 'He really did love children. And within a few
weeks, Scott and I were living with him.'

Audree knew about Dennis's relationship with Carol,
but it had to be kept a secret from Murry, who disapproved of unmarried couples living together. In the beginning it hurt Carol to have to hide the truth, but she soon
learned that Dennis was desperate to please and appease
his father, so she stayed out of the way. 'No matter how
hard Dennis tried,' Carol said, 'no matter how perfect he

150

was, no matter how hard he tried to emulate Murry, he could never win Murry's outward love.'

5

Living with Marilyn in his own apartment, Brian had total freedom from family restraints for the first time. A little like Alice let loose in a Hollywood Wonderland, he was finally able to make a new set of friends without parental interference. This wasn't too difficult, since Brian now enjoyed a certain prominence in the Los Angeles music-business scene and all the cognoscenti wanted to meet him. A whole new cast of characters began to emerge in Brian's life. Some were other musicians he had met through business contacts, some were just high-level groupies – what Marilyn Wilson would come to call the 'drainers.' As Brian saw it, all these people were hipper, smarter, and more clever than he. According to Marilyn, 'They had the gift of gab . . . Brian came from Inglewood, Squaresville . . . All of a sudden he was in Hollywood – these people talk a language that was fascinating to him. Anybody that was different and talked cosmic or whatever . . . he liked it.'

The New Best Friend in Brian's life from this period, and the one who would leave the deepest and most lasting mark on him, was a young man in his early twenties named Loren Schwartz. He was a small, good-looking guy a few years older than Brian, married to a pretty girl named Linda. An aspiring music-business agent, Loren met Brian at one of the many Hollywood studios where Brian recorded. Loren had gone to Santa Monica City College and lived in a small apartment at the back of a building on Harper between Hollywood and Santa Monica boulevards. One of his school chums described him as a 'new-wave Jewish intellectual. He was very skillful at asking people what "the sound of one hand clapping" was. You'd think this guy was really *out there*. He could impress people with his intellect, which was genuine, but wasted. Loren was something of a social manipulator. He turned Brian on to all this literature. Well, Brian just got overawed by it.' Loren's literature included *The Little Prince*, by Antoine de Saint-Exupéry, the poetry of Kahlil Gibran, the collected works of Hermann Hesse, and the writings of Krishna. At the time these were trendy works, widely read by college kids, but a far cry from anything Brian had ever read in Hawthorne. It all seemed deeply mystical and terribly important to him.

At a time when the drug culture would soon flourish into everyday prominence, there was already a plentiful supply of grass and hashish at Loren Schwartz's apartment. Four or five nights a week, a circle of friends would meet there, with candles and incense, the latest and hippest music, a kilo or so of marijuana, and a Sara Lee cake to satisfy the munchies. According to Loren, the drugs always had some special cachet about them, such as marijuana allegedly given to him by George Harrison, or hashish Jim Morrison had sent back from a monk in the Himalayas. The scene at Loren's, according to one of the participants, 'was a little like Paris in the days when the impressionist painters met at coffee houses.' Among the players were David Crosby, shortly to become famous as part of Crosby, Stills, Nash and Young; Jim McGuinn and Chris Hillman of the Byrds; a session musician named Van Dyke Parks; and Tony Asher, an aspiring songwriter and bright young advertising jingle writer with the Carson/ Roberts agency.

It was early winter of 1964, and under Loren's auspices Brian smoked marijuana for the first time. One night, when he and Marilyn had been married only a short while, she was waiting for him at her mother's house on Sierra Bonita Drive. Brian arrived late, as usual. But there was nothing usual about the way he looked. 'His eyes were all glassy and he was acting real funny, like real spacy,' Marilyn said.

'What's wrong with you?' she asked him. 'What is it?'

'Oh, I tried this marijuana cigarette and it got me really . . . high.'

Marilyn rolled her eyes and her heart sank. 'Who had ever heard of a marijuana cigarette?' she later said. At the time, Marilyn put grass in the same category as heroin. 'The most I'd ever heard of in my life was taking aspirin. All I knew was that suddenly Brian was not himself.

'Who gave you that?' Marilyn demanded angrily. 'Who gave you that cigarette?'

When Brian told her it was his new friend Loren Schwartz, she demanded he never see him again. But her pleas were useless. Brian looked forward to the gatherings at Loren's house, and continued to smoke pot – a deep, dark secret that was kept from the rest of the band and his family, but one that would have a radical effect on him within the next few weeks.

6

The pressure from Capitol for more Beach Boys product was unrelenting. With the exception of the Beatles, the Beach Boys were Capitol's highest-grossing act. In just two years, their first six albums had sold nearly six million copies. As the calendar year of 1964 ended, their seventh album, *The Beach Boys*, hurtled almost straight to the number 1 position. Their sixteenth single, 'Dance, Dance, Dance,' was also headed for the top ten of the singles charts. As far as Capitol was concerned, Brian Wilson was the horn of plenty. They continued to 'encourage' him to produce and record as many songs as he wanted.

But the pressure was clearly taking its toll. Toward the end of 1964, while sustaining a hectic composing and recording schedule, newly married, Brian hit the road for what would be his last tour for over a decade. Said Brian, 'I was run-down mentally and emotionally because I was running around, jumping on jets from one city to another, on one-night stands, also producing, writing, arranging, singing, planning, teaching – to the point where I had no peace of mind and no chance to actually sit down and think or even rest. I was so mixed up and so overworked.'

On December 23, 1964, at the start of a small western tour to promote 'Dance, Dance, Dance,' Brian Wilson had his first publicly acknowledged psychological episode. Things had been going badly for weeks. He hated going out on the road. Brian was especially reluctant to go away at this time because he and Marilyn hadn't been getting along, after only three weeks and two days of marriage. They were having the typical squabbles that many young marrieds endure; but to Brian they seemed tragic. Marilyn accompanied the boys to the Los Angeles International Airport to say good-bye. It was two days before Christmas and the airport was a madhouse, filled with tens of thousands of passengers traveling before the holidays. The sound of Christmas carols piped over the public-address system was drowned out by the noise of the crowds. The atmosphere was hectic and tense. Brian later claimed that as the group huddled together in the airport waiting room, just before boarding the plane, he saw something that drove him over the edge. 'I saw Marilyn staring at Michael,' he said. 'So I assumed she loved Michael. I wasn't hallucinating, I was seeing what I was seeing. I saw them stare. Oh boy, I didn't like that at all. I don't like someone liking Michael and not me. My ego gets real crushed and then I get real juiced up.'

Marilyn laughs nervously at this accusation, but asserts, 'Brian was very jealous at the time. But if I was looking at anyone, it would definitely not have been Mike Love.'

The plane had only been airborne for five minutes when Brian turned to Al Jardine in the seat next to him. Eyes glazed with terror, Brian said in a small, strangled voice, 'I'm going to crack up any minute!' Al told him to 'cool it' and tried to calm him down.

'Then I started crying,' Brian said. He put a pillow over his face and began screaming and yelling, alarming everyone on the plane. 'I just let myself go completely,' Brian said. 'I dumped myself out of the seat and all over the plane. I let myself go emotionally.' Some would say Brian purposely let himself lose control so be would never have to go out on tour again. Regardless of his reasons, Brian put on a harrowing display.

When the stewardess came over to see what was wrong,

Brian started screaming 'She doesn't love me! She doesn't love me!'

After a while, the group managed to calm him down, but he spent the rest of the ride white-knuckled and teary. He even refused his meal, which confirmed to the rest of the group that Brian was seriously ill. When the plane finally landed in Houston, Brian didn't want to get off and begged to be taken right back to LA.

They checked into their hotel, and in the solitude of his room Brian was able to regain some composure. 'That night I cooled off and played the show. The next morning I woke up with the biggest knot in my stomach and I felt like I was going out of my mind. In other words, it was a breakdown period. I must have cried about fifteen times [that] day. Every half-hour I'd start crying. Carl came to my hotel room. I saw him and I just slammed the door in his face. I didn't want to see him or anybody because I was flipping out. Nobody knew what was going on. I wouldn't talk. I just put my head down and wouldn't even look at anyone. That night the road manager took me back to LA.'

In her new house in Whittier, Audree Wilson received a phone call from accountant Dick Cummings, who was on the road with them. 'He said Brian was coming home and that he had been crying and breaking down and just couldn't carry on.' Cummings said that Brian wanted her to pick him up at the airport, but 'he made it very clear that only I was to meet Brian, not his father.' Audree was waiting at the terminal when Brian got off the plane. 'He was a total wreck,' she said. 'He got in the car and I said, "Where do you want to go? Do you want to go to our house or to your apartment?"'

Brian refused to be taken either place. Instead, he wanted to go back to the house in Hawthorne where he

156

had grown up, which they still owned and kept vacant. Audree drove him there and they let themselves in. There was something dark and eerie about the deserted house now. They went to Brian's old bedroom and sat down and talked. 'He was in a bad state, crying; then he stopped and he talked a lot . . .' For the first time, Brian was able to unleash all his inner terrors to his mother, and nothing was ever the same for him afterward.

For the next week Brian relaxed at home while Marilyn pampered and reassured him. After he felt a bit more collected, he went to the studio to meet with the rest of the band. The boys had been waiting patiently for him to start work on their eighth LP, *The Beach Boys Today*. 'We were about halfway through the album,' Brian said, 'and one night I told the guys I wasn't going to perform on stage anymore, that I can't travel.'

Here Brian's narrative becomes slightly hysterical. What follows is a transcript of a tape he made with Earl Leaf at the time. When he told the group of his decision, Brian claimed, 'They all broke down. I'd already gone through my breakdown, and now it was their turn. When I told them, they were shook. Mike had a couple of tears in his eyes. He couldn't take the reality that their big brother wasn't ever going to be on the stage with them again. It was a blow to their sense of security, of course.

'Mike lost his cool and felt like there was no reason to go on. Dennis picked up a big ashtray and told some people to get out of there or he'd hit them in the head with it. He kind of blew it, you know. In fact, the guy he threatened to hit with the ashtray was Terry Sachem, who became our road manager within two weeks.

'Al Jardine broke out in tears and broke out in stomach cramps. He was all goofed up, and my mother, who was there, had to take care of him.

157

'And good old Carl was the only guy who never got into a bad emotional scene. He just sat there and didn't get uptight about it. He always kept a cool head. If it weren't for Carl, it's hard to say where we'd be. He was the greatest stabilizing influence in the group . . . He cooled Dennis, Mike, and Al down.

'I told them I foresaw a beautiful future for the Beach Boys, but the only way we could achieve it was if they did their job and I did mine. They would have to get a replacement for me' – Brian corrected himself – 'I didn't say "they," I said, "we," because it isn't them and me, it's "us."'

Brian's sweet magnanimity aside, this was the beginning of the attitude that what was best for Brian wasn't necessarily best for the rest of the group, a position that would become increasingly threatening to the rest of the members as time went on.

Of course, Murry had no sympathy at all for Brian and let him know it. Al Jardine remembered, 'It affected his father very intensely. His dad was really uptight about it. He felt that Brian was copping out or . . . that he was dodging responsibilities and gave him a pretty rough time.'

Privately, Marilyn was happy that Brian would not be going out on tour anymore. He was away from the groupies and the temptation of other women on the road, and she enjoyed having more time to spend with him at home. Said Marilyn, 'Onstage it was just too painful for him; it really hurt his ear. That was one factor, but the main reason at the beginning was that he couldn't tour and write at the same time.'

Brian's first replacement on the road was a session guitarist named Glenn Campbell, who had worked with the Beach Boys in the studio and who could sing Brian's high parts on stage. In February 1965, with Glenn Campbell on the road with them, the Beach Boys netted $98,414 for fourteen one-nighters – quite a sum – but Campbell was reportedly paid a straight salary and only stayed with the group about three months. 'I'm too much of an individual,' he later said, when he went on to become famous in his own right. 'I didn't like being responsible for something done by a group. That's the way I felt being with the Beach Boys. If the Beach Boys did something, then I did it [too], and I didn't like that at all. I wanted to do what I wanted to do.'

Campbell was replaced by Bruce Johnston, a handsome young man who would eventually be incorporated into the Beach Boys lineup as a permanent member. A native of Los Angeles, Johnston was an orphan whose real name was Billy Baldwin. He had been adopted by a wealthy vice-president of the Rexall drug chain and grew up in Beverly Hills and Bel Air. In high school he had been in a band with Phil Spector, who asked him to play with the Teddy Bears on a session that turned out to be his first hit, 'To Know Him Is to Love Him.' Later, Bruce was in a group called the Rip Chords, who had a minor hit with the song 'Hey Little Cobra.' More recently, he had been making records with Terry Melcher, Doris Day's son, under the name Bruce and Terry.

'In 1963 I was working at Columbia Records, across the street from where [the Beach Boys] were recording . . . and I kind of met them through making similar records . . . A couple of years passed and I was asked by Mike Love to find somebody to replace Brian . . . on a tour. So I called a few people and they wanted someone yesterday. I said, "Look, Mike. I'll come. I don't play bass, I play piano, but I suppose I could sing all the parts if you show me what to do." So an hour later I was on my way down to New Orleans. That was in April [on the 9th] of 1965 – I performed with the group, completed the tour, and came home. They asked me to go on another tour, so I said, "Well, all right." I was still working for Columbia Records as a record manager, and I was kind of reluctant to leave because I felt that Bri would come back into the group. But when I came home from the second tour, they asked me to sing on the next album, *Summer Days* (*And Summer Nights!!*) The first song that I sang on was "California Girls."'

The Beach Boys' concert booklet later read, 'Bruce Johnston is very clever, very healthy, very ambitious, and very rich . . .'

A genius musician, but an amateur human being. – Tony Asher, on Brian Wilson

Seven

1

Early in 1965 Brian and Marilyn moved into a new apartment together on Gardner Street, just two blocks from her parents' home on Sierra Bonita. It was a two-bedroom duplex, which Marilyn furnished modestly. Several weeks after they moved in, Brian arrived home one day and said, 'Guess what? Loren's got some of this LSD and he wants me to take it with him.'

'Don't you dare!' Marilyn screamed, though she hardly knew what LSD was – except that it was bad.

'He said that I have a very bright mind and this LSD will really expand my mind and make me write better.'

'Don't you dare!' Marilyn insisted, near tears.

'I really have to do it,' Brian said. 'I have to do it, I have to try it.'

Despite Marilyn's fierce objections, Brian made plans to take his first trip with Loren. They set aside a special day for the event, and Brian told Marilyn not to expect him home. At the time, LSD was not a widely used drug. Most of the supplies available in California were made by the famous San Francisco psychedelic chemist called 'Owsley,' whose laboratories were turning out a full-strength, powerful acid – so strong that in later years the dosage would be cut in tenths. But this was the acid that Brian ended up taking with Loren Schwartz.

When Marilyn saw Brian the day after his first trip, he looked drained and exhausted. 'I'll never do it again,' he swore.

'But what happened?' she asked him. 'What was it like?'

Tears welled in his eyes, and suddenly he was crying and hugging her. 'I saw God,' Brian told her. 'I saw God and it just blew my mind.' Over and over again Brian repeated the phrase 'my mind was blown,' but Marilyn had no idea what that really meant, or even harbored the suspicion that perhaps something had actually happened to his mind. As far as Marilyn knew, he only took the drug one more time with Loren. But she later realized that over the next few years, Brian took LSD many more times – perhaps dozens – when it was slipped to him by a variety of people who became his New Best Friend.

Within a fortnight after his first LSD trip, Brian seemed to be stoned on marijuana all the time. 'He was just not the same person I fell in love with. He had started changing little by little. He was not the same Brian that he was before the drugs . . . These people were very harmful, and I tried to get that through to Brian, but he was like a kid. You tell him "no," and he's going to do it. More and more Loren had a hold over him.'

According to Marilyn Wilson, Loren Schwartz began to rule Brian's life. 'Brian was just completely taken with him,' she said. Feisty and dedicated, Marilyn kept up an active campaign for Brian to end their friendship. 'He would always want me to go over to Loren's house, and I would say, "No, I'm not comfortable with those people."'

When the fighting over Loren became explosive, Marilyn threw up her hands. 'I decided he was acting too weird for me to deal with. I said, "I've had it." I decided we should have a little separation. So I went out on my own and found a small apartment on Detroit Street.' The first day she lived there, Carl came to see her. 'He begged me, "Please, Mare, I don't want you and Brian to break up."'

But it didn't seem as though Brian cared at all about this separation. 'I think he was too involved with the drug thing,' Marilyn said. 'He wasn't devastated at all.' They were separated for a full month before Marilyn heard from him. 'One night there was a loud banging on the door. It was Brian, and he was crying, "Please, Marilyn, let me in! Let me in!" I had never given him my address and somehow he had found it out – Carl probably gave it to him.' Marilyn felt sorry for him and let him in. For once he didn't appear to be stoned.

'Please, honey,' he begged her. 'I'm sorry, really I am, Mare. I miss you terribly. Let's go find a house together and buy it. I know you want a house, and I can afford it now. We can become a happy family and have children and we'll live just like regular people . . .'

But Marilyn wasn't ready to go back with him so easily. She said she wanted some time to think about it, and several weeks went by before she consented to give the marriage another try. One morning Brian picked her up at her Detroit Street apartment and they went to meet a Beverly Hills real-estate agent. They bought one of the first houses they saw. 'It was way on top of Beverly Hills on Laurel Way,' Marilyn said. 'Half of it looked down on the valley and half over Beverly Hills and LA.' They paid $185,000, and moved in a few weeks later, in late summer of 1965. The house on Laurel Way became Marilyn and Brian's first real home together, and for a while at least, things seemed to go well.

While Brian busied himself composing new Beach Boys material, Marilyn set about fixing up the house with the help of decorator Lee Polk (wife of director Martin Polk)

– and Brian's overriding advice. The master bedroom had flocked red wallpaper. The huge four-poster bed, with a headboard of carved angels, was blanketed in a leopard-print spread. In the bathroom hung a plastic picture of Jesus, whose eyes opened and closed when you moved. In the shag-carpeted living room several 'Lava Lamps' slowly undulated, while nearby, inexplicably, was a display rack of children's dolls in their plastic shipping tubes. On the walls were Kean prints of dark-eyed children, along with cheap prints of the Mona Lisa and Blueboy. The large dining room was furnished with an immense, Spanish-style table covered in a dark blue cloth and surrounded by high-backed chairs. The kitchen had black-and-white houndstooth-check wallpaper and striped window shades, like an 'Op-art painting,' according to one visitor. The den was a small room prepared in a bright orange, blue, yellow, and red wall fabric, with a jukebox loaded with Beach Boys singles and Phil Spector tunes. A pair of mechanical parrots, dyed fluorescent colors, sat in a huge cage. Two dogs, Louie (named after Brian's pal, Lou Adler), a dark brown Weimaraner, and Banana, a beagle, completed the scene.

But their home was far from the perfect picture of domesticity. Brian's fascination with Loren Schwartz and drugs did not end, and soon Loren was a daily visitor to Laurel Way, where the air was always permeated with the scent of marijuana.

2

Meanwhile, Murry knew nothing of his son's drug use. He was living in Whittier in a new, expensively decorated house with a circular driveway and an expansive view of the valley, purchased with the enormous publishing royalties that continued to flow in. The new house had a large music room, with an organ and piano, and a huge stained-glass window with a visual depiction of a 'Sea of Tunes.' Renovations on different areas of the house were continuous, just as they had been in Hawthorne. Curiously, Murry had bought Audree her own home just around the corner from his own. This was a kind of stalemate separation; Audree and Murry loved each other, but they could no longer live together. Even after spending the day with Murry, Audree would go to her own house to sleep. After a trip to Japan, Murry hired a Japanese secretary, which raised a few eyebrows – friends referred to her as his 'geisha.'

After recovering from the blow of being fired, Murry decided the ultimate proof that he had 'made' the Beach Boys would be to do it again without them. 'Those ungrateful little bastards,' he told friends. 'I'll start a group that will be bigger and better than the Beach Boys.' That group was a bunch of teenage musicians who had gone to Hollywood Professional School with Carl – Eddie Madora and Marty DiGiovanni, and their friend Rick Henn, who went to Uni High. Murry named them the Sunrays and taught them how to harmonize by giving each a tone to sing and making them practice vocalizing it for hours. He hired professional song arranger Don Ralke to arrange songs for them, and he pulled strings to obtain a recording contract, which enabled the Sunrays to be distributed on Capitol's subsidiary label, Tower Records. 'Murry wanted us to be a Beach Boys clone group,' Henn said. He even wanted the Sunrays to tour with the Beach Boys and be their exclusive opening act, but the Beach Boys objected so vociferously that Murry dropped the idea. He told them, 'Hey, after all I did for your careers you're going to shit on me like that?'

Murry took his new band on a 'station tour' to introduce them to all the disc jockeys he had met through the Beach Boys. At each station he gave the disc jockey a little present of costume jewelry for his wife. He made the Sunrays rehearse a few bars from the classic song 'Still,' and insisted they sing at every station, changing the lyrics to include the station's call letters: 'We love you KBOZ.' When the Sunrays objected to this corny approach, Murry returned gruffly, 'You boys are getting very big-headed.'

The Sunrays' first singles, released in March 1965, were straight rip-offs of the Beach Boys popular car songs. 'Car Party' and 'Outta Gas' had music and lyrics written by Murry, of course. The songs got little local airplay and were generally ignored, but the next single, 'I Live for the Sun,' released in June 1965, took off and made the charts. Written by Murry and produced by Ralke and Murry, 'I Live for the Sun' was a local top-ten hit. But the Sunrays' next song, 'Andrea,' made a weak showing. Murry and the Sunrays put out four more, increasingly obscure singles into 1966.

Murry wouldn't let the group play in Los Angeles proper because he claimed they would become 'jaded by the Hollywood scene' that he hated so much. 'The only time we ever performed in Hollywood,' said Rick Henn, 'was at the Hollywood Bowl with the Beach Boys, and they resented the shit out of that.' According to Henn, 'Somebody sabotaged the gig.' There was a circular stage, and after the previous group, the Lovin' Spoonful, finished playing, the Sunrays began to set up their equipment. Suddenly, the huge circular stage began to revolve. One of the guitar players got his leg caught, and it was almost cut off. The rest of the group jumped off the stage just in time. They did a forty-five-minute gig with only fifteen minutes' worth of songs. 'It was a real nightmare.'

'Still,' released in January 1966, became the Sunrays' last record. By then they were perceived as a dying group, and were relegated to tours of roller rinks that Murry booked for them in the northwest. 'It was embarrassing as hell,' Henn said. 'The tours were happening less and less, and everybody looked down on us as Beach Boys clones.'

One day, when things looked particularly bad, Murry ditched the Sunrays. He said, 'That's it, boys. I can't help you any more, you're on your own.'

'I think he just abandoned us because he knew that it was a sinking ship,' Henn said.

Not long after Murry left the Sunrays, they were booked into one of the Hollywood clubs Murry despised. Murry heard about about the booking and called Henn on the phone. 'I knew as soon as I left you, you would go Hollywood,' he said.

3

The Beach Boys' first single of 1965, 'Do You Wanna Dance?' performed admirably on the charts, reaching number 12 in its eight-week run, although it broke no new ground musically. The album it came from, *The Beach Boys Today!*, was the first album Brian was able to produce without any road activity. The increased polish and depth of his production techniques showed clearly. However, the album was not one of Brian's best works, consisting mostly of a mélange of uninspired car tunes and even a comedy cut with the voice of Earl Leaf discussing kosher pickles. Good times for the group would not return until April, when Capitol released the single 'Help me, Rhonda' (featured on *The Beach Boys Today!* in a longer, sloppier version). This song was a wonderful Brian Wilson composition, an irresistible sing-along in which a spurned young man beseeches his new girl, Rhonda, to 'help me get her out of my heart.' Complemented by Brian's falsettos and Mike's 'wop-wop-wop' bass line, the song was a smash hit, logging fourteen weeks on the chart, and becoming the Beach Boys' second number 1 single.

On July 5, 1965, Capitol released the Beach Boys' *Summer Days* (*And Summer Nights!!*) album. This so-called 'quickie' album, which Capitol pressured them into as a follow-up to the smash hit 'Help Me, Rhonda,' was recorded in April through June of that year. A single from this LP, 'California Girls,' became one of the more remarkable and enduring hits of Brian's career and a solid, number 3 chartbuster. Throughout the next several decades this musical ode to California beauty was used as the background for countless TV commercials and jingles, and became a major hit for David Lee Roth in 1985.

> Well, East Coast girls are hip
> I really dig those styles they wear
> And the Southern girls with the way they talk
> They knock me out when I'm down there
> The Midwest farmers' daughters really make you
>   feel all right
> And the Northern girls with the way they kiss
> They keep their boyfriends warm at night
> I wish they all could be California
> Wish they all could be California
> I wish they all could be California girls

Despite Brian's tremendous musical accomplishments, the shadow of the Beatles had fallen across him, obscuring any pleasure he may have felt. To make it worse, Brian loved the Beatles' music and was in awe of their musical progression. The Beatles were now on Brian Epstein's promised summer assault, playing sellout shows as they toured the country. On the liner notes of the *Summer Days* (*And Summer Nights!!*) album, Brian mentions that he's writing at a coffee table in the living room, while his friends are sitting around singing Beatles songs.

Brian was to include three Beatles songs ('I Should Have Known Better,' 'You've Got to Hide Your Love Away,' and 'Tell Me Why') on the next LP, *Beach Boys Party!*, which Brian decided should be recorded live. So as not to make the album just another concert LP, they recorded it at a 'party' that the Beach Boys conducted in their own studios.

This superb album was recorded in several different sessions. It included background sounds recorded at an actual party held at Mike's house, and later, freewheeling vocal sessions at Western's studio 2, where the Beach Boys' wives, girl friends, and friends were present. Down the hall at another studio, Jan and Dean were having their own recording session, and stopped in to say hello. 'They were all sitting around trying to think of another song to do,' reported Dean Torrance. 'So they asked me what I wanted to sing. I said 'Barbara Ann' [a song written by Fred Fassert that Jan and Dean had done on one of their own albums a few years before], for what reason I don't remember.' Although Jan and Dean had been forbidden by their own company to perform on other records, with the threat of having their royalties held up, Dean helped out on the session anyway. At the end of 'Barbara Ann' Carl's voice can be heard saying, 'Thank you, Dean'; and indeed, Dean's suggestion turned into a tremendous international hit. As Dean said, it took just 'three minutes to cut a huge, best-selling record.' Released in November of that year, 'Barbara Ann' became a favorite overseas, reaching number 2 on the American charts. The *Beach Boys Party!* album reached number 6 and spent a well-deserved six months on the charts, boosted in small part by Capitol's promotional ploy of preparing one million bags of potato chips with reproductions of the cover of *The Beach Boys Party!* on them, which they supplied to record dealers, to be given away with the purchase of an album.

The *Beach Boys Party!* album spawned another new beginning. Mike Love met his second wife at the session. Mike had been seeing a girl named Pam Rexroad, who invited a girl friend to the session. Suzanne Belcher was a stunning young woman – a seventeen-year-old San Fernando Valley College student with dark hair and eyes, and a gorgeous figure – just the way Mike liked it. The girls had been promised a real party, but when they got to the studios, they were surprised to find a rather sterile atmosphere. Mike went across the street and came back with a couple of cases of beer and wine and some potato chips. By the time the session was over, Mike had asked Suzanne for her phone number. At the time, Suzanne had a steady boyfriend in the National Guard and she refused Mike's requests to date her. She finally accepted when Mike asked her to join him for lunch with the Beach Boys' booking agent, Irving Granz, who would allegedly help Suzanne get a job at the William Morris Agency. No job was ever offered during lunch, but Suzanne was hooked. Mike was charming, funny, and attentive. On the way back from lunch, they drove to Malibu to look for a piece of property for Mike to buy. At the end of the date, Mike bought Suzanne a carton of cigarettes as a gift – a gesture that would soon take on ironic significance.

Some thought it was a little soon for Mike to find a new love. Only recently divorced, he was still involved in a messy paternity suit that had come to public light a few months earlier. On March 25, 1965, the story had hit the front page of section D of the Los Angeles *Herald Examiner*. A pathetic photograph showed a twenty-two-year-old secretary, Shannon Harris, holding her three-month-old daughter, Shawn. That day Miss Harris had charged in a paternity action before Superior Court Commissioner Frank B. Stoddard that Mike Love had fathered her child. Harris, with long dark hair down to her shoulders and dressed in a herringbone suit, held the little baby in her arms as she told the commissioner that she had first met Mike two years before, on March 25, 1963, and they celebrated their meeting exactly one year later by 'engaging in a romantic interlude,' according to the published report.

Mike reportedly admitted he had made love to Shannon

171

Harris, and that he sent her certain love letters (which were not produced in court), but he denied that he was the father. Shannon Harris's attorney, Jack Ritter, asked for temporary child support and medical expenses pending the paternity trial. But Mike Love and his attorney, George E. Wise, alleged that there were other men in Harris's life and that Mike's relationship with her had ended before he could have fathered the child. After the initial publicity, the case died down, and Mike reportedly settled the suit by giving the child a few hundred dollars a year in support plus the right to use the name Love when she was eighteen. The paternity suit was eventually forgotten, and none of the group ever expected the subject to come up again.

The incident didn't slow down Mike's new relationship with Suzanne Belcher. After only two dates and ten days of knowing each other – with Mike bragging he had $70,000 in the bank – he asked Suzanne to marry him. They flew to Las Vegas on October 15, 1965, where they were quietly married. Then Mike had to rush home for a Beach Boys appearance on 'The Andy Williams Show.' Mike took his new bride with him and the rest of the Beach Boys on a long Asian tour, which included Japan, Hong Kong, and Honolulu.

With the other Beach Boys gone, Brian started work on a new album, which would turn out to be the watershed of his career.

4

Late in 1965 Brian Wilson heard the newest Beatles album, *Rubber Soul*. 'I was sitting around a table with friends, smoking a joint,' Brian said, 'when we heard *Rubber Soul* for the very first time, and I'm smoking and I'm getting high, and the album blew my mind because it was a whole album with all good stuff! It flipped me out so much I said, "I'm gonna try that, where a whole album becomes a *gas*." '

Brian went into the kitchen and told Marilyn, 'I'm going to make the greatest rock-and-roll album ever made.'

Almost immediately Brian began composing small fragments of mood music, which he called 'feelings.' As the bits and pieces began to fit together, he thought about finding a lyricist for the new album. One thing was certain – he didn't want to use Mike Love. Since retiring from the road, Brian had begun to put more distance between himself and the rest of the group. Once again, Brian found an outside lyricist. His choice this time was as peculiar as it was fortunate. He called on one of the bright young men he had met at Loren Schwartz's house, Tony Asher. When they first met, Asher had been a fledgling songwriter trying to peddle his songs. 'In those days,' Asher said, 'everybody would play their songs at the piano. For some reason, I played a couple of tunes for Brian.' Brian must have been very impressed, because now, a year and a half later, he tracked Asher down by getting his number from Loren Schwartz. By this time Asher had given up the music business and was writing copy for an advertising company, Carson/Roberts, whose clients included Gallo wines. 'I was really just interested in a regular income,' he said. 'I am a pretty conservative guy.'

At first Asher thought it was a joke when somebody told him Brian Wilson was on the phone for him. Brian was in something of a panic; the pressure was on from Capitol, which was eager for a new album. There had been no new material since the *Beach Boys Party!* LP, and Capitol was anxious to keep the flow going. There was reportedly the threat of a lawsuit if Brian didn't produce another album soon. 'We were supposed to have done it months ago,' he told Asher, 'and I haven't even started it. I've done only one or two tunes and I hate them. How would you like to write some tunes for me?'

'You could have knocked me over with a feather,' Asher said later. 'That was like saying, "How'd you like twenty-five thousand dollars?"' Asher managed to wrangle a three-week leave of absence from his advertising agency, and began the task of writing the lyrics for what would become one of the greatest albums in pop-music history.

The next Monday morning Asher drove his 356 Porsche up to Laurel Way, expecting Brian to be ready to go to work. Instead, Brian was in bed. It took most of the day to get Brian up and at the piano, with Marilyn supplying a steady flow of food from the kitchen. Asher realized the album was going to take longer than three weeks. He thought Brian was a nice guy, but something of a Hawthorne hick, who found it next to impossible to express himself verbally. Sometimes Brian's lack of sophistication manifested itself in small ways, such as ordering only shrimp cocktail and steak no matter where they ate, for fear of experimenting with other foods. Other times, his

174

childishness was more pronounced, as when he halted work to watch 'Flipper' on TV and wept at the tender moments. Asher found Brian's life-style – in bed till noon, then kibitzing around the house for hours – extremely difficult to take. 'The only times I actually enjoyed myself or even got comfortable with Brian was when I was standing by the piano working with him. Otherwise I felt hideous!

'I wish I could say he was totally committed. Let's say he was . . . um, very *concerned*. But the thing was, Brian Wilson has to be the single most irresponsible person I've ever met in my life.' Asher remembers uncashed royalty checks totaling over $100,000 lying around the house. When word got out that Asher was working with Brian, he began to receive phone calls from frantic attorneys and from Broadcast Music Industries (which collected Brian's royalties) begging him to get Brian to sign papers or return phone calls.

Brian's increasing use of drugs compounded his erratic behavior. Asher remembers that he would often lose control while listening to playbacks of his own music, and would go from hysterical laughter to crying jags. 'He had fits of this just *uncontrollable* anger. Then he'd fall apart and start crying during playbacks of certain tracks . . . What I saw appalled me,' Asher said. 'I remember how he interacted with women, the kinds of sexual fantasies he would talk about, and his apparent need to get involved with Marilyn's sister, Diane. He openly discussed the conflicts he was feeling . . . not knowing whether he loved Diane more than Marilyn . . . could it be possible he loved them both, could it be possible that he had married the wrong one . . .'

One day Loren Schwartz brought some hashish to Brian's house and they decided to make hash brownies.

'We got this brownie mix and put the hash in,' Asher said. 'Loren was in charge. The question was, "How much do we put in?" We had been smoking some and our judgment was already off. We put half in and then we put some more in, and then we ended up putting it all in. We cooked it up and put them on a tray, and in the meanwhile we smoked more dope and ate three brownies each. They tasted great – when you're stoned brownies are hard to resist. Forty-five seconds later we said, "It's not working yet," so we each had four more . . . We started to get so stoned it was terrifying. I really thought we were going to die. There was a tapestry above the fireplace with a medieval embroidered bird and the bird just took right off and started flying across the room. I was hallucinating and I was petrified. I was on an elevator going up fast, and I had the sense that I was only a fourth of the way up. We all piled into a car and drove to a Mexican restaurant. How we got there alive, I don't know . . .'

Asher wrote most of the actual lyrics for the new album, called *Pet Sounds*, although all of the songs were based on Brian's concepts. During work sessions Asher would make up 'dummy' words while they were composing, and rewrite real lyrics on his own at night. The next day he would come in and Brian would decide whether he liked them or not. In a few instances, Asher contributed to the music too, as in 'Caroline No,' 'I Just Wasn't Made for These Times,' and 'That's Not Me.'

Although the songs Asher wrote on *Pet Sounds* are credited equally, Asher hardly got equal compensation for his efforts. When Brian first asked Asher to help him with the album, Asher didn't bother to ask about royalties. After all, it was a great honor to be asked to collaborate with Brian no matter what the royalty arrangement was. Asher was well aware that royalties between lyricist and composer were split fifty-fifty; at the time the standard royalty rate was two cents to the publishers and one cent split between lyricist and composer. But when the album was finished and Asher discussed the matter with Brian, he was surprised to hear Brian claim, 'I wrote all the music.' Asher was sent to Murry to work out the details. Tony Asher's summation of Murry was this: 'I've got to say that he came across to me as a really sick man. Pathetically so, in fact.' Asher wasn't going to argue, and simply agreed to one-quarter of a per cent. Over the years, he earned an estimated $60,000 from his work on the album.

Pet Sounds is the first album on which none of the Beach Boys played instruments. Diane Rovell was hired to be Brian's production secretary, and set about hiring the finest session musicians in the industry to play on the album. Brian would write the musical arrangements himself, and start each song with the basic tracks. Most of the recording for *Pet Sounds* was done 'live' – that is, the instruments and musicians were assembled at one time in a studio where the music was played in ensemble, instead of having each instrument on a single track to be mixed together later. 'Brian was producer, writer, and arranger,' engineer Jim Lockhart said.

Brian would occasionally play tracks over the long-distance phone lines for Michael in Japan, and when the other members of the group returned to LA, they found that most of the tracks were complete. Brian was ready for them to plug in their vocals – and they didn't like it. They objected to Brian's preconceived notion of what the vocals should sound like. Mike Love reportedly considered this Brian's 'ego' music. But Brian held firm; *Pet*

Sounds was *his* masterpiece. 'It took some getting used to,' Alan Jardine admitted. 'When we left the country, we were just a surfing group. This was a whole new thing.' The vocal tracks were arduous to lay down, and Brian made them work harder than ever to perfect them. Mike hated Brian's role as taskmaster. 'Who's gonna hear this?' he asked. 'The ears of a dog? But Brian had those kind of ears, so I said, "Okay, we'll do it another time." Every voice in its resonance and tonality and timbre had to be right. Then the next day he might throw it out and have us do it over again.' Brian even brought in outside singers, including Terry Melcher, to work on some of the tracks. He would sometimes let the group do the vocals the way they wanted, then, after they left the studio, he would wipe the vocals off completely and finish the track himself, since he could sing all the parts.

At the unheard-of cost of $70,000 for production, *Pet Sounds* was brilliant – not only for its innovation, but for its melancholy innocence. A searching album about growing up and the pain involved in the realities of adulthood, *Pet Sounds* is introverted, thoughtful, and childishly curious. There is something odd about the album, lonely and alienated. The tone of the album went beyond sensitive into a realm of something nearly pathetic – the whimper of a tortured young mind. *Pet Sounds* caused critic Nik Cohn to write years later that Brian wrote 'sad songs about loneliness and heartache. Sad songs even about happiness.' Critic Richard Goldstein later noted, 'Everyone sang about loneliness as though it came from disappointment in love. But Brian sang about it as an active pursuit.'

The titles alone could be woven into a psychodrama about Brian's state of mind at the time: 'Don't Talk (Put Your Head on My Shoulder),' 'Let's Go Away for

178

Awhile,' 'God Only Knows,' 'I Just Wasn't Made for These Times,' and 'That's Not Me.' The songs for the most part were under three minutes. Many remain classics of their kind. 'Wouldn't It Be Nice,' in particular, is a song expressing the longing for the age when one could do what one wanted, get married, have children – and stay overnight together. 'God Only Knows,'[1] was perhaps the most beautiful, a song about the love felt for someone who transforms life for you. ('God only knows where I'd be without you . . .') There was also 'Caroline No,' a song about a young girl who personifies Brian's loss of innocence.[2] The album ends with a remarkably forlorn and melancholy sound effect, Brian's two dogs barking in the faraway distance and the fading sound of a lonely railroad train. The title *Pet Sounds* was Mike's contribution, suggested in the hallway of Western Records while they were adding the vocals.

This was Brian's first fully realized album. When it was finished, he brought it home, put it on the stereo, and lay down with Marilyn in bed. 'Oh boy, he was just so proud of it,' Marilyn recalled. 'People weren't ready for it – it was too much of a shock, but a lot of people who understood it really loved it.'

[1] At first Brian was nervous about including the word *God* in the title, which had never been done in a pop song before.
[2] Obviously written for Carol Mountain, although Marilyn claims it was written for her.

5

Before they even heard *Pet Sounds*, the older, conservative executives at Capitol were becoming increasingly worried about Brian's erratic behavior and the apparent dissention within the group. Nik Venet, who was still Capitol's liaison to the Beach Boys, found Brian's behavior extraordinarily vexing. At one Capitol meeting, Brian arrived with a set of eight cassette tapes made in loops. Each tape repeated a simple phrase over and over again like 'No comment,' or 'I like that idea.' Venet also remembers running into Marilyn and Diane at a music-business party on the lawn of a producer in Beverly Hills. Brian was sequestered somewhere inside the house, and Marilyn kept saying, 'Brian really wants to speak to you. Don't leave without seeing him.' Venet waited half an hour. Brian came out and said, 'Don't go yet, I want to talk to you,' and then disappeared back inside the house. Half an hour later Brian came out of the house again and said, 'Don't go yet, I want to see you,' and disappeared a second time. Venet eventually gave up and left.

One day Brian called Capitol executives and told them he had a new single for immediate release, a brilliant single they would love. He showed up at the offices with a tape of 'Caroline No,' the song that would close the *Pet Sounds* album, just before the barking dogs and fading sound of the train. Although 'Caroline No' was a beautiful song, the people at Capitol knew it was not a hit. Yet, hoping to encourage Brian to complete his forthcoming album, they released the song on March 7, while 'Barbara

Ann' was still on the top of the charts. As they expected, 'Caroline No' peaked at 32 on April 30.[3]

After nearly ten months of preparation on *Pet Sounds*, the executives at Capitol were unsure whether Brian would finish his new album on time for a scheduled release – or finish it at all. They prepared a 'best of' compilation package for release. According to Nik Venet, the schedule of this album had absolutely nothing to do with whether or not they would like the forthcoming *Pet Sounds*. Capitol's only concern was to keep up the flow of Beach Boys product. When the chief executives at Capitol finally heard *Pet Sounds*, they didn't like it at all. There were no cars, no blondes in bikinis, no beach. They heard no single, no commercial hits. Their first reaction was to refuse to release it. 'I thought Brian was screwing up,' Venet said. 'He was no longer looking to make records, he was looking for attention from the business.' Most of all, Venet saw *Pet Sounds* as a very specific way of getting back at Murry. 'He was trying to torment his father with songs his father couldn't relate to and melody structures his father couldn't understand.'

On March 23, 1966, just two weeks after the release of the unsuccessful 'Caroline No,' Capitol chose to release the song 'Sloop John B.,' from the *Pet Sounds* album, as a single. Although Brian and the Beach Boys liked the song, they had little faith that it would become a major hit. 'Sloop John B.' was a traditional folk song arranged by Brian, and the only song on the album suggested by another member of the group – Al Jardine. Much to everyone's surprise, the single shot up the charts, making giant leaps from 112, to 68, to 38, to 13, 8, 4, and finally

---

[3] This is the only Beach Boys song released credited as a 'Brian Wilson Single.'

on May 7, to number 3. Luckily for Brian, this was a month-long period when not one Beatles single appeared on the charts.

The entire *Pet Sounds* album was unveiled to the world on May 16. It was the first Beach Boys album without striped shirts and surfing or automobiles on the cover. On the front were photographs, taken at the San Diego Zoo, of the boys dressed in cardigan sweaters and feeding goats. The back showed them dressed in traditional Japanese regalia in pictures taken on their recent Asian tour. Statistically, *Pet Sounds* didn't do too badly – it spent a total of thirty-nine weeks on the charts, peaking at number 11 only five weeks after its release, with well over half a million units sold. Although the musical cognoscenti, including important disc jockeys, felt that *Pet Sounds* was a masterpiece, for the most part the public was confused and disappointed in it except for 'Sloop John B.' The Capitol executives were right about one thing – the public expected a particular kind of song from the Beach Boys, and none of those songs were present on the album. However, *Pet Sounds* found its own special audience – a growing number of disenfranchised, lost, and sensitive people throughout America. To them the album became the theme music for a time of painful transition. In England the reviews and reception for *Pet Sounds* were nearly ecstatic. But at home, *Pet Sounds* was still considered a loser.

Capitol didn't even bother to promote *Pet Sounds*. Instead the advertising thrust and sales force went into the 'best of' compilation package. '[*Pet Sounds*] was probably ahead of its time,' said Al Couri, head of promotion, 'and yet it didn't sell. The retail activity was not as good as previous Beach Boys albums.' Only eight weeks after the release of Brian's precious *Pet Sounds*

LP, Capitol released *The Best of the Beach Boys*, which quickly went gold. 'You've got to understand that Brian was so impulsive, compulsive, you never knew what was coming next,' Venet said. 'The "best of" package was put together while Brian was working on *Pet Sounds*. There was a great love at the time of Beach Boys product . . . There were [salesmen] out there that could sell Beach Boys product and the [customers] were asking for it. The *Pet Sounds* album was supposed to be ready a long time before, and it wasn't going to be ready. The whole company was geared up to the "best of" package. Everything had been locked in, magazine advertising, the separations for the cover had been printed and stacked in a warehouse.' *The Best of the Beach Boys* compilation far outshone *Pet Sounds* in terms of sales, with a total of seventy-nine weeks on the charts, topping out at number 8 on October 24, 1966.

6

By this time the Beach Boys had already left the accounting firm of Cummings and Currant and had signed with one of the big powerhouse business-management companies in Los Angeles, Julius Lefkowitz and Company, whose offices were located in the CEIR Building at 9171 Wilshire Boulevard. Lefkowitz's brother Nat was president of the William Morris Agency in New York, and the Lefkowitz company in Los Angeles handled many elite literary and show-business clients, including James Michener, Gregory Peck, Danny Thomas, and Danny Kaye, as well as several music groups, such as Buffalo Springfield and Sonny and Cher, giving the company access to approximately $500 million in funds. Lefkowitz, around fifty at the time, was a smart and savvy businessman, whose approach with the Beach Boys was to make long-term investments with the short-term spurts of income they were experiencing. But the Beach Boys were hard personalities to deal with, and spent their money as they pleased, accumulating an array of expensive cars and homes. In fact, Lefkowitz assigned a full-time employee in the accounting department, Stanley Shapiro, to keep track of his clients' 'rolling stock,' or automobiles, of which the Beach Boys collectively owned twenty-six at this point. 'People like the Beach Boys were a pain in the ass,' Shapiro said, 'because no matter what they had, they didn't want to give up dollars and cents for investments. They preferred to spent it on toys.' According to Catherine Pace, who worked as the Beach Boys' bookkeeper during that period, 'The boys were like children . . . and they would do crazy things,' including never being on time for meetings with Julius Lefkowitz. 'You can't be Beach Boys all your lives,' Lefkowitz told them, but they didn't want to hear that.

The accountant in charge of their portfolio at Lefkowitz was Nick Grillo, a young, industrious fellow in his late twenties. Grillo was a clever businessman who had an easygoing rapport with the Beach Boys and a tremendous appreciation of their music. He was more interested in personal management than in straight investment, and early in 1966 Mike Love suggested that Grillo leave Lefkowitz and become their personal business manager. 'As part of the deal,' Grillo said, 'they would fund whatever the costs were in terms of personnel, and I would have a staff composed of an accounting side and a personal-management side. I would oversee their entire operation. For this I would get X number of dollars a year, plus a percentage of the override, but they would be responsible for funding the day-to-day activity.' The Beach Boys were already dealing with a concert-promotion company called American Productions. Retaining the name, Grillo took charge of concert promotion, as well as of all the Beach Boys' business finances. Grillo and the Beach Boys opened up spanking-new offices on the eighth floor of a new tower at 9000 Sunset Boulevard.

The 9000 building was seething with rock and show-business management firms, representing groups such as Paul Revere and the Raiders and the Byrds. Directly across the hall from the Beach Boys' new offices, Derek Taylor, one of the most famous publicists in the business, moved in. Taylor was famous for one act, and one act only – the Beatles. He had met them early in his career as a journalist from a Manchester newspaper, wrote about them often, and was finally signed on by their manager, Brian Epstein, as press officer. He had left the Beatles the previous year, and set up his own publicity company in Los Angeles. Taylor had a great capacity for alcohol and marijuana, as well as a reputation as a kind of psychedelic visionary. In a world where publicity was considered so much hot air, Taylor was extraordinarily talented. He was blessed with charm, wit, and intelligence. Journalists loved him, and the feeling was mutual. Taylor was able to convey a message about the groups he handled better than anyone else. The Beach Boys quickly became his clients. Ironically, Taylor's famed connection to the Beatles was most important to the Beach Boys.

Taylor first got to know Brian and the Beach Boys during the preparation of *Pet Sounds*, and many consider Derek Taylor's influential word in England to be the cornerstone for the album's success there. 'I lived in Hollywood then,' Derek said, 'but my British links were

185

strong, and with *Pet Sounds* out and the Beatles increasingly flattering about the Beach Boys . . . and with [a new single] on the way, we started to pump information into England about this tremendous band, with their new plateau. Soon everyone was saying "genius," and the beauty of it, as with the beauty of anything, was that it was true.'

'Genius' thus became the noun now constantly applied to Brian Wilson, a tag he began to carry with great weight. Throughout the Los Angeles music-business community, Brian was suddenly considered a 'genius,' despite the failure of *Pet Sounds* on his home turf. Brian became determined to prove the appellation accurate. His next single, he felt, would vindicate the failure of *Pet Sounds*. It was a single he was especially enthusiastic about. Truly the work of a 'genius,' it was a song he called a 'pocket symphony.' Its title: 'Good Vibrations.'

Eight

1

The Age of Aquarius had come to Los Angeles.

Everywhere you turned was a new breed of teenager collectively known as hippies. Bearded, barefoot, bedecked in bells and beads and bell-bottom trousers, they were as ubiquitous as they were hairy. In San Francisco the hippies had settled mainly in the Haight-Ashbury district; in Los Angeles they had invaded the Sunset Strip directly below Beverly Hills, and *Time* magazine reported 'Hippiedom has transplanted Shangri-La a go-go.'

Indeed, the former teen mecca of Sunset Strip had become a hippie haven. Good-bye prosperity; hello peace, flowers, and LSD. The stores up and down the Strip that had catered just a few years before to affluent young teenagers were now replaced with 'head shops,' dimly lit, incense-scented stores that sold drug paraphernalia, day-glo posters, and hand-strung beaded necklaces. Expensive clothing boutiques gave way to shops filled with tie-dyed T-shirts, bell-bottom pants, and wide-ribbed corduroys. There was a surfeit of all-night health-food restaurants, motels with hour-long rates for swingers –

called 'hot-sheet' motels – and a new dance club, the Trip, where the glowing dance floor was called an 'infinity space.' Signs in the windows of more establishment restaurants implored NO BARE FEET. Along the strip, on the concrete median that separated east and west traffic, the hippies sold their wares: necklaces, incense, and a radical 'underground' newpaper called the *LA Free Press*. Love was free too, as a new era of promiscuity was ushered in, with sex becoming a gesture of friendliness. Vocabulary changed drastically. The exclamation 'Wow!' became an all-purpose word, and everyone was called 'man.' Hippies no longer slept, they 'crashed,' usually coming down from drugs. People didn't get nervous, they were 'uptight,' and when the 'narcs' arrested you, you were 'busted.' Soon the freewheeling bikers joined the hippies on the strip, with their Harley-Davidson motorcycles, Nazi regalia, and cutoff denim jackets.

Here was the rub for the Beach Boys: the new hippie movement was almost exclusively white; the blacks were already disenchanted, remaining outside of society. *Time* had only a year before reported that the Beach Boys were the only 'white' (-sounding) pop band – almost all the others were a blend of R&B, or English with R&B roots. Simply put, Brian Wilson's entire audience of affluent white middle-class kids had been swept away in a wave of change. Gone completely were the trappings of the classic California life-style, the sun-bleached surfers and expensive cars. Now the badge of honor was awarded to the poor, to those living in socialist communes. Overnight, surf and car music was dead, and *Pet Sounds*'s gloomy introversion was of little help. Overnight, the Beach Boys were suddenly the epitome of square.

The new social wave was galvanized into a cohesive force by opposition to the growing war in Vietnam.

Moreoever, rock music was now being written as much for content as for entertainment. A new magazine published in San Francisco, *Rolling Stone* (whose first issue included a free roach clip), coalesced the idea that rock musicians were modern-day minstrels, responsible for delivering socially relevant messages. They wrote anti-establishment, antiwar, pro-love songs, and songs that spoke of the magic of drugs. San Fransicso was a hot bed of this kind of music, and a local promoter named Bill Graham had converted an old dance hall called the Fillmore into a showplace for groups with strange and alluring names: the Grateful Dead, Big Brother and the Holding Company, the Jefferson Airplane, Iron Butterfly. On glorious sunny Sundays, Golden Gate Park was the site of free concerts and mass love gatherings called 'be-ins.'

By mid-1966 the hippies of Sunset Boulevard had formed an alliance against what seemed an obvious enemy – the Los Angeles Police Department. In their leather boots and military-like uniforms the police were formidable opponents. At the behest of a local councilman, who claimed the strip was 'a dangerous powder keg, ready to explode,' a 10:00 P.M. curfew was issued for anyone under eighteen. Each night the LAPD cruisers would roll down the broad boulevard with loudspeakers, announcing, 'Attention, it is now past ten P.M. and anyone under eighteen years of age will be arrested.' American International Pictures began production on a film called *Riot on Sunset Strip*. But the confrontations on Sunset Boulevard were no joke, aggravating the growing youth unrest. When real-estate developers announced plans to tear down Pandora's Box, which had become a symbol of the hippie culture, the tension brimmed over. Led by Chief William Parker and Sheriff Peter Pitchess, the leather-booted, jodhpur-clad police formed a 'flying wedge' on Sunset Boulevard and mowed down the hippies, who were armed only with flowers and beads.

In response, Jim Dickson, manager of the Byrds, formed an organization called Community Action for Fact and Freedom, or CAFF. Backed by some of the major recording artists of the day, CAFF took space for its headquarters in the office of the Beach Boys' publicist, Derek Taylor. But the Beach Boys were not drawn into the fray, perhaps because the group at this time was almost continuously on tour, away from Los Angeles. More important, they were locked in a time warp – 1959 in 1966. Still wearing striped shirts, indulging in expensive cars, clothes, and the joys of young women on the road, the Beach Boys had no social consciousness. Only Brian was provoked and fascinated by what was happening around him, and actively sought to include himself in the 'scene.'

One prominent member of CAFF was David Anderle, a tall, handsome young man whom the underground papers referred to as 'the Mayor of Hip.' Twenty-eight years old, Anderle was clever and industrious, with a superior business sense. Born in east LA and raised in Inglewood, he attended the University of Southern California drama school and then went to work at MGM records, where he signed the handsome Irish singer Danny Hutton as well as Frank Zappa and The Mothers of Invention. By 1966, Anderle had left MGM and was managing Danny Hutton. Meanwhile, Hutton had met Brian in the studios, and together they had produced a single called 'The Farmer's Daughter' for a quickly forgotten group called Basil Swift and the Seegrams. Brian remained a lifelong fan of Hutton's, and the two became close friends.

Coincidentally, David Anderle had met the Wilson family years before, when his cousin, Bill Bloom, became friendly with the younger Wilson boys in Hawthorne. Anderle met Brian again around the time of *The Beach Boys Today!* album, when someone brought him up to the house on Laurel Way. 'It was very groovy,' Anderle said. 'I really liked Brian right away . . . because there was something there that I had not seen in many people in my lifetime. And [then] I was out again.' A year later, Danny Hutton took Anderle to Brian's house, where Brian had finally finished his forthcoming masterpiece, 'Good Vibrations.'

At the reported cost of more than $50,000, this three-minute-and-thirty-five-second song was recorded over a period of six months, using ninety hours of tape in nearly twenty different sessions at four different studios: Western, RCA, Gold Star, and Columbia. There was a host of new sounds on the recordings: cello, fuzz bass, clarinet, harp, and a strange new instrument called the Theramin, which made an eerie, wailing sound and was traditionally used in horror films. 'We had a slew of musicians working on it,' remembered Chuck Britz, who engineered the song. There were still no lyrics, although Tony Asher had written several verses for it while working on *Pet Sounds* with Brian.

Brian had long been concerned about 'vibrations' of different sorts. He first heard the word from his mother, who tried to explain why dogs bark at certain people and feel comfortable with others. 'My mother used to tell me about vibrations, and I didn't really understand too much of what she meant when I was a boy. It scared me to death . . . So we talked about good vibrations with the song and the idea, and we decided that on the one hand you could say . . . those are sensual things. And then

191

you'd say, "I'm picking up good vibrations," which is a contrast against the sensual, the extrasensory perception that we have. That's what we're really talking about.'

According to Chuck Britz, 'Good Vibrations' virtually jelled in the first session with Brian, but as soon as the other Beach Boys heard it, they had suggestions and changes. Eventually, Mike Love was elected to write new lyrics. Unsure of himself, Brian listened to suggestions from every quarter and tinkered with the song. 'There was a lot of "Oh you can't do this, that's too modern" or "That's going to be too long a record,"' said one observer. Under pressure from the rest of the group, Brian was never really happy with 'Good Vibrations.' When Mike Love first heard the song, he described it as 'very heavy R&B . . . it sounded like Wilson Pickett would be recording it.' At one point Brian gave a version to Capitol Records for release, then changed his mind the next day and took it back. Eventually, the song seemed like a problem with no answer. Discouraged and beleaguered, Brian put the track aside for a while and considered selling it to Warner Brothers as an R&B single.

When he played the song for David Anderle one night at Laurel Way, Anderle thought it was so beautiful, 'it destroyed me.' Later, on the way home in his car, Anderle couldn't get the song out of his mind. When he got home, he called Danny Hutton. He suggested to Danny that the track might be right for him. The next day Anderle called Brian and asked him to sell the track for Hutton to record. Anderle's enthusiasm for the cut changed Brian's mind and made him decide to finish it, and also cemented one of Brian's most important friendships – Anderle was now his New Best Friend.

'Good Vibrations' became the Beach Boys' biggest hit to date, selling over 100,000 copies each day in its first week of release. In England it was an immediate smash, appearing on the charts at number 6 and leaping to number 1 a week later. A London *Sunday Express* headline proclaimed, THEY'VE FOUND A NEW SOUND AT LAST! Within a few weeks, the Beach Boys topped the *New Musical Express* readers' poll as the most popular group in England, one place ahead of the Beatles. In America, the reaction was less certain, but almost as good. 'Good Vibrations' appeared on the charts at 81 on October 22, a week after its release, then jumped to 38, 17, 4 on November 12, and hung in at number 2 for three weeks. On December 10, like a giant Christmas gift, the song hit number 1.

Yet from then on in, it was all downhill.

2

David Anderle, Brian's New Best Friend, was a conduit to the new hip society emerging in the LA recording business. Brian's circle of friends enlarged to encompass a whole new crowd. Some of these people were 'drainers,' whom a close observer at the time remembers as 'the usual trailings of sycophants trying to get close to power. Like white on rice, like a cheap suit, they were all over the place.' But some of these followers were talented and industrious and a few truly loved Brian, not just for his talent, but for his naïveté and warm generosity. Among these people were Brian's longtime friend Lou Adler, who had recently produced the Mamas and the Papas; Terry Melcher – the blond, moustachioed son of Doris Day and boyfriend of ingenue Candice Bergen – who was a record producer for the Byrds and Paul Revere and the

Raiders; Jules Siegel, a gifted writer covering the music business for the *Saturday Evening Post*, who had written a well-received piece on Bob Dylan; Michael Vosse, a warm, articulate friend of Anderle's from the USC drama school, and a part-time stringer for Jules Siegel; and Paul J. Robbins, who wrote free-lance pieces for the *Los Angeles Free Press*. With this new cast of characters, the scene at Laurel Way turned into a creative caldron of ideas, drugs, and activity.

During this period Brian decided to redecorate his house. His new decorating ideas were in keeping with the time – at least the times of a rock star. He placed a call to Nick Grillo at the office and insisted that the den – where his grand piano now sat – be filled with several tons of sand, so that he could feel the sand under his feet as he composed. The next day carpenters arrived and built what amounted to a giand sandbox around the piano. Then a truck hauled several tons of sand up to the house and dumped it in. Soon afterward, the office got a call from a harried saleswoman in the children's department of a large store in Century City. The woman got the Beach Boys' bookkeeper, Catherine Pace, on the line and said, 'I have a young man here who's crawling through our tree house. He wants to buy it and he says you will send me the money.' The young man turned out to be Brian. Catherine Pace said she would send the money right away, and when the tree house was delivered to Laurel Way, Brian put it in the entryway of the house. You had to crawl through it to get inside.

Physical health took on sudden importance, and for the next week Brian decided that all the furniture should be moved out of the living room, and the floors lined with gym mats. An assortment of gym equipment was moved in, only to sit unused and dusty for months. Next, a portable, enclosed sauna was installed in the hallway just outside the living room. There was a small ventilation hole in the wall, and every now and then Brian would thump on the wall. Marilyn, who sat outside waiting for his signal, would blow marijuana smoke through the hole into Brian's mouth. Finally, in the room with the beautiful view of the city, a tent was erected consisting of nearly $30,000 worth of fabric. It had velvet floors, huge cushions, and an assortment of hookahs. The first time Brian went into the tent with his friends, they realized there was no ventilation, and it was so hot and stuffy they never used it again. Vegetables, too, were in vogue at Laurel Way – Brian wanted Marilyn to start a garden of organic vegetables and sell them to motorists through a window in the kitchen.

Brian's friend Terry Melcher lived in Beverly Hills at 10050 Cielo Drive in a huge, rented house with a beautiful manicured lawn where he often gave parties for the crème de la crème of the LA hip. On this emerald lawn, David Anderle and Terry Melcher introduced Brian to his next collaborator, Van Dyke Parks. Van Dyke had first met Terry Melcher at a recording session where he was hired to play the piano. Van Dyke was a short, elfin young man with a brilliant mind and an unfailingly sarcastic sense of humor. He spoke in a torrent of punning, polysyllabic words, in sentences so melodious they were almost a musical leitmotif. The youngest of four sons of a Jungian psychiatrist from Pennsylvania, Van Dyke had originally come west as a child actor. After attending Carnegie Tech, he returned to California, where he lived at Seal Beach and occasionally worked at the Balboa Ballroom, a 'folkie playing guitar in coffeehouses up and down the coast' as he put it. In the early sixties he met David Anderle at MGM, where he made an obscure record called 'Sunshine.' When Brian met Van Dyke at Terry Melcher's house, he was instantly fascinated by Van Dyke's golden tongue and sense of style.

'He called me up out of a clear blue sky and said, "Let's write a tune together,"' Van Dyke said. Although flattered, Van Dyke was concerned. He had heard that Tony Asher had disassociated himself from Brian and the Beach Boys despite the critical praise he received for the *Pet Sounds* lyrics. 'I think Tony Asher was a foil to Brian and that Brian wanted another foil when he asked me to write with him.' At first Brian asked Van Dyke to finish the lyrics of the still incomplete 'Good Vibrations,' but Van Dyke didn't want to step into a muddled situation, and suggested they start afresh on Brian's next project. Brian explained that his next project, tentatively entitled *Dumb Angel*, was going to be a recording of such magnitude and encompassing vision that it would be bigger and better than *Pet Sounds*. It would be greater in scope than anything the public had ever heard – including the Beatles' latest LP, *Rubber Soul*, which had taken the recording industry by storm. Brian's new album would have threads of music interwound from song to song to fill a vast tapestry. The album would establish a new arena of accomplishment in the recording industry, or, as Brian put it, 'I'm writing a teenage symphony to God.' If Van Dyke decided to help, the lyrics could express the interests both of them had in American history, which the music would complement in a variety of forms, from campfire music to labor songs to western folk music and Latin jazz. Van Dyke couldn't resist.

The first time Van Dyke went to Laurel Way, he rode a small motorcycle he had managed to buy secondhand. He had no driver's license because he couldn't afford the fee. Indeed, the day Van Dyke and Brian had met at

Terry Melcher's house, Van Dyke was penniless. 'I was living in a garage apartment on Melrose near La Brea. I had no bathroom at the time, and I was vaulting the pay toilet at a Standard station around the corner. I was also using the bathroom of a hardware store.' Van Dyke was the only one of Brian's acquaintances who was personally insulted by Brian's monetary indulgences. He was horrified by the piano in the sandbox. 'It wasn't funny, a grand piano set in a sandbox. I found it offensive. Absolutely repugnant.' As for the tent, 'I didn't understand how so much fabric could be spent like that. My father was a heavy Calvinist, and economic propriety and frugality never left me.'

When Brian learned how poor Van Dyke was he immediately got on the phone with Murry, who was still handling the Beach Boys' publishing. 'I've got a guy here named Van Dyke Parks who's a wonderful worker and he needs a car. Let's buy him one.' Van Dyke was amazed. 'And he'll need some money.' Brian told Murry, 'about five thousand dollars.' Brian turned to Van Dyke. 'Would that be all right?' he asked.

Stupefied, Van Dyke said, 'Yes, that would be fine.' The check arrived later that day while Van Dyke was working on one of the songs. 'There were no stipulations about what the five thousand dollars represented,' Van Dyke said, 'but what it meant was my undying loyalty to Brian Wilson.'

In some ways Van Dyke Parks was the most brilliant lyricist Brian ever chose, and in some ways he was the worst. Van Dyke wrote in an impressionistic stream that was far too complex for the average listener to comprehend easily. Even with a lyric sheet his writing was obscure. Although Van Dyke's lyrics were evocative and beautiful, they were eons beyond anything the Beach

197

Boys' fans could appreciate. While in another short year many rock groups would be experimenting lyrically, this unexpected jump from the car and surf lyrics – or even the melancholy, but simple lyrics of *Pet Sounds* – was most perplexing to all who heard them. Still, Van Dyke was determined to aid Brian, as foil or friend, in producing his incredible new album.

The first order of business was the purchase of the necessary drugs. Brian arranged for and bought over $2,000 worth of the finest Afghani hashish. 'We smoked a lot of it and got into a good place with the black hash,' Brian said. 'We went ahead and lay on the floor recording with the microphones about a foot from the ground. We were so stoned we had to lie down. We got to the point where we thought this was the way to record. We got halfway through the album before we decided to stand up because we got sleepy.'

Over twenty songs were prepared for the new album, some comprised of several musical fragments strung together, with passages repeating and echoing each other. According to David Anderle, they recorded enough songs for three albums, but the material changed continually, and the events surrounding the album differed so much according to each person's point of view, that no one can be certain. Van Dyke and Brian started with a song called 'Heroes and Villains,' first written in fragments and then strung together into one song. Those who heard the original version thought it was stronger and even more important than 'Good Vibrations,' but as with all the cuts, the original version was never to be heard by the public. There was 'Barnyard,' about a farm in the Old West, and 'Cabin-essence,' about a log cabin in the woods. There was also a beautiful a cappella song called 'Our Prayer.'

Another, 'Do You Like Worms?,' featured the lyrics 'Rock, rock, roll, Plymouth rock roll over, roll over,' ending in a music-box version of the 'Heroes and Villains' theme.

The album cover prepared by Capitol included names of tunes called 'Wonderful,' 'I'm in Great Shape,' 'Child Is Father of the Man,' and 'The Elements,' which was an entire suite consisting of segments titled, 'Fire,' 'Air,' 'Water,' and 'Earth.' In yet another song, according to Van Dyke, 'we were trying to write a song that would end on a freeze frame of the Union Pacific Railroad – the guys come together and they turn around to have their picture taken.'

But perhaps the most beautiful and important song of all was 'Surf's Up.' Composed in a single evening, 'Surf's Up' is as obscure as it is poignant. It has a lilting, rolling melody, and its lyrics are a phantasmagoria of images. Brian once tried to explain the song's meaning: 'It's a man at a concert,' Brian said. 'All around him there's the audience, playing their roles, dressed up in fancy clothes . . . The music begins to take over. "Columnated ruins domino." Empires, ideas, lives, institutions – everything has to fall, tumbling like dominoes . . . "Canvas the town and brush the backdrop." He's off in his vision, on a trip. Reality is gone . . . "A choke of grief." At his own sorrow and the emptiness of his life, because he can't even cry for the suffering in the world, for his own suffering. And then, hope. "Surf's Up!" . . .'

During the preparation of *Dumb Angel*, Brian's creativity was fueled with not only hashish but also a prescription amphetamine called Desbutol, which was reportedly purchased in the black market, and – although never in the presence of David Anderle or Van Dyke Parks – occasional psychedelics. Under this barrage of drugs, Brian's state of mind became fragmented and out of control.

Ideas for new projects came in powerful spurts, distracting him for long periods from *Dumb Angel*. These myriad concepts soon began to overtake work on the album itself, as even the album's name changed to, simply, *Smile*. Other new distractions that kept him away from the piano and the studios were health foods; a preoccupation with his swimming pool – Brian installed a sliding pond leading from the roof of the house into the pool; whipped-cream fights during which Brian would get high by breathing the empty aerosol cans into his mouth; and chants – meaningless sounds repeated *ad nauseam* until, to the stoned mind, they sounded like music. Said Derek Taylor, '[Brian] used to talk a lot of totter about health food [while he was] digging into a big, fat hamburger. And gymnasiums! I was fitter than he was . . . Going on about vitamins. I thought maybe he was just being amusing, you see. Having a meal with him was like the Mad Hatter's tea party; "Have some tea, there isn't any."'

One night, while Marilyn prepared dinner for Brian's new group of friends, he sat at the dining table with his guests, idly tapping utensils on a white china plate. 'Listen to that!' he suddenly said. 'Come on, let's get something going here!' He encouraged his dinner companions to take their utensils and bang on the table, plates, and glasses. 'That's absolutely unbelievable!' Brian exclaimed. 'Isn't it unbelievable? That's so unbelievable I'm going to put it on the album.' It was forgotten the next day. On another occasion, Loren Schwartz, who was still very much a part of Brian's inner circle, told Brian about the caftans everyone was wearing. Brian was so taken with the idea that he immediately stopped working on *Smile* and spent the afternoon with Loren looking for an available store where he could open up a robe shop.

Brian and David Aderle would often pop five Desbutols

and sit up all night looking at the stars. One night Brian decided they needed a telescope. When Anderle said that no telescope store would be open so late, Brian told him they would have to *buy* a telescope store so they could have one whenever they wanted. On another occasion Brian embarked on a hunt to purchase a Ping-Pong table in the middle of the night.

Soon to be abandoned was an idea for an album of just sound effects, which Michael Vosse was put on the payroll to record. These sounds would include the gurgling of water, from fountains, taps, and the ocean; the crunching of gravel; the sounds of animals, and sounds of chewing and swallowing – all cut together to form an entire album based on water. There was also an entire album devoted to humor, which Brian actually recorded with photographer Jasper Dailey, and which was rejected by A&M Records. 'Brian was consumed with humor at the time and the importance of humor,' Aderle said. 'He was fascinated with the idea of getting humor onto a disc and hot to get that disc out to the people.' But there wasn't very much interest in this project at Capitol Records, and this fact led to one of the grandest, albeit most intelligent ideas, of the era: the formation of the Beach Boys' own record company, Brother Records.

Brother Records was already a major topic of discussion between the Beach Boys and Nick Grillo. Grillo was involved in intensive negotiations with Capitol to upgrade the Beach Boys' royalty before their old contract lapsed. He was not thrilled to learn in October 1966 that Brian wanted David Anderle to be put on the payroll, forming Brother Records. 'Anderle came out of the thin air for me,' Grillo said. 'He didn't have the credentials that would warrant making him the head of a record company.' Of all the Beach Boys, Mike Love was the most receptive to the idea of a separate record company. Love wanted the Beach Boys to have more control, and his support for Anderle, whom he respected as a businessman, lent the idea weight. The others were also enthusiastic, seeing Brother Records as an opportunity for each of them to discover and record their own artists and thereby emerge from Brian's shadow.

One of the first things Anderle did in conjunction with Nick Grillo was to hire Abe Somers, a top Los Angeles lawyer who was well known in the record business. Checking through old royalty statements from Capitol, Anderle discovered that 'at that point Brian had never been paid a producer's royalty,' which he claimed 'was bizarre. Everything was changing then. Artists were now starting to be treated a lot differently, and it was my feeling that Brian should be treated right.' A lawsuit was threatened, but Capitol did not seem cowed at first; their agreement with the Beach Boys had another two years to run, and they saw no reason to pay additional funds, particularly without any new hit material forthcoming. So the Beach Boys took Capitol to court. The suit, filed in Los Angeles Superior Court, alleged 'withholding of royalties due' totaling $275,000.

Meanwhile, Anderle held meetings with several other record companies to try to get a distribution deal for Brother Records. He even met with Atlantic Record's president, Ahmet Ertegun, but there were no takers in sight.

3

As summer drifted into fall, and then into winter, *Smile*
was still not finished. It became apparent to Capitol,
which had already printed 468,000 album covers, which
were sitting in a Scranton plant, that *Smile* would not be
available for Christmas release. Brian's behavior continued to grow more peculiar, although none of his intimate
circle seemed concerned. This was a time when outlandish
behavior was not only accepted, but lauded. No matter
how far-out Brian got, his actions were never considered
signs of a deteriorating mental state, but just symptoms
of drug use or general eccentricity. After all, Brian had
been declared a 'genius,' and geniuses were *supposed* to
be eccentric. 'Thinking back,' Anderle said, 'there was so
much weirdness going on that was whimsical and humor-
ous, those signs certainly didn't alarm me. Brian wasn't
the only one. We were all strange, doing strange things.'

During that fateful autumn, Brian became obsessively
concerned that Murry was planting eavesdropping devices
in his home and automobile, ostensibly to find out not
only what Brian was doing in his personal life, but what
his new music would be like. Instead of suggesting to
Brian that this was an irrational fear, and that not even
Murry was capable of doing such a thing, the people
around him took Brian's suspicions seriously. Indeed,
Murry seemed to have such an adverse effect on Brian
that when he called ahead to say he intended to visit the
house on Laurel Way, Brian would vomit in fear. Brian
was so convinced that Murry was 'bugging' the house that
he began to insist on having all important business meet-

ings held in the swimming pool. A stock of bathing suits was kept in the pool house, where harried associates and business executives would have to change before climbing into large rubber rafts to discuss important matters with Brian. Eventually, he hired a professional detective agency to 'debug' his house and car. 'Magically,' said Michael Vosse, 'they found a bug in Brian's car. To this day I think they brought it with them to get the job.' The detectives were placed on the payroll for a while, and insisted that all of Brian's close friends change their phones to unlisted numbers.

One evening Brian was sitting in his living room with Stanley Shapiro from Jules Lefkowitz's office, discussing old relationships, when the topic of Carol Mountain, his high-school flame, came up. Brian had recently heard that she was married to a physical-education teacher and still lived in Hawthorne. 'Why don't you call her up?' Shapiro suggested. Brian got on the telephone at once and started calling every Mountain listed in the Inglewood–Hawthorne area, until he finally located Carol's parents. He hurriedly explained who he was, and asked for Carol's address, which the girl's mother trustingly gave him. Two minutes later Brian was out of the house, driving to Hawthorne in his Rolls-Royce, intending to get Carol Mountain to come back to Laurel Way with him. 'It was the funniest thing I had ever seen in my life,' Shapiro said. 'The two of us were bombed out of our minds. He's standing on the doorstep ringing her doorbell and Carol Mountain opened the door with rollers in her hair. Brian explained to her who he was, and when she heard that he was Brian Wilson of the Beach Boys she was really surprised – she never knew.' Brian tried to convince the surprised woman to come back to the house with them, but naturally she didn't want to go. 'In the middle of all

204

this, her husband showed up,' Shapiro said. 'Brian said a few things that didn't sit right with the guy, and before you knew it there was an altercation and the guy started yelling, "I'm going to get my gun." Brian took off running and came back to the car, and the two of us tore out of there.'

That same autumn, Brian's deep, paranoid obsession with Phil Spector began in earnest. While Brian's competition with the Beatles was heartfelt, it had always been a friendly one. Now suddenly Brian thought Phil Spector was out to control or destroy him in some way. Brian would go to the record store and buy ten copies of Spector's hit song 'Be My Baby' and literally wear out the grooves playing them, listening for hidden meanings and messages. Spector was having his own problems by this time. He had become a virtual recluse. Surrounded by bodyguards, he hid behind the gates of his Beverly Hills mansion, venturing outside only when shielded by the dark-tinted windows of a limousine.

The situation came to a head one night when the usual group of Brian's friends, including David Anderle and Jules Siegel, was at the house waiting for him to come home. Marilyn was painting her fingernails when Brian arrived at the house, shaking and upset. Everyone asked what was wrong.

'It's Spector, man. He's really after me,' Brian said.

'Why? What happened?' Marilyn asked.

Brian said he had walked into a movie theater where *Seconds*, a new film starring Rock Hudson, was playing. The movie was about an older man who undergoes head-to-toe plastic surgery and has a second chance in life. As the movie starts, Brian explained, 'The first thing that happened was a voice from the screen that said, "Hello, Mr Wilson."'

'So what?' Anderle said.

'*So what*?' Brian repeated, wide-eyed. 'It completely blew my mind! Don't you see how weird it was?'

'But wasn't that the name of the character in the movie?' someone asked.

'That's not all,' Brian went on, his agitation growing. 'Then the whole thing was there. I mean my whole life. Birth and death and rebirth. The whole thing. Even the beach was in it, a whole thing about the beach. It was my whole life right there on the screen.' Brian also noticed that the street number of the house where the movie character lived was the same as the number of his house in Hawthorne.

'It's just coincidence,' Anderle offered.

'No it wasn't. It was mind-fuck. Spector's mind-fuck. Haven't you heard of "mind gangsters"? It was Spector who set it up. It was a Columbia movie and Spector records for Columbia.'

'Brian,' Marilyn said calmly. 'You don't think that Spector made them write the movie that way just to frighten *you*.'

But that was exactly what Brian thought.

David Anderle tried another tack. 'Listen, Brian, why would John Frankenheimer [the director of the film] make a movie just to terrify you?' he asked.

Brian said. 'Think about this. John Frankenheimer is Jewish. Phil Spector is Jewish. If Phil Spector went to a fellow Jew and appealed to him on a fellow-Jew level to help him destroy Brian Wilson, don't you think he'd do it?'

Anderle, himself a Jew, was so insulted he couldn't speak. The veins stood out on his forehead, and it was all he could do to control himself. It took him several days to forgive Brian.

Brian then walked briskly into the den and went over to his jukebox. He punched a few buttons and the sound of Spector's 'Be My Baby' came blaring out into the room. He played the song over and over again, at least twenty times. As the song played, he sat down at his desk and began to draw diagrams with a felt-tipped pen. 'Spector started the whole thing,' he said. 'He was the first one to use the studio. But I've gone beyond him now. I'm doing spiritual sound, a white spiritual sound. Religious music. Did you hear the Beatles album? Religious, right?'

Everyone looked at each other in amazement.

'That's the whole movement. That's where I'm going. It's going to scare a lot of people. Yeah.' Brian hit his desk. 'Yeah,' he said again, and smiled.

4

There was one other crucial moment that some believe helped tip Brian over into a netherworld. It was the outcome of the Derek Taylor 'Brian is a genius' campaign. CBS television was doing a prime-time documentary series called 'Inside Pop: The Rock Revolution,' and had assigned David Oppenheim, a young producer from their New York office, to assemble an hour-long show, hosted by conductor Leonard Bernstein, about the important new voices in the world of rock-and-roll. 'Some person in New York was very high on Brian Wilson,' Oppenheim said. 'I was very curious about him and his music.'

Oppenheim set off for Los Angeles, and soon after arriving drove up the hill to the house on Laurel Way. He just walked in and said who he was. 'It was a kind of informal drop-in place,' Oppenheim said. 'There were always people around . . . Brian at the time had his piano put in the sand, and in the back there was a tent. I was invited into the tent. I went in once or twice but never understood what it was about. Brian was looking at the TV set with just the color, detuned, and lots of vegetables around. Marilyn was nice, receptive and warm, and made sure I had a drink. I never understood Brian and her together. It was a strange, insulated household, insulated from the world by money . . . A playpen of irresponsible people. If they'd had to feel the road and the gravel under their feet, they would have had to behave in a very different way, but this wasn't necessary.

'A film crew and I went to Columbia Records's studios with Brian and his friends, and they were doing tiny little pieces that made no sense in and of themselves . . . just a few notes . . . also the sessions didn't make a scene that was at all interesting . . . I had hoped to get Brian masterminding a recording session, but instead it was terribly spread out . . . Brian was a little spacy, but he didn't seem drugged. We filmed a piece called "Surf's Up," and he accompanied himself at the piano. After that we tried to talk with him but didn't get much out of him. Some guy said, "He's not verbal." He was odd and he seemed odder. I had heard the stories before we got there about how crazy he was. Van Dyke seemed brilliant, intelligent, off-the-wall, and smashed.'

Later, they filmed a sequence in the pool. 'We got an underwater camera and they went down that slide into the pool and the camera went down underneath with them. The camera crew was in the swimming pool.'

The completed show aired soon afterward. It began with Bernstein talking about the discoveries that rock musicians were making both musically and in lyrics, mentioning Tandyn Almer, Janis Ian, and Brian among others. Bernstein did not call him a genius – Oppenheim used the word in the introduction to Brian's number – but Bernstein said 'Surf's Up' was 'too complex to get all of it the first time around.' However, it was perceived that Leonard Bernstein had called Brian a 'genius,' and for Brian this was a proclamation, an investment as king of the heap. Now Brian was under tremendous pressure to live up to his reputation.

In autumn 1966, with 'Good Vibrations' high on the charts, the touring revenues of the Beach Boys were quickly approaching $2 million annually. To cash in on the Beach Boys' sudden renewed popularity, the touring segment of the group – Carl, Mike, Dennis, Alan, and Bruce Johnston – embarked on a worldwide tour through the Midwest of the United States, then on to Sweden, middle Europe, and Great Britain. Early one morning, shortly after the tour had begun, Michael Vosse received a phone call from Brian. 'I'm worried about the tour,' he said. 'I think the boys need more rehearsing.' In particular, Brian was concerned about the way his masterpiece, 'Good Vibrations,' would sound when played live in concert. Brian asked Vosse to pick him up and drive him out to the Los Angeles airport, where they would catch a plane for Chicago and then drive to Ann Arbor, Michigan, where the group was rehearsing for a concert the following night.

When Vosse and Brian arrived at Chicago, they spent the first hour riding around in a taxi cab while Brian interviewed the driver about rock-and-roll and his various thoughts about youth. The driver, although perplexed, was happy to get the large fare and spent the time talking into Brian's Nagra recorder. After spending the night in a Chicago hotel, Vosse and Brian drove to Ann Arbor the next morning. It was a pretty autumn day, but Brian had no time to enjoy the weather. He put the boys through a grueling rehearsal, stopping them every few seconds to make recommendations. The concert that night went off splendidly – the boys gave a spirited, almost perfect performance. Brian watched from backstage, and when the last encore had been played, the rest of the group literally dragged him out on the stage for a bow. Brian was both upset and tickled – he had not wanted to break his vow of never appearing onstage again. When the spotlight picked him out and the audience realized who he was, a high-pitched frenzy erupted. As Brian stood frozen, the audience leaped to their feet and gave him a standing ovation.

On the way back to Chicago's O'Hare Airport, Brian got stoned on grass, and by the time they boarded the plane he was very high. Sitting in the first-class compartment next to Mike Vosse, Brian was upset and quiet. Something was obviously on his mind. When the stewardess offered him a menu for dinner, Brian decided he wanted *all* the entrées on it. The stewardess tried to explain politely that he could only choose one, but Brian made such a fuss she finally consented, giving him what he wanted. Only an hour into the flight he had another idea: he wanted to call Marilyn. He summoned the stewardess and told her he had to make an emergency phone call. The stewardess explained that it was impossible; there were no phones on the plane. But Brian insisted, relentlessly, and after much consultation with the chief flight attendant as well as the pilot, it was agreed Brian's message would be radioed to the nearest airport on the ground, where an airline official would make the phone call for him. The message was this: Call Marilyn at home and have her assemble as many of Brian's friends as she could in the next several hours and have them waiting at the airport, along with Guy Webster, a photographer who had photographed the Beach Boys many times.

When the plane landed, nearly twenty of Brian's friends were waiting at the terminal. Guy Webster lined the large group up against the while-tile wall of the terminal, and photographed them with a wide-angle lens, like an eerie graduation photograph. For the next few months a giant blowup of the photograph hung on Brian's living room wall. In just as much time, all of the people in the photograph would become strangers.

5

Meanwhile, word from Great Britain was thrilling. The Beach Boys arrived to find Heathrow Airport swamped with fans, and Capitol's EMI headquarters was besieged with reporters waiting for a press conference. Throngs of teenage girls appeared wherever the group went, tearing at their clothes. Paul McCartney phoned, John Lennon and George Harrison came to visit them at the Hilton, and they were introduced to the Rolling Stones. Mike Love called Brian in Los Angeles to tell him that the same kind of frenzy that greeted the Beatles was happening to them. In celebration, four Rolls-Royce Phantom VII limousines were purchased in a London showroom, one for Dennis, Carl, and Mike Love, and a fourth for Brian at home, at a cost of $32,000 each.

In Los Angeles, Brian was finishing work on *Smile*.

One of the most peculiar incidents involving the production of *Smile* occurred on November 10 at the Gold

Star Studios on Santa Monica Boulevard. It happened during the final session for 'Fire,' which was to be included in 'The Elements.' Brian had assembled, at great cost, an enormous string session to help record the 'Fire' segments. He had already sent the violinists home once because, while sitting outside the studio in his Rolls-Royce, he had decided the 'vibrations' weren't right for that night's session. Van Dyke Parks, who was with him in the limousine, was so dismayed by this decision that 'I avoided the "Fire" sessions like the plague. I didn't want to embarrass myself. I thought it was regressive behaviour.'

When the string session was reassembled, Brian insisted that everyone in the studio wear a fire helmet, including all the middle-aged violinists, the engineers, Marilyn and Diane, and anyone else who happened to walk into the studio. Brian sent a roadie, Arnie Geller, to a toy store to buy them. When Arnie returned, producing the red helmets from the trunk of Brian's Rolls-Royce, the session musicians all donned them and began to play.

Brian remembered, 'I walked in [to the studios], and there was a janitor named Brother Julius who lived in a little bungalow in the backyard. Before I walked in, I said, "Brother Julius, could you start a little fire in the bucket and bring it in the studio?" Well, he hit the ceiling. He said, "What do you want me to do that for?" I said, "I want these guys to smell smoke." You see, I was flipping. I wanted to smell smoke.

'So there were the musicians smelling smoke with fire hats on. They were all firemen. *Rooooar, rooar.* The violins were screeching up, reaching upward, rolling down . . . *Whoooorrr . . .*'

Those who were there say the track was a terrifying internal whine. Jules Siegel, in his article 'Goodbye

Surfing, Hello God!,' said the music summoned up 'visions of roaring, windstorm flames, falling timbers, mournful sirens and sweating firemen, building into a peak and crackling off into fading embers as a single drum turned into a collapsing wall . . .'

'It was sick,' Brian said, 'I mean, it was sick. Weird chords, it wasn't the straight eight and all that. I started thinking, Oh God, I'm flipping here. But I like it.' After twenty-four takes Brian was satisfied. Carrying the tapes out of the studio, still wearing his fire hat, he said, 'I'm going to call this "Mrs O'Leary's Fire," and I think it might just scare a whole lot of people.'

According to Brian, later that night, 'We got the news that a place nearby burned down. Well, I thought I started the fire. I thought that for some magical reason what we were doing in the Gold Star [started fires].' Brian had his staff of cronies research the number of fires in and around Los Angeles that week. Discovering that there was an 'unusual' number of fires, he decided it was his music that had caused them. Brian then tried to destroy the 'Fire' tapes by burning them, but when the tapes would not ignite, they were locked away in a vault, where they reportedly remain to this day.

'I don't have to do a big scary fire like that,' he said. 'I can do a candle and it's still fire. That would have been a really bad vibration to let out on the world, that Chicago fire. The next one is going to be a candle.'

One day Jules Siegel and his girl friend arrived at the recording studio to visit a session and found their way barred by a security guard. Michael Vosse was sent out to explain the exclusion to Jules. 'It's not you,' Vosse said. 'It's your chick. Brian says she's a witch and she's messing with his brain so bad by ESP that he can't work. I'm really sorry.' Jules Siegel never came by again.

6

The touring segment of the Beach Boys knew nothing of Brian's strange behavior. When they returned to California to put the vocals on the new record, the scene they found waiting infuriated them. It was as if a whole group of strangers had infiltrated and were taking over the Beach Boys. Anderle, whom they had trusted to start Brother Records for them, seemed to be the leader of the pack. They now began to deeply resent him, suspecting him of encouraging Brian to leave the Beach Boys and go out on his own. 'Sure I was an interloper,' Anderle said, 'and I'm sure they saw me as somebody who was taking Brian away from them. And somebody who was fueling Brian's weirdness. And I stand guilty on those counts . . . I was an interloper and I was definitely fueling his creativity. No holds barred. No rules.' And when the others heard the music, they were furious. Mike Love was the most vocal and vehement. 'You're going to blow it, Brian,' he said. 'Stick to the old stuff. Don't fuck with the formula.'

Facing the other Beach Boys, Brian felt a sense of tremendous responsibility. 'I think he was pressured by the group,' said one close observer of that period. 'And by knowing that everyone in that group was married, and had children and a house. I think he felt like more of a *benefactor* than an artist . . . He was a creative force and there were five other people – five other families – relying on his creativity.' The Beach Boys had seen infiltrators before – Gary Usher, Tony Asher, Loren Schwartz.

Not long after the Beach Boys returned from Europe,

Van Dyke Parks got a phone call from Brian inviting him to a session. He knew something was up. 'I was stunned. Usually I did not go to sessions . . . but Brian called and said would I come to the session and help Mike with the lyrics . . . there was some question about them. Well, I was frightened for a second. I realized that Brian wasn't anything more than a one-man Trojan horse.'

Van Dyke got into his car and drove warily down to the studios, where Mike Love and Brian were waiting for him. The problem seemed to be that the lyrics were too abstract and obscure. Mike began to grill Van Dyke on what each individual lyric meant. Reportedly, the line 'Columnated ruins domino' was particularly vexing – though no more vexing than most of the rest.

'I have no excuse, sir,' Van Dyke told Mike sarcastically. Insulted and hurt, he refused to explain what any of the words meant, or claimed he didn't understand them himself. 'I remember leaving with the sensation that I wouldn't be asked back. Yet I somehow thought that *Smile* would be finished, and I didn't want to do anything that would contravene it. It was like watching a balloon let loose from a child's hand . . .'

David Anderle was the last to go. As Brian's behavior grew more peculiar and childish, so did Anderle's frustration. Anderle was trying to make Brother Records a reality, a task that necessitated a stronger sense of day-to-day responsibility and punctuality than Brian was able to muster. Perhaps the most wrenching moment of all came one night at Anderle's apartment. As a surprise, David had been working on an oil portrait of Brian. Because he couldn't ask him to pose, Anderle had painted it from memory. One night he invited Brian to the small, one-room apartment he rented above a garage on Twenty-eighth Street near the University of Southern California.

215

It was nearly two in the morning when Anderle, his wife Sheryl, and Brian arrived there. The painting stood in a corner, covered with an old bedspread. David announced a surprise and uncovered it. He remembered, 'The room got very quiet. There was a definite feeling that came over us. I walked away from Brian and sat down on the bed with my wife. Brian stood in front of the painting for a long time, perhaps for as long as an hour. He examined every inch of it. When he finally spoke, his reaction wasn't what I expected.'

'You captured my soul,' Brian said. 'It's like the American Indians who have their soul captured.' Brian grew increasingly distressed, claiming that the number of objects in the painting, the circles and designs placed in the background for decorative relief, were numerologically important, relating to different stages in Brian's life. He became so upset that eventually Anderle called Michael Vosse to pick Brian up and take him home.

In the car with Vosse, Brian was even more upset. 'This painting business had been going on for thousands of years, huh?' he asked. Vosse didn't know what to say. He too was fired a few weeks later.

A final incident involving Brian and Anderle took place several days later. The lawsuit Anderle had helped implement against Capitol Records was coming to a head – depositions were being taken and it was a time of serious tension. 'I brought an attorney up to Brian's house,' Anderle said, 'and Brian would not come out of the bedroom.' Anderle tried to get Marilyn to bring him down, but he would not come. Anderle told Marilyn, 'I will not do business this way. I will not be one of those guys in Brian's life who is treated this way.' But Marilyn was helpless, and eventually Anderle went up to the bedroom door himself and knocked. 'Brian?' he called out. 'Listen, Brian, if you don't come out of this room, I'm gone. This isn't kid time anymore. Do you hear me, Brian?' But there was no answer.

Anderle never saw Brian again on a professional level. The painting of Brian to this day hangs in Anderle's living room, but he has never painted again.

I'm not a genius.
I'm just a hard-working guy. – Brian Wilson

I think it was the drugs. – Dennis Wilson

Nine

1

Capitol Records didn't officially announce that *Smile* had been abandoned until May 2, 1967. Many things dealt the final blow to *Smile* – Brian's inability to finish the album, the drugs, the lyrics, and family squabbles – and finally, the release of two new Beatles singles, 'Penny Lane' and 'Strawberry Fields,' so wondrous and different-sounding that Brian was crushed. He was still recording on April 10 when Paul McCartney, on a surprise visit to Los Angeles to see his girl friend, Jane Asher, stopped in to one of Brian's sessions. Within a few hours they had co-produced a song called 'Vegetables.'[1] At that session Paul spoke enthusiastically about a new Beatles album to be released the following month – *Sergeant Pepper's Lonely Hearts Club Band*. When Brian finally heard that album, he was shattered. The greatest album in the history of rock-and-roll had already been recorded.

Derek Taylor, writing for *Disc and Music Echo* magazine in England, broke the news of *Smile*'s cancellation overseas: 'In truth, every beautifully designed, finely wrought, inspirationally welded piece of music made these

---

[1] Some claim Paul only observed the session and did not co-produce it.

last months by Brian . . . has been SCRAPPED. Not destroyed, but scrapped. For what Wilson seals in a can and destroys is scrapped.' Music critic Greil Marcus was later to point out that the Beach Boys' artistic reputation would be forever based on unheard, unreleased music.

Brian's confidence was severely shaken, as was evidenced by his next, disastrous decision. That June a massive festival was to be held at the Monterey Fairgrounds, to celebrate the new music and new philosophy that gripped the nation's young people. The idea for the nonprofit festival came early in April from Los Angeles promoter Ben Shapiro, Los Angeles scene maker Alan Pariser, and Derek Taylor. The three set up an office on Sunset Boulevard to coordinate local acts and sell advertising space in a concert booklet. Soon the original organizing committee expanded to include Terry Melcher, Johnny Rivers, John Phillips of the Mamas and Papas, and Lou Adler. With the help of San Francisco promoter Bill Graham, a number of popular groups was enlisted to perform, and TV rights were sold to ABC to help finance the festival. The San Francisco hippie commune known as the Diggers volunteered to help feed concertgoers and arrange for Free Clinic doctors to treat the expected acid casualties. The list of acts included Janis Joplin, Otis Redding, Ravi Shankar, The Who, Laura Nyro, Buffalo Springfield, and the Byrds, among many others.

Naturally, California's native sons, the Beach Boys, were asked to perform. Although they readily accepted – and even loaned the festival the use of their sound system – they were secretly gripped by fear at the thought of appearing – fear they would be laughed off the stage by the young audience, fear that their growing musical anachronisms would show. 'You know,' Brian told Michael Vosse, who was working on the Monterey committee while acting as an informal liaison for the Beach Boys, 'the idea of a show with the Beach Boys and the Mamas and Papas is okay. But all those people from England who play acid rock – if the audience is coming to the concert to see them, they're going to hate us.'

Brian's final decision not to show up at Monterey may have been made one night about two weeks before the festival, at Alan Pariser's house. Vosse had brought Brian there to meet Pariser for the first time, and Brian seemed distant and uncomfortable from the start. After some small talk, Pariser said casually to Brian, 'I don't even know what you guys are doing. I haven't heard from you in a while.'

'Brian's mouth flew open,' Mike Vosse said. 'He was so insulted. Just at the climax of all this tension, the door flew open and in came . . . a guy who was a chiropractor . . . a pushy hippie-type. He took one look at Brian and said, "Terrible back, we're going to have to do something about that." Before Brian knew it, he was on the floor on his stomach, screaming in agony as the chiropractor worked him over.

'He was absolutely terrified,' Vosse said, 'but too scared to tell him not to do it . . . He was totally humiliated and in pain.'

When Brian left that night, Pariser said, 'If I don't see you before then, I'll see you at Monterey.'

And Brian said, 'I doubt it.'

The Monterey Pop Festival turned into the most important rock-music event prior to Woodstock. Fifteen thousand people were expected at Monterey; 50,000 showed up. The feeling was celebratory, and the event would long be remembered as the dawn of the age of rock festivals. The Beach Boys were scheduled to close the show on Saturday night, a plum position in the lineup. Their decision not to play was announced only at the last minute, infuriating many of those who had worked so hard to make the festival happen. The official story was that their inability to play had to do with Carl's personal problems, but everyone involved thought the same thing – they were scared. At the last minute, Otis Redding took their spot, and the Beach Boys' no-show became the talk of the festival. On Sunday night, during his spectacular performance, Jimi Hendrix told the audience, 'You heard the last of surfing music . . .'

The decision not to appear at Monterey had a snow-balling effect. The Beach Boys' self-exclusion from the festival was seen as a damming admission that they were washed up, unable to compete with the 'new music.' On December 14, an article in *Rolling Stone* – which at the time was considered a kind of bible – truly sealed their doom. Written by *Rolling Stone* publisher Jann Wenner, the article tore into the Beach Boys – their image as well as their music. Extolling the virtues of the Beatles, and their amazing leap from *Rubber Soul* to *Sergeant Pepper*, Wenner explained how the British fans only two years before had placed the Beach Boys ahead of the Beatles in popularity polls. Wenner pointed out that Brian's publicity people compared him to Lennon and McCartney. 'Except,' wrote Wenner, 'no one is John Lennon except John Lennon and no one is Paul McCartney except Paul McCartney and the Beach Boys . . . are not the Beatles.' Wenner went on to say that the label 'genius' was 'essentially a promotional shuck' that Brian himself believed. He gave faint praise to 'Good Vibrations,' which he said was not really rock-and-roll. Wenner called the group 'totally disappointing' live, and concluded, 'The Beach Boys are just one prominent example of a group that has gotten hung up in trying to catch the Beatles.'

2

Brian sold the house on Laurel Way. 'He wanted a bigger home,' Marilyn said. 'You know, he was making a lot of money, and we started looking for a real house.' The tent was disassembled, the recording equipment moved out. A contractor was hired to haul out the several tons of sand from the den, where it had been irretrievably soiled by the dogs. An era was over.

That April Brian and Marilyn moved into a four-bedroom home on Bellagio Road in Bel Air. They paid $320,000 for the mansion, which had once belonged to Edgar Rice Burroughs. 'We bought the house without even looking at the upstairs,' Marilyn said. 'We saw the whole downstairs and the yard, but the people who owned it didn't want us to go upstairs because something was going on up there that day. I said to Brian, "I can't buy a house without looking at the bedrooms. I've got to see my closets, I've got to see the bathrooms." But Brian said, "Oh, don't worry about it, it will be fine." I trusted Brian, and what Brian said went – that was it.'

The house boasted a large living room, a formal den with a fireplace, and a hidden study that could be entered through a secret door behind a bookcase. There was a fountain in the inner courtyard and a spiral staircase in the entrance foyer. Marilyn and Brian had some minimal construction done – they removed the old flagstone from around the swimming pool, replacing it with mosaic tiles, and built a tall brick wall around the perimeter of the acre-and-a-half grounds. The psychedelic and hippie paraphernalia from Laurel Way was thrown out, and Marilyn decorated the new house in tasteful pastels and with fashionable furniture. All that remained from before was the grand piano on which Brian had composed *Pet Sounds*, and the four-poster bed with its headboard of carved angels. To keep strangers away, a new electric gate was installed with an intercom and a sign that read STAND BACK – SPEAK NORMALLY. At first Brian wanted to repaint the house a bright magenta; the painting was only half finished when the Bel Air Residents Tenants Committee started a suit to stop him. The house was painted a simple beige.

With the Beach Boys now in a weakened position, the lawsuit against Capitol was quietly dropped, and an arrangement was made for Capitol to distribute Brother Records. Meanwhile, hurried recording began on a replacement album for *Smile*, which would be titled *Smiley Smile*. But Brian was no longer interested in leaving the house on Bellagio Road to go to the studios – so the mountain was brought to Mohammed. A makeshift studio with remote equipment was constructed at Bellagio Road. Engineer Jim Lockhart remembered, 'They had one large room which had been a music room for the former owner and there was a hallway and an office. All the consoles and tape machines were set up in the office. There was a closed-circuit television so you could see what was going on.' Because there was no soundproofed studio *per se*, the recording took place all over the house, including the tiled showers and the bottom of the swimming pool, which had been drained for repair.

This time, the other Beach Boys were never far away, and they showed up at the house almost every day to assist with the recording. Compared to the grand vision Brian had for *Smile*, *Smiley Smile* was a throwaway album. A few cuts were salvaged from *Smile*: 'Vegeta-

bles'; 'Earth,' from the 'The Elements'; and 'Wonderful.'
'*Smiley Smile* was a very simple album to make,' Carl
said. 'It took a couple of weeks at Brian's house. Tops,
two weeks.' The entire album was mixed in one overnight
session at the Wally Heider studios, and it was the first
LP to bear the words, 'Produced by the Beach Boys'
instead of 'by Brian Wilson.' 'It was a bunt instead of a
grand slam,' said Carl.

Of all the songs Brian prepared for *Smiley Smile*, the
only one he really cared about was 'Heroes and Villains,'
which he had written earlier with Van Dyke Parks. The
song now opened the album – side one, first cut. There
were already several versions of this song, one of them
almost seven minutes long. Yet it was obvious to everyone
who heard it that 'Heroes and Villains' was more than
salvageable. It had the quality of inventiveness that
marked 'Good Vibrations.' Although the song described
the Old West, its lyrics reflected many of Brian's feelings
about his past year in Los Angeles.

> I've been in this town so long,
> that back in the city
> I've been taken for lost and gone
> and unknown for a long, long time

When an abbreviated three-minute-and-thirty-six-
second version of 'Heroes and Villains' was finished,
Brian held on to it for a long time, afraid to release it. He
had been consulting with a female psychic-astrologer
named Genevelyn, who came up to the house frequently.
By that June she felt the time was right to present the
new song to the world. Terry Melcher remembers Brian
clutching the single in his hand and calling all the members
of the group to ask them to assemble for the world
premiere of the record. By 11:00 P.M. that night, Brian

ian Wilson in grade
hool, age 12, and in
nior high school. *Peter
eum Collection*

Brian *(center)* was an all-round athlete in high school, but never
good enough to satisfy his father. *Peter Reum Collection*

Brian in a dramatic slide to base. Unfortunately he's 'out'. The ball is already in the catcher's mitt. *Peter Reum Collection*

Carl and his date at his high school prom. *Peter Reum Collection*

Alan Jardine as he looked in spring of 1960. He first approached the Morgans to record a folk song. *Peter Reum Collection*

nnis *(center)* in a school photo taken in ring of 1960. Dennis preferred surfing to ool. *Peter Reum Collection*

an Jardine, a high school shot-putter. *Peter Reum Collection*

The graduates:
Brian and Carl Wilson;
Diane and Marilyn Rovell.
Peter Reum Collection

Audree and Murray Wilson arrive at the airport in Sacramento, where the Beach Boys experienced their earliest popularity. Audree is carrying a carton of promotional records to give to local disc jockeys. *Peter Reum Collection*

One of the earliest photographs of the Beach Boys, taken at Capitol Records soon after signing the first contract. *Left to right:* Mike Love, Dennis Wilson, David Marks, Carl Wilson, Brian Wilson. *Maggie Montalbano*

Dennis helps with the roast in the kitchen of the Wilsons' Hawthorne house. *Peter Reum Collection*

Mike, Brian and Carl stand next to a paneled wall covered with album covers and photographs in the Wilsons' den. *Peter Reum Collection*

Brian poses with Capitol Records' in-store display of Beach Boy records. *Peter Reum Collection*

Young, debonair Mike Love, with most of his hair still on his head. The competition for girls was between him and Dennis. *Peter Reum Collection*

Suzanne and Mike Love, February 1967. *Peter Reum Collection*

Mike Love in his 1890s' look. The photo was taken by Debbie Keil at a Beach Boys rehearsal. *Peter Reum Collection*

The Honeys in the mid-sixties. *Peter Reum Collection*

The Honeys today. *From left to right:* Diane, Ginger and Marilyn. *The Honeys*

May and Irving Rovell. They turned their home over to the Beach Boys. May was on 24-hour kitchen duty – and loved it. *May and Irving Rovell*

On their first trip to
London, the Beach Boys,
holding a few slats of wood
in parody of their original
surfboard photo, pose
outside the EMI offices.
Peter Reum Collection

Brian and Roger Christian,
who wrote the lyrics to
some of the Beach Boys'
best automotive songs.
Peter Reum Collection

Brian onstage at the Hollywood Bowl, 1963. The next year he would quit touring. *Capitol Records*

The Beach Boys' first film appearance, in Paramount's *The Girls on the Beach*. The 1965 film also featured The Crickets and Lesley Gore. *Paramount Pictures Corp.*

Dennis Wilson and his first wife,
Carol. *Peter Reum Collection*

Linda and Alan Jardine with
Mike Love. *Maggie Montalbano*

Brian gives Dennis and Al the pitch for their harmonies in the studio. *Peter Reum Collection*

Brian, Dennis, Mike and Carl arrive at the Honolulu airport in July 1963. *Fudgie*

At Western Studios, 1967.
From left: Carl and Annie
Wilson, Annie's brother
Billy Hinsche, and cousin
Steve Korthof. *Peter Reum
Collection*

Bruce Johnston first joined
the Beach Boys in April of
1965. A falling-out with
manager Jack Rieley caused
him to leave in 1972, but he
was back for good in 1978.
Peter Reum Collection

Earl Leaf photo of Brian
en at one of the many
ner parties at the Laurel
y House. *Peter Reum
lection*

Marilyn Wilson at the dinner
table on Laurel Way, 1967.
Peter Reum Collection

Brian at the electric organ in the house on Laurel Way. Behind him
is a store display of dolls enclosed in plastic bubbles. *Peter Reum
Collection*

Brian directing musicians at United Studios A control room, December 9, 1968, in a photo taken by Jasper Dailey. *Peter Reum Collection*

Brian donned a fire chief's hat for the 'Fire' segment of the 'Elements', from the ill-fated *Smile* album. Brian believed the music started fires around Los Angeles. *Peter Reum Collection*

Van Dyke Parks at a recording session. He met Brian at Terry Melcher's house. *Peter Reum Collection*

January 25, 1967. A string section was hired to record the 'Fire' segment of *Smile*. The musicians were later sent home because the 'vibrations' weren't right. *Peter Reum Collection*

Mike Love

Dennis Wilson *Carl Wilson*

Al Jardine *Bruce Johnston*

*BEST WISHES
FROM THE BEACH BOYS —*

A Capitol Publicity photo from the late sixties when the Beach Boys were desperately trying to look hip. *Maggie Montalbano*

Sheryl and David Anderle relax late at night in the studios during a *Smile* session. *Peter Reum Collection*

Published here for the first time, the infamous group photo taken at Los Angeles Airport just before Brian's total retreat from the world. Within a few months he would stop speaking to almost everyone in the picture. *Standing:* Danny Hutton, Mark Volman, Dean Torrance, Diane Rovell, Annie Hinsche Wilson, Brian and Marilyn Wilson, Mike Vosse, David and Sheryl Anderle, Gene and Barbara Rovell Gaddy, Dick and Carol Maier. *On floor:* June Fairchild, Van Dyke and Durry Parks. *Guy Webster*

Brian, Nick Grillo, and Mike Love proudly show off their new
Warner Brothers contract. The photo was taken July 27, 1970.
Peter Reum Collection

Dennis, Laurie Bird and James Taylor on the set of *Two-Lane
Blacktop*. The movie was Dennis's big shot at an acting career.
Universal Pictures, Peter Reum Collection

Barbara Charren and Dennis
Wilson in the early bloom of
love. Friends said she was
the best thing that ever
happened to him. *Peter
Reum Collection*

Tandyn Almer at the
keyboard in Western
Studios, circa 1970. *Peter
Reum Collection*

Terry Melcher, son of Doris Day, was Manson's real target. The Tate-La Bianca murders were meant only as a warning. *Connie Pappas*

Charles Manson *(below right)* and his 'family' were Dennis Wilson's long-term house guests. Dennis later told the District Attorney that he didn't remember anything significant about their time together. *UPI/Bettman Newsphotos*

The Love Brothers: Stephen, Mike and Stanley. *Peter Reum Collection*

Mike Love meditates live onstage. *Peter Reum Collection*

Rocky Pamplin in Australia.
Fudgie

Brian stands in front of the
house on Bellagio Drive on
his way to the Grammy
Awards in 1977. *Fudgie*

Debbie Keil gave Brian refuge from business and family, much to
Marilyn Wilson's chagrin. *Carolyn W Poulin*

Rocky Pamplin's
Playgirl centerfold.
Playgirl Magazine

Fred Vail and Dennis in
1977 at Dennis's house
in Venice, California.
Fred Vail

Brian and his mother, Audree. *Peter Reum Collection*

Mike Love, the consummate showman, took the Beach Boys loc into new dimensions. *Fudgie*

Stephen Love rides the waves in Hawaii in 1980. *Lee Lucas*

Dr Eugene Landy and Brian backstage at the Washington D.C., concert on July 4, 1984. *Fudgie*

Brian at almost 300 pounds in the parking lot behind Brothers Studio in Santa Monica. *Fudgie*

Carnie, age 17, and Wendy, age 15. *Marilyn Wilson*

Shawn Love Wilson, in January 1985, waits outside Los Angeles Superior Court, where she successfully petitioned the court to declare her Dennis's lawful heir. *UPI/ Bettman Newsphotos*

A recent photo of Marilyn Wilson, who lives in a large home in Encino, California, with the children, Carnie and Wendy. *Marilyn Wilson*

Dennis Wilson and Karen Lamm on the beach in Malibu. Together they were the perfect young California couple. *Guy Webster*

Karen Lamm in a recent photo. She forgave Dennis too many
times for her own good. *Guy Webster*

was ready. An incredible procession of Rolls-Royces and limousines set out from Bellagio Road to KHJ-Radio in Hollywood. But when the cortège of automobiles reached the studio gate, the security guard refused to let them in.

Finally, after a long argument with the guard, who called his superiors, the five cars were allowed inside the gates. Brian and the Beach Boys found their way down the long fluorescent-lighted hallways to the small soundproofed booth where the disc jockey was broadcasting live out over Los Angeles.

Brian made a simple speech. 'I'm Brian Wilson and I'm holding the new Beach Boys single, "Heroes and Villains." I'd like to give you and KHJ an exclusive on it.'

The disc jockey looked at Brian and the small, seven-inch, disc he was holding, and shrugged his shoulders. 'Sorry,' he said. 'I can't play anything that isn't on the play list.'

'It really killed Brian,' Melcher said. A fierce debate ensued. The rest of the group forced the reticent disc jockey to call the station manager, who screamed at him. 'Put it on, you idiot!' The disc jockey put the song on, and 'Heroes and Villains' was released to the world.

'Heroes and Villains' was the first Beach Boys single released since 'Good Vibrations' the previous October. It was also the first piece of the extraordinary new music that everyone in the Los Angeles music business had been waiting to hear since the *Smile* project was announced ten months before. The reaction was decidedly mixed. It was special, yes, and different – but was it commercial? That question could be answered only by the public. 'Heroes and Villains' first appeared on the *Billboard* charts on August 5 at number 61, leapfrogged to number 33 on the twelfth, reached its pinnacle of number 12 for two weeks around Labor Day, and then one week later fell off the charts forever, its novelty gone. 'Heroes and Villains' was, by everyone's estimation, a failure. It was the last Beach Boys single to break below the top twenty for nearly a decade.

In July, Capitol released a compilation album of old tunes called *Best of the Beach Boys – Volume 2*, and although it was on the charts for twenty-two weeks, it only broke 50. It seemed even repackaging was no longer working for the group. On September 18, 1967, *Smiley Smile* became the first official release of Brother Records, distributed by Capitol. Although it was on the *Billboard* charts for twenty-one weeks, it never broke into the top forty, and the album spent the majority of its chart time wavering between 100 and 197. Just two months later, the Beach Boys quickly released another album, *Wild Honey*, although pointedly on the Capitol label and not on Brother Records. This album was to become a favorite for hardcore Beach Boys fans, considered by many to be a 'soul album,' lauded for its simplicity and rawness (the longest cut on it was only 2:42). But it too was a commercial failure. It was most notable for Carl's increased role as producer. Carl passed the album off as 'music for Brian to cool out by. He was still very spaced.' After a fifteen-week run on the charts, *Wild Honey* reached only number 24. Word was out – the Beach Boys were in serious trouble.

3

Marilyn Wilson was pregnant. That August the Beach Boys and their wives had gone to Hawaii for three weeks, to shoot a promotional film to be released in conjunction with the upcoming *Smiley Smile* album. The child was conceived in tropical, romantic surroundings, and was due in spring of 1968. Marilyn was hoping for a girl, but Brian didn't seem to care. While Marilyn contentedly redecorated one of the many rooms to create a nursery, Brian retreated into the master bedroom, where he slept all day. Soon he had a refrigerator installed in there, and rarely came downstairs at all. Sometimes, because the 'vibrations' weren't right in the master bedroom, he would sleep in one of the other rooms, frequently switching from one to the other several times in a night. Ironically, with the remote studio downstairs in the music room, the recording sounds easily penetrated the floorboards, making the Beach Boys' presence inescapable. Brian began to feel, more than ever, that the Beach Boys were a monster of his own making – there was no escape from them. He worried about money, and wanted to go out on his own, but he felt it was too late. He still wanted to work, and when Danny Hutton formed a group called Redwood, Brian managed to produce a tune for them called 'Darlin'.' But when the Beach Boys heard the song, they took it for themselves.

Brian was worn and devastated. On April 29, 1968, his first child, a girl named Carnie, was born. 'It was around then that I started really getting worried about Brian,' Marilyn said. 'There was suddenly a difference between having fun and having sick fun. I don't think I really saw, or let myself see that, until after Carnie was born. I remember her lying in the crib and Brian being weepy. I was worried before that, but once you have a child you look at things differently.'

Retreating further and further, less and less interested in friends and going out, Brian stayed in bed later into the day, until he finally took to bed altogether. He would stay there for many years.

Carl was now emerging as the level-headed, dependable Wilson brother, growing calmer and fatter with the passing years. Professionally, he was esteemed as a first-rate live guitarist, though the confines of playing Beach Boys songs rarely gave him a chance to display his talent. Carl was the last of the Beach Boys to fall in love and marry. Annie Hinsche was a sweet, dark-haired, fifteen-year-old with a round face and a bright smile. The daughter of a well-to-do casino owner from the Philippines, Annie had been born in Manila and moved to Los Angeles with her family when she was five. She grew up in Beverly Hills and was no stranger to the show-business world – her brother Billy was already on the record charts as part of the rock group Dino, Desi, and Billy. Annie met Carl at the Los Angeles airport, where she had gone to accompany a girl friend who was dating Bruce Johnston. Carl was only eighteen at the time.

'He had a great sense of humor, and we hit it off,' she said. 'He was also very sensitive and perceptive. It was really love at first sight.' In Salt Lake City, where the Beach Boys had gone to perform that weekend, Carl asked Bruce to call his girl friend and ask if she could bring Annie to meet him at the airport on his return. Annie was waiting at the gate when the plane landed, and Carl drove her home in his brand-new Aston Martin. He gave her an engagement ring two months after meeting her on her sixteenth birthday, December 27. When she wore the ring to the Marymount School in Beverly Hills, where she was a sophomore, the nuns told her she either had to leave school or give back the ring. Annie discussed it was her parents and they decided she should choose Carl over school. They were married just two months later, on February 3, 1966. By the time he was married, Carl had already bought his first big house at 1902 Coldwater Canyon, for a modest $100,000. It was a contemporary, U-shaped house, with a patio in the center and a swimming pool in back. It too was decorated by Lee Polk.

At the time, Carl was involved in a protracted legal battle with the government over his draft status. The problem came to a head in 1967 when he was arrested in New York for refusing to be inducted, claiming to be a conscientious objector. Carl said the arrest was 'a hype,' and insisted that the authorities had forewarned him of it. 'They called me a few days before and said, "Okay, listen, there's a warrant for your arrest. You just come in to the office in New York and we'll arrest you. Then we'll release you on a personal-recognizance bond, and you'll go back to LA and take care of it."' According to Carl, when he presented himself to the authorities, they 'really wanted to do a news thing' and had a photographer waiting. They 'actually arrested me and did a hoked-up trick, held me in jail for a few hours . . . It's cost me thirty thousand dollars to fight this thing so far. Imagine what it would be like for somebody who didn't have the money.'

Of all the Beach Boys, Mike Love had perhaps changed the most. Professionally, his nasal vocals had turned into something of a trademark, and he had become the consummate stage frontman. Perhaps because he was self-conscious about not playing an instrument, he would prance, jump, and dance across the stage, giving the audience something to look at. More than anyone else in the group, Mike clearly enjoyed performing live and touring. Mike's vision of himself as a celebrity included his personal life. In the summer of 1967, after living in a small house in Manhattan Beach for a year, he and Suzanne moved to a house at 1215 Coldwater Canyon in Bel Air, which, Mike bragged, 'cost about three number-one records.' Formerly owned by internationally known auctioneer Milton Wershow, the house was handsome and imposing, with a large tiled pool surrounded by gardens of lemon and tangerine trees. From the living room, which one visitor described as 'the width of an airplane hangar,' there was a breathtaking view of the twinkling city below. For a few months before the furniture arrived, the living room was bare except for the lavish lemon-yellow carpeting that Suzanne had installed as soon as they moved in – they called it the 'Yellow Valley.' To make this picture of seeming domestic tranquility complete, on December 27, 1966, their daughter, Hayleigh, was born; and seventeen months later, on May 23, 1968, a son, Christian. By this time Mike owned a vintage yellow MG convertible and a large white Jaguar, in which he would tool down the hill to the Daisy, a celebrity disco in Beverly Hills, where he danced all night and rubbed elbows with Barbra Streisand.

But within Mike's marriage things were not so glamorous. The couple hadn't been together very long before Suzanne discovered that Mike was given to violent fits of temper, sparked by what he saw as her transgressions, such as cigarette smoking. His reaction must have seemed particularly ironic to Suzanne, since Michael had given her a carton of cigarettes on their first date. Suzanne quickly realized that Mike's temper tantrums went beyond the momentary flare-up of a man under pressure from a demanding career. Once, when she was pregnant with Hayleigh, Mike hit her. They had just checked into the Fountainbleau Hotel in Miami after a concert in Memphis. In the room above them, Dennis started throwing chairs out of his window onto the roof below to let off steam, incensing Michael. Suzanne went downstairs to the pharmacy, and when she came back to the room, Mike had discovered a pack of cigarettes, hidden in her suitcase. After the beating, Mike was apologetic and charming, but Suzanne lived in inceasing fear. On a trip to England, Mike hit her so hard she sported a black eye for a week.

Dennis's wife Carol remembers one incident when Christian and Hayleigh were little. 'They were disturbing this man who claimed to be all peace and love. He came down and hit [Christian] so hard that he flew across the room. I actually went after Mike with a frying pan, I was so outraged that a person could get that violent.'

Al Jardine, the stable, quiet – some say boring – mainstay of the group was happily married, living with his wife Lynda in a beautiful house and small ranch in the Mandeville Canyon area at 1820 Westridge Road. They had dogs, horses, and even a pet monkey – and 'Monkey' became Alan's nickname around the office. On the road he worked hard, was prompt for concerts, and read books on ecology. He eschewed drugs and drink. Dennis once described Alan as 'a man waiting for a bus.' Throughout the Beach Boys' early fame, Alan had been an employee of the group; now he was finally made a full financial partner in the firm.

Dennis was having the best time of all – or at least the wildest. Rock stardom agreed with his personality, his ego, his foolish generosity, and his lust. He did not care much for the hard work of recording, and session drummer Hal Blaine had long been handling most of the chores involved. But Dennis did like the glamour of touring, the jet planes, limousines, and adoring crowds. At home he had attracted his own circle of admirers. Some, as in Brian's life, were drainers while others appreciated Dennis, bringing excitement and vitality. Brian's friend Terry Melcher had become part of Dennis's circle. Dennis had also befriended a former employee of Julius Lefkowitz, Stanley Shapiro, whom he had nearly run over one day while driving in Century City.[2] After Shapiro bawled him out about his recklessness, the two became fast friends. Shapiro quit his job at the Lefkowitz office, and came to work for Dennis. One of Dennis's first gestures was to buy Shapiro a new wardrobe in one of LA's most expensive clothing stores. But Dennis's closest friendship was with a self-styled talent scout and sometime actor named Gregg Jakobson. Jakobson was born in Los Angeles and had gone to Venice High School (with photographer Guy Webster). He had met Dennis in Hawaii through Bruce Johnston and Terry Melcher, who were still performing together. Jakobson married Carol Costello, daughter of comedian Lou Costello, and lived not far from Dennis, just over the hill in Benedict Canyon.

Dennis's wild side was growing even wilder. His newest

---

[2] Stanley Shapiro's father was Bernie Shapiro, the investment counselor for Lefkowitz.

love was dirt bikes. 'He had a feeling about himself that he was invulnerable, and nothing could hurt him,' said Shapiro. On one occasion, Dennis decided to ride his bike up to and inside Brian's Bellagio Road house. 'There were tufts of carpeting shooting out from behind him as he rode up the stairs,' Jakobson said. 'We'd be riding on motorcycles and he would buy out all the whipped cream in the supermarket, literally all of it, hitting the nitrous oxide gas and throwing the cans over his shoulder,' said Jakobson.

Dennis had adopted Carol's son, Scott, when the child was eighteen months old; a daughter, Jennifer, was born around the same time, in 1967. He was a wonderful father, when he had the time or interest. In 1965 they had moved to a large tan house with white trim at 2600 Benedict Canyon Drive on two and a half acres of land. They gutted the house and renovated it completely. The living-room ceiling was lifted to a towering thirty feet, and one of the four bedrooms was transformed into a music room for Dennis. Lee Polk also decorated this house, except for the red velvet bed and matching headboard Murry gave the couple as a gift the first Christmas they lived there. Murry also donated the quartz rock, taken from outside his house in Whittier, that was installed around the fireplace. In the backyard was a stable with a pony named Skipper for Scott, and horses for both Carol and Dennis – Rusty and The Big Black. Cars came and went with spendthrift speed – an XKE; a Ferrari that had once belonged to murdered singer Sam Cook; another Ferrari, this one red; a British racing-green Austin Healy followed by a green Corvette convertible and a bright yellow Cobra that Dennis sometimes raced.

The first two years of the marriage, according to Carol, were wonderful. 'I had a blast. He was terrific,' she said.

But soon the day-to-day reality set in. Some of Dennis's behavior, though not malicious, was difficult to take, such as his foolhardly generosity. 'I once came home and our washer and dryer were gone.' When she questioned Dennis, he told her he had met a man who lost his job and had five kids. Dennis decided to give the washer and dryer to them.

By the end of 1967 it was clear to Carol that their marriage was in serious trouble. 'For me it was the drugs,' Carol said. 'I was not into drugs, and with two little children, that was really hard for me. The drugs started right after Jennifer was born, maybe while I was pregnant. Murry was really against drugs, and at first so was Dennis. This was one way Dennis could be separate from everybody else and get the love he wanted from Murry. I would say a big part of Dennis's problem was that he could never connect with his father or please Murry.'

But of all the problems Carol had with Dennis, his extramarital affairs hurt the most. While Dennis was extremely prim and moral about Carol – she joked that she was the only woman on the beach in a turtleneck bathing suit – he had another standard for himself. Dennis cheated on Carol without apologies or apprehensions. He bragged to his friends that the night his daughter was born, he made love to another woman on the lawn of his house. Frequently he would come home from touring with a case of gonorrhea, contracted from a groupie on the road. He and Terry Melcher and Gregg Jakobson formed a club called the Golden Penetrators. 'They considered themselves roving cocksmen,' Carol said. 'It was mostly guys hanging out and getting stoned.' Gregg Jakobson donated his old car. 'They even painted this old car gold, drove it up our driveway, and parked it on the side of our hill. It hurt, of course. You don't like thinking of your husband belonging to a club called the Golden Penetrators. It was tough.'

When the fights with Carol became onerous, Dennis would disappear for days, usually sleeping at Gregg Jakobson's house. The marriage took a disastrous turn with the death of one of the horses. Dennis claimed that Carol had starved it to death; Carol said it had gotten pneumonia and had to be put to sleep. The horse's death caused an irreparable rift. Much to Carol's relief, early in 1968 Dennis finally rented his own place, an enormous house at 14400 Sunset Boulevard. Once a hunting lodge owned by Will Rogers, it had vast, manicured grounds with trees so rare they were registered. The house was wood-paneled, with handmade furniture, and out in back was a swimming pool the shape of the state of California.

Murry and Audree's marriage continued to have its ups and downs. Audree loved Murry, and could see the misguided but well-meaning man so often hidden from strangers by his gruff exterior. But even for Audree, Murry was often difficult to take, and she spent much of her time at her favorite son Carl's house before Murry bought a second house for her to live in. Still, Murry and Audree were extremely dedicated to one another.

One major breach occurred when Murry discovered that his sons were smoking marijuana. 'I remember Carl and Brian telling me,' Audree said, 'we were walking through the airport – they had just come back to Los Angeles from someplace – and [they told me about smoking pot]. I just choked because at that time it was such a new thing to me . . . I knew nothing about it except, "Oh, stay away! Dangerous! Bad!" And of course, their father, oh Jesus, he just went wild cause they all told him – they were very honest. I wished they had never told

235

us.' Murry forbade Audree to have anything to do with them. 'It was a terrible time in my life,' she said. 'He wouldn't allow them to come over until they would say, "I'll never touch another marijuana cigarette again." I only got to see them sort of sneakily because he didn't want me to go to their houses. Instead of asserting myself and saying, "Go to hell, they're my sons," I did what he told me.' Murry finally relented on Christmas Day of 1967. 'All of a sudden,' Audree related, 'he said, "You can have the family for Christmas," and I was ecstatic. I was so thrilled – they all came and had a wonderful day. But the important thing that I remember was the pain of the months he wouldn't allow them to come to my house.'

The worst was to come in January 1967, when Audree went on a short vacation to Las Vegas with her brother, Carl Korthof. Carl, who had been trying to cut down on his drinking because of a serious heart condition, had been introduced by his nephews to a much less lethal high – marijuana – and had brought some with him to Las Vegas. By this time Audree was no stranger to marijuana. One morning while her brother was in the other room, he had a sudden and fatal heart attack. In a panic, Audree called for an ambulance. When the police and paramedics arrived, the first thing they saw was the marijuana on the living-room coffee table. Already beside herself with shock at her brother's death, poor Audree was now arrested and 'put behind bars,' according to Carl's son, Steve Korthof.

Said Steve, 'I flew to Vegas with my mom and Murry, and Murry didn't know anything about [Audree's arrest]. They were going to Vegas to identify my dad, and when they got to the hotel I already knew. I didn't say a word. They were told that Audree was at the police station. So Murry says, "Police station? I guess she went to file a report." When he got down to the station and went to the normal department where she should have been, he found out she was [being held] in the narcotics division. "What?" he said. When he found out what happened, he totally flipped out . . . oh Jesus, when he found out . . .' It took a long time for him to forgive Audree for that one.

During this period Murry was still promoting various new ventures in the music business. He had recently re-teamed with Rick Henn, of the Sunrays, who said he 'sort of became Murry's Brian.' One of Murry's projects was to write unsolicited jingles for television commercials, 'because he felt the sponsors needed his help,' according to Rick Henn. 'Little did Murry know that no advertising agency takes outside input.' Murry wrote and recorded a Kentucky Fried Chicken commercial and a Taco Bell commercial, among others – all were politely turned down. The only song of Murry's to be heard by the general public was one he wrote with Brian under the pseudonym Reggie Dunbar, called 'Break Away.' The Beach Boys released the song as a single in June 1969, without much success.

But to Murry, his most important project was the LP entitled, *The Many Moods of Murry Wilson*. Murry wrote and produced most of this album, with Don Ralke doing arrangements. However, Murry still fancied himself a talent scout and showcased a new discovery on the LP – a forty-year-old plumber named Eck Kynor who had helped with the renovations on Murry's Whittier house. Kynor was represented on the album by tunes called 'The Plumber's Tune' and 'The Happy Song.' Also included on the LP were tunes entitled 'Leaves' and 'Betty's Waltz' (with an assist from Audree). Capitol released the album in October 1967.

That December Murry took Audree to England, where

237

the album was also released, and embarked on his own self-styled one-month promotional tour. Interviewed in a luxurious suite at the London Hilton, Murry told a reporter from *Disc and Music Echo* that 'after "Good Vibrations" Brian lost a lot of confidence. He didn't think he could ever write anything as good as that again . . . With [my] LP I'm going to nudge my boys' competitive spirit. Show them that the Beach Boys don't have all the talent in the family. Brian may find new rejuvenation in his confidence as a result. They may all find new spirit to stay at the top.

'I call them my "Monsters,"' Murry laughed. 'But they've never let me down. How could I be anything other than proud of them?'

4

While Murry was in England promoting his own album, the Beach Boys were rehearsing for a UNICEF benefit to be held in Paris on December 15 and rebroadcast on TV to 250 million people around the world. The benefit boasted a program of international stars, including Marlon Brando, Richard Burton, Elizabeth Taylor, Burt Lancaster, and Lena Horne. On the first day of re-hearsals, John Lennon and George Harrison accompanied their recently acquired guru, the Maharishi Mahesh Yogi, to hear Ravi Shankar play. The Maharishi was sitting cross-legged in the audience with the two Beatles when Dennis Wilson wandered in and made a beeline for them. Dennis shook the Maharishi's hand. 'All of a sudden,' Dennis said. 'I felt this weirdness, this presence this guy had. Like out of left field. First thing he ever said to me

[was] "Live your life to the fullest." So the next day I went over to his room, and he said, "Tell me some words of your songs." So we told him the lyrics of "God Only Knows" [which Tony Asher wrote] and he goes, "That's the sun rising and the stars and the planets and it connects with . . ." So I said, "God, this is great!" And he said, "We'd like to initiate you into the program." I said, "What does that mean, how much?" And he said, "We'll just do it to you tomorrow morning."'

The rest of the Beach Boys had already flown on to London. 'So I called Michael and all the guys in London. "C'mon down here to Paris. We're all gonna meditate." And then I got my mantra, and as the Maharishi was giving them to us he said, "What do you want?" I said, "I want everything. Everything." And he laughed and we meditated together. It was so wild.'

The Maharishi Mashesh Yogi was a small, brown-skinned man who seemed to offer instant spiritual relief and salvation, a modern-day psychic Band-Aid with fast results that appealed not only to Dennis but to Mike Love and the other members of the group. The Maharishi spoke of Jesus, of God, of eternal happiness and peace – he seemed for all the world a mystical, Eastern sage. But the Maharishi was far from an unsophisicated hick from the Himalayas. College-educated, with a degree in physics, he had studied Sanskrit and learned the scriptures with a well-known Indian sage named Guru Dev. Reportedly, the title 'Maharishi' was self-adopted. Sometime in the late fifties he began to preach his brand of mystic salvation to sold-out audiences in various Western countries.

Most of the world learned of the Maharishi through the Beatles. Leaders of the burgeoning youth movement, the Beatles were under enormous pressure to find the 'truth' and the 'meaning of life.' When the Beatles first went to hear the Maharishi lecture at the London Hilton, they were fascinated. They promised to travel to the Maharishi's Himalayan ashram as soon as possible. The trip took place early in February 1968, when Mike Love also went to India. Of all the Beach Boys, Mike Love was the most influenced by the Maharishi. 'When I heard about TM,' Mike said, 'I consciously took steps to expand my awareness . . . I didn't want to live life at the same level twenty years from now . . . And one of the greatest things that interested me was that [the Maharishi] said, "You don't have to give up your Rolls-Royce . . . and forsake all your pursuits of material pleasures . . . to develop inner spiritual qualities." That sounded real good to me.' Indeed, Mike Love looked at meditation as a way to wash his spiritual laundry; he could 'clean up' the bad karma from his other deeds.

For Mike Love, the trip to India marked the start of a lifelong passion for meditation. For the Beatles, it was the beginning of the end of their interest in Eastern mysticism. While the Beatles were in India at Rishikesh, the Maharishi suggested they tithe 10 to 25 per cent of their income into a Swiss account in his name. At the time the Beatles were considering starring in a film about TM to promote the Maharishi's university, and when a Beatles aide arrived in Rishikesh to negotiate the deal, he found that the Maharishi not only had a full-time accountant, but was also haggling with him about points in the profit structure. Moreover, the Maharishi had announced that the Beatles would appear with him on an ABC television special in America to help publicize his movement. Although the Beatles management told ABC this was not true, the Maharishi insisted it was. Eventually the Beatles had to insist he stop using their name for his benefit.

When the Maharishi persisted, George Harrison shrugged it off, saying that since the Maharishi was not a worldly man, he could not understand the ramifications.

Mike Love was so taken with not only Maharishi, but the celebrity-studded scene in Rishikesh, that he was determined to make a movie about it. He called Nick Grillo several times in Los Angeles, demanding that Grillo advance him a considerable sum of money to rent or purchase film equipment, as well as a helicopter. 'He was driving us nuts,' Grillo said. For Grillo, the idea was out of the question; money was tight, and the boys weren't touring. But Mike was so determined that he demanded Grillo get an advance from the next Capitol royalty check. When Grillo refused to comply, Mike wrote a 'threatening' letter to Alan Livingstone, then president of Capitol Records, insisting he get the money. 'We all said no,' Grillo explained, 'and Mike was very upset about it – there were a lot of harsh words, to say the least.'

While Mike was at the ashram in Rishikesh, a scandal erupted that is still a highly contested incident to this day. Allegedly, the Maharishi had made advances to an American nurse who was also studying with them, and to whom he had served the forbidden meal of chicken. By this time Ringo and Paul had begun to doubt the usefulness of Transcendental Meditation and had already left the ashram – only George and John were left there with their wives. The scandal about the nurse and the Maharishi destroyed John's belief, and the next morning he and George left the ashram for good. The Beatles were through with the Maharishi, but Mike Love's faith was not shaken. When he returned from the ashram to Los Angeles late in the spring of 1968, he was still a firm believer and proselytizer, encouraging everyone in the office to meditate and join the TM movement. Mike managed to convince the rest of the group that it would be a good move for the Beach Boys to tour America with the Maharishi – a kind of spiritual California rock-and-roll package to be booked into large college auditoriums.

5

While discussion about a tour with the Maharishi continued, the Beach Boys needed desperately to replenish their quickly dwindling company funds. In April 1968 they set out on the road, with funds advanced to them by banker Joe Lipsher. 'It was the answer to all our dreams,' Grillo said. Although it was a small tour of primarily the Southeast, with only seventeen dates, 'we would see net big bucks,' Grillo said. This was because the Beach Boys were basically promoting the tour themselves. Said the road manager, Richard Duryea, 'At that point we were hiring the halls and paying for the newspaper ads, paying for the radio spots, fronting the whole tour.' In an attempt to spark audience interest, the Strawberry Alarm Clock and the Buffalo Springfield were added to make the bill more eclectic. The Beach Boys were on a plane to Memphis, Tennessee, at the beginning of the tour, when they learned of a national tragedy: Martin Luther King, Jr, had been assassinated. Later in the day, when the Beach Boys were setting up their equipment, the National Guard arrived, informing them that no audience was expected at the concert, and that there was a curfew in effect to curtail expected racial violence. 'We flew on to the next city,' Duryea said, 'Greenville, North Carolina, and we ended up waiting in a Holiday Inn for a couple of days while all the other cities that we scheduled went dead because no one wanted to go. We had to wait until it blew over, and we finished the tour as best we could. Even then people didn't come because they were concerned about violence.'

'Some dates we played to half-houses,' Grillo said. 'Some dates only twenty-five people showed up.' Eventually, the remainder of the tour was cancelled, after only four performances, and every penny the Beach Boys had borrowed went down the drain. 'Devastating,' Grillo said, 'a fucking nightmare.'

The Maharishi tour was supposed to remedy all that. 'We were licking our wounds from the other tour,' Grillo said, when just a month later, on May 3, the Beach Boys set out on a seventeen-day tour with the Maharishi in a private rented plane. The Maharishi had certain demands, including elaborate flower settings wherever he went, as well as fresh fruit and other dietary needs that the Beach Boys were obligated to filfill. Billed as 'The Most Exciting Event of the Decade' by the New York promoter, the shows took place in huge concert halls and stadiums, instead of college auditoriums as originally planned. On opening night, at the Singer Bowl in New York, 'more police showed up than audience,' according to Richard Duryea. The fans were completely uninterested in hearing the Maharishi, and those who might have turned out for the Beach Boys alone, stayed away. 'There was a date at the Spectrum in Philadelphia where quite a few people showed up to see the Beach Boys, but when the Maharishi came on, they all left. No one cared, which is what everybody told Mike would happen. You can't slug your audience around like that and ask them to pay a high-priced ticket to hear this guy talk.' On a typical tour date, the Maharishi opened with a long, boring, unintelligible lecture while the audience booed and yelled for the Beach

243

Boys. 'The Maharishi laughed,' said Duryea. 'He was laughing all the time. He got his money.'

Grillo called it 'another diaster.' Quoted in an article by Carl Fleming in *Newsweek*, Jardine summed it up: 'The only people that are going to make money on this tour are the florists.' The tour was cancelled halfway through, at a loss approaching half a million dollars.

The culmination of the Beach Boys' official business relationship with the Maharishi was an album, called *Friends*, released that June after the miserable tour, Known as the 'TM album' by fans, it was one of their worst-selling albums by far – a boring, emotionless LP. This low-key album was, according to Al Jardine, 'just a collection of cuts. It was done in Brian's house.' Beach Boys biographer David Leaf called the album, 'so laid back as to be almost soporific, which gives an accurate insight into what Brian Wilson was up to . . .' Indeed, Brian's solo contribution to the album was called 'Busy Doin' Nothin'.'

On June 15, in London, the Beatles formally renounced their association with the Maharishi as a 'public mistake.' Mike Love would continue to be a lifelong follower.

6

Across the nation the Beach Boys' concert grosses plummeted. Promoters were reluctant to book them, considering them passé. In an effort to keep more of their proceeds, the Beach Boys had changed their arrangement with Irving Granz at William Morris. At the end of 1967, they formed their own promotion entity, called American Productions, but would look to Granz to fill in dates they could not book. 'I was under pressure,' said Grillo, 'because the guys would not go on the road. They were spending money, Brian was in the bedroom locked up, and their wives wouldn't go on the road because they were fucking other women . . . How do you go on? It was difficult.'

Yet they still made other investments. One of them was a major real-estate deal in the Simi Valley, north of Los Angeles. It was a good guess that the Simi Valley would soon become one of the next major development properties around the city, and under Grillo's direction the Beach Boys purchased over six hundred acres of income-producing farmland at between $6,000 and $8,000 an acre, with orange and lemon groves that would cover the cost of the real-estate taxes. Brian, who had the largest, most stable income of all the Beach Boys because of his publishing revenues, invested the lion's share of approximately $250,000 in the Simi Valley, owning 62 per cent of the deal. 'It was a brilliant investment,' Grillo said, 'that would make the guys into multimillionaires . . . The balloon payment was down the road . . .'[3]

At the same time, the group gave up the lease at 9000 Sunset Boulevard and worked out a favorable deal with Bernie Shapiro, the real-estate investment counselor for Julius Lefkowitz and Company, for a lease-option agreement on the Mannis Fur Building at 1654 North Ivar Street in Hollywood. 'The deal was very favorable,' Grillo said. 'We were paying a monthly fee [of only $1,500]

[3] At the time, tax laws allowed an immediate five years of 'pre-paid interest' on property purchases to be deducted from income taxes. The idea was to purchase property and use the prepaid interest as a down payment. The property would then immediately be put on the market, and hopefully sold at a vast profit before the five years' interest was due to the government. Many Hollywood stars became wealthy from this tax loophole.

against the purchase price of the building . . . [Shapiro] agreed to put together the upstairs the way we wanted it, renovating it to suit us . . . he paid for all that . . . It was based on the premise that we would eventually buy the building. We were expecting X number of dollars coming in from various deals.' The two-story building offered six thousand square feet of office space upstairs, and the downstairs tenants were Albert Hosiery and Sir George Smorgasbord. Grillo's office, which had previously been a humidified fur vault, now had an electric sliding door. The new place included a small rehearsal studio, accounting offices, room for the fan club, and even a sauna. The only drawback was there were no windows. 'It was a tomb in more ways than one,' said their old friend Fred Vail – and a tomb it would soon become.

Ten

1

It was nearly three o'clock one morning in late spring of
1968 when Dennis returned from a recording session to
his newly rented home at 14400 Sunset Boulevard. He
had not left the outside spotlights turned on, and as he
pulled his silver Ferrari GTB down the long, curving
driveway, he was surprised to see that the house was well
lit inside, seemingly full of activity. He stopped the car
near the rear of the house. As he got out, the back door
swung open and a small man emerged. He was a remarkable vision, like a hippie from a gothic horror movie. He
as a slight fellow, scarcely more than five feet tall, and a
bit hunchbacked. He wore a work shirt, jeans, and fringed
buckskin shoes. His dark, shaggy hair was shoulder-
length, and even in the shadows Dennis could detect a
strange, almost crazed look in his dark eyes. Dennis
instinctively felt a chill; something told him this was no
ordinary housebreaker, and no ordinary hippie. Without
even knowing why, he heard himself ask, 'Are you going
to hurt me?'

The man looked wounded. 'Do I look like I'm going to
hurt you, brother?' he asked. Before Dennis could
answer, the man dropped to his knees. Dennis stood

247

there, frozen, as the man leaned forward and kissed his sneakers reverently.

'Who are you?' Dennis asked in wonder.

'I'm a friend,' the man said, and invited Dennis into his own house. As they went in the back door, Dennis noticed a black school bus hidden by the trees. The words *Hollywood Productions* had been painted sloppily on its side.

Dennis was shocked – but not unhappy – to find the house occupied by a dozen or so young girls. They were smoking pot and had helped themselves to liquor and whatever food was in the refrigerator. A few of the girls were topless. The stereo was on, blasting Beatles songs.

Dennis immediately recognized two of the girls – one who said her nickname was 'Yellerstone,' and another who called herself Marnie Reeves and had long brown hair and beautiful blue eyes. He had twice picked them up hitchhiking in Malibu – the first time a month before, the second earlier that day. Marnie had told him that she had been born and raised in Inglewood, virtually Dennis's childhood backyard. Earlier that day he had driven them to 14400 Sunset Boulevard to show them his gold records. As he hoped, he ended up having sex with both of them, and he had bragged about the incident that same evening in the studio. He would soon find out the experience had given him gonorrhea. Much later, he would find out that 'Yellerstone''s real name was Ella Jo Bailey, and that Marnie Reeves's real name was Patricia Krenwinkle.

Patricia Krenwinkle came forward when she saw Dennis and said, 'This is the guy we were telling you about. This is Charlie Manson.'

Charlie Manson, as the girls had told Dennis earlier that day, was a musician of great power and talent. He was also a philosopher, a leader and prophet. As it turned out, the two men had a lot in common. Manson was a musician; so was Dennis. Manson hated the blacks; Dennis didn't care much for them either. Manson liked young, innocent-looking girls; they were Dennis's favorite, too. Manson spun a vivid and convincing scenario about the apocalypse that was soon to come. In the near future, Manson told Dennis, there would be a worldwide race war – black, red, and yellow against white. Manson had formed a 'family' – a loving army for security and protection against the coming war. Manson and his followers would arm themselves and live safely in the desert until the wars passed. Said one of Dennis's friends later, 'If you didn't have a basis for reasoning, if you were not a very deep-thinking person, you could really be taken in by this guy because what he said was a lot of half-truths.' Manson lived on other people's fears, and he sensed fear in Dennis. Confused, depressed about his impending divorce, and very stoned, Dennis was the perfect prey for Charlie. Not only that, Charlie held the strongest lure of all for Dennis: wild, free, orgiastic sex. That very night, the orgies started. Charlie's dictum was sex seven times a day – before and after each meal and once in the middle of the night.

Manson orgies were a very organized affair. 'It was more like a business transaction,' said Stanley Shapiro. Manson himself handed out the drugs, usually psychedelics – LSD, STP, mushrooms, or whatever was handy – and made sure that he took a much smaller dose than anyone else so he could remain in charge. According to Paul ('Tex') Watkins, Manson's second-in-command and procurer of young girls, 'Everything was done at Charlie's direction.' As Charlie began to strip, so did the girls. Then everyone would lie down on the floor and, under Charlie's directions, take twelve deep breaths with their eyes closed, rubbing up against each other until everyone was touching. Charlie would proceed to literally direct the orgy, suggesting positions and sexual acts. 'He would say, "You take off your blouse," said one of Dennis's friends who was brought over to 14400 Sunset to participate, '"and now spread your legs."' Watkins told police, 'He'd set it all up in a beautiful way like he was creating a masterpiece in sculpture.'

At the moment Charles Manson met Dennis, he was thirty-three, an illiterate burglar, car thief, forger, and pimp; a drifter and ex-con who had spent seventeen years – half of his life – in various prisons. He had last been released from Terminal Island prison in the spring of 1967. The morning of his release he begged the prison officials to let him stay, afraid he could not adjust to the outside world. But they forced him to leave, and he roamed the streets of San Francisco, sleeping in doorways, until a friend got him a room in a transient hotel. He spent his days wandering Telegraph Avenue, playing his guitar, and eventually met a girl named Mary Brunner, then twenty-three. He moved in with her and they had a child.[1] It was the San Francisco peace-and-love movement that helped Manson coalesce his free-love Family philosophy. Dr David Smith, who had worked with the Family at the Free Clinic in San Francisco, said, 'Sex, not drugs, was the common denominator.' During the summer of 1967 Manson procured a school bus, piled into it his expanding Family – which now included Mary Brunner, Ella Jo Bailey, Lynette 'Squeaky' Fromme, Patricia Krenwinkel and three or four young boys – and started wandering for a year. They lived in Mendocino, Big Sur,

---

[1] Manson's children, as well as other Family children, were placed in foster homes by the courts, and their real identities and locations are sealed in court records.

Mexico, Nevada, Los Angeles, Topanga Canyon, Malibu, and Venice. Shortly before meeting Dennis, Manson and his Family had been living in a deserted ranch once used as a movie location, the Spahn Movie Ranch in Chatsworth, in the Simi Valley.

Dennis was sufficiently impressed by Charlie and his girls to ask them to move in with him, thus beginning what the media would later call Manson's 'Sunset Boulevard' period. Living with Dennis was paradise for Charlie and his band of locusts. Dennis's self-styled brand of generosity was just what Charlie needed. Charlie helped himself to anything that belonged to Dennis: cars, clothing, money, food, and a couple of gold records – the latter Charlie gave away as gifts. Yet, although they were living in high style, some aspects of the Family's behavior remained the same, such as their food-collection activities. Despite the enormous deliveries to the house every day by the Alta Dena Dairy, of parcels including yogurts and ice cream, and generous cash supplements from Dennis to buy food, Manson still sent the girls on nightly 'food runs.' On these scavenging hunts, the girls would pile into Dennis's Rolls-Royce in the middle of the night and visit a selection of closed supermarkets, where they would search the garbage dumpsters for decaying foods that were waiting to be picked up by private sanitation companies. Dennis thought these food runs were a lot of fun and made some of them himself, sometimes driving the girls a hundred miles an hour up and down Sunset Boulevard in his Ferrari.

That summer Dennis began an affair with a beautiful fifteen-year-old girl named Diane Adams, who was on vacation from boarding school. One weekend, while staying with her father in Encino, she heard that Dennis Wilson, the Beach Boy, was living in a house on Sunset

251

Boulevard and went there to find him. Diane, whose nickname was 'Croxey,' drove her Nassau-blue 1965 Stingray into the driveway of 14400 Sunset and found Dennis running across the lawn dressed in silk lounging pants. For the rest of the time that Dennis lived with Charles Manson and the Family, Croxey Adams was his girl friend.

'It was very bizarre,' Croxey said. 'They were sleeping all over the house. Charlie had these girls providing for him – sewing, cooking, doing anything he wanted . . .' According to Croxey, daily life with the Family was calmer than anyone would have expected. The girls would lounge around the pool, dividing up the household chores. A group of them worked in the kitchen and baked bread for the evening meals, while others took turns watching the children. Croxey didn't fit in with this group from the start, and although Manson made a persistent effort to have her join the Family, she resisted him. Her only interest was in being with Dennis, whom she remembered as 'the greatest stud at twenty-three.' Because of her separateness from the Family, Charlie and the other girls mistrusted her greatly. Croxey wouldn't take orders from Charlie, and she couldn't take the group sex seriously. When Manson started to choreograph, Croxey would find herself giggling and trying to hold it in, which interrupted the flow. Manson would get furious with her and throw her out. 'I would try to stop [the orgies]. I would start cracking up. I would get out of those things and say this is not for me.

'Charlie had a passion for me,' Croxey said, but she refused to sleep with him. 'I slept every night on a little antique love seat, my legs and head up so that Charlie couldn't sleep next to me. I wouldn't sleep anywhere where he could crawl next to me. He was such a creep,

252

and I would say, "Would you get away!" I said, "I'm here because I like Dennis," and Charlie would say, "You're not allowed to have crushes. Everybody is supposed to love everybody." Sometimes it would get so intense I would leave and go home. It's not very complimentary to know that Charlie Manson has a crush on you. I told Dennis, "You better get these people out of here, because I have a feeling you're going to get busted."'

But Dennis wasn't afraid of getting busted. He liked Manson and the Family so much that he bragged about his friendship with them in a 1968 issue of an English music magazine called *Rave*. 'Fear is nothing but awareness,' he told the writer, mimicking Manson's mumbo jumbo. 'Sometimes the Wizard frightens me – Charlie Manson, who is another friend of mine, says he is God and the devil! He sings, plays and writes poetry . . .' Moreover, Dennis thought he had made a great musical discovery in Manson, and wanted him to record for Brother Records. Although he was later to claim that 'Charlie didn't have a musical bone in his whole body,' Dennis was quite impressed with Charlie's song-writing ability at the time, and tried to help Charlie's musical career get off the ground. One of the first people he introduced Manson to was Gregg Jakobson. 'One day Dennis called me up,' Jakobson recounted, 'and said, "Hey, Gregg, you should have been down here. Some guy pulled in with a big black bus . . . and he's got about thirty girls." Charlie later told me that the only reason why he used to travel with all those girls was to attract guys. He was always recruiting.' The following night Jakobson went to Dennis's house and was overwhelmed by the scene – a host of subservient, half-naked young women, catering to Dennis's and Manson's every whim. Jakobson's first impression of Manson was that he was 'intellectually stimulating.' 'He had a very powerful intellect,' Jakobson said. 'He could discuss almost any subject, just like he said [later, in court] he had a "thousand hats" and he could put on any hat at any time. In another situation he would have been capable of being president of a university . . .' Over the next year, Jakobson had more than a hundred philosophical conversations with Manson, and got to know him as well as anyone outside of the Family.

One night Dennis and Gregg took Manson and some of the girls to the Whiskey A Go Go on Sunset Boulevard. 'Charlie started dancing, and I swear to God, within a matter of minutes the dance floor would be empty and Charlie would be dancing by himself. It was almost as if sparks were flying off the guy.'

Jakobson was so taken with him that along with Dennis, he touted Manson to others – such as Rudy Altobelli, a business manager for show-business personalities. Altobelli owned several properties in Los Angeles, including an enormous mansion at 10050 Cielo Drive. Altobelli lived in the guest house behind the mansion, and rented the main house to Terry Melcher and his girl friend, Candice Bergen. Altobelli met Manson at a party at Dennis's house that summer, and listened to a tape of Charlie's music. 'They were telling me about his philosophy and his way of living and how groovy he was.' But Altobelli had no interest in Manson, and declined to help Manson's career, as did John Phillips, of the Mamas and Papas. The only one of Jakobson's friends to show any real interest in the man was Terry Melcher. Jakobson was convinced that Melcher's production company should record Manson, and brought Melcher to meet Charlie at Dennis's house several times. On one occasion Dennis drove Melcher home to 10050 Cielo Drive, while Charlie

254

sat in the backseat, softly strumming his guitar. Eventually, on August 9 of that summer, Jakobson arranged for Manson to have a preliminary recording session at a Van Nuys studio, but not much was accomplished.

2

It wasn't long before Dennis started to bring Charlie up to the Beach Boys' offices and introduce him to everyone. After all, the philosophy of Brother Records was supposedly that each member of the group should be allowed to discover new acts and record them, and Dennis had found one. He didn't find much suppport for Manson at the office, however. 'He just gave us all the creeps. He was very sullen,' said bookkeeper Catherine Pace. 'He would hang around and plunk away on the guitar, just one tune – *plank, plank, plank* – one string he would plank away, this mastermind . . .' Manson was so filthy they called him 'Pig Pen' – but not to his face.

Nick Grillo was obligated to take Manson more seriously than the rest, because Dennis insisted. 'Charlie was a very bright guy, and his major concern was public acceptance of his music,' Grillo said. 'Dennis was enamored with Charlie, and the other members of the [Beach Boys] were enamored with the fact that he had twelve or thirteen women. The other guys were looking to get laid . . .' Indeed, Croxy Adams remembered, 'They would come over to the house because they were all eyeing the situation. The Beach Boys loved it.' Grillo, however, suspected the worst about Charlie, and asked a friend of his at the district attorney's office to check Manson out for him. Grillo was told only a limited amount of information: that Charlie had robbed a supermarket with a gun, had served some time, and was on probation. 'He was looking to connect with something to fulfill the probationary situation [to have a job] . . . it was important to Charlie . . . it would give him some credibility and relieve him of the probationary responsibility . . .' Finally, after much urging on Dennis's part, Grillo called Stephen Despar, the new engineer at Brian's house on Bellagio Road, and said, 'Crazy Dennis has some friend he wants to record. You can work at night. Dennis will bring him in and they'll work till two or three in the morning, and it shouldn't take too long.'

Stephen Despar was a twenty-four-year-old electronics wizard who had built the Beach Boys' traveling sound system. At that time there were three fully equipped systems, which the Beach Boys had hoped to lease out to other touring rock groups at a profit. One of these systems had been sent to Monterey for the festival before the Beach Boys decided not to show up, and Despar served as one of the main sound technicians for the concert. Recently, he had been elected to build 'a full-fledged recording studio with the capacity of any other' at Brian's house, as an improvement over the mobile equipment that had been installed previously. 'This studio was supposed to be available so whenever Brian wanted to come down and record, it would be there,' Despar said. Despar designed the recording system, and the Beach Boys hired a studio builder named Henry Mancini to contruct it. Mancini arrived one morning with nine carpenters and finished the job that night. 'It was a temporary kind of construction,' Despar said. 'The big window that overlooked the fountain in the courtyard was covered, a hole was opened in the wall above the fireplace so you could see out of the control room, and the final revision was the installation of a thirty-cubic-foot speaker encloser and custom-made monitors.' Despar estimated the total cost at nearly $150,000.

At first Brian didn't even come down to see the new studio, but he could still hear all the sessions through the floorboards in his bedroom above. 'Eventually it got the better of him, and he came down,' Despar said. 'He was in his pajama bottoms and must have weighed about two hundred pounds. He said, "Hi, Steve. I thought I'd come down and look at this place."' Despar gave him a tour and showed him how the new board worked. 'Then he noticed there were coffee stains on the rug, and he didn't like that. The next day some carpet installers came and replaced the carpet with another rug of the same color.' Soon afterward Brian said he wanted to paint the walls. 'I want red and green and orange and pink and blue,' he said. Despar purchased acoustical paint and Brian painted the panels himself. His final decorating touch was the purchase of a $1,500 alabaster lamp.

According to Despar, Brian would come down to the studio 'in waves.' All of a sudden the door would fly open and Brian would be standing there in his bathrobe and say, 'Hey guys, I've got an idea! Listen to this line.' He'd play a little tune on the organ and then disappear into his bedroom again. One night Despar and Brian discussed Brian's deafness and his subsequent inability to record in stereo. Despar had a suggestion: when Brian was in the studio, they would pipe the sessions over the speakers in mono while recording in stereo. After this, all the Beach Boys records would be produced in stereo.[2]

It was to this new studio – while Brian was upstairs in

[2] Brian did manage to produce several songs in the studio that summer – but not for the Beach Boys. Instead, he recorded a double-sided single for Marilyn and Diane and their cousin Ginger.

his bedroom – that Dennis brought Charles Manson. According to Despar, a demonstration tape would be recorded 'That would be shopped around by American Productions.' It was also assumed – at least by Manson – that Terry Melcher would help him get a contract with a major label.

'Dennis was really taken in by Manson,' Despar said. 'He went on for days about how much he loved Manson and how he wanted to help him out, saying that he really had talent, and that he was terribly misunderstood.' When Manson finally showed up at Brian's house for his first professional recording session, he was completely unprepared. 'He brought nothing,' Despar said, 'except half a dozen girls, and they stayed in the studio with him and smoked dope. I guess I got on Charlie's good side, because the first thing that happened was he pulled out a cigarette and didn't have a match, so I went to the kitchen and got a match for him. He was very impressed that someone would actually go to the trouble just for him. He made a big thing about that.'

Charlie had just one caveat about his music. He used to say, 'I don't care what you do with the music. Just don't let anybody change any of the lyrics.' Between six and eight songs were recorded, some of which were 'pretty good,' according to Despar. 'He had musical talent . . . Dennis really should have been producing him, but he only came in a couple of times, and then he would leave.'

Eventually, Manson's true nature started to come across, and Despar got nervous. 'What struck me odd was the stare he gave you. It was scary. We were in there two or three nights, and then he got pretty weird. [He] pulled a knife on me, just for no reason really, just pulled a knife out and would flash it around while he was talking. I called Grillo and said, "Look, this guy is psychotic, I don't think without a producer you're going to get anything on him. And the guy is just too weird for me. I don't know if I'm going to say something and that's going to tick him off and he's going to pull a switchblade on me." Grillo told Despar that the six or eight songs they had already recorded were enough, and called off any further recording sessions.

According to Gregg Jakobson, 'Charlie couldn't make it with those people [at Brian's house]. They were too stiff for him.' 'Stiff' was an understatement – they were frightened to death of him. Marilyn in particular hated Charlie and the girls he brought around, especially one girl called 'Sadie Glutz' (Susan Atkins). Marilyn once called the office and told Catherine Pace, 'Kathy, please, I want you to buy us an ultraviolet toilet seat for the bathroom.' When Catherine questioned her further, she said, 'Dennis is bringing those crummy girls up here with Charles Manson, and I'm afraid they're going to give us or the children some diseases.' But there was no such thing as an ultraviolet toilet seat, and Marilyn had to make do with thorough washings with disinfectant when they left. Once, Tex Watkins 'borrowed' one of Brian's sports cars without telling them. Marilyn, furious, had Diane track them down, give them hell, and get the car back.

Dennis's estranged wife, Carol, had meanwhile noticed an extreme change in Dennis. He seemed to be continuously in a drugged stupor, as though completely overwhelmed by his new friends. 'He invited me [there] a lot and I never went, and I think the reason I didn't go is because I knew what was going on,' Carol said. 'I didn't want to walk around where there were naked girls and sex happening at all hours of the day and night and stuff like that.' Carol had several conversations with Manson on the phone. 'He would call and say, "Come on, we want you to be here,"' but she always made some excuse. Carol did, however, go to the house on a few occasions to pick up her children, Scott and Jennifer, who visited their father on the weekends. One weekend Carol arrived at the house to discover that all the water had been drained from the California-shaped swimming pool, and that there were several young girls sitting at the bottom of the empty pool with an elderly, white-haired man. (This was Family member Ruth Moorehouse's father, himself a nonviolent sometime member of the Family.) After that, Carol never let the children go back to visit with Dennis.

Before long Dennis's wardrobe, including all his flashy Rodeo Drive outfits, was added to the communal Manson Family clothing pile. Manson ordered the girls to cut up all the clothing into large swatches and sew them into robes for everyone to wear. 'One day Dennis walked into our house in Benedict Canyon,' Carol said. 'I'll never forget him coming down the dark hallway. He was barefoot and wearing a robe they had made for him out of patches of clothing. I just looked at him and said, "If you will pack all your things right now and move out of here, I'll file for divorce tomorrow."' Dennis packed and Carol filed for divorce soon afterward.

Dennis did manage to get his mother to visit the house. 'Dennis was at the recording studio in Brian's house,' Audree said, 'and he said, "Will you take me home?" I was very hesitant because I thought, Oh God, Murry's not going to like this. But I took him home and he said, "Will you just come in and meet them? Come on, they're nice." And I said, "Dennis, promise me you won't tell Dad."

'So I went in, and Charlie Manson was walking through

260

this big yard with a long robe on, and Dennis introduced me. We went into the house, and I think three girls were in the house, just darling young girls, I thought. I zipped through the house, got back in my car, and left. And wouldn't you know that Dennis told his Dad? . . . Murry didn't like it. He was pissed . . . I did think [Manson and the Family] were a bunch of leeches. Dennis . . . could never stand to see anyone who needed anything or anybody who had any kind of problem. He was right there.'

Manson and the Family drained Dennis of over $100,000 that summer. This included money spent on food and clothing, bills for wrecking Dennis's uninsured $21,000 Mercedes-Benz, and constant bills for doctors' visits to cure the Family of gonorrhea, which kept reinfecting Dennis. The doctor bills were sent to Catherine Pace at the North Ivar Street office, and she summarily paid them from Dennis's account. Dennis also picked up the bill to fix Susan Atkins's teeth.

As the summer progressed, Dennis began to grow disillusioned with Manson. As Gregg Jakobson described the situation, 'Ultimately Dennis and Charlie went head-on, because they both had the same energy. Only, Dennis was more heart-cultured. They attracted each other immediately and then immediately repelled.' The turning point may have come one day when Charlie pulled a hunting knife on Dennis, put it to his throat, and said, 'What would you do if I killed you?' Dennis just shrugged and said, 'Do it!' Manson lowered the knife.

The Beach Boys toured heavily throughout the late summer and early autumn of 1968, and Dennis was in and out of Los Angeles. He never really had the courage to tell Manson and the Family to leave his house. Instead, early in August, three weeks before his lease expired, he moved to a small rented house on the hillside just above the Pacific Coast Highway in the Palisades, leaving the big house at 14400 Sunset to the Family. The rent was not paid, and eventually the Family was thrown out.[3] The maid who worked there sued Dennis for back pay. Charlie was not particularly upset by Dennis's actions – he simply moved back to the Spahn ranch, where he had been before. However, he did show up at Dennis's new house in the Palisades whenever he needed something. Fred Vail remembers Manson arriving one day and saying, 'We're getting low on food and we need stuff for the Family.' Dennis told him to help himself. Charlie proceeded to empty out the refrigerator, and then Dennis's clothing closet. 'He took out every shirt and pair of pants that Dennis had,' Vail said, 'bundled them up and threw back in the back of a jeep. He left one shirt hanging on a hangar in the corner.' He also appropriated the jeep, which belonged to Gregg Jakobson. Jakobson's wife, Carol, wanted to report it stolen, but instead Dennis and Jakobson simply drove out to the desert and got it back. On this trip Jakobson ran over a scorpion, infuriating Charlie, who began a lecture that the life of the scorpion was more important than a human life.

On another occasion, Charlie arrived at the house looking for Dennis and found Croxey Adams instead. He demanded she have sex with him, and she refused. 'I said, "Get out of here and leave me alone,"' Croxey said. 'He pulled out a knife and said, "You know I could cut you up in little pieces . . ."' Croxey ran out of the house and down the road to the Coast Highway before she gathered the courage to go back and confront Manson. 'I belittled him so much that he left,' she said. 'I told him, "Go

---

[3] Some say Nick Grillo hired plainclothes detectives to do the job.

ahead! Go ahead, you wimp! Try and get it up, you motherfucker! You're a punk peon! You got me in a spot, so go for it, buddy! Get out that knife and kill me! Slice my throat! Slice it!"' Faced with the challenge, Manson seemed cowed. He put the knife down and left. It was nearly a year before Croxey would realize how lucky she had been.

In September, Manson paid another visit to Dennis and Gregg and demanded they join the Family full-time, but both demurred. It mollified Manson somewhat when Dennis played one of Manson's songs, 'Cease to Exist,' for the Beach Boys, and they recorded it for inclusion on their next album, *20/20*, their last album with Capitol Records. The Beach Boys' twentieth album, it was a disparate collection of tunes, mostly leftovers from recent records, and almost completely devoid of Brian's production input. 'It was recorded all over the world,' said Despar, 'on both sides of the US, in England, France, and Germany.' *20/20* became an opportunity for each group member to contribute his own music. Bruce Johnston called it 'a very un-Brian album.' The album was notable for the inclusion of Carl Wilson's first major production, the beautiful song 'I Can Hear Music' (written by Jeff Barry, Phil Spector, and Ellie Greenwich); the 'Cabinessence' track left over from the *Smile* album; a telling Brian Wilson composition entitled 'I Went to Sleep'; and the Manson song. Reportedly, Manson was aware of the strife within the group, and wrote 'Cease to Exist' as a tonic. The lyric was easily changed to 'cease to resist,' and the title to 'Never Learn Not to Love.' Charlie was furious that his lyrics had been changed. Even so, on December 8, 1968, the song was released by Capitol Records on the 'B' side of the first single from the soon-to-be-released *20/20* album, backing 'Bluebirds over the

Mountain.' The single never got past number 61, but the Beach Boys had put Charles Manson on the charts.

3

That winter, Dennis moved into a small, one-room garage apartment below Gregg Jakobson's house in Benedict Canyon. When it got too cold at the unheated Spahn ranch, Manson and the Family moved, too – to a two-story house on Gresham Street in Canoga Park, where they would prepare for Helter-Skelter.[4] This was the term Manson now used to describe his race wars, having heard the phrase on the newly released Beatles record, the so-called *White Album*, which now played incessantly at Gresham Street. During this winter, Manson's anger with Terry Melcher was ignited. According to accounts given by Family members (but denied by Melcher and Jakobson), Melcher had promised to listen to Manson's new songs at the Gresham Street house. The girls even baked cookies for him one night, but Melcher didn't show up. Manson never forgave him.

In March 1969, Manson went to 10050 Cielo Drive to find Melcher, and learned from Rudy Altobelli – who was then occupying the guest house in the back – that Melcher had moved out. Although Altobelli knew that Melcher had gone to his mother Doris Day's house in Malibu, he told Manson he did not know where to find him. On the way out, Altobelli asked Manson why he hadn't stopped

[4] Dennis later told friends he visited Tex Watkins in this apartment and smelled a terrible stench. When he asked Watkins what it was, Watkins told him there was a 'dead body in the closet.' Dennis thought he was joking.

at the main house. Manson said he had, but the new occupants, who had moved in on February 15, had sent him back to the guest house. The new tenants were movie star Sharon Tate, pregnant with her husband Roman Polanski's child; Jay Sebring, a successful hairstylist and one-time boyfriend of Sharon's; Abigail Folger, heiress to the Folger coffee fortune; and Folger's boyfriend, Voytek Frykowsky, who had been introduced to her by Polish novelist Jerzy Kosinski.

Jakobson finally convinced Melcher to see Manson that spring, when Manson had moved back to the Spahn ranch. 'My idea,' said Jakobson, 'was for a film, not just a record. I said to Terry, "This guy should be captured on film. You're never gonna capture this guy on tape." It'd be like having footage on Castro while he was still in the mountains or something. This guy was a real rebel – it had to be movie footage. This crazy guy with all these girls and music, but his music was visual, too. You had to see the guy sing his songs, not just hear him on a tape. I wanted to do a documentary, at least . . . it would be like a B movie.'

Jakobson brought Terry Melcher to the Spahn ranch on April 18, 1969, to hear Charlie sing in his natural setting. Charlie sat on a rock and sang while the girls, all naked, sat around him humming a background chorus. After the performance, Melcher gave Manson $50 to buy some feed for the horses on the ranch, but 'wasn't impressed enough to allot the time necessary' to Manson's career. Family members, however, claimed that Melcher discussed a recording contract with Charlie, but that Charlie refused to sign any papers, since he thought his word was good enough. Melcher later denied ever discussing a formalized recording situation with Manson. Melcher did, however, come back to the Spahn ranch again on June 6, this time with recording engineer Michael Deasy, who had a mobile recording unit. According to Jakobson (who later wrote about the experience under the pseudonym of Lance Fairweather for *Rolling Stone*), Melcher *was* 'impressed the first time he went to the ranch.' However, on Melcher's second trip an ugly scene took place. They were all sitting by a stream where Charlie was singing when a drunken old Hollywood stunt man who lived on the ranch began waving a gun. Charlie yelled, 'Don't draw on me, motherfucker!' and 'Beat the shit' out of the man in front of Melcher and Jakobson. That incident completely put Melcher off.

4

On August 9, 1969, the occupants of 10050 Cielo Drive were massacred in one of the most sadistic and terrifying crimes committed in this century. On the very next day, Leno and Rosemary LaBianca of 3301 Waverly Drive, near Griffith Park, were slaughtered in a similar manner. While the identity of the murderers still remained a mystery to the police, Dennis and his friends hoped fervently that their most frightening assumptions would not turn out to be true. But one thing was undeniably clear – the Tate murders had been committed in the very house where Melcher had lived. Their fears may have seemed farfetched; in any event, they decided not to come forward and contact the police.

A few days after the Tate murders, Manson and twenty-six members of his Family were arrested in a daybreak raid on the Spahn ranch. They were charged with auto theft – they had been stealing Volkswagens and turning

266

them into dune buggies. The police had no idea who they had arrested or that there was any connection between Manson and the Tate murders. Almost all those arrested in the raid gave false names, and to make matters worse, the warrant had been misdated. A day later all the suspects were released to roam free.

Manson appeared at Dennis's apartment at Gregg Jakobson's house not long afterward. Dennis was playing the piano when the door flew open – and Manson was standing there, looking like a crazed wildman. He demanded $1,500 in cash from Dennis so he and the Family could move farther into the desert, this time to the Barker ranch, in the rugged area south of the Death Valley Monument. When Dennis nonchalantly asked Manson where he had just been, Manson told him, 'I been to the moon.' Dennis gave Manson all the money he had on him and Manson left, disgruntled. By this time Manson had apparently learned that Melcher was living in Malibu in his mother's beach house. One morning, Melcher awoke to find that the telescope kept outside the house had been moved to the far side of the deck in the dark of the night. Presumably, this was on one of the Family's 'creepy crawly' expeditions, in which they went to the homes of sleeping people and silently moved the furniture around to show they were ubiquitous. In fact, Manson called Jakobson one day and asked if Melcher had a green telescope on the deck at Malibu. When Jakobson said he did, Manson replied, 'Not anymore, he doesn't.'

While the police investigation continued into the Tate–LaBianca murders, Dennis and his friends lived in constant fear. 'One evening,' related Stanley Shapiro, 'I was in Gregg Jakobson's house, within a day of the Tate murders, and Gregg was not home. Dennis was scared to death and had to go to Canada to play a concert with the Beach Boys. While he was gone, Charlie Manson called numerous times to talk to him, and he was pissed [that Dennis wasn't in]. Later, there was a knock at the door and it was Manson. He had a .45-caliber automatic pistol stuck in his waistband and he said, "Where's Dennis?"'

Manson was told that Dennis was out of town and could not be reached.

'Oh yeah?' he raged. 'Well, you tell Dennis I've got something for him.' Then Manson pulled the .45 out of his waistband and took out the magazine. He popped a bullet out of it and threw it on the floor. 'When you see Dennis, tell him this is for him. And I've got one for [his son] Scott, too.'

Fred Vail remembered, 'We were in Canada, and after the show we went back to the hotel, and there was a message from Carol: Scott was missing! They were up in the mountains, looking in ditches for him, and Carol was getting frightened. Scott was gone for six or eight hours and Dennis was really worried. He said, "I want a jet right now. I'm going home."' But not only were there no private planes available, the group had no money to pay for one, and Dennis was booked instead on the next commercial flight. Just before he boarded the plane, they received another call from Carol: Scott was safe. He had gone to a friend's house to spend the night and had forgotten to call.

It wasn't until November 19 that the police tracked down Manson and the Family at the Barker ranch, and in a dawn raid arrested him and the entire Family for car theft. This time the arrest warrants were in order, but the police still did not connect Manson and the Family to the Tate–LaBianca murders. It was only after Susan Atkins bragged to her roommate in jail about the murders that

268

the police realized the murderers were already in custody. Within a few days, the entire story came spilling out on TV.

'Right after that, the district attorney wanted to see Dennis,' Shapiro said. 'In fact, they waited for him at the airport [returning from a tour], and took him into custody. He was pissed off and blamed me for telling the DA where he had gone.'

Dennis told the DA nothing that day. He was afraid for his family's safety as well as his own, knowing that, although Manson was in jail, there were still many Family members out on the street. 'The next day was [Dennis's] birthday,' Audree recalled, 'and he was at Carl and Annie's. I went there and we had dinner. And we were all very quiet. And somebody said something and Carl said, "I don't think we should talk about it." So we just watched television and had a very quiet evening. We were totally terrified. I remember Carl saying, "Mom, let's all go back and stay at your house." And I said, "Carl, everybody knows where I live. What good would that do?" So I stayed at their house for a couple of nights.'

Several nights later, at Gregg Jakobson's house, Dennis was paid a visit by Family member Squeaky Fromme, who told Dennis that if he didn't give up the tapes Manson had made at Brian's house, she was going to kill him. According to Stanley Shapiro, 'Dennis just scoffed at the whole idea. I said, "Dennis, do you have those tapes?" And he said he had already turned them over to the DA, which was bullshit.' In fact, when Nick Grillo had heard the news on TV, he locked the tapes in a vault, where they remain to this day.

Susan Atkins later admitted that although the Family knew Melcher had moved out, the 'reason Charlie picked that house was to instill fear into Terry Melcher, because

Terry had given us his word on a few things and never came through with them.' Atkins also told the police that the 'only reason why we were going to that house was because Tex knew the outline of the house.'

Terry Melcher testified at the Manson trial. He told prosecuting attorney Vincent Bugliosi that he was so terrified of Manson, he had been under psychiatric treatment and was constantly accompanied by a bodyguard since December 1969. Melcher had to be given a tranquilizer before taking the stand, and was reportedly relieved when Manson smiled at him after he testified.

Gregg Jakobson was a key witness at the trial, bravely coming forward to tell the whole story, explaining what at first seemed to be incomprehensible motives for the murders. Later, during Jakobson's custody battle with his wife, Carol, Bugliosi wrote a letter in his behalf.

Dennis never testified at the Manson trial, pretending to remember little of what had happened. He was interviewed by the district attorney, and did explain how he had met Manson, and some of the subsequent events. Dennis lived in fear of Manson and the Family for years afterward, but for some reason, although reporters always questioned him about this period, he never discussed it. During an interview in 1976, Dennis said, 'I don't talk about Manson. I think he's a sick fuck. I think of Roman and those wonderful people who had a beautiful family and they fucking had their tits cut off. I want to benefit from that?'

The public thinks of us as surfing Doris Days. – Bruce Johnston

The Beach Boys, unfortunately, had become dinosaurs. – David Leaf, *The Beach Boys and the California Myth*

Eleven

1

The Beach Boys sued Capitol Records on April 12, 1969, formally severing their seven-year relationship with the company. According to the group, the audit of Capitol's books, begun in 1967, had disclosed an alleged underpayment of royalties of over $622,000, based on an outdated 'breakage' clause,[1] as well as $1,418,827.92 in producer's fees for Brian Wilson. In a peculiar move, penalizing both sides, Capitol *deleted* the Beach Boys catalog, making it next to impossible to buy any of their old records, and completely cutting off the flow of royalties. The Beach Boys were now adrift without a recording contract.

Nick Grillo, under enormous pressure to keep the group going, scrambled to find another recording company, but none of the majors was interested. According to Grillo, 'Brian was notorious at this point,' and record-company executives were afraid to take a chance with him. Grillo felt it was unfair to base the entire value of

---

[1] The recording industry traditionally based payment on revenues less 10 per cent. This automatic 10 per cent deduction began when records were breakable and many were destroyed in shipping.

the Beach Boys on Brian – there was enough talent in the rest of the group, especially Mike and Carl, to produce commercial albums without him. But Brian was the legendary 'genius,' and the legend now had it that he was also a reclusive drug casualty. Because the Beach Boys' popularity remained consistently high in Europe – particularly in Great Britain – and Brian's reputation was less blemished overseas, Grillo tried to land a foreign, worldwide deal with a European company before attempting to convince a US company to take a chance with them. The boys went off to tour Europe, where they were still selling concert tickets and where the revenues would keep them from bankruptcy. As a business ploy, their tour was to end in Germany – the Deutsche Grammophon company was sincerely interested in giving them a contract, and the chief executives would be attending the final concert. Grillo, who had already traveled with attorney Abe Somers to see the Grammophon executives, hoped to close the deal after their triumphant concert in Germany. A major contract was outlined, 'but the trigger,' according to Grillo, 'was that we had to have an American distributor for our records.' There was a long shot that Polygram would sign them in the US, but they were 'trepidatious about the Beach Boys delivering product, and the domestic side of the deal was falling apart.'

However, when Grillo and Abe Somers arrived in England, they were greeted with the terrible news. Brian had given an interview to an English rock newspaper, confessing that the group was teetering on the edge of bankruptcy. 'If we don't pick ourselves off our backsides and have a hit record soon, we will be in [even] worse trouble,' he was quoted as having said. He went on to say that Grillo had predicted the Beach Boys would soon have to file a chapter 11 proceedings in Los Angeles. 'We all know that if we don't watch it and do something drastic, inside a few months, we won't have a penny in the bank,' Brian concluded.

'It was devastating,' Grillo said. 'Here we were going to meet with the Germans, and that information was released to the press. The whole deal fell apart.'

Back in Los Angeles, various bankers became 'angels' to the group, loaning money to keep them afloat, holding checks instead of bouncing them, and generally giving Grillo and the boys time to land a new record deal. Whenever possible, the group was booked on the road for concerts, where the revenues would repay their bank loans, but traveling expenses were high and concert prices were low. Things got so bad that road manager Richard Duryea and Fred Vail, now their promotion man, began to charge the group's plane tickets on their personal credit cards.[2] To make matters worse, the Beach Boys' wives didn't want them on the road all the time.

Somehow, the group members themselves didn't take their predicament seriously enough. They continued to spend – 'profligate' Grillo called them – and to expand. That year a new group called Flame was signed as an act for Brother Records. Flame was a black South African group from Durban consisting of three brothers – Ricky, 'Brother,' and Steve Fataar – and their friend, Blondie Chaplin. Mike and Carl had discovered them one night playing at a club in London, and everyone thought the addition of black members would increase the Beach

---

[2] Vail was fired with thousands of dollars' worth of charges still left on his credit cards. The Beach Boys were 'unable' to pay him at the time, and his credit was ruined. It took an obligatory seven years to get his credit rating in order. Dick Duryea had a similar problem; however, he took the money owed him out of proceeds from concerts while on the road. The Beach Boys then told everyone he was a thief.

Boys' cachet. Plans were immediately set in motion for Flame to record an album for Brother Records, and they were signed up as the Beach Boys' opening act. Later, they would play with the Beach Boys as sidemen. Meanwhile, Mike's middle brother, Stephen, a recent graduate of the University of Southern California with a master's degree in business administration, was hired to assist Nick Grillo in the office. Finally, Rene Pappas, a young, attractive former booking agent at the Ashley Famous Agency, was hired as 'director of personal appearances.'

With all these additional expenses, Grillo was constantly searching for ways to shore up the boys' sagging finances. A newly formed entertainment company called Filmways, with ready investment capital, was looking for projects, and Grillo was able to negotiate a clever deal with Filmways president Dick St John. Grillo had already discussed the possibility of the Beach Boys going into business with Wally Heider, who owned a successful recording studio on Selma and Cahuenga avenues in Hollywood. Heider intended to open a second studio in Los Angeles, as well as a third in San Francisco, and Grillo convinced Filmways to put up all the capital to buy the Heider studios. Thereafter the Beach Boys would record all their records with Wally Heider. In return the group would own 25 per cent of the studios. Not long after the deal was closed, Brian decided he didn't like the sound at Heider's, and within two years they were 'bumped out of the deal' by Filmways. 'They paid us off,' Grillo said, 'for about three hundred thousand dollars net for our twenty five per cent.'

However, Filmways was also interested in building a library of music-publishing rights – considered one of the soundest show-business investments – and Grillo went to speak to Murry about selling a piece of Bri-Mur publish-

274

ing, which owned Sea of Tunes, the complete catalog of Beach Boys songs. 'Filmways wanted to buy out the catalog,' Grillo said, 'but the group would still retain a fifty per cent interest in perpetuity in the publishing, and that would revert to the guys after Filmways recouped the entire amount of money they paid.'

But at the moment, Murry Wilson wasn't interested in Filmways's offer – although he had been seriously contemplating selling Sea of Tunes himself. Murry had already decided that Brian and the Beach Boys were finished. Some would say he reveled in the idea. As far as Murry was concerned, Brian's songs were so specific to the Beach Boys that they would be next to worthless to anyone else. More important, Murry had a basic, jealous distrust of anyone involved with the Beach Boys, including Nick Grillo, and he was shopping around to find his own deal. Murry's deal, not surprisingly, turned out to be one that would completely devastate Brian. According to Chuck Kaye, then vice-president of Irving Almo Music, the publishing arm of A&M Records, 'It was a wonderful deal' – for Irving Almo. 'Seven hundred thousand dollars for one hundred per cent of the songs,' Kaye said. 'At the time everybody thought I was crazy. The trend in music was English rock, like Black Sabbath and Led Zeppelin. The Beach Boys were history, the squarest music.' But Kaye had absolute faith in Brian's music. 'He was a musical genius with a sense of pop music behind him better than anybody I had ever come in contact with.' As for Murry, 'He was a sick fuck, that's who that guy was. He reared a brilliant genius of a son, raised him as a total neurotic. Look what could have been and what is.'

When Murry told Brian that he negotiated a deal with Irving Almo to sell 100 per cent of every song he had ever written – Brian was distraught. He begged Murry not to sell the catalog, but Murry insisted it was a good deal at a good price. 'Murry wanted to be mean,' Grillo said. 'Murry was Murry. He acted like a total prick.' The rest of the band was just as upset as Brian – they appealed to Murry, begging him to accept the Filmways deal instead. Mike Love even called Chuck Kaye at Irving Almo to somehow scotch the deal, but Kaye held firm, as did Murry. 'The cash deal was equal [to the Filmways deal],' Grillo said, 'but there was something about Murry, in that mean state. He told the boys that Filmways would screw them down the road and he had to go with Irving Almo, that they were more reputable, that Filmways was a new company and they might never pay. He came up with a zillion excuses.'

In November 1969, Sea of Tunes and all of Brian's compositions – his children and his spirit – were sold. Murry was paid, according to Chuck, in a single cash payment. 'The guys didn't see one dime,' Grillo said. 'I never forgave Murry for that. Brian was heartbroken.'

'It killed him,' Marilyn said. '*Killed* him. I don't think he talked for days. He was tortured, he couldn't believe his father had done that to his songs. That's like saying to Brian, "Your songs aren't going to become anything any more than they ever were, and therefore I'm going to get the money out of them now." Brian took it as a personal thing. Murry not believing in him anymore. That's what destroyed him.'

As it turned out, selling Sea of Tunes was Murry's single worst business move. Sea of Tunes would become one of the most valuable music catalogs in existence, generating millions of dollars of income over the years. The total worth of the catalog is now estimated at $20 million. Brian's songs have become advertising staples, used to sell everything from soft drinks to shampoos, breakfast cereals, granola snack bars, and automobiles. Every day dozens of Beach Boys songs accompany commercials played on TV and radio, accruing huge sums of royalties that Brian would never see.

Around that time drummer Hal Blaine received an unusual call from Brian, who wanted to come by to see him. Brian arrived with a carton 'filled with [his gold] records,' said Blaine, 'and wanted me to have 'em all.' Brian had given up.

Now came an even crueller twist of fate. Once Irving Almo owned the catalog, they naturally wanted to generate some recording activity with it. One of the most blatant attempts to have one of the tunes 'covered' was the Carpenters' version of 'Don't Worry Baby,' which met with little chart success. While it was generally agreed that the Beach Boys melodies were timeless, Chuck Kaye had the idea that perhaps if the lyrics were updated – changed from car and surf themes – other artists would be more likely to record 'cover' versions of them. At that point, it didn't seem at all sacrilegious to change the lyrics of these songs; no one guessed that in a short time they would be considered classics. When Dennis Wilson heard about this, he suggested that his friend Stanley Shapiro write the new lyrics. Although Shapiro had absolutely no previous experience as a lyricist, he was hired for the job by the A&M artists and repertoire department. Shapiro went through the catalog during the first week and made a curious discovery: the 'lead sheets' – printed music of the songs – were almost all incorrect. 'Every time someone tried to play the music, it didn't come out right,' he said. It seemed the problem had developed because Brian didn't write music – early versions of his instrumental recordings had been submitted to freelance copyright music writers to be transposed onto paper. The music that had been filed for copyright was only a rudimentary facsimile of Brian's original music.

Shapiro took this problem directly to Brian. Brian seemed pleased that someone cared enough to get his old songs covered – even if he would only share in 'mechanical' composer's royalties and not the more lucrative publishing rights. Brian told Shapiro that he had his own tapes of just the instrumental tracks of the songs, and that Shapiro could use those to facilitate the rewrites.[3] Brian had recently become friendly with Tandyn Almer, a songwriter who was highly regarded for the complicated and beautiful lyrics that he had written for the song 'Along Comes Mary,' a hit for the Association. Brian suggested that he, Tandyn Almer, and Stanley Shapiro all collaborate on new lyrics. After several weeks of writing and rerecording, Shapiro took the songs, fully recorded with new lyrics and vocals by the three of them, back to David Bayard Nelson, the A&M executive in charge of the project. Nelson loved the tapes. 'Damn, this is great stuff,' Shapiro claimed he said. 'Who are those voices? Who's that at the piano?'

Shapiro said, 'This is the problem,' and told him about going back to Brian and getting Tandyn Almer to help rewrite the lyrics. Shapiro explained that the credit for the new lyrics would have to be split three ways. According to Shapiro, Nelson was furious. 'What the heck do I want to cut them in for?' Nelson asked him. Nelson reportedly worked himself into a rage, telling Shapiro that they had once thrown Tandyn Almer off the A&M lot for being disruptive, and that 'they wouldn't have Brian Wilson walk in their lot in a million years.' Accord-

---

[3] An LP of these tracks called *Stacks of Tracks* was released in December 1976 on Capitol Records. This rare album has since become a collector's item.

ing to Shapiro, 'They were afraid he'd want to throw up circus tents and have parades running through the place.' Shapiro turned and walked out of Nelson's office, and the lyrics were never rewritten.

2

In recent years Dennis's wild behaviour increasingly rankled Mike's quiet, meditative pose, while Mike's 'holier than thou' attitude irritated Dennis immeasurably. Mike, the hardworking frontman, was more than a little aggravated by the screams and cheers Dennis would get simply from appearing on stage. The lowest blow was served when Mike discovered through office gossip that Suzanne – whom he was divorcing – was reportedly having an affair with Dennis.[4] Suzanne and Mike were legally separated, and Mike had promised a bitter custody battle over their two children. Suzanne was so afraid of Mike that she had a restraining order put against him so he could not come to their home and harass her.

One day Suzanne got a phone call from Dennis, who was temporarily staying at the Beverly Hills Hotel during the period after Manson. Dennis invited Suzanne over for a drink, and later in the evening they were lying on the sofa together, kissing, when the door opened suddenly and Bruce Johnston was standing there. He said, 'Aha!' and left almost immediately. Mike counterfiled against

[4] By this time, office gossip was rife with intramarital affairs, so much so that a weekly 'newsletter' was circulated among the office staff – a satiric scoresheet of who was doing what with whom. Although most of the information in this newsletter was a joke, there was more than an element of truth to some of the allegations.

Suzanne, alleging adultery, and hired a private detective to follow her. When the divorce trial started, Bruce Johnston testified in Mike Love's behalf. According to one close member of the Beach Boys family, Suzanne was painted as a 'drug-addict hippie' who took LSD and writhed on the floor while having conversations with the devil. (Suzanne passed that incident off as a stomachache.) Other evidence introduced in court alleged that Suzanne had endangered the lives of their children by driving through a red light while under the influence of drugs. Mike was summarily awarded custody of the children. The large house in Benedict Canyon was sold and the proceeds were reportedly donated to the Maharishi. All Suzanne received was a $15,000 settlement. She never remarried and was rarely allowed to see her children until they were teenagers.

Mike was going through some rather difficult personal times of his own. In early spring of 1970 he embarked on a strenuous fast, and everyone in the office noticed he had begun to act strangely. 'People kept telling us, "Keep your eye on Mike! Keep your eye on Mike!"' said Fred Vail. During that period the rock performer Little Richard was appearing at the Coconut Grove in Los Angeles, and a contingent of the Beach Boys went to see him. After the show they went backstage and invited Little Richard up to Brian's house, where Bruce and Carl joined them for a pleasant evening spent in the music room. The next day they received a strange phone call in the office. Reportedly, Mike Love had gone to Little Richard's room at the Ambassador Hotel and accidently exposed himself. Everyone wrote the incident off as some whimsy on Mike's part, but Rene Pappas's sister Connie, who was going out with Mike, remembers that Mike's behaviour at the time was indeed bizarre. He appeared on a local TV show and 'he was an embarrassment,' she said. 'He was taking his clothes off on the show, really getting out there, and they pulled the cameras off him.' Connie also recalled that Mike was seeing a chiropractor at the time who he said would 'take the demons out of his solar plexus.'

One day Mike came up to the office on North Ivar and explained that he was feeling okay, but everyone said, 'Mike, do us a favor, you might be fine, but let's just go see a doctor. We'll set up an appointment after office hours and no one will know.' According to Fred Vail, Mike abruptly said, 'Okay, let's go.' He got into his rented car, and Vail followed him in his Thuderbird. They drove to a doctor's office on Hollywood Boulevard near La Brea.

'Mike was carrying around a two-gallon glass jug of apple juice everywhere he went,' said Vail, 'kind of like a security blanket. Apparently the doctor realized Mike was right on the edge, and he was about to give him a sedative when Mike saw what was coming and became very neurotic. He jumped up and fled the room.' When he came out of the reception room, where Vail was waiting, he threw the jug of apple juice at him, and it smashed against the wall. A second later Mike was gone. He leaped into his car and took off with Fred Vail following him. 'He was flipping out, and we went everywhere; it was like the Steve McQueen chase in *Bullitt*. We're going up and down hills and around corners and through red lights in Hollywood, and we ended up somewhere near Venice where Mike pulled into a gas station to get gas.' While he was filling up, Vail called Mike's brother Stephen and told him what was happening.

Stephen and his father, Milton, were waiting at Mike's house in Manhattan Beach when Mike and Vail arrived. Everyone insisted Mike go for medical treatment, and

281

when he refused they tried to force him physically into a car. Mike became violent and nearly bit a chunk out of his brother's shoulder. Eventually they managed to restrain him and forcibly put him into the back of Fred Vail's car. The three men drove Mike to the Edgemont Hospital in Hollywood. The orderlies and the nurses helped him out of the car and got him inside, but Mike was fighting and they had to use a straitjacket. Vail wrote out a $350 check to get him admitted. He remained there 'about a week' under observation, then was moved to a convalescent home for another week until he recovered. Connie Pappas went to see him at the Edgemont Hospital. 'I vividly remember him being in a straitjacket,' said Pappas. 'It was pretty, pretty scary.' Connie Pappas broke up with Mike soon afterward. In later years Mike would explain away the incident, saying he had been 'tainted by the Wilson blood.'

3

In the late summer of 1969, Dennis was waiting in line at the Bruin Theater in Westwood to see *Midnight Cowboy* with his friends John Vincent and Stanley Shapiro. The line snaked around the corner, past the windows of the local branch of a popular restaurant chain, the Hamburger Hamlet. Dennis happened to glance in the window. Not more than ten feet away, behind the cashier's counter, stood one of the prettiest women he had ever seen. He mentioned the girl at the cash register several times to his friends until the line started to move. No one thought anything about it until a few nights later, when Dennis was out cavorting with Stanley Shapiro and asked if they could go into the Hamburger Hamlet for dinner.

While they ate, Dennis could not take his eyes off the girl behind the cash register. 'She's beautiful, huh, don't you think?' Dennis kept asking Stanley, who was by now accustomed to Dennis's sudden infatuations with women. 'I'm going to go up there and talk to her,' he said. Dennis left the table and went to the cashier's desk to ask for change.

The girl behind the desk was twenty-three-year-old Barbara Charren. Born and raised in Indiana, she had moved to Los Angeles with her parents when she was ten years old. She had long dark hair, beautiful blue-gray eyes, and a sweet, Mona Lisa-like smile. There was a warm, charming quality about her, as well as an intelligence that intimidated Dennis. Barbara Charren well remembers Dennis coming up to the cashier's desk that night. 'He acted like a three-year-old kid with a crush,' she said, 'fumbling for his money and staring, acting nervous. I had no idea who he was, but I thought he was real cute.'

The Hamburger Hamlet in Westwood quickly became Dennis's favorite place to eat dinner. He would come by with a friend as often as three times a week and try to make conversation with her. 'I didn't take him seriously at all,' Barbara remembered, 'and then all of a sudden he stopped coming in, and that's when I paid attention.' A few weeks later Dennis showed up again and Barbara asked him where he'd been.

'Have you ever heard of a group called the Beach Boys?' Dennis asked her.

'Sure,' Barbara said. 'Everybody knows who the Beach Boys are.'

'Well, I'm with the Beach Boys and we were just on tour. I'm the drummer,' he said.

By the end of that conversation, Dennis had enough confidence to ask her out on a date, and Barbara liked him enough to accept. It was the beginning of the soundest, most heartfelt relationship of Dennis's life. The night of their first date Dennis borrowed Brian's Rolls-Royce and asked a friend to pick up Barbara (since he had recently lost his driver's license for various driving offenses). Barbara was driven to Dennis's tiny apartment below Gregg Jakobson's house on Beverly Glen, where she found Dennis at the piano, working with Jakobson on a new song called 'Forever.' It was a beautiful love song, about a love that would last an eternity, and it became the song of their relationship. Later that night they went to Pink's Hot Dog Stand for dinner, and Barbara was completely charmed.

Barbara Charren quickly became the center of Dennis's world, stabilizing his life after his traumatic divorce from Carol and the ugliness of his relationship with Manson. They showered each other with attention and affection, and the two could not bear to be apart. For Barbara, Dennis was a fascinating combination of lost little boy and sexy young man. A night out with him was a whirlwind of activity and excitement. He was funny, unpredictable, and full of boundless energy. They called each other 'Big Poop' and 'Little Poop.' 'Dennis made you feel alive in a way not many people do,' Barbara remembered. 'Dennis impacts on your life. There's the other side of it too – the crash landing. But in the beginning he's always there and it's exciting, something most people never got to feel in their lives, and it really shakes you.' Less than four months after they started going out, Dennis asked Barbara to marry him as soon as his divorce from Carol was final. They planned the wedding for April 1970, and made reservations at the

284

Hana Lei Plantation Hotel in Hawaii. However, when the date rolled around, the divorce from Carol wasn't yet legal – there was a sixty-day waiting period till he was free to marry – so they decided to go to Hawaii anyway and pretend it was their wedding. In Hawaii Barbara became pregnant with their first child, and they were married when Barbara was four months pregnant, on August 4, 1970. A son, Michael was born on February 19, 1971.

About this time, a new movie was being cast – *Two-Lane Blacktop*, directed by Monte Hellman. Singer James Taylor was to star, along with another, as yet unnamed male. The producers hoped to snag another big name from the recording industry for this 'road movie' about a cross-country race between a gray 1955 Chevrolet and a GTO. When Dennis heard about the film, he asked Nick Grillo to arrange an interview for him and Fred Vail drove him to the audition. During the ride over, Dennis got cold feet. 'Maybe I shouldn't even audition,' he said, but Vail encouraged him to go in. Dennis's audition left much to be desired as far as acting ability was concerned, but his personal appeal was evident, as was his physical attractiveness. Two weeks later, Dennis was astonished to learn that he had gotten the part. The rest of the Beach Boys, more than a little jealous, heard the news within an hour. Dennis was going to be a movie star.

4

By January of 1970 Nick Grillo had been able to set up a recording contract with Warner Brothers Records to distribute Beach Boys products on the Reprise label. Other Beach Boys products would be distributed by

Starday-King out of Nashville, Tennnessee. The Warner Brothers deal was for only two albums, to be delivered eighteen months apart, with a handsome advance of $205,000 per album. The cornerstone of the deal was Mo Ostin, the venerable president of Warner Brothers Records and a long-standing Beach Boys fan who had been convinced by Grillo that Brian would be able to produce and write. According to David Berson, Ostin's executive assistant at the time, 'Mo loved them.' Moreover, Ostin believed that the Beach Boys held a special place in American musical history – they were too important, both to American culture and the music business in general, to be abandoned because of a losing streak. Naturally, on the business side, it was important to Warner Brothers that Brian become an integral part of the recording process. Brian's services as producer and composer were written into the contract, although, curiously, he never got around to signing the contract himself.[5] But around the Burbank offices of Warner Brothers, few people actually believed that Brian would be able to pull it together, and the deal was commonly known as 'Mo's Folly.'

Sure enough, the first album the group submitted to Warner Brothers was rejected. Originally titled *Add Some Music*, from the single titled 'Add Some Music to Your Day,' the album didn't have an all-important hit single and was thought to be weak by Warner executives. 'It seemed like an amazing thing to do,' said Berson, 'to say to the Beach Boys, "This is not the kind of an album we want to pay for." Contractually we didn't have any right to reject albums.' Now, feeling more insulted and disgrun-

[5] In the Beach Boys' corporate structure, three out of five votes was legally binding for the group. David Berson made sure Brian's signature was obtained when the contract was renewed.

tled than they had with Capitol, the Beach Boys edited out five songs from the album and replaced them, retitled the album *Sunflower*, and convinced Warner Brothers to take a chance with it. The single 'Add Some Music to Your Day' was bought by wholesalers at a promising rate – one of the highest-selling orders that Warner had ever received. But the single received little or no radio airplay, and sat in record bins gathering dust until it was returned. The album, released August 31, fared no better – it turned out to be the worst-selling album to that point in the Beach Boys' career. As usual, England had the opposite reaction – the public loved the album, and *Sunflower* was acclaimed in the British press as 'the Beach Boys' *Sergeant Pepper*.' The group left for Great Britain to perform at sell-out concerts, where they were mobbed by fans. At home, however, their reputation as has-beens solidified.

Although Brian spent most of his time in bed, he ventured out occasionally, sometimes to visit his friend Danny Hutton, or to shop at the Radiant Radish, a health-food store in which he had invested during the summer of 1969, with his cousin Steve Korthof and road manager Arnie Geller. An offshoot of Brian's preoccupation with vegetables, and financed for only $15,000, the Radiant Radish was located in West Hollywood across from the Black Rabbit Inn. Occasionally, late at night, dressed only in pajamas and bathrobe, Brian would go to the store and raid the vitamin supplies, making off with as much as a thousand dollars' worth of stock. At other times he would wait on surprised customers. One night *Rolling Stone* writer Tom Nolan stumbled in after a late movie to discover the store deserted, except for Brian. When Nolan tried to buy a bottle of vitamin B-12, Brian refused to sell it to him unless it had been prescribed by a

287

doctor. Fred Vail remembers Brian going to the store one night to count the day's grosses. They were just a few dollars shy of $600 – the best tally so far – and Vail bought a bottle of vitamin C to push them over. 'Here was this genius songwriter,' said Vail, 'a real spokesman for the sixties, and the six hundred dollars was the only thing that mattered to Brian for the day.' But the store was poorly run and under-capitalized, and when Brian grew bored with it he closed the shop on July 29, 1970.

The same night the Radiant Radish closed, Brian was scheduled to help promote the *Sunflower* album with his first full-length radio interview in months. Along with Mike Love and Bruce Johnston, Brian went over to Pacifica Radio, KPFK, where they were interviewed by Jack Rieley, a tall, rotund, deep-voiced announcer with long dark hair. Brian had first met Jack Rieley at the Radiant Radish when he walked in one night and introduced himself: 'Hi, I'm Jack Rieley from NBC News.' Rieley said he was a former Peabody Award-winning journalist and Brian was struck by Rieley's gift of gab. 'We took a liking to the guy,' Brian said, and agreed to do the interview. They covered the usual topics: why Brian recorded only in monophonic and what unreleased tracks still remained from the *Smile* album. Brian also discussed the Beach Boys' current business and recording problems. But more important than the interview itself was the impression the interviewer made on Brian.

A little over a week later, on August 8, Jack Rieley wrote the Beach Boys a six-page memo about their career dilemma. Divided into three sections, the memo's main points were '(1) What are the causes of the problem; (2) What have been the effects of the problems; and (3) What is the solution to the problem.' The ego-pumping, soothing memo, which encapsulated the Beach Boys' well-known struggle for public acceptance and relevance in an era of hip rock-and-roll, was full of references to 'heavy, trippy' music, 'funky' music, and 'lack of recognition of your profound creativity.' Rieley recommended a publicity-promotion campaign to educate the public, which included a promotional mail-out to disc jockeys. The memo ended with the sentence, 'The creativity of the communications man has to match the creativity of the musicians and the producer in order to meet with the success you guys deserve and must have.'

There was really nothing new in the memo, nor any bright ideas, and it was not even written in the style of a Peabody Award-winning journalist. But it was clear that Rieley had tremendous clarity of thought and that he wanted to be involved with the Beach Boys in an important way. Mike Love and Carl liked what Rieley said, and although they hardly knew what a Peabody Award was, Rieley's credentials seemed impressive. The Beach Boys trusted and believed in Jack, and suddenly, before anyone else could voice an objection, Jack Rieley was in charge of public relations and general direction of the Beach Boys at a reported salary of $600 a week.

John Frank Rieley III was born in Milwaukee on November 24, 1942, and was the elder of two sons. He grew up in the community of Bayside with his brother James and graduated from Nicolet High School in the suburb of Glendale. After attending Beloit College in Wisconsin for a short time, he got a job in the news department at a local Beloit radio station. Bright, a smooth talker, and a good salesperson, Jack grew bored quickly and liked to keep on the move. He worked at another radio station in Wilmington, Delaware, and then moved to San Juan, Puerto Rico, where, he told the Beach Boys, he had been news director for NBC. At one point he returned to Milwaukee, and then went to New York to form his own company, Hand Music, and recorded a group called Space. He also said he had once been executive administrator to the Democratic party of the state of Delaware and that he was a personal friend of Robert Kennedy. He moved to Los Angeles in the late sixties and wound up at KPFK, where he was a disc jockey and announcer when he met the Beach Boys.

'Jack Rieley did not amuse me,' Nick Grillo said grimly. 'I think we might have worked well together, but it became a situation in which the more power the guys gave him, the more he abused it. There were a number of things that were happening at the time, the most important of which was that the Beach Boys and I were falling out of love. Nothing was happening in their careers, and they refused to listen to career guidance. They were just sitting back and waiting for a new voice, and Jack Rieley was that voice.'

5

On Labor Day weekend of 1970 a telegram arrived at the Beach Boys' offices from Van Dyke Parks. Van Dyke had been working on the board of the upcoming Big Sur Folk Festival, which was being organized by Joan Baez. That year the festival would take place at the Monterey fairgrounds – the same location as the festival the Beach Boys had decided not to play, with such disastrous results. Many connected with the group felt that now the Beach Boys had a chance to make it up. But not everyone was for it. Mike Love was especially worried about Joan Baez's prominent sponsorship of the festival. 'Oh my

God,' he said in all seriousness when he heard about it. 'How can we play up there? I think she's a commie.' A tug-of-war quickly ensued over whether or not the group should play Big Sur. One of the stumbling blocks, as far as the Beach Boys were concerned, was that A&M Records intended to make a live recording of the festival. Some group members thought they should only play if the recording could be released on Brother Records. This was a ludicrous demand, considering the state of the Beach Boys' recording careers, yet they insisted Grillo make the proposal. As a result, they were practically uninvited to the festival and only Rene Pappas's gentle diplomacy ensured them a spot on the bill.

Jack Rieley was all for having the Beach Boys play at Big Sur. He knew the festival would receive media attention and hoped the rock world would discover that the Beach Boys were not just a good, enjoyable live act, but a terrific one. While audiences expected a nostalgia act, the Beach Boys were indeed much more. Alive and vibrant onstage with a tight, solid sound, their show was near-dazzling.

As Rieley hoped, the Beach Boys received rave reviews at the festival, and almost immediately afterward Jack encouraged them to book themselves into a four-night appearance at the Whiskey A Go Go, the small but venerable rock club on Sunset Boulevard. Although the Whiskey's fame had decreased since its heyday in the sixties, it still provided an excellent local showcase for the Beach Boys to prove their stuff. This was their first Los Angeles performance in four years and much to the surprise and delight of everyone involved, the Beach Boys packed the house all four nights. According to Bruce Johnston, 'the line went three blocks up [around the corner].' The group even managed to get Brian onstage for one set, but his appearance lasted no more than a few minutes. Stoned and spiraling into his increasing paranoia, Brian claimed the sound of the giant speakers caused a painful buzzing in his ear. He disappeared backstage, halfway through the performance.

As the months went by, Jack Rieley's control over the group began to solidify, while the antagonism between him and Nick Grillo came to a head. Grillo ran the office with businesslike precision – some might say military precision – and Rieley was the antithesis of Grillo. Hypochondriacal and frequently sick, Jack Rieley would often not show up for work at all, missing meetings and sometimes disappearing for days at a time. Such behavior was more than Grillo could tolerate, and the battle lines were clearly drawn. Yet Grillo was not able to fire Rieley, and indeed Rieley was so manipulative that Grillo seemed as much in danger of being fired as Rieley did. Said one observer, 'The situation in the office made Justinian's court seem like a kindergarten.'

Whenever Rieley's position needed some shoring up, some remarkable occurrence would take place. Ricky Fataar needed immigration papers to work in the United States and Rieley produced a personal letter from Robert Kennedy welcoming him to the country. But the most remarkable of these incidents took place in Laguna Beach, a lovely community some ninety miles south of Los Angeles. One summer Sunday a group consisting of Bruce Johnston, Connie Pappas, her sister Rene, and Jack piled into Mike Love's Rolls-Royce and went to Laguna to have lunch. Although no one had decided in advance where they were going to eat, Rieley was paged to the telephone while they were having lunch. He came back to the table a few minutes later, flushed and excited. 'I've won the Pulitzer Prize!' he exclaimed. Congratulations went up all around, and a bottle of celebratory

292

champagne was ordered. The next day in the office it was all anyone could talk about: Jack Rieley had won the Pulitzer Prize for journalism for his work as bureau chief of NBC-TV in Puerto Rico.

When you love someone as much as I loved Brian, you begin to accept more and more. Maybe more than you should. – Marilyn Wilson

Twelve

1

The four nights the Beach Boys played the Whiskey A Go Go in November 1970 had one other, far-reaching repercussion, aside from raising the value of their stock among the LA cognoscenti. In the audience that night, a young man named Michael Klenfner was fascinated and delighted by the group's performance. Klenfner had been listening to the Beach Boys' music ever since he was a kid growing up in Brighton Beach, Brooklyn. From the time he was a teenager, Klenfner had been in the music business, beginning as a candy seller and security guard at the Fillmore East and working his way up to various administrative positions for promoter Bill Graham. A tall, burly man with a warm outgoing personality, Klenfner was on a working vacation in Los Angeles the night he caught the Beach Boys at the Whiskey A Go Go. After returning to New York, he approached Graham about booking the Beach Boys at the Fillmore East, but Graham was not interested. Graham considered the group passé, yesterday's music, and, in the vernacular of the music business, a 'stiff' for ticket sales. Graham said that he had once booked the Beach Boys, and after the concert they had demanded a stub count, impugning his honesty.

But Klenfner didn't stop with Graham. Convinced the Beach Boys were too good a live act to pass up – even if they might not be a big money-maker initially – Klenfner decided the public would have to be educated. He next approached his good friend Chip Rachlin, then a twenty-one-year-old junior agent at the Millard Agency, which was the booking arm of Graham's organization. Himself a Beach Boys fan, Rachlin was intrigued with the idea of bringing the group to New York. He asked if Graham would mind if he and Klenfner, along with two partners, were to book the Beach Boys into a local hall and promote their own concert. Graham was convinced they would 'stiff,' but wished them luck anyway. Rachlin called Carnegie Hall and found an open night on February 24. Then he called American Productions and spoke to Rene Pappas, who convinced Jack Rieley of the importance of trying to break New York. The agreed guarantee was $9,000 for two shows, with a top ticket price of only $5.50. If the two shows sold out, the total take would be $28,000.

As Graham had predicted, the ticket sales were slow and painful. The second show hardly sold at all and had to be cancelled, but by the evening of the performance, only thirty tickets were left unsold. Pete Fornatele, a respected local disc jockey on WNEW-FM radio, who had remained a loyal Beach Boys fan and continued to air their music over the years, was asked to emcee the show. Fornatele walked out on stage with a surfboard, and gave a simple and eloquent introduction: 'Growing up wouldn't have been half as much fun without these guys: the Beach Boys.' The two-hour show, simply put, brought down the house.

Rachlin followed the Beach Boys to Boston, where they played Symphony Hall to a meager crowd, and tried to convince the group to let him continue to book them. With aggression and fresh blood, he argued, he could help turn their career around. Rachlin suggested they do a series of two-hour shows as they had at Carnegie Hall, covering their whole career and including their latest music. Rachlin promised no glamorous fees – in most places they would see no more than $1,000 guarantee until the ball got rolling. He asked for a two-year contract. What he got was a telegram, a week later, which confirmed that he had ninety days to prove himself. Rachlin would stay on for seven years and some six hundred shows.

The group rented a Trailways bus and set out on a three-week tour, which in seventeen dates would gross $50,000 – if they were lucky. 'They still had the headline mentality,' Rachlin said, 'and they were uncomfortable with the bus.' But they were all ready for hard work, especially Mike Love, who was willing to do two shows a day if possible. Rachlin booked them on a northeastern tour of colleges, where they had a better chance of selling tickets than in big cities, where groups needed a hit record. The highest-paying date that first tour was a $5,000 guarantee at a thousand-seat movie theater in Worcester, Massachusetts, for three shows in a day. Rachlin didn't bother to tell the group that it was a porno theater, but when the boys found out they played anyway. At Bucknell University they sold only eleven hundred seats in a three-thousand-seat gym at only $3 a seat. Rachlin was so depressed he sat under the bleachers during the concert. At a hockey rink in a college in Manchester, New Hampshire, the box office told them they had sold out. When Rachlin spied a shoe box sitting on a shelf in the office with tickets to two thousand unsold seats that had been overlooked, he didn't mention it. In

Portland, Maine, the group played to a half-filled movie theater whose owner couldn't even pay the $1,000 guarantee. They had to leave immediately after the performance because the janitor had to sweep up the popcorn left on the floor of the theater from the show before.

Mike tried to talk Michael Klenfner into meditating with him every day, but Klenfner refused unless Mike told him his mantra, which he knew Mike couldn't do. 'I would constantly ask him if his mantra was "cash,"' Klenfner said. 'Mike would say, "Oh you Jew boys!" and laugh.' Klenfner would say, 'I'm Jewish? I'm going to change your name to Loveinsky.' Klenfner, who basically did not like Mike Love, thought he 'was a pretty evil guy, kind of like a secret-service agent, with a real military attitude.'

The most important date of the tour was April 27, 1971. The Grateful Dead were playing several nights at the Fillmore in New York, and because of Klenfner and Rachlin's entrée there, the group was able to convince the Dead's leader, Jerry Garcia, to jam with the Beach Boys at the end of one show. Klenfner saw the potential of exposing the Beach Boys to the Dead's 'hip' kind of audience, and he was instrumental in getting Mike, Carl, and Jerry Garcia to sit down and talk. Rieley was dead-set against the idea, and Klenfner thought Mike Love was scared the kids would laugh at them. 'It took an hour of yelling at Jack Rieley to convince him it was an important move,' Klenfner said. 'Mike Love would put up a fight about everything and then claim it was his idea.' It was finally agreed that the Beach Boys would appear on the final night of the Dead's venue, after the last encore.

'The Dead had been playing for three hours that night,' Rachlin remembered, and by now it was eleven o'clock. A heavy stench of pot hung over the auditorium, and it was a good guess that of the twenty-seven hundred members of the audience, twenty-seven hundred of them were tripping – as was *de rigueur* for a Grateful Dead concert. 'The audience was so stoned that nothing could have taken them higher,' Rachlin said. After the Dead's last encore, Garcia said into the microphone, 'Now we'd like you to welcome some fellow Californians.' Pause. 'The Beach Boys.'

There was dead silence from the audience, at which point the group walked timidly onto the stage and took up their instruments. The Fillmore was suddenly hushed. Then unexpectedly from the back of the auditorium, someone started to applaud, and slowly, like a wave, row after row began clapping, clapping, until the wave hit the stage and the audience was on its feet cheering. Absolute pandemonium rang through the auditorium. The Beach Boys launched into 'Heroes and Villains,' 'Help Me, Rhonda,' and all their greatest hits, and the audience loved it. The bootlegged tape of that concert became legendary in the rock-and-roll business. *Billboard* wrote of their performance. 'From their opening "Heroes and Villains" to the closing "Good Vibrations," the Beach Boys combined the best of their many standards with different material and treatment, producing a contemporary feel.' The rock critic for *Crawdaddy* wrote, 'They were brilliant . . . their excellence that night equaled any rock performance I have ever seen.'

Word spread through the music industry. The Beach Boys were coming back. On May 1, with Jack Rieley's prodding, they played the May Day antiwar demonstration in Washington, DC, and on June 22, two days after Brian's twenty-ninth birthday, they played the closing of the Fillmore. Rachlin and Klenfner were having less and less trouble booking them. 'That first year they worked about seventy-five dates and grossed about $300,000 which is not a whole lot, but it started,' Rachlin said.

By July 25 of that year, when the Beach Boys released their next Warner Brothers album, *Surf's Up*, their resurgence was in full swing. *Rolling Stone*'s review of the album said, 'The Beach Boys are back. After suffering several years of snubbing, both by rock critics and the public, the Beach Boys stage a remarkable comeback beginning with the release of *Surf's Up*, an LP that weds their choral harmonies to progressive pop and which shows youngest Wilson brother Carl stepping into the fore of the venerable outfit.' Although Brian had relatively little to do with *Surf's Up*, with the exception of his tragically beautiful contribution of ''Til I Die,' the album was more cohesive and better produced than the recent few before it. Influenced by Jack Rieley, the album contained several ecological ('Don't Go Near the Water') and student-revolution songs, including an old Jerry Lieber–Mike Stoller tune called 'Riot in Cell Block Number Nine,' transformed into 'Student Demonstration Time' with new lyrics by Mike Love. Bruce Johnston contributed the second-best composition of his career, a love song entitled 'Disney Girls' that was a lush evocation of a simpler, sweeter time.[1] 'Feel Flows,' an airy mixture of jazz and Moog synthesizer by Carl, was another outstanding cut. But perhaps the most special was the title song, written by Brian and Van Dyke Parks for the long-lost *Smile* album. The strangest contribution was without doubt 'A Day in the Life of a Tree,' featuring Jack Rieley as lead singer, which many suspected was one of Brian's devilish put-ons. *Surf's Up* hit number 29 on

---

[1] Bruce Johnston's most memorable song is 'I Write the Songs' which was recorded by Barry Manilow and has since become a pop-music classic.

the charts at its peak, making it the Beach Boys' best-selling LP in years and renewing Warner Brothers' faith in them. The release of the album was followed on August 19 by a live broadcast on ABC-TV of a Central Park concert that nearly filled Sheep Meadow, and then on September 24 a triumphant return to Carnegie Hall.

2

Despite the Beach Boys' newfound popularity, road expenses continued to be enormous, and profits small. Back in the offices on North Ivar in Hollywood, tension was running high. The vortex of the inner-office problems seemed to be Jack Rieley. Rieley was suspected of troublemaking, setting the group members against each other in petty arguments, and interfering in crucial Beach Boys business. The worst example of this kind of behavior involved the group's relationship with Warner Brothers, which had agreed to renew their initial contract for several more albums. Warner Brothers had learned that as part of the group's settlement with Capitol Records, the Beach Boys had retained complete ownership of the last five albums they recorded for the company – everything from *Pet Sounds* on. Warner wanted to distribute these albums as part of the new deal. Another important element in the deal became the *Smile* album. It had become legendary at this point, and Warner Brothers wanted to put it out. 'After literally months of negotiations with Nick Grillo,' said David Berson at Warner, 'Jack Rieley called me up one day and said, "Look, I now manage the Beach Boys and I've been managing them quite sometime, in fact.

300

They're totally unaware that negotiations have taken place with you." '

Rieley naturally wanted to jack up the price for the new deal Grillo had set up – $90,000 for the five Capitol LPs and $300,000 per new album (according to Grillo). When confronted with Rieley's allegations that Grillo was no longer managing the Beach Boys, Berson said he 'yelled and screamed and said they had a deal and a moral commitment and I was going to sue them. The result was they signed the agreement. Even Brian.' According to Grillo, Rieley had actually been negotiating the price *down*, but this was a hotly contested allegation.

The office back-stabbing was heightened when a member of the staff found a stack of stationery from Robert Kennedy in Jack Rieley's desk drawer. Thinking now that perhaps the letter welcoming Ricky Fataar had been a fake, Grillo and Rene Pappas decided to look further into Rieley's credentials. Rene Pappas still had connections through her previous job at the Ashley Famous Agency in Beverly Hills, where she worked with several newscasters as clients. She asked a close friend at NBC to check the personnel files and find out exactly what Rieley had done at the Puerto Rican bureau and how he had won his Pulitzer Prize. Rene said, 'I got a call back from [my friend] who said, "a) We have no Puerto Rican bureau, and b) this Jack Rieley has never worked for NBC in any capacity." '

With this shred of deception to work from, the same private detective that had trailed Suzanne Love during her custody battle with Mike Love was hired to investigate Rieley. Although Grillo claims Rene hired the investigator, Rene denies this. 'I could much less afford to pay my own rent,' she said. 'This was all paid for by Nick Grillo. What I did was I was the liaison between the [office and the] detective, because Nick was afraid that even his secretary wasn't loyal and it would get out that this was happening.'

Several weeks later, a six-page report was delivered to Rene Pappas. According to the report, Jack Rieley had not won a Pulitzer nor a Peabody Award and had never worked for NBC News. However, the report claimed that Jack was in the employ of a Washington, DC, right-wing conservative organization called the Stern Concern. Reportedly the Stern Concern was hoping that Rieley would infiltrate rock-and-roll groups that might have subversive intent. This report was photocopied and summarily hand-delivered to each of the Beach Boys' homes the next day.

'I will never forget that day,' Rene said. 'I was sitting with Nick Grillo in his office when Jack Rieley walked in. He was green, red and purple. He said, in effect, "Since Rene has done this terrible thing, it was decided among the boys that Rene must be fired."'

Rene turned to Nick Grillo who was sitting behind his desk, for a response. 'Wonderful gentleman that he was,' Rene said, 'he sat there quietly and didn't say a word. Eventually he said, "Yes, Jack, you're right."' And Rene was fired the next day.

Despite the revelations in the report, Jack Rieley's control over the group continued to solidify throughout the year. Rieley was able to take credit for every success, carefully sharing the credit with others as necessary. For every failure, Rieley was able to assign blame elsewhere. Ultimately, he stayed on the good side of Brian, who had the final say, and Carl and Mike Love, who were his supporters. But from the start Bruce Johnston, more sophisticated and less gullible than the rest, mistrusted Rieley and his intentions, and as the year progressed Johnston and Rieley began to openly dislike each other.

Said one observer, 'Bruce was definitely the one who most clearly saw what Jack Rieley was up to.' Said another, 'Bruce was raising the flag early about Rieley and felt he should have been fired.' The turning point came when Bruce was reportedly shown a letter that Rieley had written to a drummer (not Dennis), which Bruce termed 'a love letter.'

When push came to shove, Bruce Johnston left the group after seven years with them, allegedly by the unanimous vote of the rest of the group, instigated by Rieley. Johnston claims he wasn't fired, but left by a mutual decision. He didn't seem to take it too personally, however, telling one reporter, 'I don't know if he was trying to get rid of me; I think he was just trying to redirect the band.'

In the office on Ivar in Los Angeles, the animosity was even stronger. According to Grillo, 'The Beach Boys were beginning to fall out of love with Nick Grillo.' For one thing, the payments on the huge Simi Valley deal that Grillo had secured for them were falling far behind. Brian even took out a second mortgage on his home to help out financially, but nothing seemed to stem the tide. According to Grillo, 'The problem was that they could not keep up with that portion of the annual payment to the principals, and they thought that I was getting a kickback. They all thought I was making out like a bandit . . . I must say that the one person that I think instigates a lot of this . . . is Mike Love.' Grillo met with the Simi Valley owners, who were waiting for their annual payment, and tried to buy time, but to no avail. The entire investment had been lost by the end of 1970. To make matters worse, Grillo and his brother, Frank Roy Grillo, tried to take the Beach Boys 'public' by floating a company called the American Recreation Corporation. 'We were never able to generate the activity only because like all the Beach

Boys' deals . . . they sat back and said, "Okay, why do you have so much?,"' Grillo said. Once, Grillo nearly had a fistfight with Dennis in a men's room in New York. The last straw was when Stanley Shapiro claimed he saw documents that showed Grillo was getting a share of the proceeds on a sale of property the Beach Boys owned for some time in Beaumont, California, to two doctors in Florida whom Mike Love had met while on tour. Grillo vigorously denied this. In a complicated tax-shelter scheme, the two doctors were to donate medical equipment to a foundation and buy the property.

The corporation had paid Grillo's fees and salaries fairly regularly during the previous year, and was only one tour or so behind, according to Grillo. But before the group went out on the road in April 1972, Grillo put approximately $40,000 of his own money into the corporation to cover expenses. On a Friday afternoon Grillo got a phone call from Stephen Love on the road. He was fired. Grillo hung up and made some fast decisions. 'Knowing how they operated, I felt I could deal with fighting with them . . . in terms of a fee, but I wanted what I'd advanced them in the form of a loan [back right away].' Grillo sat down with the corporate checkbook – which he had power of attorney to sign – and wrote himself a check for the money owed to him. 'It was specifically for that amount of money, and nothing more. I don't give a fuck what anybody says. Whatever I advanced to them for the tour, I wanted back. I felt I would have to go head-to-head with them for my fee.'

Over the weekend, someone in the office called Stephen Love on the road and told him about the check Grillo had written to himself. By Monday morning, the bank had been notified and the check stopped. 'When the tour was over,' Grillo said, 'I said to Stephen Love, "I

304

don't want to go to litigation over this situation. You guys made a decision. I think you buried me, Rieley buried me. What I want back is what I loaned the group and what is owed to me to date in terms of my fee."' Grillo claims that Stephen Love offered him fifty cents on the dollar. 'I did not loan them fifty cents on a dollar,' Grillo said. 'I did not work fifty cents on a dollar and I want a hundred cents on a dollar. I told him, "I'll give you thirty days, and if I don't get a favorable response I'm going to sue."'

Grillo took the matter to court, as did his brother. In court papers he alleged breach-of-contract, specifically naming Rieley and Stephen Love, as well as the Beach Boys' lawyer, Abe Somers. Grillo asked for $35,000 out-of-pocket reimbursement, $182,000 for payment of services, and $10 million in damages. According to Grillo, he realized his money in litigation, except for the damages. The Beach Boys have continued to bad-mouth him for years, blaming Grillo for the loss of the Simi Valley property, for their bad touring times, and for just about every other financial woe they ever had. Grillo now lives in Los Angeles, where he is a movie producer.

Jack Rieley was now managing the Beach Boys.

3

Brian's psychological state had deteriorated further into what was unmistakably mental illness. However, it was hard to tell how much of his behaviour was out of true craziness and how much was Brian's clever faking to control the band and keep it away from him. He had periods of deep depression when he became suicidal. One day he dug a grave in his backyard and fantasized about jumping off the roof into it. On another occasion he threatened to drive his Rolls-Royce off the Santa Monica Pier, and once he actually did jump off the pier – but luckily Dennis was nearby and pulled him to safety. He said that killing himself was the best way to kill off the Beach Boys, for by now he hated the idea of the group – it was a monster he had created, and the unrelenting symbol of the demands and pressures weighing on him. He was stoned most, if not all, of the time, and now weighed over 210 pounds. His friends Tandyn Almer and Danny Hutton were not much help in encouraging his mental health, as they still found Brian's behaviour amusing. Brian spent many days by himself sleeping in the tiny chauffeur's quarters at the back of the house. Some nights he frequented the massage parlours along Santa Monica Boulevard and even wrote a song, 'Marcella,' for one of the girls.

Marilyn Wilson tried to keep the household going, maintain her sanity, and raise her children. Although a second child, Wendy, had been born on October 16, 1969, Marilyn's romantic and sexual life with Brian had virtually ended, and their personal difficulties were compounded by Brian's increasing fascination with her sister Diane. Diane had never worked, except for her sporadic career as a member of the Honeys and as a studio assistant to Brian, hiring musicians for sessions. Her entire life was spent as an adjunct to her younger sister Marilyn, who had authority and power as Mrs Brian Wilson. Still, Marilyn was more than generous with and loyal to Diane, sharing everything with her, including the love of her husband.

Yet another love interest developed in Brian's life – a young girl named Deborah Keil. Debbie Keil was pretty and winsome, with long blond hair and huge blue eyes. A telephone operator, born in Kansas, she had been a longtime, hardcore Brian Wilson fan who had first met the Beach Boys in Atlantic City after traveling there to attend one of their concerts. When she was nineteen, she moved to Los Angeles to be close to Brian, and got a nonpaying job working for the fan club. Marilyn highly disapproved of Debbie's presence – once the girl was forced to hide in the office sauna when Marilyn came to visit. She was fired after Marilyn discovered that Brian had driven her home one day from the office. But that didn't keep Debbie away. She worshipped Brian and was there for him, whenever he needed her, with no complications or demands. She was brazen in her affection for Brian, and mistakenly saw Marilyn as a competitor instead of the long-suffering wife at the end of her rope. Debbie's relentless pursuit of Brian was terribly distressing to Marilyn, and she tried to keep Debbie a respectable distance from the household, often to no avail. Brian would call Debbie whenever he was lonely and invite her over.

Even more bizarre was Brian's desire for Marilyn to have an affair with another man. He chose Tandyn Almer for this role, and encouraged Tandyn to make love to Marilyn. 'Brian spent months at Tandyn's place, day and night,' Marilyn said. 'In fact, I remember sleeping at Tandyn's house for two or three nights in a row.' During one summer Tandyn stayed at Brian's house for a month, and Tandyn once went to bed with both of them. 'It's just funny,' Marilyn said. 'It's no big deal.' This relationship came to a bad end one day when Brian went shopping at Tower Records on Sunset Boulevard with Stanley Shapiro and arrived home to find Tandyn and Marilyn romantically involved by the swimming pool. Brian complained bitterly about this incident, but almost immediately forgave Tandyn and took him back into the circle. But not for long. 'We had a giant fight and he was gone,' Marilyn said. Marilyn accused Tandyn of taking a piece of recording equipment out of the house on Bellagio Road without permission and sent 'two guys to get it back. They kicked doors in and they took guns and they broke open the door and smashed it in and they said, "Give us the stuff back," and he gave it back quick.' (Actually, Brian would have given away anything he was asked for, and this piece of equipment had been sold, not to Tandyn, but to someone who lived in Tandyn's house.)

4

At this time, a new album, *Carl and the Passions – So Tough*, was released by Warner Brothers. Brian had practically no involvement in the album, except for the donation of the song 'Marcella' and a song he had written with Tandyn Almer called 'You Need a Mess of Help to Stand Alone.' Curiously, Warner Brothers turned *Carl and the Passions* into a double-album set by packaging it with *Pet Sounds*, one of the albums the group got back in the settlement with Capitol. *Carl and the Passions* made a dismal showing on the *Billboard* charts, peaking at number 50.

On February 24, 1972, the Beach Boys were scheduled to play at the Grand Gala du Disque in Holland, an event broadcast on Dutch television. The Beach Boys had been to Holland before – in December 1970 – and had pleasant memories of the trip. On their way to Amsterdam, they had found themselves fogged in at Heathrow and had taken a jet from Gatwick to Brussels. They were then driven by a fleet of Mercedes-Benz automobiles to Amsterdam. Meanwhile, their audience had assembled in the auditorium and was waiting patiently, hearing the step-by-step account of the group's progress. The Dutch audience was worked up into a frenzy by 5:15 A.M. when the Beach Boys finally reached the hall, and the crowd went berserk. Although the Beach Boys were exhausted, nevertheless this was one of the band's best concerts and most appreciative audiences. Now they were looking forward to going back to Holland. Before Rieley worked with the Beach Boys, he had never been to Europe. After their arrival, he fell in love with Holland and was determined that they should all move to Amsterdam to live and record. Thus started the Great Holland Fiasco.

Actually, while Jack Rieley has been blamed for the decision to move to Holland, it was the group's general consensus that a change, a move from Los Angeles, would be refreshing and creative. In Holland, there was no traffic, less drugs, and a place where the most exciting entertainment was a choice of 'Flipper,' 'Zorro,' or Rod McKuen on television at night. However, brother Brian said he didn't want to go. Brian had not gone far from home for more than a day in many years.

The wives and children of the rest of the Beach Boys were more than happy to be off to Holland, where the surf was never up. The move began in early spring. Eventually the entourage included Dennis Wilson, Barbara, and their son; Carl and Annie and their two sons; Audree Wilson; Annie's brother Billy Hinsche; Carl's housekeeper and his two dogs; Mike Love and his third wife, Tamara, and their maid; Al Jardine, his wife, and their maid; Ricky Fataar with his wife and her parents; Blondie Chaplin and his girl friend; engineer Steve Moffit, Moffit's secretary, and her son; engineer Gordon Rudd and his wife; friend and road manager John Parks and his girl friend; Tom Gellert; Rieley's friend Russ Mackie, who was being billed as photographer and traveling attaché; Rieley's secretary, Carole Hayes, and her husband; and a PR man from Hollywood, Bill de Simone.

Marilyn tried to get Brian on the same plane with her, but realizing this might be a long-drawn-out chore, she went over first with Wendy and Carnie and the housekeeper. The office staff twice managed to get Brian as far as the Los Angeles Airport, but he insisted on turning back, claiming he had forgotten things. The third time he was brought to the airport, his escorts thought he was safely on the plane and called ahead for Marilyn to collect him in Amsterdam. But when the plane landed, he was not in his seat; they found only his passport and plane ticket, as if he had vanished in midair. Now nearly hysterical, Marilyn called Los Angeles. Friends were sent to Los Angeles Airport where they discovered Brian sleeping deeply in an airport waiting room. He had boarded the plane, found an excuse to get off at the last moment, and it had left without him. Brian was put on the next plane.

The group started out living in hotels until more permanent accommodations could be found. In all, eleven houses were rented within a thirty-mile radius of central Amsterdam. Brian and Marilyn moved to Laren; Carl was in Hilversum; Mike and Al in Bloemandaal. Once settled the group rented nine Mercedes, one Audi, purchased three Volkswagens and one van. Offices were set up at Jack Rieley's duplex apartment, a furnished summer rental, in the children's room, which was filled with stuffed animals on the tables not more than a foot and a half high. A telex clattered away in the corner. Phone calls had to be placed through an international operator in the United States, located, oddly enough, in Pittsburgh,

310

Pennsylvania. So many calls were placed from Holland daily that the international operators knew the number by heart.

The Beach Boys originally hoped to use Dutch recording facilities but either they were all booked or there were none that they liked. Instead, they decided to build their own studio in a converted barn in Baambrugge. This was sheer folly – a nearly impossible, incredibly expensive idea; but the group rushed into it with total enthusiasm. Steve Moffit, the engineer of *Carl and the Passions – So Tough* was alerted in mid-March to break down the studio at Bellagio Road and ship over the twenty-four-track quadrophonic console. Moffit was given a deadline of June 1 to assemble the studio in Baambrugge. Since none of the manufacturers in the United States could supply him with additional consoles and equipment in time, he decided to try to create his own studio from scratch. The idea was to fashion a modern studio in Los Angeles, disassemble it, ship it, then reassemble the studio in Holland. Moffit constructed the new studio in the back of a two-hundred-square-foot warehouse in Santa Monica, where assemblers worked in shifts around the clock. Then each component was shipped to Amsterdam in crates which cost $5,000 each to ship. The crates filled almost every one of the four flights a day from LA to Amsterdam. Every time a piece broke down, they had to ship it back again. The racks for the limiters, Kepexes and Dolbys were so heavy, they cracked the tarmac in Amsterdam, and the gross weight of all the shipped parts was 7,300 pounds.

When the studio was finally reassembled, nothing worked. Moffit then flew to Holland, where he spent eighteen hours a day for the next four and a half weeks trying to get the equipment running. This ruined the

311

touring schedule the Beach Boys expected to keep in Europe, severely limiting the needed income to cover the expense of living in Holland. In the interim, the group tried to mix down a live tape from their recent European dates by having Moffit detach a 3M sixteen-track mixer from their new equipment and move it to a studio in Amsterdam. It immediately blew up, smoke pouring out, and finally a representative from the Minnesota Mining and Manufacturing Company, which had made the machine, was flown to Amsterdam from London to repair it.

Brian Wison celebrated his thirtieth birthday in Holland. He was melancholy and morose most of the time, spending every day in the house, listening continuously to Randy Newman's new album *Sail Away*. Somehow the sound and feel of this album inspired Brian, and he wrote a strange 'fairy tale' called 'Mount Vernon and Fairway' to contribute to the upcoming *Holland* LP. The story derived from the nights he spent at the Loves' when they still lived in the big house on Mt Vernon and Fairway. As Brian explained it, late at night in Mike's bedroom, when the rest of the household was asleep, 'I'd have a transistor radio under the covers so we could listen to the late-night R&B on KGFJ and KDAY. You [know the] part in the fairy tale about the prince's "magic transistor radio"? Well, that came from *that*.'

Brian explained the rest of the story line in his own inimitable fashion: 'The fairy tale? Okay, lemme tell you. Well, we were in another country; we were in Holland, and I just sat around and drank apple sap – that's like apple cider – and just sat around and dreamed. And one night I was listening to that Randy Newman album called *Sail Away*. So I started playing the album and I was sitting there with a pencil and I started writing. And I found that

312

if I kept playing the Randy Newman album, I could still stay in that mood. It was the weirdest thing; I wrote the whole fairy tale while listening to that album. It was the weirdest little mood I created. I was thinking about Mike Love's house, and I just wrote, "There was a mansion on a hill," and then later on, in my head, I created a fairy tale.'

Predictably, nobody in the group appreciated this bit of whimsy, however brilliant it might have been; 'Nobody was ready for that,' Brian said. 'Nobody. I remember, Carl said, "WHAT?"'

Brian quickly hurtled back into a depressed state. Carl, realizing how hurt Brian was, took the bits and pieces of the song to the studio and put it together while Brian lay in bed. When Brian heard the finished product, he was overjoyed. 'It was really a thrill; the first time we'd ever done anything that creative.' However, the group thought the piece was too long for the album, and their opinion depressed Brian further. In the end, the group convinced Warner Brothers to include the twelve-minute, six-part song as an additional record the size of a single to be included with the album as a special 'bonus.'

When the *Holland* album was finally submitted to Warner Brothers for release, the company hated it. In reality, the album was not very good. There was an especially long and pretentious three-part song written by Mike Love, and Alan and Lynda Jardine called 'California Saga: Big Sur; the Beak of Eagles; California' that took up most of side one. Side two was equally disappointing, including 'The Trader,' written by Carl Wilson with lyrics by Jack Rieley; 'Leavin' This Town,' composed by Ricky Fataar, Carl Wilson, and Blondie Chaplin; and a forgettable tune called 'Funky Pretty,' composed with a little help from Brian, with lyrics by Mike Love and 'additional lyrics by Jack Rieley.' The only outstanding part of the album was a small segment of the 'California Saga' and a pretty song called 'Clear Cool Water.' Warner Brothers immediately rejected the LP for lack of a single. 'It was bloodshed,' said a Warner executive. 'Everybody went wild.' The Beach Boys had just spent eight months in Holland, gambling every penny they had, and each member of the group thought he had contributed a small masterpiece. Now Warner thought the album was 'soft.'

'When it was delivered, it didn't seem that it was . . . well, it seemed like a pretty weak album,' said David Berson. In fact, having heard what *Holland* sounded like, Warners realized that perhaps they shouldn't have accepted *Carl and the Passions – So Tough* either. '*Carl and the Passions* was a real disappointment, maybe because it was released in tow with *Pet Sounds*; but for whatever reason, it didn't do very well.' Then came *Holland* and the Warner executives thought, 'Gee, two weak albums in a row – it's going to be very bad,' Berson said.

Mo Ostin suggested to Berson that perhaps they could turn to Van Dyke Parks for help. At that time, Van Dyke was working for Warner Brothers in a staff position as director of audio visual services, making $350 a week. Mo contacted him and told him he was thinking about dropping the Beach Boys from the label altogether. Van Dyke said, "But Mo, you can't do that. These boys have spanned presidencies. They're an important American institution." So David [Berson] came down to my office to play the record to prove it was no damn good.'

According to Berson, Van Dyke immediately said, 'I have the answer to your problems.' It seemed that Van Dyke had in his possession a cassette of a song he had written with Brian on a recent visit to his house on

314

Bellagio Road. 'It was a rare visit. In a five-day rush at that house, I came out with one song. I called him up out of the clear blue sky and at some point he said, "Let's write a tune." It was better than having him stare at the angels on his headboard and write tunes about them.' Van Dyke said this was the single that would save the *Holland* album. He loaded the cassette on his office stereo equipment and Berson sat in a chair while an amazing dialogue came out of the speakers.

First Brian's voice, plaintive, low: 'Hypnotize me, Van Dyke.'

Van Dyke: 'Cut the shit, Brian. You're a songwriter, that's what you do, and I want you to sit down and write a song for me.'

'Hypnotize me, Van Dyke, and make me believe I'm not crazy,' Brian pleaded. 'Convince me I'm not crazy.'

'Cut the shit, Brian, and play the tune,' Van Dyke said.

'What's the name of the tune?' Brian asked.

And Van Dyke said, 'Sail on Sailor.'

What followed was a small masterpiece, in league with 'Heroes and Villains' and 'God Only Knows.' They sang the entire tune together with only Brian accompanying on the piano. 'Sail on Sailor' was the last masterpiece to come out of Brian and the Beach Boys. Ironically, when Mo Ostin and David Berson told the group they wanted to put 'Sail on Sailor' on the *Holland* album and release it as a single, it became impossible for them to get Brian into the studio. When Brian finally got around to working, he started his usual procrastination, tinkering with the song, trying to make it perfect, as he had with 'Good Vibrations' and *Smile*. Finally, the rest of the group did not allow Brian into the studio to work on it at all. The finished song credits Brian, Tandyn Almer, and Van Dyke Parks as 'composers,' with lyrics by Jack Rieley and Ray

315

Kennedy. Blondie Chaplin sings the lead. Berson remembers that the initial tape of 'Sail on Sailor' that Van Dyke played for him in his office was much better.

Even so, 'Sail on Sailor' got the most airplay of any Beach Boys song in years, and helped to sell the *Holland* album, which got mixed reviews. It entered the album charts on January 20, 1973, and made a steady climb, hitting 37 at its height and logging twenty-six weeks on the charts – although most of that time it remained high above the number 100. 'Sail on Sailor' hit a tepid 79 at its best. Curiously, the song reappeared on the charts in April, May, and June of 1974 and reached number 49 its second time around.

When the group packed to return to the United States after spending eight months in Holland, Jack Rieley refused to go with them, saying he had decided to run the Beach Boys' careers from Amsterdam. This naturally infuriated the group, and the problem was compounded by another situation that had arisen during their stay. It was reportedly noticed by members of the group that Jack's young male assistant seemed to be living with him. In the homophobic enclave of the Beach Boys, enough of a shadow had been cast.

Carl made the trip back to Holland and fired Rieley. For some time now, Stephen Love, Mike's younger brother, had been waiting in the wings to take over as a manager.

Jack Rieley was heard from again five years later, when he contacted David Berson, Chip Rachlin, various Warner Brothers employees, and members of the Beach Boys to tell them he was dying of cancer. He asked everyone for a loan, and his impending death was so 'heavy' that most people sent him whatever they could afford. This became a hotly discussed situation, and for

316

several years people wondered what actually happened to Jack Rieley. He turned up again in Los Angeles in 1982 and spent some time with Dennis Wilson. Rieley claimed he had been miraculously cured of his cancer by a Laetril treatment he could get in only West Germany. As of this writing, he is living in Amsterdam, Holland.

I was his lover, she was a best friend. I mean, if I couldn't trust my own sister, who could I trust? – Marilyn Wilson

Thirteen

1

Dennis Wilson did not become a movie star. *Two-Lane Blacktop* opened to less than respectable reviews, and neither James Taylor nor Dennis was acclaimed for his acting ability. Dennis wound up hating the experience – the subtle ego competition with Taylor and the demanding schedule that required him to get up at six in the morning to face a long, boring day on the set. Besides, rock drumming paid better than acting. The $25,000 Dennis received for his role in the film was gone within a month.

Back with the Beach Boys, Dennis felt continually thwarted in his role as a musician. The tension between him and the other members of the group, especially Mike Love, had reached a new peak. Little if any song-writing material that Dennis submitted for inclusion on the new Beach Boys albums was considered seriously. This attitude was truly unfortunate, because Dennis was now blossoming into an accomplished songwriter. But he was brash and abrasive on a personal level, and it was difficult to take him seriously. When Dennis was out on the road, he indulged in all manner of childish behavior, smashing rental cars as though they were amusement-park bumper cars, dropping the complimentary fruit from hotel windows to watch it splatter on the sidewalk below. In every

318

bar and restaurant, he would buy a round of drinks for all the patrons. Dennis was ever the foolish, big-time spender looking to be loved.

Dennis's marriage to Barbara had long since gone awry. Barbara was more than most men could have hoped for in a wife and friend. Their second son, Carl, had been born on New Year's Eve of 1972. But there was no stability in the relationship, and no promise of improvement. They had already moved fourteen times since they were married, and the frequent relocations had naturally unnerved Barbara and the children. When Dennis lost his temper, anything was liable to happen. During one argument, he punched his fist through a plate-glass window and cut his hand so severely he was unable to play the drums. Ricky Fataar had to take over onstage drumming tours for him for nearly a year. Being replaced on tour depressed and angered Dennis even further. One night, while driving to a restaurant with Barbara and some friends in his latest Rolls-Royce, Dennis was stopped by the police for a traffic infringement. He was so obstreperous (and licenseless) that they hauled him down to the station house and kept him in the clinker overnight.[1]

'Dennis was impossible to live with by now,' Barbara said. 'He was having an affair . . . at the time, and it was very painful; but somehow I was able to swallow it and think somehow it's going to get better. It was awful, just awful.' Barbara convinced Dennis to see a female psychi-

---

[1] Dennis later told friends that he was raped by a black man while in jail that night. He also told friends that he had once stopped to help a stranded motorist and was dragged into an alley by three black men and raped. And on another occasion, he claimed he was raped by a black handyman on his boat, the *Harmony*. He would also later claim to be raped by a black man in the alley behind his first wife Carol's house in 1982. Obviously, this was a recurring fantasy, and whether or not any of these stories is true remains unknown.

atrist, and Dennis went for several sessions. The doctor reported that Dennis was suffering from tremendous guilt because of his fame and money, and that he felt he didn't deserve his riches and feared he would always live in the shadow of his brothers. After he terminated therapy, Dennis told Stanley Shapiro that the only reason he went every week was to see if he could talk the doctor into sleeping with him.

'I was graced with the knowledge there was nothing I could do,' Barbara said, 'nothing I had to take personally anymore. The illusion was gone, and I got to see Dennis for who he was and me for who I was. I either had to accept it the way it was or move on.' Within a year, Barbara would decide to move on.

One of the few positive things Dennis had done in recent years was to try to grow closer to his father. Although Murry loved Dennis in his own way, he continued to criticize the way Dennis led his life. It was important to Dennis to come to terms somehow with Murry – this man he loved so much and was never able to touch, this man who had hurt him so deeply and never seemed to give him a modicum of respect. Through Dennis's efforts, they had become friends over the last year. There were now brief periods when the two got along well. 'Every Thursday night,' Barbara related, 'Murry and Dennis would be on the phone together throughout the boxing matches on TV. It was like a connection they had together, talking on the phone like two guys about the fights. That was a highlight of their relationship, that they connected during those couple of hours the fights were on.'

After speaking to Audree at her house on Mother's Day of 1973, Dennis called his father. Murry had been seriously ill for over a year with a stomach ailment called diverticulitis, and just two weeks before had suffered a serious heart attack. Murry was mainly confined to bed, although he had recently been able to attend a Beach Boys concert, where he announced backstage that he was finishing an opera that he intended to have the boys perform. On Mother's Day, however, Murry was singing quite a different tune. 'I'm just going to live about a month,' he told Dennis, to which Dennis replied, 'Aw, Pa, cut it out.'

A few days later they were on the phone again, Dennis complaining he had nothing to show for years of being a Beach Boy, not even a car 'worth having.'

'I'll give you my Thunderbird,' Murry told him gruffly. Murry loved his Thunderbird like a loyal old mistress.

'Yeah, and what are *you* going to drive?' Dennis asked him.

'I don't need a car,' Murry said. 'I'm dying.'

'Yeah, I'm *sure* you're going to die,' Dennis said sarcastically. 'You're always dying.'

Later that evening, Stanley Shapiro picked Dennis up and took him to Will Wright's Ice Cream Parlor in Westwood. They were in the midst of devouring huge sundaes when Dennis started to cry. Tears rolled down his cheeks, and Shapiro said, 'What the fuck's the matter with you?'

'I think my dad is going to die. I think he's dying,' Dennis said.

'But your old man's always talking about dying,' Shapiro said.

Dennis just shook his head. 'Somehow this time I think it's real.'

Murry also spoke to Brian occasionally on the phone. Murry told him he had written a new song, 'Lazzaloo,' which he wanted the boys to record. According to Brian,

321

the song was five and a half minutes long, about a 'guy who goes to Turkey and meets a Turkish girl.' Murry had some great ideas for sound effects. 'When we [sing] "we made love all night long," you go "*aaah*,"' Murry said. Brian played along and said they would record the song.

On the morning of Monday, June 4, 1973, six weeks after Murry's near-fatal heart attack, ever-loyal Audree Wilson was in the kitchen of Murry's house, waiting for her husband to wake up. She sat at the table drinking coffee, watching the hands of the clock. I wish he'd wake up, she thought. I wonder if he's really okay.

Finally, she heard Murry stirring, and went into the bedroom. 'We had a great talk,' she said. 'He was in a good mood. We talked for quite a while, about so many things. He said to me, "I'm so glad I've never had to take nitroglycerin." And I was glad too, because I knew that would be frightening. That's for the pain.'

Murry was feeling so good that day he decided he wanted to take a walk. Although he had been out of bed several times and had walked around the house, he hadn't been outside since his heart attack. Audree suggested she make cereal for breakfast, and then they would drive down to Whittier Boulevard and Murry could stroll with her. She was in the kitchen when she heard him yelling for her. 'I started dashing down this long hallway. He was in the bathroom sitting on the toilet and he said, "Nitroglycerin," so I grabbed it and said, "Put it under your tongue." But he just sat there, very pale. And he said, "Cold water." So I got a cloth with real cold water on it and kept touching his forehead. Then I held it on the back of his neck and he still just sat there. I said, "Are you okay?" And he said, "I don't know."'

Audree stood up to hold him, but Murry just toppled over, facedown. Using all her strength, she managed to turn him over, but somehow she knew he was already gone. She patted his cheek and said, 'Baby, baby,' but she could tell he couldn't see her. 'All I said to him was, "Baby, baby, I love you."'

Audree went into the bedroom, called the fire department, walked out of the house, locked the door, and waited in her car for the ambulance to come. Later, in the hospital waiting room, a doctor came out and said, 'We're doing everything we can.'

Audree said, 'I'm sure you are.'

Audree called Carl when it was all over. Carl had gone up to the family cabin at Big Bear Lake, and she reached him there. Carl left immediately for Audree's house, but not before calling Brian. Marilyn answered the phone. 'Mare, Dad is gone,' Carl told her. 'You have to tell Brian.'

Marilyn composed herself and went up to the bedroom, where Brian was sleeping. She sat on the side of the bed and shook him gently. 'Brian, I have to tell you something that you're not ready for. It's really going to hurt, but your father's gone.'

'My father is gone?' Brian said, trying to make sense of the words. 'My dad is . . . My dad died?' He laid his head back and broke into tears. 'My dad . . . my dad . . .' he sobbed.

'We all went to his mother's house,' Marilyn said. 'I said to Brian, "Come on, we have to go," and he said, "Okay." He immediately got up and we got in the car and went to Whittier. They were all there. Dennis, Carl, all of them.' Eventually the family retired to the Big Bear Lake cabin and spent a few days there together.

For Dennis, the only way to know that Murry was really gone was to see him in death. He took Barbara to the morgue with him. 'He wanted to see Murry dead,'

Barbara said. 'Dennis needed to see Murry that way to somehow digest the fact that he was gone. He couldn't get over the fact. Murry was just lying on a table in the morgue but they hadn't fixed him up or anything. He was still all cut up from the autopsy.'

Dennis did not go to the funeral. According to Barbara, 'He was having an affair with one of his best friends' wife at the time and he took her to Europe with him.'[2]

Brian, too, fled Los Angeles. 'Going to the funeral would have been a reality,' Marilyn said, 'but Brian didn't live in reality. Brian lived in fantasy.' It made Carl furious; he didn't expect any better from Dennis, but he thought Brian owed it to Murry to stick it out. For Audree, however, it made perfect sense that Brian had to go away, and she forgave him immediately. Marilyn stayed in Los Angeles to attend the funeral, and Brian went to New York with Diane, ostensibly to promote a new Honeys single he had produced called 'Shyin' Away.' 'I couldn't go,' Marilyn said. 'I knew I had to be there with the family. So Diane was his sidekick sometimes. Honestly, *honestly*, there is no way that I thought they were doing anything. When he was with Diane, I knew he was safe. I know it's peculiar, and I felt funny about it, but I felt if he's going to go off with anybody, let him go with someone I trust. I knew that my sister was not going to take my husband away from me.'

In New York, Brian did several interviews with Diane at his side. He told *Record World* magazine, 'The real reason that we're here is that my father died . . . I went through a little bit of a change . . . I haven't been feeling too good because he died, you know. I went through a

---

[2] Typically, Dennis would forever remain irreverent about Murry's death, telling all his friends that when Murry died, his head landed in the toilet bowl.

shock and I wanted to leave town. I said, "Come on, Diane. Let's go to New York and promote."'

The interviewer tried to move Brian away from the subject of his father, but he kept coming right back to it. 'You know, since my father died, it's been a lot different. You know, I feel a lot more ambitious. It really does something to you when your father passes away. Takes a while to get over it, too. I got a new perspective on life. I'm gonna try a little harder now . . . It's makin' a man outta me.'

But Murry's death did not make a man out of Brian. Brian retreated even further, and did not return to the studio to produce more material as promised. Tired of the hordes of strangers and drainers who showed up at her house at all hours of the day and night, Marilyn had the studio dismantled and removed. From the release of the *Holland* album in January of that year Brian would contribute no new Beach Boys material for the next three years. Instead, he became even more self-obsessed. His fondness for cocaine grew to prodigious proportions, as did his intensely close relationship with Danny Hutton. When asked in later years what he did exactly during that period, Brian answered, 'Drugs and hanging out with Danny Hutton.' Indeed, Brian would spend much of his time at Danny Hutton's small, 'gingerbread' cottage in Laurel Canyon, and on several occasions Marilyn had to send friends there to climb the fence that surrounded Hutton's house and bring Brian home forcibly. 'He would get *real fried*,' said one observer at Hutton's house. Yet no professional help was sought for Brian – his problem was perceived as drug abuse, not mental illness. Audree Wilson told one reporter, 'It would get to the point where Marilyn really thought Brian needed help; then he seemed okay, and she'd sort of forget about it, not necessarily talking to him about it at all.'

Eventually, in September 1973, Marilyn's frustration culminated in a cataclysmic argument with Diane, who was banished from Bellagio Road. At the same time, Debbie Keil maintained her friendship with Brian as quietly as possible. By the end of 1973, Brian had moved to the chauffeur's quarters in the back of the house, where he spent most of his days in an escapist's sleep.

2

When the Beach Boys delivered their next album to Warner Brothers, it was again 'rejected.' It was a live album that 'didn't make sense to me,' according to David Berson. 'They took the album back and made a whole new album,' Berson said. The second album, too, was almost rejected, but Warners and the Beach Boys fiddled with it until it was acceptable. 'It was a two-record set and it was a much better album,' David Berson said. 'When I played the album track-by-track some of the tracks on the first album were stronger, but it was a single record instead of a double record. I frankly thought it was something they threw together to deliver.' When *The Beach Boys in Concert* LP was finally released, it turned out to be the only Warner Brothers Beach Boys album that went gold – technically. 'It did not go gold because it sold enough copies to push a single-record package into the realm of a gold record,' Berson explained, 'but because it was a double-record set and had a great retail price. It went gold if you prorate the sales via the price . . .'

As part of the Beach Boys' settlement with Capitol, the group had retained the rights to the unfinished *Smile* album. These tapes were expected to be delivered to Warner Brothers no later than January 1973, or $50,000 would be deducted from the next advance to the group. Stephen Love sent a memo to the group members to this effect; but *Smile* was not forthcoming, and the $50,000 was subtracted from the next check. With no new product in sight, Warner Brothers released a series of reissues. In May 1974, they reissued *Pet Sounds*. On July 15, *Wild Honey* backed with *20/20* was put on the market, and on October 5, 1974, *Friends* and *Smiley Smile* were re-released, all greeted by minor sales. In a move that would have seemed to flood the market even more with unwanted Beach Boys product, Capitol Records decided to reissue their own compilation of favorite Beach Boys songs. Mike Love willingly consulted with Capitol on this album, helping them choose the songs and even suggesting the title *Endless Summer* to take the curse off the image of a 'best of' package.

Astonishingly, when the album was released on June 24, it went hurtling to the top of the record charts. Capitol, wisely, put together a strong television promotion and advertising campaign for *Endless Summer*. Backed by the Beach Boys' constant touring and their rediscovery by a new generation of music listeners, this campaign gave the album tremendous impact. *Endless Summer* hit the number 1 position on October 5, 1974. It stayed on the charts for an astounding seventy-one weeks, dropped off, and had a second wind the following summer as it went back up the charts to reach as high as number 20. After falling off the charts during the winter months of 1975, it was back yet again for another breathtaking sixty-seven weeks. *Endless Summer* became the talk of the recording industry as it went double platinum. Its success drove the Warner Brothers executives crazy, and even 'freaked Brian out.' As Brian told a Los Angeles disc jockey, who showed a copy of the record charts to him with *Endless Summer* in the number 1 position, 'It's going to be a little freaky for me to see that, but nevertheless, I can accept [it]. It seems weird. It gives me a shock . . .' Capitol had the good sense to package quickly another 'best of' album entitled *Spirit of America*, released in April 1975. This record leaped to number 8 on the charts that summer, and logged an impressive forty-three weeks on the *Billboard* charts.

With Stephen Love now at the group's financial helm as business manager, the Beach Boys entered a new era of financial prosperity, not experienced since their earliest years. Janet Lent-Coop, a one-time secretary and book-keeper who had been with the boys for five years, was named as administrative assistant.

Stephen Love seemed in many ways the antithesis of his brother Mike. He was a quiet, introverted, well-educated man whose primary interest was in figures. 'He worked very hard for the Beach Boys,' Janet Lent-Coop says. 'His whole heart and soul was in what they did.' First, he fired the bookkeepers, and managed to bring the accounts payable as up to date as possible. Stephen hated the Ivar Street offices – they were impractical, claustro-phobic, and dark because there were no windows. He moved the Beach Boys' offices to 3621 Rosecrans Avenue in Manhattan Beach, a small, two-story building behind a gas station, not far from where Stephen himself lived at 4201 Ocean Avenue. Although the offices were hardly glamorous, the rent was right. Since the studios had been moved out of Brian's house, new facilities called Brother Studios were opened in a leased building at 1454 Fifth Street in Santa Monica. Initially, Brother Studios was owned by all the Beach Boys, but it was later sold to Dennis and Carl, who ran the business for many years at a deficit.

The Beach Boys' resurgence in popularity was augmented by twenty-nine-year-old James William Guercio, who had been the guiding force behind the group Chicago and a successful record producer for several groups including Blood, Sweat, and Tears. A former guitarist for Frank Zappa's group, The Mothers of Invention, Guercio had become a millionaire moviemaker with the film *Electra Glide in Blue*. Guercio ostensibly joined the Beach Boys on tour as a bass player to replace Blondie Chaplin, who had reportedly been fired after 'onstage inebriation,'[3] but it quickly became evident that Guercio would play a much more important role in their careers. Guercio was a friend of Dennis, who suggested that perhaps Guercio could make some suggestions and changes to improve their stage performances. More important, Guercio became a stabilizing force, almost a 'Dutch uncle' to whom the individual members of the group could go with their problems. Guercio resolved conflicts with what seemed a Solomon-like wisdom. He quickly moved up the ranks into a full managerial position and his company, Caribou, was officially named as the Beach Boys management arm. With Stephen Love in the office as business manager and Guercio out on the road, the Beach Boys suddenly experienced a reincarnation, selling out even the largest halls. Their nightly guarantee leaped to the $25,000 range and then even higher. Perhaps the crowning

---

[3] Chaplin also had a near swing-out with Stephen Love at a Madison Square Garden concert after Stephen refused to allow Chaplin's wife and girl friends up on the stage at the end of the concert. When Chaplin said, 'Fuck you' to Stephen, Love threw Chaplin against a wall, took his gum out of his mouth, wadded it up, and threw it in Chaplin's face.

touch was when *Rolling Stone* voted the Beach Boys 'Band of the Year.'

In May 1975, under Guercio's direction, the Beach Boys teamed up with Chicago in one of the most successful tours in rock-and-roll history. It was a twelve-city odyssey that would gross $7.5 million and play to a total of over 700,000 people, despite a general recession, which had hit the rest of the music business hard. It seemed almost miraculous that within a year the Beach Boys were back on top, grossing as much money without any new recorded product as they had in their best days with Capitol Records.

But James Guercio and Caribou Management didn't stay with them for long. The following spring Guercio was relieved of his business responsibilities with the Beach Boys. An intimate member of the Beach Boys family claims Caribou was fired because it was getting 10 per cent of the gross of both tour and record income, while the ICM talent agency was receiving another 10 per cent to book the group. Various group members felt Caribou was being overpaid on the concert end of things because the group was already on its way up from the end of 1973 and Guercio didn't have anything to do with their renewed popularity. Initially, it was claimed, the disparity would balance out in the end because it was alleged that James Guercio promised he would get more productivity out of Brian. When this didn't happen, Stephen Love reluctantly fired him. However, many observers suggest the Beach Boys followed an old pattern of jettisoning personnel when their financial situation improved. Now Stephen Love took over as *de facto* business manager.

3

By this time Dennis Wilson had found the new love of his life, the *Harmony*. A sleek, impressive sailing vessel, built by the Azuma boat company in Japan in 1950, the *Harmony* was originally christened the *Watadori*, which means 'bird of passage.' The boat was constructed with materials from all over the world, including teak from Burma, mahogany from the Philippines, and brass fittings made in Scotland. With a sixteen-foot beam and four large plate-glass windows, the boat had an air of spaciousness below deck. Dennis needed $50,000 to buy it, and Stephen Love helped him get 100 per cent financing through a local bank. Dennis put the boat in drydock and began to pour tens of thousands of dollars into its renovation.

On Saturday night, October 5, 1974, after working on the boat all day, Dennis went for dinner to Mr Chow, a chic Chinese restaurant in Beverly Hills. As he sat with his friend Steve Kalenich, Dennis noticed, at a large round table across the room, one of the most beautiful girls he had ever set his eyes on. Yes, for Dennis there were lots of beautiful girls, and each of them was more beautiful than the last, but this girl was different. It wasn't simply that she was blond and had blue eyes so electric they shone across the restaurant; it wasn't simply that her figure was provocative and she radiated an animal sexuality (like his own). This girl had poise, a worldly, aloof sophistication that was rare, particularly in the world of Hollywood starlets. His hair streaked from the sun, dressed in jeans and a baby-blue tanktop that said 'France' across the front, Dennis stared at her. Occasionally, but not often, he caught her staring back.

The girl was Karen Lamm, Dennis was told, a twenty-two-year-old model and actress. Karen, who was dining with her girl friend, actress Candy Clark, wondered who the handsome, wild-looking guy in the 'France' T-shirt was and learned he was Dennis Wilson of the Beach Boys. But neither had the courage to say hello that night. Karen and her friend had just come from a screening of *Vrooder's Hooch*, which starred one of Karen's boyfriends, Timothy Bottoms. At one point Dennis walked across the room in his tight Levi's and Karen turned to Candy Clark and said, 'Hmmm, real cute. I want to go out with that guy.' And Candy said, 'Me too. Well, all's fair in love and war. Let's see who dates him first.'

And Karen said, 'I'll top you. I'll marry him.'

Later that night Dennis was joined at his table by agent John Burnham, whom Karen coincidentally also knew. When she got home she phoned Burnham and asked, 'What do you know about Dennis Wilson?'

Burnham said, 'I know that Dennis didn't shut up about you all night long.'

Burnham arranged a double date for them for two weeks later, after Karen finished shooting a 'Manhunters' TV episode. On Friday, October 18, Dennis arrived at Karen's house on his newly purchased Harley-Davidson motorcycle. He came in, bashfully put his head on her shoulder, and Karen immediately smelled a couple of beers on his breath and didn't like it. 'Back off,' she said.

The couple met Burnham and his girl friend Heidi at Mr Chow's for dinner. Dennis was nervous. He got the sense that Karen was making a large amount of money from modeling and acting and wasn't the least bit

332

impressed that he was a rock star. During dinner he began to drink to get up his courage, switching from margaritas to straight tequilas. Eventually he got pretty loose, and at one point he reached across the table and grabbed Karen's right breast. 'Great tits!' he exclaimed, like a little boy. Quickly glancing around the room, Karen could tell many people in the restaurant were staring, and she nearly fell to the floor trying to shove his hand away.

Flushed with embarrassment, Karen let out a little cry as she stood up and ran into the bathroom. What am I going to do with this fool? she thought. For a moment she considered looking for the rear exit to the restaurant and leaving him there, but eventually she regained her composure and went back to the table. Dennis was sincerely apologetic and spent the rest of the meal pouring on the charm.

Later, when he dropped her off, Dennis asked if he could come in. She said yes. For the first time that evening, Karen felt she was getting to see the real Dennis Wilson. 'He didn't make a big play,' she said. 'He was just low-key and charming. We sat around and talked about music, his life, the entertainment business. We took out all my old family albums and photographs of me through the years and went through them.' Dennis told Karen that money was tight within the Beach Boys' organization,[4] and that he was living in a $160-a-month apartment at 3109 Ocean Front Walk in Venice. He seemed reluctant to go back there that night, but Karen 'wouldn't let him stay,' she said, 'although I was very attracted to him.'

In her diary that night, she wrote, 'Dennis changes under pressure. Hah, nobody laughs when you're alone . . . and an ass. Very sexy, boyish grin.'

[4] It really wasn't, but he was spending it as fast as he made it.

Two days later Dennis came by Karen's house while she was rehearsing a scene with a girl from her acting class. Saying he would amuse himself in the music room until she was through, he began to play the piano. 'This amazing sensitivity came through, this sober, sensitive feeling that was romantic,' Karen said. 'I stopped rehearsing and went back and sat down next to the piano. Dennis played for a long, long time.' Later they went out for dinner, and on the way home Dennis bought her a Halloween pumpkin as a gift. Dennis said to her, 'I'd like to stay tonight,' and Karen smiled.

'You can stay,' she said, 'but you'll have to stay in the guest room.' She made up a bed for him and went into her own room, but she couldn't sleep. Later, she went to the guest room and knocked on the door, where Dennis, too, lay awake. She said to him, 'I've changed my mind.' He never left.

'It was magic,' Karen Lamm said. 'He spun my head around. I was in a trance after that.'

Karen Lamm was born Barbara Karen Perk on June 21, 1952, in Indianapolis, Indiana. When she was five years old, she was adopted by her stepfather, James Sullivan. By the age of fifteen she had blossomed into an extraordinary beauty, dropped out of high school (to finish at night), and started a modeling career in Indianapolis and Chicago that was almost instantly successful. At seventeen she met composer–pianist Bobby Lamm of the rock group Chicago at the Whiskey A Go Go. She married him a year later on December 18, 1970, at the Self-Realization Fellowship Center on Sunset Boulevard in Los Angeles. They moved to a rented house in Studio City, where Karen discovered she had a lot to learn about being a rock star's wife.

'We were on the road three hundred days a year,'

Karen said, 'which was a strain. Besides, I was too young to be married. To live with a musician you've got to have a certain confidence in yourself and a strong bond with the man. I didn't have an understanding of what life was about.' While Lamm was touring Germany with Chicago, Karen found his datebook and realized he was seeing other girls. In May 1971, after only five months of marriage, she filed for divorce.

She moved into her own small rented house and started diligently studying acting with Lee Strasberg. She quickly became one of his favorite students, and her beauty, combined with raw talent, started to land her acting jobs. Her first movie role was in the 1973 film *Scarecrow*, which was quickly followed by two starring parts in national commercials for Ford Pinto and Royal Crown Cola. Major advertising campaigns for Clairol and Maybelline came next, and in 1975 she was put under contract by Benson and Hedges. A famous photograph of her holding a broken extra-length cigarette appeared in magazines and on billboards around the world. With her career well under way, Karen moved to a larger house at 1850 Beverly Drive, which she decorated beautifully with art nouveau lamps and furniture and a large brass bed in the bedroom. It was here that Dennis eventually moved in with her.

For Dennis, Karen Lamm was quite a girl to reckon with. She was no pushover and was not at all in awe of him. She had her own successful career and depended on him for nothing. He was hardly the first famous man she had gone out with. Not only had she already been married to a rock star, but Dennis knew she had dated many celebrities, including Tim Matheson and Jan-Michael Vincent. Yet Dennis's double standards didn't cease in his relationship with Karen. Although he was head-over-heels in love with her, that wasn't going to stop him from sleeping with any pretty little thing he laid his eyes on. But if he thought for one second that Karen was fooling around with anyone else, Dennis became irrationally jealous. Karen was to discover the extent of Dennis's wrath only a few months into their relationship.

One day in January 1975, Dennis returned to Karen's house from a Beach Boys tour to find Elliott Gould stretched out on the sofa watching TV, the straps to his overalls hanging around his waist, and Karen in a nearby chair in her bathrobe. Although this was in reality an innocent situation, Dennis was infuriated, his rage compounded by the fact that Gould was wearing a T-shirt Dennis had recently given Karen that said, 'I am a Blonde Bombshell.' Gould, sensing the explosive tension in the air, made some polite conversation and quickly excused himself. Dennis and Karen had it out after he left, and Karen thought the subject had been laid to rest for good. But a few days later Gould and a friend of Karen, actress Patti D'Arbanville (the recent girl friend of 'Miami Vice' star Don Johnson), asked Karen to meet them at the Bistro, one of Beverly Hills's most exclusive restaurants. Karen left a message for Dennis saying that if he was interested he should meet them there for dinner. Dennis arrived at the restaurant in a snit. 'He reached across the table at the Bistro,' Karen remembered with a shudder, 'grabbed Elliott by the jacket and tie, and said, "You stay away from Karen, she's *mine*."'

Karen raced out the door in tears.

But for Karen and Dennis, passion and heat were the perfect formula for love. Their relationship seemed only to strengthen through each tumultuous event. 'We were so in love with each other,' Karen said, 'when everything is so intense, one little thing just triggers you off and you go off the deep end. When you put two dynamos together, you are going to get a dynamo.'

Indeed, each fight was like an episode from a gothic soap opera. After one lovers' spat, Dennis had begun moving his clothing out of Karen's house when she decided to help him. Outside in the driveway Dennis became so enraged that he punched her in the stomach, ripped off her diamond earrings, and stepped on them. Karen ran inside and locked the door. Dennis stood in front of the house taunting her. 'What are you going to do now, honey? Get your gun?'

'I said, "That's a fucking good idea!" I thought, I'm going to scare the shit out of this guy.' Karen went to the bedroom and got the licensed .38 revolver she kept next to her bed, for personal protection, opened up the front door, and assumed a combat stance.

'Don't you think this crazy little girl won't do it!' she shouted. 'I'm tired of your bullshit! You get your goddamn butt off my property.'

Dennis said, 'You're crazy. That gun doesn't scare me. And you know the Mercedes I gave you? A tow truck will be here to get it!'

Karen aimed the gun at the Mercedes 450 SL that Dennis had given her and said, 'You know what I think of that car?' and pulled the trigger. She put a hole in the car a half-inch from the gas tank, shattering the rear lights and nearly blowing it up.

Dennis left on tour the next day. He called every day from the road, apologizing for what had happened. When he returned, he phoned her and asked, 'Do you want to see our new home?'

'What new home?' Karen asked.

Dennis told her he had rented a two-story, five-bedroom house for them at the beachfront community of

Trancas, at 32184 Broad Beach for nearly $3,000 a month. Karen packed her belongings and moved in with him there. For a while, their life together was dreamlike. They bought two Irish setters, Christian and Wagner, and that Christmas, under the tree, Karen found four boxes of Chloe outfits. Later, Dennis gave her a necklace of pear-shaped diamonds, and before they went to sleep that night, she found a heart-shaped diamond ring sitting on the marble commode in the bathroom. Karen bought Dennis a telescope, and a little catamaran. Later, he anchored the *Harmony* just off shore, and they swam out to it every morning and ate breakfast. Sometimes Dennis would put on his wet suit and spear fresh halibut for lunch. Their photographs started to appear in the papers as they became rock-and-roll's favourite twosome. 'We were unmistakably the perfect couple,' Karen said. 'It was an extraordinary relationship.

Of course, the rest of the Beach Boys didn't think so. Not one of them liked Karen or the influence she exerted over Dennis. She was as headstrong and tough as any of them, and did not show the kind of deference the group members had come to expect of their women. She could drink as hard as the best of them, and when she wanted, could cuss as well too. Once, at a concert in Oakland, she even managed to insult promoter Bill Graham. By then Karen was singing backup harmonies with the Beach Boys for fun. Between the last number and the encore, she had gone off stage and given one of her friends her backstage pass. When she tried to get back on stage, a black security guard roughly grabbed her and said, 'Where do you think you're going?'

Karen lost her temper for a moment and said, 'Get your hands off me, nigger!'

Graham, incensed, insisted Karen apologize for what

338

he termed her 'bigotry.' Karen looked Graham straight in the eye and said, 'I'm no bigot, I had lunch with Huey Newton!' The humor of the remark was lost on Graham.

Later, for having insulted Karen, Dennis told Graham, 'Go fuck yourself!' Graham refused to allow him on stage until both he and Karen apologized. After that incident, Graham refused to book the Beach Boys ever again.

Dennis did not have many intelligent, understanding friends with whom he could discuss his problems. Over the previous year he had become especially close to Carl's wife Annie's father, 'Pop' Hinsche. 'Pop', who was pushing eighty by this time, was a wise and warm father figure to Dennis. But by mid-1976 'Pop' Hinsche was fatally ill, and when he died of cancer on May 7, Dennis took the news hard. It seemed there was no anchor in his life, that he was drifting. Dennis decided it was time he and Karen married. 'He wanted to marry me about two weeks after we met,' Karen said. 'But I knew better. He loved the romance of being married but hated the confinement. We were supposed to get married many times, but I would always pull out at the last minute. The idea scared me. I didn't want to get married to get divorced. But after "Pop" died, he seemed lost. So I said, "OK, let's get married."'

On May 21, Dennis and Karen, along with Audree, her sister Gwenn Korthof, and Karen's brother Jeff, flew to Hawaii and took a boat trip down the Fern Grotto River on Kauai where they were married. This time, Dennis said, the marriage would last forever. For a short time everything seemed perfect. Although they had no children, Dennis's relationship with Karen was the most important one of his life. No other woman galvanized Dennis the way Karen did – or incensed him. Their relationship burned with such intensity and heat that it nearly incinerated them both.

They killed the Golden Goose. –
Stanley Love

*I never considered him sick. Because what
is sick to most people is they just don't know
how to accept the unusual, the eccentric.* –
Marilyn Wilson, 1976

Fourteen

1

Brian was a very sick man by the beginning of 1975, and
he had long passed the point where even his most loyal
supporters could dismiss his behaviour as either eccentricity or the effects of simple drug addiction. Brian now
weighed 240 pounds. He did not shower or shave. He
seldom went out, and would appear in public in his
pajamas and bathrobe. Once he even climbed onto the
stage of the Whiskey A Go Go, uninvited by the group
who was playing. His preferred drug was cocaine, and his
access to it seemed uncontrollable, even though all his
money had been cut off and he had no checkbook. His
well-meaning friends were not much help in this matter.
In order to alleviate Brian's cash-flow problems, Terry
Melcher and former Beach Boy Bruce Johnston, who
now ran an RCA-funded production company called
Equinox Records, gave Brian a contract to produce thirty-
six sides with an advance of $23,000. But Brian refused to
finish any of the tracks – the studio seemed to scare him –
and his access to the $23,000 was wisely cut off by the
Beach Boys.

More than occasionally, Brian found a way to purchase and snort heroin, after which he would be 'nearly catatonic' for days. Reportedly, the children found his drug stash, but Brian was not concerned. Marilyn, already pushed past the breaking point, was desperate for help. She finally decided to consult a psychiatrist herself, but after only a few sessions the doctor told her that Brian was clearly the person in need of treatment. Yet Brian refused to get counseling of any kind. One morning in the spring of 1975 Marilyn called Stephen Love at his office and told him that she was going to put Brian in a psychiatric hospital and divorce him if he didn't voluntarily get medical treatment. Some believed that the best possible thing for Brian would have been for him to receive intensive psychiatric care in a hospital setting. But in some ignorant, convoluted way, that idea seemed to be an admission of defeat and an embarrassment to the Beach Boys. Stephen Love suggested that instead of taking any drastic action, they hire his younger brother, Stanley, to assist Marilyn in trying to straighten Brian out at home.

Stan Love was twenty-six and a professional basketball player. Six feet four inches tall, macho and tough, Stanley nevertheless had a good-natured, almost sweet quality about him. In 1961 he had graduated from the University of Oregon, where he was a leading scorer in the Pacific Eight conference and was named an All-American in his senior year. After college he was chosen in the first round of the NBA draft by the Baltimore Bullets, and his contract was negotiated by Nick Grillo and Stan's brother Stephen. Later he played for the Los Angeles Lakers, but was laid off early in 1975, when Stephen called him to ask if he wanted to take on the chore of rehabilitating Brian. Although Stanley had no experience with this kind of situation, he had always idolized his cousin Brian. He said he would do whatever he could to help. An extra incentive was the salary Stephen negotiated for him with Marilyn: $50,000 a year, plus perks, half paid by the Beach Boys, half by Marilyn and Brian personally.

Stanley arrived at the house on Bellagio Way one day in April 1975. 'It was the first time I had seen Brian in years,' Stanley said. 'He was lying curled up in a ball on the floor, shaking and crying, because he and Marilyn had just had a tremendous blowout, a yelling contest. I knew that little kids were usually intimidated by my height, so when I walked in I immediately sat down on the floor with him for about an hour, to make him feel a little more comfortable. Brian was right on the verge of a nervous breakdown – drug saturation, everything. It was dangerous, really. I mean, you push that guy much further and he would have freaked out.'

Stanley's priority, aside from keeping Brian away from drugs, was to get him to wash. 'He was gross. He wouldn't take showers because he was afraid of what would come out of the shower head. He didn't know what would happen, and that scared him. "Could be too cold, could be too hot, could be *gas*!" is what he thought. Then he said, "Maybe *nothing* will come out. Oh no! What does that mean? *Nothing*!"'

After convincing Brian it would be safe to bathe and coaxing him into the shower, Stanley tried to get him to lose some weight. A huge padlock was installed on the refrigerator. Then the coffeepots were thrown away. 'He'd go down and fill a coffee cup halfway up and then put in five tablespoons of instant coffee and stir that sucker up and fill the rest with hot water and then try to drink it as fast as he could to get the [caffeine] rush,'

342

Stanley said. 'Everything he did was to orchestrate a rush, a high, a kick.'

Cigarettes were another high for Brian, literally as many as he could smoke, sometimes five packs a day. Marilyn, who also smoked at the time, would safely lock hers away, but Brian would either take the car keys and drive to the market (licenseless) to buy a carton or wander out on Bellagio Road to flag down passing cars and bum smokes. A guard was hired for the front gate to keep Brian from wandering out. Then Stanley and Marilyn walked up and down Bellagio Road and rang the doorbells of the neighboring houses. 'Brian Wilson is not feeling well,' Stanley explained, 'and we're involved in a program for his rehabilitation. In case you see him wandering down the street, or he comes by asking for money or cigarettes, would you kindly call us so we can come and get him?'

But it wasn't long before Brian discovered a new method of obtaining controlled substances. Stanley claims Brian was privy to what he called the 'Beverly Hills Home Delivery Service.' According to Stanley, Brian only had to leave cash in the mailbox, and whatever drug he wanted would appear in exchange during the night. Marilyn fiercely denies even the possibility that this was true, as Brian had no money of his own.

Finally, a psychiatrist was found, and Brian embarked on a three-day-a-week appointment schedule. The treatment turned out to be a total farce, since Brian frequently refused to go to appointments, and when he did attend sessions he was less than cooperative. According to Stanley Love, this first psychiatrist soon refused to treat Brian, and recommended him to a 'meditating' therapist in San Diego. Again, Brian refused to be driven to sessions, and therapy soon ended.

343

Throughout this period, Debbie Keil continued to visit Brian at the house, steering as clear of Marilyn as possible. Her visits were often solicited by nocturnal calls from the phone Brian had installed in the chauffeur's quarters. Brian used to refer to her as his 'golden-haired angel coming in at night.' She spent hours talking with him, consoling him, careful never to make any demands. Brian was truly fond of her, and even wrote a song for her called 'The Night Was So Young.'[1] But Debbie was soon to learn that she was competing with someone for Brian's attention – Diane. Diane had made up with her sister and was now allowed back into the house. One night, Brian called Debbie in her apartment and invited her over. Debbie was getting dressed when she received a second phone call from Brian telling her not to come. Now determined to find out what was going on, Debbie drove to Bellagio Way at about 1:00 A.M. and let herself into the open house to discover Brian, shirtless, talking with Diane. Marilyn was asleep in the master bedroom. Diane disappeared downstairs while Brian locked himself in a bedroom. Debbie stood in the hallway knocking on the door, calling to Brian. The noise awakened Marilyn. 'There was Debbie Keil in my hallway. God knows how she got in my house. She was knocking on the door saying, "Let me in, Brian. Let me in!" Brian was saying, "Go away! Let me alone! I don't want to see you!" I went up to her and said, "Get the fuck out of here . . . before I kill you!" That's when I realized something else had been going on.' When she escorted Debbie downstairs, Marilyn was even more surprised to discover her sister Diane in the kitchen.

Stanley Love was asked how a two-hundred-and-forty-

[1] The song appeared on the Beach Boys' *Love You* album.

pound, unwashed, emotionally disturbed man could wind up with three women fighting over him. He replied, 'These weren't your average surfer chicks. And anyway, you're talking about Brian Wilson, a symbol of talent and wealth.'

At the end of the summer, Stanley got an offer to play basketball for the Atlanta Hawks and left his job in the Wilson household. Brian quickly retreated to his room, where he lay in bed stuffing himself with food and drugs, beating his toes against the headboard of carved angels and humming his own songs, California dreaming.

2

Eugene Landy is also the stuff of California dreams. Within a month of Stanley Love's leaving, Marilyn began to search around again for a therapist who could deal with Brian. Through the cousin of a friend she was told about Eugene Landy, a psychologist who had experience working with drug problems. Marilyn first went to consult with Landy in his offices in a two-story mocha-colored building on South Robertson Boulevard, directly across the street from Pips, a private backgammon club. Although the wooden sign above the doorway to the building proclaimed FREE (The Foundation for Rechanneling Emotion Through Education), an hour with foundation president Landy – $90 – was no more free than a session at the backgammon boards across the street.

Landy was a short, smiling man, with dark, unkempt hair. Warm and likeable, he spoke with a heavy cadence akin to that of comedian Jackie Mason. His office had grass-cloth covered walls; a low, square orange coffee table; and two brown lumpy sofas. As soon as Marilyn laid eyes on Landy, she liked him. 'I got semi-dressed up, and when I walked into his office there was this guy in jeans and boots and I loved it. I said, "This guy is great! He's as eccentric in his world as Brian is in his own." I knew that it would click, that I was talking with somebody who was well known for working with people who had taken drugs.'

Eugene Landy was born November 26, 1934, in Pittsburgh, Pennsylvania. A self-described 'sixth-grade dropout,' he attended night school and earned a high-school diploma. Landy told *Rolling Stone*, as well as this author, that he had worked for a circus, produced a radio show, and worked as a promotional man for RCA, Coral, Decca, and Mercury records, and also at Republic Pictures for a time. Landy also told *Rolling Stone* he had worked for the Peace Corps, Job Corps, and VISTA before becoming a psychologist. But jazz guitarist George Benson sheds further light on Landy's background.

George Benson also grew up in Pittsburgh, one of six children in a family so poor they had no electricity. He was first 'discovered' at the age of seven while playing the ukulele in the street for change. 'When I was ten years old,' Benson said, 'a guy came to my house and convinced my mother to let him manage me . . . this guy . . . was a very zealous young person. Man, he could sell anything. My people developed a distrust for him when he made them sign a power of attorney that they didn't understand and he got all my mail and all my checks. He dressed things up a bit. He was a guy that people hated to see coming, but once he got to talk to you, you were done. I didn't like his style, but I always liked his go-getterness

. . . He was a very good-looking kid, girls were all he would talk about.

'He finally introduced me to this very wealthy woman who managed an apartment building . . . and lived in the penthouse. It was fantastic. This woman bought me a new guitar and a new outfit. Well, at the time I didn't understand the whole thing, but later I began to understand. They wanted me to go to New York to cut a record. To get permission to go to New York, they had to convince my principal at school that they were going to send a tutor along with me – a very attractive nineteen- or twenty-year-old girl. Now, the other woman was middle-aged, and had money, and that's why he had her. This agent of mine was a very handsome person . . . She and this [agent] were very good friends, and I assumed later that was the relationship. I was just a kid, I knew nothing. We stayed at one of New York's most famous hotels, the Savoy Plaza. She rented a suite and we went to these fantastic dinners, and I got very ill. The evening I got sick, we had been to the Copa and had a big dinner there, and I ate steak and lobster or crab and they had to rush me back to the hotel. They had a doctor come up, and they had this violent argument that woke me up. I remember this woman coming in and saying, "George, I don't expect you to understand anything I'm going to say, but something has happened . . . and I'm getting ready to go to Pittsburgh. You can come with me, and when I bring you back I promise you'll cut a record; but if you say no, I'll understand." And I said my mother had entrusted me to [my agent]. After she left, we moved from that fantastic hotel into a [bad one]. We ended up going back to Pittsburgh, but a few months later we went back to New York and cut a record for RCA Victor. He got me a single deal. The single didn't make it, and very soon after that he took off. He did what he said he was going to do. The last thing he told my mother before he left was, "I'm going to be a *millionaire*, and George is going to be rich too, if you put him in my hands." He was moving from Pittsburgh to Hollywood. He was setting up what he called "Landy Productions." That was his big thing, "Landy Productions." "It's gonna be big," he'd say. "I'm gonna be rich." That's all he talked about. That was my manager. We called him Eugene Landy.'

In a way, Landy did set up 'Landy Productions.' At age thirty, according to Landy, he returned to school. He attended Los Angeles State College, where he majored in psychology and received a bachelor-of-arts degree in 1964. Afterward he attended the University of Oklahoma, where he received a master-of-science degree on June 4, 1967, and the following year a PhD. In 1970 he received a California license for private practice. Landy became a 'director' of the 'young people's' adolescent program at Gateways Psychiatric Hospital and Community Health Center and a senior lecturer in psychology at the University of Southern California. In 1971 Simon and Schuster published his book *The Underground Dictionary*, which contained phrases of drug abuse and street language such as 'roach position,' 'kick ass,' and 'knock up.' According to Landy, 'My background is basically that of a hyperkinetic, perceptually disoriented, brain-damaged person. I'm also very bright, very intuitive, very sensitive, and I'm quite capable of reading what most people are thinking or doing.' At various points in his career Landy treated Alice Cooper, Rod Steiger, and Gig Young.[2]

According to Landy, from Marilyn's first description he felt that Brian might be a paranoid schizophrenic. Landy

---

[2] Gig Young later shot himself to death in his New York apartment.

told Marilyn that in order for treatment to work, Brian would have to want to have therapy, so he devised a plan. Landy arrived at the plush beige house on Bellagio Road one day in October 1975. Marilyn took him up to the bedroom where Brian, a huge bulge under the sheets, lay on his back with a pillow over his head. Marilyn introduced Landy, and when Brian tried to sneak a peek at Landy from under the pillow, Landy spun around like the Phantom of the Opera unmasked, so Brian couldn't see his face.

During the following three weeks Landy made two trips a week to the house and met with Marilyn, hoping to get Brian interested. Each day before the session, Marilyn would write Landy's name and her appointment time on a large red chalkboard next to the refrigerator. Then they would lock themselves in the den and talk. Landy's initial drama had provoked the right mechanism in Brian. After the eighth visit, Brian himself answered the front door when Landy arrived.

Landy said to him, 'Who are you?' and pushed past him. Marilyn and Landy locked themselves in the study. Five minutes later Brian was pounding on the door, according to Landy, begging for his own appointment.

Landy swiftly took almost total control of Brian's life. Scott Steinberg, a young aide whose mother was Landy's office bookkeeper, was hired to keep watch over all of Brian's activities. A list was made of 'banned' individuals who might have had a negative influence on Brian. The list included some of Brian's closest friends. 'One night,' Landy said, 'Brian called me about going out to coffee with Terry Melcher and I said no, because of [Brian eating too many pancakes with Terry in the past], but I also said Terry Melcher was *persona non grata*, and I told Terry to get the hell out of the house.' Then a rigid

349

schedule of exercise and productive activity was designed. The only trouble was, Brian wasn't interested in following a schedule, and quickly returned to his bed.

'I had to be crazier than Brian,' Landy explained. 'There is only room enough for one crazy person in Brian's head, and that's got to be me. I have to be the ultimate power in this situation. That's how I got into this dance. Brian said, "Make me." I said he had to get out of bed and start living a normal life, and he said, "Make me." How do you make a guy get out of bed after so long? Explain it to him first? No. You throw water on him first. That's just what I did. I warned him, and then threw water on him and he got up.'

This was just the beginning of Brian's rude awakening. He had met his match. Landy was not about to sit back idly and allow him to be 'eccentric' as his friends and family had done for years. 'Look,' Landy said, 'I can't let Brian blackmail me. He's manipulated everybody for a long time, and I have to confront him at every turn.' At one point Brian threatened to beat Landy up if he didn't 'get off his back,' Landy said. Landy took off his shirt and told Brian to hit him. 'I'm forty-two years old, and I said to this big guy, "*Do it!* Take your best shot if you're gonna do it!" [Brian] said he couldn't hurt me.'

Landy supervised every aspect of Brian's daily life. In the morning, Brian was brought to Rancho Park to jog. Later he was made to bowl at lanes on Pico Boulevard. Often, Brian would refuse to pick up the bowling ball. 'If he doesn't do the bowling, then he continues to bowl,' Landy said. 'If he just sets the ball down and won't do it, then I'll hire three heavy-duty dudes – the big ones (hah!) who will stand there and say, "You may not bowl, but we're renting this alley by the minute and we're gonna stay here until you do." And we'll stay there! I give you

350

my word that within a period of time he will decide that it is easier to bowl than to sit there. *And I give you my word: Brian Wilson will bowl over a hundred!* and he'll compose again! . . .

'It doesn't matter who he is,' Landy went on. 'I don't give a fuck whether he's a Beach Boy or a beach bum . . . I'll make him go to work as a welder, if he has to. We'll see how many crazy people there are in Brian's head!'

The rest of the group, including members of the Warner Brothers publicity department, got a chance to see first-hand what *New Musical Express* journalist Nick Kent would call Landy's 'bullying tactics.'[3] The group attended a $5,000 steak dinner at Ernie's restaurant in San Francisco to celebrate the Joffrey Ballet's having choreographed Brian's music of 'Little Deuce Coupe' at the War Memorial Opera House. At first, Brian didn't want to go to the performance at all, telling Landy he was afraid the audience would boo his music. Later, at the party, with a hundred people in attendance, Brian had only been in the restaurant five minutes when he told Landy he wanted to leave. 'We were all sitting around a long, elegantly set table, and Brian said he was sick and had to go to bed, that he would throw up if I didn't let him go,' Landy said.

Landy stood up and pointed to the table in front of Brian. '*Throw up!*' he screamed. '*Throw up!*'

Brian sat at his place and sheepishly went on with dinner. 'But I had to be ready to get the table the hell out of there if he threw up on it!' Landy said.

According to Arnold Horowitz, one of Landy's assist-

---

[3] Kent wrote: 'He forced Wilson to act the role of the responsible member of society; bullied him into writing songs; bullied him into going onstage with the group . . . and bullied him into performing humiliating solo performances . . . To get full mileage out of this specious ploy, Brian was made to do interviews, most of them farcical.'

ants at the time, Landy's methods were based 'upon very very heavy reality confrontation on a very consistent basis . . . Gene, in addition to being eloquent at times . . . is . . . *dramatic*.'

At first, the treatment was perfectly all right with Marilyn, although the rest of the group, formally introduced to Landy at a meeting at Brian's house, had reservations. Brian was indeed up and around. Brian was losing weight. Brian was composing, daily, during ninety-minute work sessions that Landy insisted he adhere to. Although Landy's fees for his 'twenty-four-hour therapy' began to increase each month, everyone involved thought he was worth it, considering Brian's progress. 'I thought it was *cheap*,' Marilyn said. But then, something strange began to happen.

The problem became obvious to the other group members when they agreed to deliver to Warner Brothers their first album of new material in nearly four years – a 'comeback' album. Thus began the ill-fated 'Brian Is Back!' campaign. The 'Brian Is Back!' campaign was Stephen Love's brainchild – he felt that a publicity campaign highlighting Brian's recovery and ability to contribute to the group, especially as writer and producer, would increase their financial value, and facilitate negotiating a new recording contract when their existing one expired. Stephen designed the entire 'Brian Is Back!' campaign and hired publicists Rogers and Cowan at $3,500 a month to implement it. The media coverage was enormous, resulting in a *People* cover, as well as major feature pieces in *Newsweek, New West, Rolling Stone*, and *Crawdaddy*.

Under Brian's fragile, distracted guidance, the Beach Boys returned to the Brother Studios in Santa Monica and began recording a new album. Dennis suggested calling the LP *Group Therapy*, but eventually the title *15*

Big Ones was agreed upon – the album would contain fifteen songs and would come out during the Beach Boys' fifteenth year of existence. At first, Mike Love deeply resented Brian's control over the album. *Newsweek* reported, 'Jardine and Love were all for letting Brian take full charge, even though Love makes no secret of resenting him. Love, who jumped rope to get in shape for the tour, recently declared, "I'm not going out on the road like some broken-down rock star."' In the end, only half the songs on *15 Big Ones* were new material.

The Warner Brothers publicity department soon learned that the only way to contact Brian was through Gene Landy's office, and didn't like the idea. Warner's publicity director Bob Merlis immediately had a falling-out with Landy. He told reporters interested in writing about the Beach Boys that he found the doctor 'repugnant.' Several journalists covering the story of Brian's re-emergence were directed to Landy for consultation, including this author. When one reporter asked Landy how much he, as a doctor, could talk about his patient, Landy immediately phoned a member of the California State Psychological Association's ethics committee for direction. Landy was told it was up to the patient, and he then phoned Brian, who told him to say whatever he pleased. Landy said, 'Brian would probably give me permission to say anything.'

At the same time, Dennis Wilson had been harping on the idea that the Beach Boys should be featured in a national television special. Stephen Love asked the ICM agency to find a sponsor and help them locate a producer and director. Dr Pepper, the soft-drink company, agreed to fund the production, and Lorne Michaels of 'Saturday Night Live' agreed to produce it for NBC-TV. The special, to be called 'The Beach Boys: It's OK,' co-starring Dan Aykroyd and John Belushi, was scheduled to air on NBC on August 5 of that year. It was to be directed by 'Saturday Night Live' contributor Gary Weis.

When Lorne Michaels started dealing with the Beach Boys on the special, he found the project next to impossible as he discovered they were 'five people who couldn't make up their minds. It was unlike most situations, where there is one central figure or manager or agent. In our first meeting somebody would suggest something and someone else in the group would knock it down.' When Michaels first heard that in order to get Brian's cooperation on the special he had to give Landy control over Brian's segments, he was affronted, and refused. After much discussion, Landy agreed to allow Brian to attend a production meeting without him at Michaels's production offices on Sunset Boulevard. Landy waited outside the conference room, while inside Brian pleasantly agreed to whatever was said to him and excused himself in eight minutes, begging off for an imaginary luncheon appointment although it was late afternoon. Landy had made his point, but the incident only increased Michaels's fascination with the project. Michaels agreed to sign a quasi-censorship agreement giving Landy approval on segments that either he was involved in or might be detrimental to Brian's psychological welfare. In return, Brian would be available for filming – with Landy at his side.

At the first production meeting held at Brian's house, with Michaels, Weis, Dan Aykroyd, and John Belushi in attendance among others, several pizzas and bottles of beer were brought in. Brian quickly drank five beers, got sleepy, and excused himself. Soon after he left, Landy, who had been sitting in the corner, scolded the group for bringing beer and pizza. 'Now, when you come back next Monday,' Landy told the group sternly, 'no beer, no food, no anything. Today somebody was very naughty and brought beer. Brian's on a diet.'

An uncomfortable silence followed, broken by John Belushi's half-apology: 'It was just a friendly gesture.'

It was exactly this kind of Svengali–Trilby relationship that observers found so uncomfortable in the Landy–Wilson pact. In recognition of Landy's unique methods, the production crew facetiously taped to the door of the editing room a sign reading, WELCOME DR LANDY – FREUD WAS NO SCHMUCK.

Lorne Michaels in particular found Landy difficult to deal with. His own staff members suggested that Landy could come off looking not his best in the special; but Michaels had other ideas. 'I am committed to not making Landy look bad in this, out of a sense of personal morality,' he said at the time. 'If somebody's putting out a fire with a Dixie cup, running back and forth to the room, it doesn't make any difference to me because at least their intentions are honorable. Whether or not I like the method they're using or whatever, to go in there and rupture that relationship in front of forty or fifty million people [on TV] would be rather stupid and gratuitously unkind.' Lorne Michaels held to his promise, and the TV show aired to excellent reviews later that summer. A few months afterward, Brian would also appear as the host of 'Saturday Night Live' in a poignant, frightened performance during which Landy stood behind the cameras holding up cue cards that said 'Smile,' and 'Relax.'

On July 4, 1976, Brian Wilson played at a concert in Anaheim, just as Landy had promised, appearing onstage for the first time in seven years. The new Warner Brothers release, *15 Big Ones*, fared better than any new Beach Boys album in years, although not as well as they had hoped. The only hit generated by the album was a cover version of 'Rock and Roll Music,' which reached a more-than-respectable number 5 on the singles chart that August, propelling the album into the top ten a few weeks later. But the reviews were less than favorable. The *Village Voice* review was especially disturbing, calling the album 'the kind of music one might expect to find at a rock star's funeral.'

By December the Beach Boys were quickly growing disenchanted with Gene Landy. Reportedly, the most disenchanted of all was Stephen Love. There were several reasons for Stephen's mistrust of the psychologist. Some who were closely involved say that Stephen disliked Landy right from the start, when Landy proposed that he receive a percentage of Brian's income. According to sources, Landy felt that the further Brian's recovery progressed, the more songs he would be able to produce and write. Because Landy would in effect be responsible for Brian's increased productivity, he felt he should participate in the increased earnings. Stephen Love reportedly thought this proposition 'stunk to high heaven.' Also, Landy would reportedly charge his hourly fee while on tour with Brian, which meant a twenty-four-hours-a-day charge, plus billing for expenses for himself and his lady friend, Alexandra. Stephen Love's strict policy had always been that any touring member who brought a wife or girl friend with him did so at his own expense. Moreover, Landy tried to control what times Brian would be available to work at the studio as well as what songs he would work on. There was even talk of Landy's collaborating with Brian on song writing. Stephen felt this would interfere with Brian's creativity far too much. There was a final argument at Brother Studios in which Landy's aide, Scott Steinberg, wanted to take Brian away from the studio to keep him on Landy's prearranged schedule, while Stephen wanted Brian to finish working on the song he was producing. Stephen lost his temper and had Steinberg removed from the studio. Brian stayed behind.

But the deciding factor occurred when Landy's monthly fee, including charges for the twenty-four-hour staff, which began at a reported $10,000, escalated to $12,000, then $15,000, then $18,000, and finally to $20,000. Stephen tried to persuade Marilyn to let him fire Landy, which by then wasn't too difficult. Marilyn was disgusted with the control Landy was exerting over her personal life as well as Brian's career. 'What psychologist or therapist writes songs?' Marilyn asked. 'So when it came to the point where it was costing around twenty thousand a month, I said, "Brian, Jesus Christ, it's costing twenty thousand a month." And Brian said, "What!?"

'So we went to Landy's office, and Brian confronted Landy, and Brian said, "You son of a bitch!" You have to understand that I have never seen Brian get physical, ever, *ever*. I saw him take his fist and start to punch this man, and I started screaming. Landy said, "*No, no, no, let him do it, let him do it!*" Landy thought it was the greatest thing. He was saying, "Come on, you motherfucker, hit me, hit me!" And then finally Brian just did it, he made Brian do it. Landy was pushing me away, saying, "No, he needs to hit me, he needs to do it, he needs to take his anger out on me . . ." That was a therapeutic session, if you can believe it.'

Reportedly, Stephen Love was not concerned that Brian would regress without Gene Landy. He had made tremendous gains and even managed to go out on the Christmas tour of 1976 without the psychologist. After Landy was fired, Brian was immediately brought to a new psychiatrist, whom he saw for several sessions. Said Brian

357

at the time, 'Now I'm seeing someone else twice a week, Dr Steve Schwartz; he's a very mild man, doesn't have much to say, just listens.' Then a tragic event occurred. One day the phone rang and a strange doctor asked Brian to come see him; when Brian arrived at the office, he was told that Dr Schwartz had been in a terrible camping accident and had fallen off the side of a mountain to his death. 'It scared Brian so bad,' Marilyn said, 'I don't think he could believe it. He didn't talk for days after that.'

Brian was clearly in need of round-the-clock supervision, and Stanley Love, whose career with the Atlanta Hawks had been short-lived, was asked to come back to work at Bellagio Road. In addition, Brian's first cousin and former Beach Boys roadie, Steven Korthof, was hired to assist him. Korthof was a short, heavyset, good-natured man in his early thirties who had grown up with Brian. Like many members of the family, he had a special respect and love for Brian. Several months later, Stanley told Marilyn that they needed yet another man to assist them, and he suggested Rushton Pamplin, an old college chum of his.

Six feet three inches tall, handsome and muscular, 'Rocky' Pamplin was a professional model. He was an expansive, volatile young man with a big temper and a short fuse. Born in Minnesota, he grew up in Florida and moved to California when he was ten years old. He attended the University of Oregon for three years, where he met Stanley Love. For several years he played professional football with the Saints and the Alouettes. When his athletic career petered out, he became a model. Two of his more prominent modeling jobs were the well-known Times Square billboard for Winston cigarettes and a nude centerfold for *Playgirl*, whose readers voted him both 'Man of the Year' and 'Man of Five Years.'

The first time Rocky walked into Brian's house to play basketball with Stanley, Marilyn took Stanley aside and said 'Where did you find this guy?' A few weeks later, Rocky was put on the payroll to assist Stanley at the handsome fee of $40,000 a year. Three weeks later, Marilyn and Rocky were having an affair. 'He was an attractive guy,' Marilyn said, 'and I had a sexless marriage. He was a gorgeous man.' He was also available. 'If you put Bo Derek in front of any guy, do you think they are going to turn her down? It was easy for me to fall into the trap.' Marilyn's major concern about the affair was that Brian should never find out, for his welfare was still uppermost in her mind. She loved Brian deeply, but her love was now more that of a sister for a brother, and Rocky was impossible to resist.

According to Rocky, his affair with Marilyn was 'hard in the first place, but the money made it easier. I made myself do it, day by day, month by month, I made myself do it.'

If Marilyn suspected she was being used by Rocky, she pushed the thought to the farthest corners of her mind. She needed to feel attractive and sexy again, and Rocky made her believe that she was. Marilyn felt that after a time Rocky began to fall in love with her, and even Rocky admits there was real affection between them. 'She was real spontaneous, a great person in some ways. But the one thing about Jewish people is sometimes they think the worst about people.' At one point, he even brought her home to meet his parents and said he was going to marry her if she divorced Brian. When asked why he did this, Rocky said, 'A fifty-thousand-dollar-a-year-job, traveling around the world in Lear jets . . .'

Rocky, Stan, and Steve Korthof were dedicated to Brian, and managed for the most part to keep him away from drugs and to keep track of his whereabouts, although the job was sometimes nearly impossible. Brian could be clever and wily, and anything was liable to happen if they took their eyes off him for one minute. Once, in Chicago in 1978, they were all staying at a hotel near the airport. Brian met a stranger in the bar, had a few drinks with him, and made an appointment to meet the man the next morning at 8:30 and go off with him to Minnesota. When Stan and Rocky awoke the next morning and found Brian missing, Rocky ran down to the lobby in his pajamas and asked, 'Did you see a guy with a beard?' He was told that Brian, barefooted, had left shortly before. Rocky raced to the airport and learned that the next departing plane was going to Minnesota. Making the logical guess that Brian would be on that plane, he convinced them to stop the plane and boarded it with a security guard. 'I walked on, and there's Brian sitting with some guy, and he says, "Rocky, what are you doing here?"'

Rocky said, 'Get off the plane, Brian.'

'No. I'm going to Minnesota with my friend,' Brian said, gesturing to the man in the seat next to him.

'*Brian, get off the plane!*' Rocky shouted.

'Okay,' Brian said quietly, and followed Rocky back to the hotel.

Other examples of Brian's drifting mental state are even more poignant. One day Paul McCartney came to visit Brian, and when Brian heard he was at the house, he became petrified, although he had met McCartney several times before. He raced outside to the chauffeur's quarters and locked himself inside. McCartney knocked on the door for twenty minutes, but Brian would not come out. All he could hear were the gentle sounds of Brian weeping.

3

With only one more album due to Warner Brothers and their contract scheduled to expire on July 1, 1977, it was now Stephen Love's responsibility to negotiate a new recording contract for the group. Stephen hired crack music-business attorneys Mike Lorimer and John Frankenheimer to help with the negotiations. At Warner, interest in the group was understandably sagging. They had not made tremendous profits from the record sales, and Warner Brothers was all too familiar with the group's internal struggles. At the same time, CBS Records was showing keen interest in signing the group, not only because the company felt the Beach Boys were prestigious, but also because of the close relationship with James Guercio and Caribou Records, which CBS distributed. Although Guercio had been fired, he still admired the Beach Boys' music and believed in their commercial potential. With Guercio's encouragement, CBS became determined to sign them. A bidding war ensued between Warner Brothers and CBS, which CBS easily won with a bid of $1 million per album, including bonus provisions. As a special sweetener, the CBS deal included a $2 million advance to the group upon signing the contracts, $1.8 million to Brother Records Inc and $200,000 to pay off working capital loans at the Wells Fargo Bank. The total worth of the deal was a handsome $8 million.

Warner Brothers knew of the CBS deal by January 1977, when the Beach Boys' final Warner album, *The Beach Boys Love You*, was submitted. Once again, the Warner Brothers executives were none too happy with the product, although the material included twelve new Brian Wilson compositions written under Gene Landy's aegis. To make matters worse, Warner had just shipped *The Beach Boys Love You* to the record stores when the CBS deal was announced on April 1. Warner was so disgusted with the Beach Boys at this point that the group members were convinced the company was doing very little to promote the album. In truth, the best promotional campaign in the world couldn't have helped *The Beach Boys Love You*, which made a feeble showing of seven weeks at the top end of the charts.

On March 1, 1977, the Beach Boys officially entered into a recording agreement with CBS, with the first album expected by January 1, 1978. In addition to the $2 million advance upon signing, the group would receive $667,667 upon the delivery of each album, shooting up to a bonus $1,167,000 if the preceding album sold more than 1.5 million copies. The basic royalty rate was a dollar per album and fifteen cents a single. In return, the CBS contracts placed many demands on the group, as was only fair. Brian was required to compose at least four songs on each album, and co-write at least 70 per cent of all the material, acting as producer or co-producer with Dennis or Carl. Although it wasn't necessary for Brian to tour, the group was required to play thirty dates a year in the United States in large arenas to back up the albums, in addition to two tours within four years in at least seven European cities, and one tour in Australia and Japan. When Brian signed the contract, he cried, knowing he would now have to go back to the studio full-time.

Suddenly, Mike Love took off for Leysin, Switzerland, where the Maharishi was running a study center. Mike believed the Maharishi was going to teach him how to levitate. But it was a most inopportune time for Mike to learn how to float, not only because of the group's pressing recording obligations, but because the trip meant that he would not be present for the negotiations with CBS on the new contract. A hotly contested incident then took place. Mike was reportedly unhappy with the 'outside projects provision,' which would not allow him to work on solo projects for the benefit of the Maharishi. But Stephen thought it ill-advised to ask CBS for clauses allowing such projects, fearing the company would be concerned that the provision would dilute the strength of the group. While Mike was in Switzerland, Mike Lorimer reportedly initiated a phone call to him to confirm that Stephen Love had his permission to sign the contracts for him. Stephen Love listened in on the extension, with Mike's knowledge, as Mike gave his permission for Stephen to sign his name, *in absentia*, to the CBS contracts. Reportedly, the contract was signed 'Michael Love by Stephen Love, as his attorney-in-fact'.

With the first CBS album due and Mike Love nowhere in sight to begin work on it, Stephen fired off a telegram to Mike, which advised, 'NOW IS NOT THE TIME IN YOUR LIFE TO BE SELF-INDULGENT AND STUPID . . .' Stephen also sent a letter to the rest of the group warning them to shape up or he would leave. The letter included the phrase 'I no longer choose to render my services to punks or incompetents . . .'

Fifteen

1

There are as many different versions of the 'firing' of
Stephen Love as there were participants.[1] Stephen Love
was perhaps the finest business and personal manager the
group ever had, but he was also the most didactic and
controlling. Stephen's rigid, albeit intelligent, approach to
organizing the group and its finances was too stringent for
the Beach Boys. 'They said he was too arrogant,' one
observer recalled. He was also a firm opponent of drug
use, as were Michael and Al Jardine, and could not
tolerate any group member or associate partaking of illicit
substances. He was outspoken in his criticism of personal
behavior. Stephen did not appreciate Karen Lamm or the
influence she had on Dennis's life – when Dennis asked
him to be best man at their wedding, Stephen refused.

By letting Stephen Love go, the Beach Boys were
repeating the same innuendo that Nick Grillo had decried
years before: 'Why do you have so much and I have so
little?' Nineteen seventy-seven had turned out to be the
biggest year in Beach Boys history. The total group gross
was running upward of $8 million, including the nearly $2
million advance from CBS on the signing of the new

---

[1] Technically, Stephen Love was not fired; he was relieved of his
managerial responsibilities and his contract simply wasn't renewed.

contracts (which was quickly put into an interest-bearing account until the first album could be delivered). Brian's income from his songwriting royalties neared the $1 million mark. Mike, Carl, Dennis, and Alan were earning close to $600,000 each. What troubled them was that Stephen Love's income was almost $300,000 for the year, before office overhead expenses. Indeed, Stephen had watched his money and made investments judiciously, and this fact alone aggravated some group members who felt he hadn't served them as well personally.

Stephen had fallen into disfavor with Carl for giving what he perceived to be poor real-estate advice. Since Annie's father, 'Pop' Hinsche, had died, Annie and Carl had been paying $6,000 a month to rent a luxurious house at Trancas Beach from the widow of Las Vegas hotel owner Del Webb. Carl now wanted to sell his Coldwater Canyon house and buy his own place at the beach. Stephen suggested that Carl set a limit on what he would pay for his new house and stick to it. When Carl made a bid on a house he and Annie especially liked, the seller turned them down, and Stephen insisted he not go any higher. A short time later the house was sold to another buyer for only $20,000 more, and Carl was reportedly furious with Stephen.

But perhaps Stephen's greatest offense was that he was entitled to 5 per cent of the CBS Records deal. On March 17, two weeks before Stephen Love's contract expired, the Beach Boys received their first check from CBS for $1,800,000. Then the real trouble started. According to Stanley Love, 'The Beach Boys have a history of not paying people, that's why a lot of their deals fall apart. If your five per cent of an eight-million-dollar contract is four hundred thousand – that's too much money for you.

They figured they could save that four hundred thousand for themselves.' Mike Love now contended that he never gave Stephen permission to sign his name to the CBS contracts, which drove Stephen wild with anger. Insiders say this change in Mike's attitude occurred when he realized that the CBS contract did not have the special riders he wanted that would have allowed him to record solo albums under their label. Meanwhile, Dennis, through his friend James Guercio, was getting a $100,000 advance from CBS to record his own solo album.

The group expected to negotiate a settlement that would allow Stephen to continue working as a consultant until his contract officially expired on March 31. In the interim, the Beach Boys needed a new, full-time manager, and Carl thought he knew just the right guy. Henry Lazarus, thirty-five, claims to have met Carl 'through friends' in Los Angeles. They had been discussing the Beach Boys' management problems for several months, and Lazarus, a loquacious, quick-thinking man, had many suggestions. Carl called Lazarus and said, 'Listen, you've been giving us the best advice of anybody,' and asked if he would take over the management post – at a reported $75,000 a year.

Born in New York, Lazarus had sold his family business, Lazarus Fabrics, a commercial drapery-fabric company, in 1974. He had moved to Los Angeles, where he purchased, coincidentally, the same Coldwater Canyon house in which Mike Love had lived with his second wife, Suzanne. He started a new company, World Wide Artists, that dabbled in the entertainment business. He then changed the name of this company to the Alchemy Company, with the slogan 'We Turn Shit into Gold,' but had toned it down to '. . . Ideas into Gold' by the time he started managing the Beach Boys. Although Lazarus had no previous experience in the music business, Carl thought he was just what the group needed.

One of Lazarus's first jobs was to settle the matter of whether or not Stephen Love had signed the CBS contracts with Mike's permission. According to Lazarus, CBS Records President Walter Yetnikoff 'asked me to get Mike's signature.' Mike was still in Leysin, Switzerland, studying with the Maharishi, and Lazarus flew there to see him. At the Grand Hotel, Lazarus entered two giant rooms 'the size of basketball courts, filled with mattresses on the floor.' According to Lazarus, this was the room where the Maharishi's students were learning to levitate, and the mattresses were there to break their falls. Lazarus and Mike met for the first time there, and according to Lazarus they got along very well. Mike even took him to meet the Maharishi, who also approved of Lazarus. Mike told Lazarus to write down his home address so he could send the newly executed contracts to him, and when he noticed the address he said, 'Why are you writing down my old home address?' Lazarus told him he now lived there, and Mike was ecstatic. 'It's written in the heavens and stars that you should be our manager,' Mike told him.

Lazarus moved the group's management headquarters into his own offices at 1888 Century Park East and started going over their books. Lazarus claimed 'there was a lot of money being stolen from the Beach Boys' at the time but declined to say by whom. He apparently found discrepancies in the group's withholding statements.[2] Laz-

---

[2] Indeed, during the dark financial days of the early seventies, Stephen Love intentionally claimed as many deductions as possible in the Beach Boys' withholding statements to give them as much free cash flow as he could. Because he knew this might cause a potential tax problem later, he had the Beach Boys sign statements indemnifying him against any future action by the IRS.

arus brought the Beach Boys to a new law firm, Fierstein and Sturman, who began by issuing a subpoena to get the accounting books from Stephen Love. That April, Stephen's loyal associate, Janet Lent-Coop, arrived early at Stephen's Manhattan Beach offices and found an 'odd-looking person' sitting behind the wheel of a car outside the gas station. This was a process server who was trying to seize the books. Stephen and Janet managed to protect Love's personal records, but everything else was turned over to the accounting firm of S. D. Leitersdorf, where several accountants looked for some irregularity in Stephen's financial management of the group. When the results came in several months later, they could find nothing wrong.

Lazarus's next task was to set up a giant European tour for the Beach Boys, which would include Germany, Switzerland, and France, both to satisfy the terms of the CBS contracts pertaining to tour commitments and to generate income. This tour was to be kicked off by a live performance at the CBS Records international convention being held in London on July 30. Attended by hundreds of CBS affiliates from different countries, the concert would solidify the record company's worldwide support of the Beach Boys. CBS even rented a private plane to fly the group to London. Although the Beach Boys were an enormous hit at the convention, an unpleasant surprise awaited them. The entire European tour was in disarray. The proper tax documents and working papers had not been obtained from the foreign governments; travel arrangements and hotel reservations had not been confirmed; the contracts had not been fully signed by promoters. It was obvious the tour could not take place. By July 21, before the Beach Boys had even played the CBS convention, Lazarus was gone. The tour was canceled, and many of its promoters sued the Beach Boys.

Later, Lazarus was formally fired. The blame for the lawsuits and enormous monetary loss was placed squarely on Henry Lazarus – and the blame for Henry Lazarus was placed squarely on Carl. A Beach Boys' employee called it the 'second Jack Rieley affair.' The estimated loss to the Beach Boys was $200,000 in out-of-pocket expenses, and an additional $550,000 in potential revenues.

The group did manage to play one concert in England that July, at Wembley Stadium, where one of the ugliest public displays to date occurred. In the middle of the concert, before an enormous audience of over fifteen thousand, Mike Love lost his temper, picked up a piano bench, and threw it at Brian. It bounced off the stage and nearly hit his own children, Christian and Hayleigh, who were sitting in the front row.

If anything could further exacerbate the growing bad feelings among the group members, it was the release of Dennis's solo album, *Pacific Ocean Blue*, on September 16, 1977. This first solo album by any Beach Boy came as a mighty shock to the rest of the group – not only because Dennis had managed to pull it off, but because the album was a small masterpiece. Dennis's years in the studio watching brother Brian had paid off handsomely. Co-produced and co-written by Gregg Jakobson, *Pacific Ocean Blue* received excellent reviews. The album sold over 200,000 copies, although it only broke the top one hundred on the charts. However, it was clearly a *succès d'estime* of which any performer could be proud, and Dennis wouldn't let any of the Beach Boys forget it. Mike Love was especially infuriated that Dennis was the first to go solo, and get such glowing reviews. According to Stanley Love, 'The Beach Boys were scared. Intimidated by it.' And some of them wanted to top it.

2

To Michael and Alan Jardine, one thing was clear; they needed Stephen Love back. Alan flew down from his Big Sur ranch that August to ask Stephen if he would consider coming back to work for them full-time, but Stephen was understandably wary. He knew that Carl and Dennis were still strongly opposed to him, and that the tension and animosity within the group were so explosive that Mike and Alan were hardly talking to Dennis and Carl. They traveled separately and even stayed at different hotels. Among the Beach Boys' staff, the two contingents were known as the 'meditators' and the 'free-livers.' Stephen did agree to discuss returning to the group at a meeting to be held in New York over Labor Day weekend at the end of a northeastern tour. A day earlier, the Beach Boys had bowled the city over with a free concert in Central Park, attended by over 150,000 people, according to police estimates.

The meeting with Stephen was held at the Sherry Netherlands hotel, where the free-livers were staying (the meditators were at the Plaza). Stephen brought with him a 'memorandum agreement' stating the terms he wanted. These were basically the same terms he had tendered to them that January, three months before his employment contract was to expire. He proposed a sliding scale of 5 per cent of the first $5 million and 7.5 per cent over that, net of his overhead expenses.

But Mike Love had a different proposal for his brother. Stephen would be employed not by the Beach Boys, but by a corporation called All American Management Orga-

370

nization, of which Mike Love and Alan Jardine were officers. AAMO would be compensated 2.5 per cent of the gross of the Beach Boys' touring revenues for providing tour management and promotional services for the group. Stephen Love would be guaranteed a minimum annual salary of $250,000 against 5 per cent of the first $5 million gross income received by the Beach Boys, and 7.5 per cent thereafter, aside from business and travel expenses. Reportedly, Stephen was not happy about being piggybacked on AAMO, but he had little choice. Stephen also wanted a $70,000 bonus for management services he had performed for the group after Caribou was fired and before he was officially named manager. When Carl and Dennis heard about AAMO and the terms of Stephen's employment, they were outraged – they would not have Stephen back under any circumstances, especially if he was to be employed by AAMO. They made it known that they were prepared to walk out of the group if Stephen was forced on them. Yet Stephen left the meeting with his employment memorandum, signed by three-fifths of the group – Mike, Al, and Brian Wilson – enough signatures to ratify it.

The next afternoon the group piled into two different limousines and headed to Newark Airport to fly to a concert in Providence, Rhode Island, on two separate planes – a prop rented from singer Ray Charles for the free-livers and a sleek private jet for the meditators. On the way to the airport, Dennis told a *Rolling Stone* reporter, 'This could be the last Beach Boys concert tonight. I see the Beach Boys coming to a close, and there's a lot of backstabbing and maliciousness going on.' According to Carl, there was even talk of 'replacements' for him and Dennis.

After the Providence concert, at a stopover at Newark

Airport on the way back to Los Angeles, Dennis and Karen joined the meditators on the faster jet for the flight home, but Carl still refused to be on the same plane with them. During the long wait for maintenance and refueling, Dennis and Karen decided to spend the night in New York and take a commercial flight back to LA in the morning. When Brian heard this, he decided to stay over with them and help paint the town, but the meditating contingent forbade him to remain behind. This infuriated Dennis, and when he saw Carl standing outside the plane, he told him they wouldn't let Brian get off. Tempers erupted and Dennis raced back on the plane to tell them the group was finished.

Now everybody poured out of the two planes for a confrontation on the tarmac. The reporter from *Rolling Stone* called it 'a scene right out of [the movie] *Casablanca*.' Both planes stood waiting, engines running, for their passengers while Mike, Stephen, and Stanley Love formed a tight circle around Dennis and his bodyguard. They stood there screaming at each other over the roar of the engines. Stanley kept repeating that Dennis 'got into this band on Brian Wilson's coattails! . . . I'm the one that's brought [Brian] around. I'm the one that keeps him from walking out in front of buses. And you're gonna quit on us after all that?'

Later, riding in a limousine back to Manhattan, Dennis said to Karen, 'What's today's date? September third? I'll remember it. The Beach Boys broke up on Al Jardine's birthday.'

But the Beach Boys did not break up. Two weeks later, on September 17, 1977, an extraordinary meeting was held at Brian and Marilyn's house on Bellagio Road to discuss the future of the group. Each contingent was accompanied by a high-powered, high-priced attorney.

Those attending were Brian, Carl, Mike, Alan, Dennis, Stephen, Marilyn, along with attorneys Harvey Fierstein, Skip Brittenham, Jeff Ingberg, Michael Allen, and David Braun (who was hired as 'special counsel' to the Beach Boys acting in Brian's behalf). Several motions were brought up to be voted on, including securing the management of All American Management Organization to engage Stephen Love as manager; securing proper recording facilities and equipment; auditing the books, and getting new office facilities. It was also suggested that Stephen Love purchase equipment not to exceed $200,000 to be installed at the Maharishi International University in Iowa, where the next album would be recorded. The meeting began on a calm note, but quickly became a shouting match as it became apparent that Mike, Al, and Brian – who fell asleep on the floor during the meeting – would vote down any of Dennis and Carl's objections.

Carl and Dennis, as well as their attorney, were hotly opposed to Mike's commissioning 2.5 per cent from the top for AAMO. They wanted the gross income 'split at the source' before anybody else got their hands on it. Mike accused Carl: 'You have lost us four million dollars over the last couple of years. Carl, you're a big-time bullshit. Nick Grillo, Jack Rieley. Hang on to Jimmy Guercio and not let him perform, and then Henry Lazarus. Wonderful.' But Carl also objected to the fact that while he had in effect produced the last three Beach Boys albums, he had received no special credit or compensation. Accusations flew back and forth for nearly an hour.

Stephen Love was quietly fuming about a remark made by Carl and Dennis's attorney Harvey Fierstein, who had called the compensation for his work with the Beach Boys 'atrocious.' Finally Stephen turned on Fierstein, who had a hunchback and was less than five feet tall, calling him a 'hideous little creature.'

With that, Carl and Dennis stormed out of the room, followed by their lawyer. But the group had been officially reunited. Stephen Love was back, and the Beach Boys would soon leave to spend the winter recording their next album at the Maharishi University in Iowa.

Going to the Maharishi University to record was a little like going to Holland, only worse. Ostensibly, it was another out-of-the-way location where there would be few distractions. It was hoped that two albums could be recorded. One album would satisfy the terms of the Warner Brothers contracts, the second would become the album due soon to CBS. As it turned out, only one album was forthcoming, and not a very good one at that. The entire group, and most of their family members, set up house in the circular dorm rooms of the university. Stanley Love described the situation as 'torture. Agony. Like being put right in the middle of nowhere, frozen and cold and small, with only one decent restaurant in town. Brian was putting in his time, but he wasn't too happy. He was depressed and on medication. We passed the time playing Ping-Pong.' The resulting album reflected the mood of the group. Released on September 25, 1978, the *MIU* album was on the record charts for only four weeks, never reaching higher than 151. Nick Kent, of *New Musical Express*, called the effort 'dreadful' and said, 'Both critics and pundits ignored the product's pitiful contents.'

3

Mike Love and his wife, Tamara, a pretty, dark young woman he met through his endeavors in Transcendental Meditation, had a baby girl named Summer (Love). But their marriage was falling apart and a divorce suit was filed. Carl's seemingly solid marriage to Annie was also in trouble, and Carl began to flirt with cocaine and alcohol. Said Annie, 'Carl had been flirting with drugs' out of a sense of profound unhappiness with the group and the managerial morass he found himself in. Naturally, Dennis was blamed for much of Carl's indulgence, as he was considered a 'bad influence.'

Indeed, Dennis seemed incorrigible. His drinking had increased along with his tolerance to it, and his philandering had grown to satyric proportions. Even the lovely Karen Lamm couldn't keep Dennis from fooling around, and within a few months of their marriage he was having an affair with a local beauty queen. Yet he was still insanely jealous of any man that Karen so much as talked to, including important business associates. Dennis once warned her that if she did a commercial with a handsome man, he would walk out on her.

The Beach Boys had already lost a prized employee as a result of a squabble between Dennis and Karen. Road manager Rick Nelson (not the performer) had been with the group in various capacities since the early seventies. Nelson had met Mike and Alan at a Transcendental Meditation center in Los Angeles and had been quickly taken into the fold. He was an easygoing road manager, although not a baby-sitter by temperament, and he usually called things as he saw them. While the group was on tour in Houston, Texas, Karen Lamm called Rick Nelson's room looking for Dennis. She had been calling Dennis's room through the night, and suspected that he was shacked up elsewhere with another girl. Nelson simply told her the truth – she was correct. Dennis was off with some girl he'd picked up and Nelson couldn't reach him. When Dennis learned that Nelson had 'turned him in' to Karen, he insisted that Nelson be fired, and Carl backed him up. Stephen Love thought this was a terrible move; Nelson was one of the best and most loyal employees the group had. Stephen even wrote a letter imploring Dennis and Carl to reconsider, but their decision stuck and Nelson was gone.[3] In his place, Jerry Schilling, a former member of Elvis Presley's 'Memphis Mafia,' was asked to take over road-management chores. Schilling would later be promoted to become Carl Wilson's personal manager.

But Karen was more concerned about Dennis's drug intake than she was jealous of his infidelities. On one occasion she found a huge bottle of cocaine on the console at Brothers Studio and got so angry she threw it all over the carpet of the control booth. When she returned the next night, the locks on the front door had been changed and the group would not let her in. She found a brick in a nearby lot and threw it through the front window. The brick was thereafter used as a doorstop, referred to as 'The Karen Lamm Memorial Brick.'

On December 30, 1976, Dennis woke up one morning and turned to Karen in bed next to him. He said, 'Honey, I don't want you to take this personally, but I don't want to be married anymore.'

---

[3] Rick Nelson later married Janet Lent-Coop and became Brian Wilson's personal business manager.

Karen said, 'Go for it, Dennis, if that's what you really want.' Then she rolled over in bed and went back to sleep. 'I thought he was kidding,' she said. But Dennis was serious. He picked up the phone at his bedside and called his lawyer. Later that day he left for Florida, where the Beach Boys were performing.

'New Year's Day,' Karen remembered, 'I found a house at 9747 Yokum Drive in Beverly Hills and moved out of the Broad Beach house. When Dennis returned to Los Angeles and discovered I wasn't there anymore, he moved into a trailer that was sitting on blocks behind Gregg Jakobson's house.' When Dennis filed for divorce, Karen hired well-known divorce attorney Marvin Mitchelson to represent her. She was worried about the $70,000 she had loaned Dennis to get him out of various financial pinches and wanted the money back. Two weeks went by before Dennis called, sheepishly asking to see her again. 'For months it went back and forth,' she said. 'Are you going to drop this divorce or what?' Eventually, he moved into her house on Yokum Drive with her. 'Mind you,' she said, 'we had a great time. It wasn't like anything was different except that he was divorcing me. Then one morning he woke up and said, "Okay, let's get married again and stop all this boloney."' The two of them went straight to the Santa Monica courthouse and tried to file the proper papers to get remarried. They were consulting with the clerk when he said, 'I'm sorry, we can't marry you. You're already married.' Dennis was so frustrated he threw the papers up in the air.

On the ride back to the house, he and Karen had a huge fight. By the time they were at the house, Dennis was furious. He took all his clothes and threw them in the back of his Ferrari. As a farewell gesture, Karen overturned a twenty-five-pound planter on the car, smashing

377

the hood. A few minutes later Marvin Mitchelson called her. He had received a phone call from the Santa Monica city clerk saying she and Dennis wanted to get married again and now Dennis's lawyer was on the phone saying that Dennis wanted to have her arrested.

'He left for a tour that day,' Karen said. 'He thought I was insane, but I joined him on tour two days later. It was a wild relationship. We were both so strong, we were both like fire, extremists, so that everything we did was done really big. When we were together we were so powerful that nothing could stop us. But when we were at each other's throats, nothing could stop us either. The love was intense, the craziness was intense, and the productiveness was intense.'

On New Year's Eve of 1977 Dennis and Karen tried heroin together for the first time. 'Dennis was saying I will never do that drug, and I said, "Come on, what are you, chicken?" Dennis tried it on my account, and I always felt deeply guilty about that. He got violently sick and so did I. We spent New Year's with our heads in the toilet and vowed never to do it again.'

But Dennis never lost his urge for heroin and began a lifelong struggle to avoid its lure. He snorted it on several occasions, only to awaken so depressed the next day that he resolved never to try it again. His resistance to heroin took strange forms. 'One night he was at a restaurant in Venice,' Karen said, 'and this surge of destruction comes over him and he wanted to try heroin again. Instead he got very drunk. Later, he told me, "Either I did heroin or I went out and burned down the car." So he chose to burn the car.' The car was a $70,000 1976 GTB baby-blue Ferrari with a tan interior. He asked a friend to drive him to where the car was parked and then drove it to a parking lot in Venice, covered the inside with charcoal lighter fluid, and torched it. The vagrants who had been sleeping in the parking lot danced around the car with him as it burned.

But that was not the end of Dennis's experience with hard drugs. Heroin would play a prominent part in the Beach Boys' winter tour of New Zealand and Australia in 1978.

4

One of Stephen Love's first responsibilities in his renewed role as manager was to arrange a three-week tour of New Zealand and Australia to comply with the terms of the CBS contract. The tour was to be promoted by David Frost's Australian entertainment company, Paradine Productions, and road-managed by Richard Duryea, who was now working for Caribou. One of Frost's most important demands was that Brian Wilson appear on tour, and he insisted on a contractual letter guaranteeing Brian was well enough to work.

Everything about this tour seemed destined for trouble from the start. Allegedly, Dennis had brought heroin with him into New Zealand at the start of the trip. When Karen saw him in terrible shape, she thought he was just drunk and left him in the hotel bar. He came back to their room in the small hours of the morning and she refused to let him in, telling him to 'go sleep it off in Carl's room.' The next morning, when she opened the door for him, he smacked her across the face, punched her in the chest, threw her down on the bed, and sat on her. He left her behind at the hotel, taking her money and passport with him. Karen talked two groupies who were hanging around the hotel lobby into driving her to the airport, where she found Dennis in the lounge, barefoot. She took his shoes and beat him over the head with them, demanding he hand over her passport and airplane ticket so she could get back to Los Angeles. She eventually went to Auckland, where the concert promoter loaned her $500 and drove her to the local hospital. Karen's X-rays revealed that Dennis had broken her sternum in three places. She immediately left for Hawaii, where she was treated at the Kaiser Hospital.

But this incident was minor compared to the trouble that started in Melbourne. Allegedly both Dennis and Carl purchased $100 worth of heroin from a Paradine employee. The rest of the Beach Boys might never have learned about this had the heroin not reached Brian. At this point Brian was doing quite well under the auspices of Stan, Rocky, and Steve Korthof. He had been away from most drugs for months and was functioning without prescribed medications. Still, it took a great deal of effort to make sure that no drugs were around, and each night, in each hotel room, Stan and Rocky made a careful sweep of drawers and closets, checking under furniture and behind pictures to make sure Brian hadn't procured some drug while they weren't watching and stashed it for when he was alone.

One night, according to Steve Korthof, 'Brian wanted to do a live radio broadcast from a station in downtown Melbourne, and a woman publicist said she'd take him to the station and watch him carefully.' Korthof let Brian go unescorted, not knowing that Dennis, in his own room, was snorting heroin. When Brian returned from the radio broadcast, he went directly to Dennis's room, where he snorted some himself. 'When Brian came back to his

380

room, he started throwing up,' Korthof said. 'I had no idea, I thought he had been drinking. I said, "Brian, did you have a drink at the bar?" And Brian lied to me and said, "Yeah, I had a drink." He went to sleep and it was over.'

The next day Stan and Rocky did a little investigating and found out about the heroin. According to Rocky, a guilty production assistant employed by David Frost told the whole story. As unlikely as this story seems, the following tale was related. The production assistant had apparently been approached by Dennis to purchase him heroin, but he wanted to give it to someone more responsible than Dennis, and sold it instead to Carl for $100 in the hotel bar. When Rocky related the story to the rest of the Beach Boys, they were understandably furious, and threatened to call off the remainder of the tour unless Dennis was sent home immediately. Naturally, David Frost was against taking any radical action, lest it erupt in ugly publicity. Late that night, after the show, the group insisted on meeting with David Frost and his partner Pat Condon in Stephen's hotel suite. Carl – evidently a little drunk – Mike, Al Jardine, Richard Duryea, Rocky, and Stan attended. Dennis was unaware of the meeting, and Brian was kept in his room with Steve Korthof.

David Frost tried to be reasonable and low-key. 'First off,' he began in measured tones, 'I thought the show was terrific and I was ecstatic as everyone else in the audience. A breathtaking experience . . . The only two points I wanted to make are that we're in the middle of a tour that's on the verge of being the most successful tour in Australia ever, record-breaking, a stunning success, due to all of you. The realities of the situation are that the fees that we pay are the result of the backing of AGC, the biggest financing company in Australia, and we would seek that they not know of any problems that are going on . . . Obviously, they've got two billion in assets, they might sue us . . . they would certainly sue you for fifty million dollars, because if anything goes wrong. . . . What I'm really saying is that without wishing to interfere in any way . . . we have a kamikaze pact . . . please delay any explosions until the tour is over because otherwise AGC . . . would just go berserk . . . We would be part of it and their trust in us would be eroded . . . If Dennis left the tour, all hell would break loose, on our heads too.'

'This is a veiled kind of threat,' Stephen Love said. 'You're threatening us with a potential lawsuit of fifty million dollars if we send the drummer home for buying heroin . . .'

A shouting match followed. 'I see this as condoning fucking bullshit!' Mike yelled. 'I'm not in the fucking Rolling Stones, goddamn it!'

Rocky told Frost, 'If I employed somebody who procured heroin for the Beach Boys, I'd be worried about a lawsuit!'

Rocky started screaming at Carl to admit that he had personally paid $100 for the heroin, but Carl denied it. 'You know what happened?' he slurred. '*I flushed it down the toilet!* I didn't buy Brian shit or spend a penny on shit.'

Rocky yelled, 'Then you didn't flush it soon enough!'

Stan turned to Frost and said, 'You wanted a piece of paper saying Brian was in good enough health to attend this tour, then your man turns around and buys heroin? How would that look?'

'Okay,' Carl said. 'It's a possibility I was drunk and gave him one hundred dollars, but I really don't think I did.'

'And one hundred per cent went down the toilet?' Frost asked.

'Yeah,' Carl said, and continued to deny that he had bought it.

After prolonged screaming and threats of taking Frost and his organization to court, Frost interjected, 'Let's stop the insults and look at the future for a minute. The point is that to try and send Dennis home causes problems. I think that he should have one last chance. I think that your moral stance is absolutely correct, but I think that this [tour] should not be destroyed because it probably would be the destruction of the Beach Boys . . . All I would say is to give him one last chance because the consequences of not doing so are awful . . .'

'Dennis is not a person who you can give a second chance,' Mike said. 'He's not the kind of person who's trustworthy. What we're considering is sending Dennis home while the rest of us finish the tour. People who like drugs lie, they're not trustworthy. I can dig it because . . . I'm an addictive personality but I'm addicted to TM and I meditate my ass off.'

Carl interjected, 'Michael, I was addicted to cocaine psychologically for many months last year and I know all about that. I was a fucking wreck. I was terrified because I thought Dennis was going through withdrawal.'

A few minutes later, Rocky tried to get the production assistant who allegedly sold the heroin to Carl up to the room so he could repeat his story, but David Frost forbade it. 'Absolutely not!' he shouted. 'That would be a disastrous backwards step.'

But Rocky was still not satisfied, and insisted, 'People are going to be penalized for their actions around here. We're not going to let Dennis slide.'

'We're going to *have* to let everybody slide,' Frost said.

Rocky erupted. 'You said you were gonna say a few words and now you're telling us what the fuck we're gonna have to do!'

'Don't talk to me like that,' Frost said, the proper Englishman. 'I haven't talked to you like that and I don't expect you to swear at me.'

'Michael, I know all about drug abuse,' Carl said. 'I abuse drugs, I do not condone them.'

'That's a weird statement,' Michael mused.

'What I'm saying is absolutely not a threat, it's a scenario,' Frost said. 'If anyone were to leave, there would obviously be a breach of contract . . . But I'm not sitting here saying Paradine would take action, I'm not saying that . . . As one of your greatest fans, it's bizarre and macabre that we're discussing this . . . This incident must not be repeated . . . it would not be seen as positive if it became public . . . Let's plow on to glory.'

'Are you going to fire [the procurer of the heroin]?' Frost was asked.

'Yes,' Frost said.

The entire room exploded as the group members objected that the production assistant was not at fault.

Still Rocky would not let up, and continued to grill Carl about who had bought the heroin. 'I happen to know the fellow's name who paid for it and I won't repeat it,' Carl said. 'I'll tell David [Frost] or I'll tell Pat [Condon], I'll tell someone else but I won't tell you about it.'

'Yeah, they'll come to you, Carl,' Rocky snarled.

'Fuck you!' Carl said.

'Fuck me, huh?' Rocky said. He jumped up and punched Carl full in the face. Carl fell to the floor unconscious. 'Don't ever tell me to get fucked!' he yelled to Carl's motionless figure.

384

'Jesus Christ! That's about it, guys,' Richard Duryea said.

'Fuck you, Duryea!' Rocky said.

'You're the one who should leave town,' Frost coolly told Rocky.

When Carl came to, he said, 'I won't look good for the photo sessions tomorrow.'

Frost couldn't wait to get out of the room. 'Sleep well, everybody,' Frost said drolly. 'Pleasant dreams.'

'It's rock-and-roll, David,' Michael said.

'Mr Frost,' Stanley called after him as he went out the door. 'It was a pleasure meeting you. I enjoyed all your Nixon interviews.'

The next night Dennis was ready to perform, completely unaware of what had happened in Stephen's hotel suite. He was shocked and outraged to hear that Rocky had punched Carl. But Dennis was not prepared for a physical confrontation and stayed as far away from Rocky and Carl as he could. Carl showed up for the concert very drunk, and in the middle of the performance he fell down and had to leave the stage. The incident made headlines all over Australia, and Carl had to apologize publicly the next day, telling the press that he had taken a mixture of medication that made him sick.

For the rest of the tour, Carl and Dennis traveled apart from the Love contingent. Their tour funds were collected separately by tour manager Richard Duryea, and they even entered the stage from different sides to keep as much physical distance from the others as possible. Even so, minor tussles occurred, such as a swift knee to the groin and a harsh bump as the group members crowded around the microphones. By now the tactic of cutting

385

each other off in the middle of solo vocals was quite common.

Even with all the sanctions against drugs on this tour and David Frost's caveat that none be made available through his staff, Brian still managed to obtain some pills. On their next-to-last night in Australia, after Stan and Rocky left him alone for the night, Brian went down to the front desk, borrowed $20 in cash against his credit card, and paid a visit to the hotel doctor. Complaining he was pent-up and sleepless from touring, Brian convinced him to prescribe sleeping pills. The next morning Stan and Rocky found Brian lying in bed half conscious, drool pouring out of his mouth. After reviving Brian, Stan and Rocky did a drug search of the room and found several bottles of pills – but evidently not all of them. On the way to the airport, they noticed that Brian's face was contorted and that he was short of breath from an obvious overdose of amphetamines. Carl's personal masseur was given a letter absolving him of any responsibility, and then gave Brian a massage to relax his muscles. On the plane home, the Beach Boys and their entourage heaved a collective sigh of relief.

The group had broken every concert attendance record in Australia.

On the way back to Los Angeles, they stopped off in Hawaii for one last concert. Brian requested that Debbie Keil be 'imported' to see him. There was some discussion about this, as Marilyn was also scheduled to come to Hawaii for a visit and a short vacation. However, since Marilyn was coming primarily to see Rocky, those in authority figured Debbie's arrival would even things out. Even so, they were afraid to put Debbie's name on the Beach Boys hotel roster list lest Marilyn see it, so they asked Debbie to pay her own fare and to check into the hotel with her own credit card, promising to reimburse her. Of course, she was never reimbursed and ended up paying her own bill. But before long, everyone in the Beach Boys organization would have a heavy bill to pay.

5

A renewed surge of bad feeling toward Stephen Love began, and this time he lost one of his most loyal supporters, Al Jardine. Al was highly critical of Stephen Love for not firing Rocky Pamplin after he knocked Carl out in Australia. But Stephen, who did not hide his contempt for Carl and Dennis, seemed to feel Rocky had been justified in punching Carl.

Moreover, everyone in the group was irritated with Stephen for the pressure he was putting on them to meet the January, 1978, deadline on their CBS contract. The group members felt the deadline could easily be extended, because their attorneys, David Braun and John Branca, had a good relationship with CBS. By this time Tom Hulett, one of the top managers and tour agents in the music business, was handling their domestic schedule for a 15 per cent fee. It seemed that Stephen Love had become superfluous to the group, and the hard feelings generated by the Australian heroin incident didn't help. It was agreed to fire him a second time, this time for good.

Stephen Love was owed $550,000 on his contract, and a settlement was reached under the guise of a consultancy contract in which the group agreed to pay him half of that, or $75,000 a year for three years, at a rate of $18,750 every three months. Although Stephen Love was reportedly not very happy with the settlement, he was relieved to be finished with the group. He packed his belongings and moved to Hawaii, where he was content, for a time.

*I was in such a hole that I swear to God
every living second of my life was just a
disastrous calamity.* – Brian Wilson

Sixteen

1

Rocky Pamplin and Marilyn Wilson continued their affair,
still a well-kept secret from Brian. By now Marilyn was
wracked with deep guilt. She loved Brian dearly, and was
in the most basic sense a moral, committed wife. But she
was also only twenty-nine years old, a lonely, affectionate
woman caught in the gothic web of an emotionally disturbed husband and a sexless marriage. Rocky Pamplin,
however, was quite clear-headed and calculating. Only a
few months into the affair he revealed a long-held desire
to have a singing career. According to Rocky, Marilyn
supported this wish, as did Brian, who promised to help
produce an album for Rocky with Marilyn's group, the
Honeys, singing backup. Rocky went into the studio and
cut several songs. The results were amateurish, but Brian
was fond of Rocky and continued to encourage the
project.

Brian had reached a new low after returning from
Australia – his emotional stability seemed to disintegrate
daily. He still managed to obtain cocaine and barbitu-
rates, no matter how closely his three caretakers watched
him. One night, on some untold mixture of drugs, Brian
began to vomit in his sleep and would have choked to
death if the sound had not awakened Marilyn, who

389

summoned Stanley to help clear the vomit from Brian's windpipe. Stanley and Marilyn spent the rest of the evening dousing Brian under a cold shower to keep him conscious.

The next day Brian disappeared. They searched throughout the house, calling all of his friends, but no one had seen or heard from him. 'He was just so drugged and miserable with himself, he didn't want to be home,' Marilyn said. Brian hitchhiked to West Hollywood and ended up in a gay bar. 'I know he was playing piano for beers,' Marilyn said. He met someone there who drove him down to Mexico. Later Brian hitchhiked up to San Diego and wandered around the city for days, barefoot and unwashed.

'He was on a binge,' Stanley said. 'A couple of guys felt sorry for him and took him home and let him stay there for a while. He got drugs from somebody in a recording studio who recognized him. They said they'd give him coke if he helped them produce a song. The engineer called Brother Records and immediately got hold of Marilyn, who hired a private detective to go down and find him. The next thing we knew, there was a phone call from a doctor at the Alvarado Hospital who said to Marilyn, "I'm treating your husband."'

Brian had passed out in the gutter and had been picked up by an ambulance. 'The cops found him in Balboa Park under a tree, with no shoes on,' Stanley said, 'his white pants filthy, obviously a vagrant with no wallet, no money.' Marilyn, Stephen Love, and Stanley went down to San Diego to take Brian home, but decided to follow the doctor's advice instead, allowing him to spend some time detoxifying in the hospital.

Marilyn returned to Los Angeles to take care of the children. While Brian was in the Alvarado Hospital they finally discussed getting a divorce. They were talking on the phone and Marilyn was only half surprised to hear Brian say, 'Mare, I think we should separate.'

'I wanted it too,' Marilyn said, 'but still it hurt. The thought of him not wanting me anymore killed me.' September 15, 1978, for legal purposes, became the arbitrary date of their separation, although Brian continued to depend on Marilyn for encouragement and stability, and kept in close telephone contact with her.

Brian never moved back into the house on Bellagio Road with Marilyn. By the time he was ready to be discharged from the Alvarado Hospital, the rest of the group was already in Miami, starting work on their long-overdue first album to satisfy their CBS contract. Through their attorney David Braun's intervention, they had received an extension on the due date, but patience at CBS was running low and the boys were under extreme pressure to produce. Said CBS Vice-President Tony Martell, 'Obviously there was the feeling that the company was screwed, because we did not know Mike Love was going to take off [to Switzerland] and that all of them would be disjointed . . . They were making money because Capitol was putting out repackages up the kazoo. They were making a lot of money on tour and making money from two companies . . . so they didn't feel under pressure to produce an album.'

Since Brian was contractually obligated to produce the CBS albums, he flew by himself directly from San Diego to Los Angeles Airport, where Stanley met him in a limousine and drove him to a private plane. Brian joined the rest of the group at Critereon studios, the lush Miami recording facilities owned by the Bee Gees. Once more, the Beach Boys were together.

The new album was to be called *LA (Light Album)*,

391

and its highlight was 'Here Comes the Night,' a twelve-minute song done in the then-popular 'disco' style, the original version of which had appeared on the 1967 *Wild Honey* album. With the disco craze reaching its height, several popular groups had changed their style to accommodate the new music, and the Beach Boys – mistakenly – jumped on the bandwagon. The group was staying at the Doral Country Club Hotel, and it was apparent from the start that Brian was still very ill and wouldn't be much help in producing the album. Eventually, CBS President Walter Yetnikoff flew down to Miami to hear how the album was progressing. Brian had prepared a demo track of some of the songs, hoping to satisfy Yetnikoff that the old Brian Wilson flair was still evident. Yetnikoff and Martell assembled in the control room at Critereon and listened in dismay to the playback. Remembered Tony Martell, 'We sat there and listened to the tunes . . . At one point, it was a little volatile, because of what we heard. They told us it was one of their finest efforts.'

According to a Beach Boys' employee who was present, 'Yetnikoff basically said, "I think I have been fucked." That was his opening statement. But Yetnikoff was great. His next statement was "Where do we go from here?" It was a very positive meeting. Yetnikoff has a very subtle sense of humor. He says something to get your attention.'

'We refused to put out [what we heard],' said Martell. 'It was not up to their capabilities by any stretch of the imagination. I think they were in a hurry . . . It bothered them that they still had obligations to us, it really did . . . They wanted to fulfill their obligations and by trying to do it fast, the product just wasn't there . . . It was typical of them to do something like that. Then they realized what had happened, one by one. They went to Walter and said, "You're right, this is not what we wanted." . . . Walter has a way with artists. He presented a logical explanation of why the company was very upset, and they had a meeting of the minds.'

According to Steve Korthof, 'Brian was real weird then, real quiet, not saying much. Real depressed. I think he just realized he wasn't going to be able to pick up the slack. Brian eventually suggested that Bruce Johnston be brought back in to help produce the album. I was in the hotel room with him at the Doral Country Club when he picked up the phone and called Bruce Johnston. He said, "Why don't you come down to Florida? I think we need you." Brian was right; they needed him, they still do. Bruce jumped in. He flew down the next day.' Bruce has been a full-fledged member of the Beach Boys ever since.

When everyone else returned to Los Angeles to continue recording at Western Studios, Brian wanted to stay in Florida by himself. The group agreed that this was out of the question and forced him to return to LA. Back in Los Angeles, Brian moved in with Marilyn's youngest sister, Barbara, but after one weekend she asked him to leave. He called a real-estate agent and rented a small house on Sunset Boulevard for $2,300 a month. The house was dumpy and dark, with a small pool in the back. The furniture came from a local rental company, and a secondhand car was purchased to chauffeur Brian around.

At first, Brian seemed to fare well alone in the house, but he soon took to drinking heavily. His behavior verged on manic. Stan and Rocky would come by every day to stay with him. Brian would say, 'Watch me walk around the pool seven hundred and eighty-five times,' because that was a number he liked. Then he would frantically walk in circles around the pool until he was sweating and exhausted. He had also developed the habit of talking out of the side of his mouth, and his right leg vibrated constantly.

With Marilyn out of the picture, Debbie Keil now had free rein with Brian. She would often visit him at his new house, and once they took a romantic trip to Palm Springs. Unfortunately, Brian discovered Debbie's diet pills in her purse, devoured them all, and refused to come out of the hotel room until they returned to LA. Back at the house, Debbie was often torn as to how to deal with Brian. When he asked for money, she knew it was to buy alcohol and would usually refuse to give it to him, but occasionally she would relent, driving him wherever he wanted to go lest he get hurt hitchhiking or run away altogether. Often Brian would disappear, turning up penniless in Watts or East LA. One morning, after they had spent the night together, Brian insisted Debbie drive him to his old house on Bellagio Road. Marilyn had always told him that if he was lonely he could visit her and the children there.[1]

Brian let himself into the house and went up to Marilyn's bedroom. The door was closed and he let himself in without knocking. Marilyn was asleep, lying on her side. On the other side of the bed, under a blanket, was Rocky Pamplin.

Brian walked over to where Marilyn lay sleeping, knelt at her side, kissed her, and said, 'I love you.' Then he walked around to Rocky's side of the bed, knelt next to him, kissed him on the cheek, and said, 'I love you.' Then he was out the door.

It took Marilyn and Rocky a few minutes to compose themselves. 'I went out to find him and saw him pacing

[1] Marilyn Wilson denies that the following incident ever took place, calling it 'total bullshit.' Rocky Pamplin, however, in direct, taped interview with the author of this book, relates the story in detail.

394

by the front gate,' Rocky said. 'I walked up to him, and he turned to me and said, "You love Marilyn, don't you?"'

Rocky said, 'No, Brian.'

Brian said that he needed a pack of cigarettes, and Rocky offered to drive him to the store. Marilyn came out of the house and got into the back of her Mercedes while Rocky and Brian sat in front. All three were silent as they drove to get Brian the cigarettes. Suddenly Brian turned to Rocky and said, 'It wasn't fair, Rocky.'

Rocky said, 'Worse than the way you've been treating your kids and wife the last ten years?'

Brian looked down at his lap and said, 'No.'

When they got back to Bellagio Road, Brian said he wanted to walk back to his rented house alone, and they let him go.

The next day Stan and Rocky arrived at the Sunset Boulevard house to find Brian plastered on muscatel. He was standing on the front porch, 'drunker than a skunk,' according to Steve Korthof, who had arrived a short time earlier. They took him inside, and he was quiet and morose for a while. Then he said abruptly, 'Watch me kick these windows in.' Brian was referring to a long row of ceiling-to-floor plate-glass windows that faced the rear of the house. He started hammering away at them with his foot. Korthof grabbed Brian and pulled him away from the glass, but he was obviously out of control. The three men managed to haul him out to the car and throw him in the back, where he was wedged between Rocky and Stan. Korthof drove them directly to the office of a Dr David Ganz, the medical doctor who had been prescribing various medications for Brian.

They brought him into the doctor's office. Dr Ganz was sitting behind the desk, smoking a pipe. For a moment, the sight of the man with the pipe in his mouth reminded Brian of Murry. Brian screamed at him, '*You Jew mother-fucker!*' and wiped everything off the doctor's desk with one sweep of his arm. While Rocky, Stan, and Steve held Brian down, Dr Ganz injected him with a sedative. Then they drove Brian directly to the psychiatric ward at Brotman Memorial Hospital, where he would stay for the next several months.

Stanley Love and Rocky Pamplin were fired by Marilyn Wilson's attorney via letter in January 1979 with two weeks' severance pay.[2] 'I stopped seeing Marilyn that day,' Rocky said. But Rocky would not leave it at that. For months to come Marilyn received obscene messages from Rocky on her answering machine, in which he called her a 'kike' and a 'Jew.' 'I told her everything I ever felt about her,' he said.

Said Stanley Love, 'If Rocky hadn't been sleeping with her, we'd still be there.'

2

On April 12, 1978, above the Roxy Theater on Sunset Boulevard, at a private club called On the Rox, Karen caught Dennis flirting with another girl. She punched him out cold. Jack Nicholson, who was sitting nearby, told Karen, 'You should leave before he gets up,' and she did.

---

[2] Marilyn Wilson claims she fired Rocky because, during an interview at which she was present, he said Brian would be producing his forthcoming album. 'Stan and I got into a big fight,' she said. 'I looked at them and said, "You . . . expect me to go along with you? I'm not going to lie about Brian for your benefit." I won't have anyone lie about Brian . . . I fired them the next day.'

That night she wrote in her diary, 'I hit him in the mouth and it felt great.' But it obviously felt better to be with him – the next day they made up. Two days later, Karen joined Dennis in Houston, where the Beach Boys were performing. She arrived at the hotel to find him 'holding court' in the hotel bar.

'He had been drinking and cocaining the whole day,' Karen said, 'and had picked up some girl. He told me to go back up to the room and wait for him. About two-thirty I called down to the bar, but it was closed. So I called the desk and asked if Dennis was around. They told me he had taken another room.' Furious, Karen went to the room and tried to break down the door, until she was stopped by a security guard. The last thing she heard through the door was a girl's voice asking, 'Should I put my clothes back on?'

Karen flew back to Los Angeles the next day, only to receive several phone calls from a contrite Dennis. On Monday, April 24, Karen learned that Dennis had been arrested in Tucson, Arizona, for 'contributing to the delinquency of a minor.' According to Dennis, he was the victim of an angry mother. According to the local papers, 'a sixteen-year-old girl was allegedly found alone in Wilson's hotel room following the Beach Boys concert at a local university. The arrest came through a tip by the girl's mother, who called the police at 3:55 A.M. to say her daughter had breached curfew and was at Wilson's hotel room . . .' Dennis later told Karen it had cost him nearly $100,000 in legal fees to get out of trouble.

Still, Karen found it in her heart to forgive Dennis yet again, and by May they were considering remarrying.[3]

---

[3] Karen is hard-pressed to explain the number of times she forgave Dennis. 'If you're worried about fidelity with a rock star, forget it. It's

She was hesitant, however, not because of his philandering, but because of his increasing use of heroin. On at least half a dozen occasions in her diary that year she noted that Dennis was either high or nodded out on the drug. However, on the morning of July 28, after she had returned from an appearance in a Michelob beer commercial at Lake Arrowhead, Dennis 'begged [Karen] to get married again because he wanted a clean slate.'

'I don't know why I did it,' Karen said. 'I always forgave Dennis, and I really, really, really, really loved Dennis. I loved Dennis more than anything in the world, and nothing meant that much to me.' That night they flew to Las Vegas and were married in a small church on the strip.

For a short time Dennis stopped using cocaine and heroin, but less than two months after they were married, he was getting high all the time. Karen encouraged him to seek professional treatment for withdrawal. On September 29 Dennis signed himself in to a hospital in Century City under an assumed name to detoxify himself. When he arrived home chipper and clean, the two hoped to make a new start together.

Dennis had been recording songs for a second solo album at the Village Recorders, the studio owned by George Hormel, Jr. One night in November 1978 he met Christine McVie, keyboardist and singer of the English group Fleetwood Mac, who was there recording background vocals as a favor for musician Danny Duma. McVie was a tall, husky-voiced, blonde woman with hard features – a far cry from Karen Lamm's classic American

---

part of the life-style. But if you really love the man, and you need each other, there's justifiable reason to try and work it out. The only absolutely intolerable thing Dennis ever did was to take drugs.'

beauty. Born Christine Perfect in Birmingham, England, she joined Fleetwood Mac after a stint as a featured member of the group Chicken Shack. She later married Fleetwood Mac's bass player, John McVie, only to divorce him in February 1978. Still, the two continued to work together in the group, which would soon hit megastar proportions, owing to both Christine's exceptional talent as a songwriter and the incomparable voice of group member Stevie Nicks. Christine was a loyal, sensitive woman with strong moral convictions, but she was also lonely and vulnerable, living in a huge four-bedroom house in Coldwater Canyon.

She had been romantically involved with Curry Grant, Fleetwood Mac's lighting director, but the affair had run its course. According to Chris Kable, who was Dennis's secretary and later worked for Christine in the same capacity, 'She took one look at Dennis and knew that he was somebody she wanted to be with. The night they met, she went home with him and spent the night with him on the boat. It was very romantic, and they were together ever after that night. She told Curry Grant she had met someone else, and he moved out.'

The beginning of this affair contributed to Dennis's slide into a completely dissolute life-style. Just before Christmas 1978, Dennis moved into Christine's house. Like many of the women who fell in love with Dennis, she was generous to a fault, and found herself giving him money almost daily. Yet she was wealthy enough that one of their friends described Dennis's role in her life as an 'expensive excuse for her to get up in the morning.' At first they spent their time between the *Harmony* and Christine's house, but within a few months, with Christine's blessings, Dennis had set up quarters in a small pool house on Christine's terraced property. He outfitted the place with a brass bed and pump organ, cushions on the floor, and an array of candles for mood lighting.

Karen was by now resigned (and a little relieved) about the impending end of her relationship with Dennis. With Dennis's enthusiastic urging, Karen began to visit him at Christine's house, where she befriended her competitor for Dennis's attention. Karen and Christine had one common bond – the misery Dennis was putting them through. Karen, a magnanimous and in some ways wise young woman, gave Christine her support. Karen's spirit helped Christine through many dark times to come.

Still, the relationship between the two women was most peculiar. Dennis tried to impart many of Karen's virtues to Christine. For instance, Dennis didn't like the way Christine dressed, and asked Karen to take her shopping for clothes. (Christine dropped over $50,000 in Charles Galley in Beverly Hills under Karen's guidance.) Karen would sometimes visit Dennis when Christine wasn't home, which led to some odd situations. One day while Karen was there, a messenger arrived with a manila envelope from a lawyer's office and Dennis wasn't home to receive it. Karen was nice enough to sign for it. When Dennis arrived home later, she discovered that Dennis had filed for divorce a second time without telling her and that the envelope she had so helpfully signed for contained her own divorce papers. When she saw what the envelope contained, she asked Dennis sweetly, 'What's this, honey?' But Dennis had no answer. The divorce became legal in June 1980. Karen received only $2,000 a month through February 1983 and $1,000 a month thereafter – not as alimony, but merely to pay back the loan Dennis owed her. Attorney Marvin Mitchelson took $19,000 of it in fees. On the bottom of the dissolution decree was a handwritten note that said, 'So sorry, Dennis Wilson.'

Dennis lived with Christine McVie for over two years, and during this time his drinking and cocaine addiction increased alarmingly. According to reputable sources, Christine McVie loaned or gave Dennis approximately $100,000 during that period, including a $20,000 loan to make repairs on the *Harmony*. Said Bob Levine, who had become Dennis's business manager in 1978, 'How can a man with any dignity live in a situation [like that]? Even though she did it without any strings in a very nice manner, [he felt] like he's a gigolo, sponging off her.'

Still, Dennis did not have enough money to pay for all the cocaine – at one point he had run up a coke bill of over $10,000 with a hard-nosed dealer. Reportedly, Dennis settled his debt by giving the dealer a 1935 classic Ford automobile – a wedding gift from Karen.

Dennis brought all his personal problems into Christine's life. At one point, on vacation in England, he thought he had stomach cancer. Christine checked him into a hospital for treatment, only to discover he was perfectly healthy. At any time of day or night half a dozen people might arrive at Christine's house at Dennis's invitation for shelter and food. Jack Rieley spent nearly a week with them in the summer of 1979. One day, Dennis's daughter Jennifer was deposited on Christine's doorstep with a suitcase and a note, and Christine took her in. Jennifer's mother, Carol, was besieged with personal problems at the time. 'I had remarried and was getting a divorce. I was having a very, very big problem,' Carol said. 'Jennifer loved living there. She always spoke highly of how nice Christine was. The problem was that Dennis was a heavy drinker. Jennifer started to experience some of the real things that go on out in life. She was exposed to drugs and drinking. After a few months . . . she didn't want to come back . . . she was having a great time.'

Dennis's stepson, Scott, also came around the house, and was soon employed as an assistant to Dennis while he was there. But relations between stepfather and stepson were less happy than Dennis's relationship with Jennifer.

With Dennis, any kind of disaster was possible. One night, because Dennis left candles burning in the pool house, or perhaps because of an electrical short, the pool house burned to the ground. There were, of course, romantic moments, as only Dennis could orchestrate them to make up for all the problems. On a trip to Hawaii with Fleetwood Mac, Dennis bought Christine an unset ruby as an expression of his love. He presented it to her in Rex's restaurant in Honolulu, where he got down on his knees in front of the whole band and asked Christine to marry him. Back in Los Angeles, Dennis was showing the stone off to her friends and he dropped it on the floor. It was recovered by Dennis's long-time assistant Chris Kable, who found it in the vacuum-cleaner bag. One July, for Christine's birthday, Dennis hired a team of gardeners to construct a heart-shaped flower bed in the backyard, and even hired a string quartet to play for her. Unfortunately, the bill for the party was sent to Christine. That same night, Dennis managed to take Scott's girl friend to bed, and the entire household was up in arms over the incident.

'He did crap to Christine,' Chris Kable said. 'He would be gone for days, and he would call her every hour while he was off with somebody else. But for whatever reasons, he didn't intentionally set out to hurt her by his actions.'

After an onstage fight with Mike Love at the Universal Amphitheater, where Dennis performed drunk and on Quaaludes, he was officially thrown out of the Beach

402

Boys, learning of the decision by telegram. Now almost broke, Dennis needed Christine more than ever – he became completely dependent upon her, both emotionally and financially.

3

At Brotman Memorial Hospital, Brian was under the care of Dr Lee Baumel, a psychiatrist he had met socially years before through Tandyn Almer. Brotman had a system of putting patients on 'teams.' Brian was first on the C team, where the rooms had little furniture and some were padded. The B team was for healthier patients, and the A team was for those who were well enough to be on their own. Brian progressed very quickly from C to B to A. He spent his time playing piano in the lounge, and drinking endless cups of coffee. When the other patients found out who he was, they all wanted to compose with him, and Brian amused himself by writing songs with a female patient.

While Brian was at Brotman, a pathetically small contingent of loyal friends came to see him – writer David Leaf, his wife Eva Easton, Debbie Keil, Fred Vail, and Chris Kable. There was also a list at the front desk of people who were not allowed in to see Brian. Among them were Stan and Rocky. Brian had finally determined that he 'hated Stan and Rocky,' according to Steve Korthof, who still was permitted to see him. 'He told the doctors he didn't want them around and that they scared him.'

But Stan and Rocky were perhaps the most loyal to Brian in their own peculiar way – they were determined to get him back and get their own jobs back in the process. 'We were only fired in [David Braun and Lee Baumel's] minds,' Stanley said. One day they showed up at the hospital and demanded to see Brian. The psychiatric aide at the desk told them it was impossible, and Rocky said, 'We work for the guy, so get out of the way.'

The aide insisted that they were not permitted to see him. 'We went behind the counter,' Rocky said, 'and said, "You little fucker, that's my cousin! Don't give me that fucking shit!"' But the aide would not be intimidated and called security guards, who escorted Stan and Rocky out. They later called Steve Korthof, who was permitted to take Brian out of the hospital on passes, and suggested they 'hijack Brian.' '"You get him out of the hospital on a pass. Don't say anything, and we'll be waiting,"' Korthof claimed Stanley told him. 'I got so angry I hung up on him,' Korthof said. 'I couldn't believe it.' Korthof did take Brian out of the hospital to visit his lawyer so he could sign his divorce papers from Marilyn.

Stan and Rocky finally saw Brian at Brotman. A few weeks after they were thrown out, they managed to slip by the desk and visit with Brian in the cafeteria, where they tried to talk him into rehiring them. Brian said to Rocky, 'You know, Rocky, you were fucking my wife . . .'

And Rocky said, 'Yeah, and you weren't.'

Then Brian accused Stan of having poked him in the chest one day.

'Brian,' Stan said, 'I poked you in the chest because I love you and you know that.'

'Well, I have to think it over about hiring you guys back.'

'Brian, now look,' Stan said. 'We know exactly what you're doing. You're trying to do yourself in. We're trying

404

to save you. We're offering you our love and our help. Now, if you want to play your bedroom game again, and destroy yourself, then go ahead.'

Brian got up and left the table.

'So he did it,' Stanley said.

Brian was released from Brotman at the end of March, and went almost directly to New York to appear at the Radio City Music Hall date of the *LA (Light Album)* tour. Released on March 16, 1979, the new album provoked outrage among Beach Boys fans. Indeed, the disco song 'Here Comes the Night' was roundly booed by the audience at the Radio City Music Hall. The criticism of that song was so great that, under pressure from the group, CBS recalled the single. Still, the *LA (Light Album)* sold over 400,000 copies worldwide, although it only managed to reach 100 on the album charts.

Back in Los Angeles, Brian stayed at the Westwood Marquis Hotel for a week, and then moved into a house in Santa Monica Canyon on Sycamore, which he rented for $1,300 a month. Before he left Brotman, a round-the-clock psychiatric nursing team of four professional aides had been arranged for him. 'There was a full-time staff,' Korthof said. 'We wrote "med notes" [reports-on-the-patient's-moods] just like in the hospital, which Jim Redman [one of the psychiatric aides] read every morning. It was very professional. It was the only arrangement outside of the hospital setting that made any sense.'

Brian's night nurse was a competent psychiatric nurse named Carolyn Williams. A warm, caring black woman with corn rows in her hair, raising three children from a former marriage, she had been one of Brian's favorite nurses while he was at Brotman. In several phone calls to Marilyn from the hospital, Brian had mentioned how fond he had become of Carolyn Williams. But no one suspected that Carolyn would soon become his girl friend. 'You know,' said Korthof, 'a guy is a guy . . . Maybe I would do the same thing . . . Little by little, I imagine, the nighttimes weren't just professional.'

Janet Lent-Coop, who was by then an officer of Brother Records, remembered the first time it dawned on the rest of the group that Brian was involved in a romantic relationship with Carolyn. 'We'd have meetings at the Brother Records office,' she said, 'and sometimes Michael would bring his girl friend. Brian was proud of his girl friend [Carolyn], and he put his arm around her during the meeting. The first time I saw it, I looked at the attorney and said, "What's going on?" Carolyn looked at me with a totally blank [expression]. Later, when I confronted her about it, she completely denied that anything was really going on. She said, "Big deal. If it makes him feel good, big deal."'

When Brian started to go out on the road again, Carolyn accompanied him, much to the mortification of the rest of the group. 'Everybody hated it,' said Korthof. 'Brian arm-in-arm with a black girl backstage. They would say, "Oh Jesus!" Al would come up to me and say, "Why does he have to put his arm around her?" But what are you going to do about two people? You can't tell them to live in a little closet. How do you tell a human being not to be with somebody else?'

Aside from the general humiliation the group felt about Brian's attachment to Carolyn Williams, they were also concerned that he would spend too much money on her – although there was no evidence that Carolyn ever took advantage of Brian financially – or even worse, marry her. The couple once went to Las Vegas together for a weekend, and the group held its breath until they came back – unmarried.

Although Carolyn Williams tried her best, life with Brian still left much to be desired. According to visitors, the house they lived in was always a mess. The floor was mottled with thousands of cigarette burns where Brian had tossed his cigarettes instead of using an ashtray. Unable to curtail his drinking, or food intake, Brian was reportedly consuming four or five steaks a day, as well as mountains of ice cream and other fattening foods. There were also rumors within the Beach Boys organization that Brian was using drugs again, in addition to the prescribed medications he was taking. He managed to find the bottle of chloral hydrate sleeping pills that had been prescribed for him and started taking them during the day. When this was discovered, Dr Baumel put Brian back in the hospital for a short stay.

Brian's renewed drug use was blamed on Dennis Wilson – indeed, Dennis had been seeing a great deal of Brian in recent months, often bringing him to visit friends in seedy neighborhoods of Venice or to various studios where they produced and wrote songs together. Sometimes Dennis would buy a huge bag of hamburgers at MacDonald's and give one to Brian for every song he worked on. Dennis might also promise Brian a gram of cocaine for every song he wrote. Dennis would lay out the entire gram of cocaine on the piano top and Brian would snort it all in one long, noisy inhalation. Fifteen minutes later he would want another.

In early March of 1982, Brian was pressured by the other Beach Boys to attend St John's Hospital in Santa Monica against Carolyn Williams's wishes. Carolyn Williams reportedly complained to a patients' legal-rights group and Brian was released in five days. Now the Beach Boys and their management were furious with her interference.

A few weeks later, on March 24, at the Lee County Airport in Fort Myers, Florida, the Beach Boys were on their way to Tampa to perform. Carolyn Williams was passing through the security check before boarding, when she was asked to open a blue denim carry-on bag as well as a black-and-brown bag. According to the booking report filed that day, security guard Charlotte Maxwell found 'a gold cigarette case which contained a razor blade, straw and a piece of clear plastic which both contained residue . . .' There was also a white piece of paper 'that contained a white substance that appeared to be a narcotic substance.' The report said that Carolyn 'grapped [sic] the white paper and deliberately emptied it out the floor.' Later, the residue proved 'positive to Cobalt Thocyanate Narcotest' as cocaine.

Carolyn insisted she was set up as a means of getting rid of her. (Intimate members of the Beach Boys' circle suspect she was right.) Carolyn spent the day and night in jail before she received an anonymous phone call warning her that she should not try to see Brian again. At one in the morning, after repeated phone calls to the Beach Boys' touring entourage, a $300 bail was paid, reportedly charged to Brian's credit card. A court date was set for April. The next day, Carolyn's arrest was widely reported in the news, and featured on 'Entertainment Tonight.' Carolyn later entered a plea of 'nolo contendere' to possession of a controlled substance. She was fined $5,000 (which Brian reportedly paid himself) and was put on probation for three years.

But Carolyn and Brian could not be kept apart once they returned to Los Angeles. Later that summer Brian asked Carolyn to move her three children and dog into a new house he had purchased at 910 Greentree in the Pacific Palisades, which Janet Lent-Coop had decorated.

By autumn, Brian's weight was 311 pounds and climbing.

<h1 style="text-align:center">4</h1>

Christine McVie's personal life was nearly destroyed by the end of 1980. She had tried, unsuccessfully, to end the relationship with Dennis several times. Each time she asked him to leave, he came back like a sheepish dog, and Christine's heart went out to him. Like Karen Lamm before her, she forgave Dennis more times than she should have, and always let him back in. But by Christmas of that year her neighbors were up in arms over the loud arguing and public scenes taking place in the street, and her own lawyers advised Christine to end the relationship. Sadly, Dennis moved out and rented his own house on Wavecrest Avenue in Venice Beach with his friend Steve Goldberg.

Stan Love was in Hawaii at this time visiting his brother Stephen. He claims he got phone calls from both Janet Lent-Coop and Carolyn Williams, telling him that Brian was in desperate straits and needed somebody to protect him from Dennis. 'Brian is out of control,' Stanley claimed Carolyn told him. Stanley learned that 'Dennis had been hanging around and he got Brian to buy maybe fifteen thousand dollars' worth of cocaine. Brian would snort up five or six grand in half an hour, and they'd have to put their hands in his mouth to stop him from swallowing his tongue.'

Stanley returned from Hawaii to see his old friend Rocky. A few nights later was Superbowl Sunday, and Stan and Rocky were celebrating on the yacht of a friend.

'We were partying,' said Stanley. 'We were on a pump.'

Rocky said, 'Stanley was going to drive me home because I was too high [to go myself] – I admit it – and [Stanley] said, "Let's go get Dennis." And I said, "Yeah, let's go cruise his pad."'

'It just happened to fall together,' Stanley said.

The two of them drove to Dennis's house and hid in the bushes outside, watching what was going on inside. According to Stan and Rocky, they could clearly see Dennis through the window, snorting coke with seven other people. Later, they followed him on a trip to the liquor store and waited for him outside. When Dennis came out of the store, they said hello and pretended they were there coincidentally, but Dennis was wary of them and went directly home.

'I said, "Let's go fucking get him . . ."' Rocky said.

When Dennis went back inside the house, a terrifying assault began. Stanley knocked down the front door with one swift kick, and he and Rocky went barreling inside. Stanley screamed, 'Freeze! We're cops!' And before anybody could move, they were on Dennis.

'We broke our hands the first couple of punches,' Rocky said. 'He doubled up, and we picked him up and dragged him through the house, beating him up for ten minutes. We let him try to run away, and then we grabbed him and threw him through a window.'

With Dennis bleeding and badly beaten, Stanley picked up the telephone, and as if he were speaking to other police officers, said, 'Okay, we've got everything under control here,' and then took the receiver and smashed it into Dennis's head.

'He knocked him twelve feet over a couch into the other room. Then we slammed his head against the bedboard twelve times,' Rocky said. 'By now the guy is

410

pleading, "Stanley, please! Stanley, please!"'

'It was one of the most brutal beatings ever,' Stanley said.

Dennis pressed charges against Stan and Rocky. They appeared in Santa Monica Superior Court on March 19, when a restraining order was placed against them. Rocky was fined $250 and Stanley $750 (although he claims that with legal fees and air fare back and forth from Hawaii his actual fine was close to $10,000). Both were put on six months' probation.

According to Rocky, when the judge handed out the fines, Dennis cried out, 'Oh no! I got beat up for two hundred and fifty dollars!'

Dennis was now on the last loop of a spiral plunge. He was unable to refuse anyone shelter or money, and the house on Wavecrest was soon filled with a collection of needy wanderers from Venice and the surrounding neighborhoods. One day Jennifer brought a friend by. She was a short, blonde teenage girl named Shawn. Dennis had heard a rumour that she was the very same illegitimate child Mike Love had fathered sixteen years before. When Dennis asked Shawn who her father was, all she would say was 'Mike.' Later, she admitted that 'Mike' was indeed Mike Love. For Dennis, now would come the ultimate revenge.

The whole pathetic thing was the child, a
beautiful child. – Bob Levine

Seventeen

1

A disgruntled CBS Records, disappointed with the sales of the previous album, expected another album as soon as possible. From November 1979 to January 1980 the Beach Boys went back to the studio to produce a new LP, *Keepin' the Summer Alive*. The group wanted Brian to return to the studios in an environment that would be comforting to him, so they decided to record the album at Western, where the earliest Beach Boys albums had been produced. According to Carl, 'Brian got hot for about three days in the studio. He was singing like a bird. All the protection he usually runs just dropped; he came out of himself. He was right there in the room.' But the productive period lasted only three days, and when the album was released, the production credit went to Bruce Johnston. By the time it was finished, over three dozen tracks had been recorded for the album. The single, 'Goin' On,' with lyrics by Mike Love, was released early in March 1980 and appeared on the charts for only three weeks. The album itself, released two weeks later, fared no better, chalking up six weeks on the *Billboard* hit list at no higher than number 76. Still, according to the terms of their contract, the group was paid $667,667 by CBS.

In 1980 there was no Beach Boys group to speak of – while the band continued to tour, they had concert dates in which Alan and Mike were the only original members present. Dennis had been kicked out of the group. Carl was busy on his own. From September to December 1980 he recorded a solo album, *Carl Wilson*, for Caribou Records, produced by James Guercio, and co-written by Jerry Schilling's wife, Myrna Smith. Although the album was distinguished by Carl's beautiful voice, which had given most of the memorable Beach Boys songs their distinctive sound, it was a commercial failure. In April 1981, Carl went on a short solo tour to help promote the album. He told one reporter, 'I was hoping my absence would encourage the guys . . . I felt that by leaving, I was in a rare position to offer them some feedback.' According to Steve Korthof, 'In 1981, Carl wasn't on the road at all with the Beach Boys. Dennis was there half the time, showing up, leaving the tours, not able to make the show. Sometimes they had only one Wilson family member onstage, and when Dennis didn't show they had nobody. Here we are trying to sell a Beach Boys show and no Wilson. It's kind of stupid. So they said, "Get Brian out here, I don't care how you do it, we need Brian on the road."'

The problem was how to do it. By now, Tom Hulett of Concerts West was managing the Beach Boys, while Jerry Schilling handled Carl Wilson's personal management. Under their guidance, an extraordinary event took place. Brian Wilson was fired by the Beach Boys on November 5, 1982, at a meeting held in their lawyers' office. Brian was presented with a letter which read, 'This is to advise you that your services as an employee of Brother Records Inc and otherwise are hereby terminated, effective immediately.' The letter added that 'this action is taken in your best interest, and is not reversible. We wish you the best

413

of health.' It was signed by Alan Jardine, Mike Love, Carl and Dennis Wilson.

Just a few weeks before, Brian had been notified that he was 'broke' and behind in his taxes by nearly $80,000, according to Rick Nelson and Janet Lent-Coop, who were now his personal business managers. Steve Korthof had also been told Brian was broke and was unable to afford Steve's salary – he was fired on October 28, 1982. Now Brian was left alone, under the total care of Carolyn Williams, who had moved her children into Brian's house.

But in truth Brian was not broke, and had not really been fired. All of this was merely a ploy to get him away from Carolyn Williams and back to Gene Landy. Suspecting some kind of plot, Brian (or somebody who could type) wrote a letter to the Bank of Beverly Hills, where his accounts were kept, and asked that all his statements, checks, and correspondence be sent to his house at 910 Greentree. The bank automatically got in touch with Rick Nelson about the letter, and Nelson told them to ignore it.

This crisis had taken six months to invent and prepare, with Gene Landy's help behind the scenes. According to Landy, Tom Hulett called him and said, 'We are worried that Brian Wilson is going to follow Elvis. We've got to do something.' He had a year or two left to live and then he would have died.

'No one thought there was hope for Brian,' Landy said, 'but four people decided to take a shot at saving him anyhow – his brother Carl; Carl's manager, Jerry Schilling; Brian's lawyer, John Branca; and the Beach Boys' manager, Tom Hulett.' According to Landy, he told them: 'There are certain conditions. I want him in a hospital first; I want to check the man out physically.'

When it was first suggested to Brian that he go back to

Landy, he refused. Asked if Brian didn't like Landy anymore, Rick Nelson said, 'That is putting it mildly. He didn't want to have anything to do with the guy.' Instead, Brian suggested that he consult with the mop-headed TV exercise guru, Richard Simmons.

In order for Landy to take Brian back, Brian had to really *want* to be treated by him again, and Brian had to make the phone call himself. Landy's position at the time was that he wasn't available to see any new patients. 'That was all part of it,' according to Rick Nelson. 'Landy masterminded the whole thing.' Said Janet Lent-Coop, 'The way to get Brian to see Landy was to tell him that he was broke and that he wouldn't be earning any money at all, from touring. He had been getting paid for not touring, and the only way for him to get that money was to see Landy. It took us six months to get ready for that meeting.'

Carolyn Williams was not thrilled with the idea of Brian going back to see Landy, and she was not party to the 'Brian is broke' ploy. 'They were willing to try and work with Carolyn,' Janet Lent-Coop said, 'but she refused to work it out because she . . . saw the handwriting on the wall. She tried to make appointments for Brian [herself] but they wouldn't let her call . . . Landy had to hear it from Brian directly.' Reportedly, Carolyn Williams attended one of the first meetings with Landy's associate, Dr Arnold Dahlke, who would assist in the new program being designed for Brian. Williams later claimed to reporters that a tape recording was secretly made of the session without her knowledge and that she found the hidden recorder and took the tape with her before she left Dahlke's office. The battle lines were clearly being drawn.

The Beach Boys felt that for Brian's own benefit they had to get him away from Carolyn Williams, so another plan was devised. In January 1983 Brian was told he needed a complete physical examination in order for Landy to treat him. He was brought to Cedars of Sinai Hospital, where, according to Landy, Brian weighed 320 pounds upon arrival and was in a chemical daze. An extensive series of tests was run, including myriad blood analyses, cardiograms, and electroencephalograms. Landy said, 'We put Brian through every test imaginable to see what food allergies he had, the levels of medication in his bloodstream. This man was on so much shit! He had forty per cent lung capacity and no liver!' Drs Murry Susser and Sol Samuels put Brian on an intravenous biomedical diet that Landy called 'heavy detox.'

Two weeks later, after the tests were completed, Brian was whisked away from the hospital on a Sunday – without Carolyn's knowledge – and taken to a rented house in Kona, Hawaii. He was accompanied by Gene Landy, his lady friend Alexandra, his associate Arnold Dahlke, and Dr Susser, who put Brian on a megavitamin treatment.

The day after Brian's arrival in Hawaii, Landy and his two associates asked him to take a walk. When Brian refused, they drove him to the beach. After a short stroll, Landy asked Brian if he wanted breakfast. Brian, who was always hungry, immediately headed back to the car, but Landy insisted they walk to a restaurant visible in the distance. 'How am I gonna get there?' Brian said. 'I can't walk that.'

'Well, we'll come back for you,' Landy said.

'You're gonna *leave* me here?' Brian asked.

'Unless you walk with us,' Landy said. And with breakfast as the lure, Brian walked.

Slowly, Landy and his crew began to reintroduce Brian to the basics of normal socialization. From table manners to relearning how to drive, Brian gradually became independent. 'When we started driving with him,' Dahlke told a reporter, 'back when he was on nine hundred calories a day, we'd give him nine hundred dollars a day in Monopoly money. If he made a mistake driving, we'd pull him over and fine him – twenty dollars for speeding, that sort of thing.'

On January 11, before he was taken to Hawaii, Brian signed a notarized letter to Carolyn Williams stating that he was leaving town on a 'retreat' and would be unable to speak with her for some time. While he was away, the letter asked, would she remove herself and her possessions from his house? Carolyn Williams was understandably hurt and angry – especially when the electricity and water were turned off in the house. Then a For Sale sign appeared on the front lawn and a moving van arrived to take all of Brian's furniture into storage. Carolyn retaliated by calling a press conference in which she displayed a telegram she claimed had been sent to her from Hawaii by Brian. The telegram read, WHY ARE OUR PHONES DISCONNECTED? PLEASE STAY HOME AND WAIT FOR ME . . . THEY FORCED ME TO COME . . . I MISS THE KIDS . . . PLEASE HELP ME GET HOME TO YOU. The press jumped on this announcement with great delight, the *Los Angeles Herald Examiner* running a headline that read, 'Brian Wilson, Please Phone Home.' *Rolling Stone* ran a column headlined, 'Was Brian Wilson Shanghaied?' In Hawaii, Brian held a press conference at the Kahala Hilton Hotel in which he told reporters, 'We are trying to get rid of her, yes, so that we can sell the house. It sure is weird.'

Later, Carolyn started a campaign against Gene Landy. She reportedly kept trying to contact Brian throughout the year, once even waiting for him outside of Landy's office. By the late winter of 1984, she would finally report

417

Landy to the Psychology Examination Committee in Sacramento, as well as the California State Psychological Association ethics committee. She accused him of violating moral and legal standards, the welfare of the consumer, and professional relationships. The results of the Association committee's findings, if any, are confidential.

By March 1983 Brian was back in Los Angeles, some forty pounds thinner. Landy moved him into one of the largest homes in Malibu colony – a seven-thousand-square-foot, six-bedroom, two-storey beach house with two kitchens and a Jacuzzi. Several aides moved in with him, including Landy's son Evan, Dahlke's son Greg, two of Greg's classmates at Sonoma State, and Evan's friend Carlos. Brian was cut off from all his old friends, including Debbie Keil; his former wife, Marilyn; and their two children.

That same March, Brian's business manager, Rick Nelson, wrote a cautionary letter to John Branca about Landy's bills. 'As of March 17th, Brian had written checks to Eugene Landy totalling $44,000 . . . Based on Landy's projections expenses will run approximately $57,000 per month, plus any other unpredictable occurrences, such as recording sessions. In addition, Brian has ongoing monthly expenses which total approximately $15,000 . . . Thus, in the nine months remaining in 1983, we will need about $650,000. This is a good $350,000–400,000 more than Brian's gross projected earnings for 1983 before taxes.' But according to Nelson's wife, Janet Lent-Coop, the money no longer mattered. 'If Landy could get Brian to produce just one hit album, it would easily be worth it.'

2

In January 1980, Brother Records Inc., under Alan Jardine's direction as corporation president, had stopped paying Stephen Love his severance fees. These fees were to have been paid under the terms of a consultancy agreement, but by 1980 relations between Stephen and the group had virtually disintegrated, except for the minimum dialogue required by Stephen's role in certain real-estate investments. When Stephen learned that his quarterly fees had been halted, he told his brother Stanley that Alan Jardine was a 'chickenshit.' Then all hell broke loose.

The multitude of lawsuits that followed is a tangled skein of yarn knotted by accusations and recriminations, bringing out the worst in all parties involved. If blood is thicker than water, then nothing is worse than bad blood between family members. Over the years, under Stephen Love's guidance, the Beach Boys had made several group investments in real estate with the help of Paul Gader, a prominent real-estate investment advisor.[1] One of these was the Spaulding Ranch, a choice piece of raw land, purchased in 1974 at a cost of $500,000 for a down payment of $250,000. The second investment was called

[1] There were sundry other real-estate investments made by the Lefkowitz office, including the Saple property, an industrial site with three buildings, which cost the boys $340,000; the Lisal properties, a ninety-one-thousand-square-foot office building leased to Liberty Savings and Loan, purchased for $2,150,000; and the Anaclara property, which was a North American Aviation plant in Anaheim and a Lockheed plant in Sunnyvale, acquired for a $100,000 down payment against a purchase price of $600,000.

419

Modal, purchased in October 1974. Its asset was a profitable Motel 6, operating in Mesquite, Texas. The purchase price was $762,000 with a down payment of $167,000. An income-producing property, Modal was a self-liquidating deal in which the income from the lease paid for the mortgage with a net cash flow. At the end of twenty years the mortgage would be completely paid off. The third investment, called the South Kona Land Company deal, involved a thirty-acre piece of property on the island of Hawaii. Only a $65,000 investment, the South Kona property was a 'symbolic' acquisition allowing the five Beach Boys to own a piece of Hawaiian real estate. The investment was viewed as an introduction to Hawaii, where, it was presumed, the group would retire in later years.

In addition, Mike Love had bought a two-acre site in Santa Barbara at 101 Mesa Lane. There was one acre in front, overlooking the ocean, where Mike lived, and one in the rear, which was undeveloped. Allegedly, Mike made a deal with Stephen to develop the 'rear five,' as it was called. Paul Gader arranged for mortgage and construction financing and Stephen oversaw the building of five houses on the land. In return he expected 15 per cent of the equity. Reportedly, Stephen signed the limited-partnership agreement in December 1976 and Janet Lent-Coop sent it to Mike's attorney in Santa Barbara, but the deal was never recorded. These circumstances are hotly disputed by both sides.

The Beach Boys didn't realize that before they had stopped sending Stephen Love his settlement checks, he had already sold the Spaulding Ranch for $1.25 million, a deal in which he was a general as well as limited partner and responsible for the management of the property. The Beach Boys finally learned of this sale in March 1980, a month after Stephen started to sue Brother Records Inc for breach of contract in Los Angeles Superior Court. Reportedly, Stephen had sold Spaulding without telling them because he became paranoid about the group and felt they might try to avoid paying him his 15 per cent of Spaulding. To make matters even more complicated, Stephen had given Stan Love a priority payment of $175,000 from the sale of Spaulding. Marilyn and Brian Wilson joined the other Beach Boys in a suit against Stephen and Stanley.

The crux of Brian and Marilyn's lawsuit was an alleged 'oral agreement' between Brian and Stanley. Stanley claimed that Brian had told him that if he was no longer in Brian's employment he could be 'cashed out' of his investment in Spaulding. Marilyn and Brian both gave depositions countering this claim, but at Brian's deposition, face-to-face with Stephen and Stanley Love, Brian became so frightened he said 'yes, yes' to almost every question he was asked. In a subsequent declaration supporting a request to appoint a court receiver, which Brian's attorney prepared for him, Brian claimed: 'At the time of the taking of my deposition in this matter I was emotionally upset . . . Further, the presence of Stephen Love and Stanley Love at the deposition was intimidating to me. I find Stanley Love physically intimidating and am physically afraid of him.' He went on to say that 'I have no recollection of any agreement having been made with either Stephen Love or Stanley Love that if Stanley Love's employment with me was terminated he would be entitled to take his money out of any limited partnership investments . . .'

Stephen and Stanley Love's depositions included a series of very personal allegations against Brian and Marilyn Wilson. Stephen Love's depositions were poten-

421

tially so harmful that they were sealed by the court in an unusual move for the protection of minors.

Marilyn struck back in court papers filed February 11, 1982, saying that Brian was 'incapable of caring for himself in any sort of a financial or business sense' and that 'it is ridiculous for either Stephen Love or Stanley Love to contend that they have discussed these matters with him and he has agreed to them. He is not capable of responsibly agreeing or disagreeing about such matters.'

When Stanley Love was asked why the depositions and claims became so personal, he said, 'Because we thought we would say the heaviest shit possible and they would wake up and say, "Whoa! Let's not get into that." It didn't work.'

As of this writing, the lawsuit has not been resolved, but the parties are reportedly working toward a settlement.

The next round of lawsuits started when Mike Love took five second mortgages out on 101 Mesa Lane totaling $600,000, without Stephen's awareness. Mike's contention was that Stephen was not obligated to know about this transaction, because when Stephen tried to point to his partnership agreements as proof that he deserved 15 per cent of the mortgages, he learned that the agreement was never recorded. In 1980 Stephen filed suit. Michael in turn sued Stephen over the sale of the Hawaiian property they owned together. Throughout the next four years hundreds of thousands of dollars would be spent on lawyers, which contributed to Mike Love's eventual personal bankruptcy. As of this writing the lawsuits are not settled.

On October 8, 1981, Mike realized a lifelong dream. His solo album, *Looking Back with Love*, was released on the Boardwalk label. Produced by Curt Becher, and recorded on a mobile unit at Mike's Santa Barbara estate, the album was mostly ignored by critics, as well as by fans.

By now Mike was divorcing his fifth wife. In the late seventies he had married Sue Oliver Damon, a pretty Hawaiian woman in her mid-thirties, in a quiet ceremony in a Lake Tahoe chapel. They were divorced two years later. He then had an affair with a pretty Korean girl, Sumako Kelley, whom Mike announced as the fifth Mrs Love. But instead, he met and fell in love with Cathy Linda Martinez and married her in 1981 at his Santa Barbara home in a ceremony performed by disc jockey Wolfman Jack, who is an ordained minister. Mike and Cathy had a son together, Michael Edward Love II. Cathy was gone in a little over a year. Mike filed in Reno, Nevada, under Nevada's non-community property law. Cathy moved into Mike's vacation home in Incline Village, Nevada.

The lawsuits, divorces, and Mike's extravagant lifestyle toppled him financially. In 1983 he filed for a Chapter 11 bankruptcy in the Central District Court of California. Among other debts Mike claimed $48,000 in taxes owed to the California State Franchise Tax Board; a $100,000 loan secured against his properties in Santa Barbara and Incline Village; and at least fifteen loans from various banks. Total debt to creditors holding security was $2,854,767. In all there were over a hundred unsecured creditors, including exterminators, his answering service, his dentist (to whom he owed $28), and a telephone bill for $1.16 from Nevada Bell. With the addition of several hundred thousand dollars in legal fees owed for divorces and sundry lawsuits, the grand total came to $2,462,737.80 for unsecured debts to creditors.

In court papers Mike claimed immediate debts payable

totalling $163,671.77. In a declaration by Pamela An
Caughill, his bookkeeper since August 1982, she stated
'Mr Love has financed his lifestyle by extensive borrow
ing. All of the properties he owns are fully mortgaged
and as a result, he has substantial monthly obligation
... His monthly loan obligations presently tota
$22,765.59 . . . [and] his total monthly obligations are i
excess of $50,000.' Pamela Caughill said, 'Mr Love
present financial circumstances are, to say the very leas
desperate.'

3

On April 5, 1983, the Beach Boys got an unexpecte
boost from the most unusual quarter. Then Secretary c
the Interior James Watt announced that the Beach Boy
would not be invited to play the Mall on Independenc
Day that year because they attracted 'the wrong element.
He added, 'We're not going to encourage drug abuse an
alcoholism as was done in years past.' A wave of nationa
sentiment and sympathy arose, from such supporters a
Beach Boys fans and fellow Californians Nancy an
Ronald Reagan. Watt was called to Reagan's office
lectured about the national treasure known as the Beach
Boys, and presented with a cast plaster foot with a hol
shot in it to symbolize his gaffe. On July 4, the Beach
Boys played Atlantic City instead while Las Vegas singe
and personality Wayne Newton graced the Washingto
concert with his presence. On July 17 the Beach Boy
were invited to the White House, where they posed fo
pictures with the president and his wife. Dennis stood i
the background, pale and bloated from drugs and alcohol

looking the worst the public had ever seen him.

Dennis's peculiar relationship with Shawn Love had blossomed into a romance. Shawn had moved into Dennis's little house on Wavecrest Avenue, a block from the ocean in Venice. There were so many other people staying in the house (with Dennis paying the bills) that at first it wasn't clear what was happening with Shawn. Hemmed in by the dozens of people crashing at his house, Dennis moved into a tiny broom-storage closet underneath the stairs that led to the second floor – there was hardly enough space for Dennis himself in the room, let alone Shawn.

According to Bob Levine, 'Dennis was thinking with his cock. He was an easy mark. When it came to young girls, he was very vulnerable. If there was one thing that acted as a drug on Dennis, it was young sex.[2] Shawn didn't care about Dennis. She really didn't. She was only trying to get into a situation where she could have close proximity to her father. All she wanted was for Mike Love to look at her and say, "My daughter."'

But Mike Love did not say, 'My daughter.' When Dennis first brought Shawn to a Beach Boys concert, Mike reportedly said, 'No daughter of mine takes drugs.'

By spring of 1982 Shawn was visibly and unmistakably pregnant, and she and Dennis moved into their own rented house in Trancas Beach, Malibu. On September 3, 1982, Shawn and Dennis had a son, Gage Dennis Wilson. Dennis, on tour in Texas with the group, took a private jet home to be with Shawn. But when he arrived in Los Angeles, he wasn't sure he wanted to see her. Instead, he called Karen Lamm. Once free of Dennis, Karen had completely restructured her life. Her career, which had

---

[2] Shawn Love refused to be interviewed for this book.

floundered under the strain and distraction of their relationship, was once again successful. She was exercising daily and neither drank nor did drugs. When Dennis called Karen on the night Gage was born, he asked if he could come see her.

'Absolutely not,' Karen told him. 'You belong at the hospital with your wife and son.'

Once Dennis laid eyes on the boy, his whole world began to revolve around Gage. He talked about him to anyone who would listen and slept with the baby next to him at night. But when the call of the wild sounded, Dennis could easily desert the infant and its mother. On July 28, 1983, he married Shawn for Gage's sake, but marriage only intensified the tension between the couple. Shawn, like all of Dennis's wives before her, could not abide his impossible behavior, and she was not going to be the one to tame him. Dennis complained to his friends that the marriage had been a mistake and almost immediately began to talk about getting a divorce. Less than four months married, he filed for one.

Shortly afterward, he called Karen Lamm again and asked her to come visit him in the Trancas house he was renting. Dennis's friend John Hanlon drove Karen out to the beach, and at first she wasn't even sure she recognized the man who answered the door. Dennis had shaved his beard and was bloated and gray. His face was jowly and his eyes lined and tired.

'Look at you!' Karen cried. 'What happened to all your muscles?'

'I have muscles,' Dennis said, smiling sadly. He pounded himself on the stomach to show her how tough he was. 'I run every day.'

'Where to? The local bar and back?'

Dennis told Karen he had kicked cocaine and would

soon be off the booze, but only a few minutes later he produced a vial of white powder and asked Karen to join him in a few snorts. Karen shook her head no, and disappointed, but resigned, soon left.

Shawn moved into the Santa Monica Bay Inn with Gage. That November, when the lease at Dennis's Trancas Beach house was up, he was homeless. Said Bob Levine, 'The concept we agreed to was that he go [to a detoxification program], spend a month, six weeks there, and when he came back, we'd find him a place.'

But Dennis never actually went to detoxify; every attempt he made was aborted for one reason or another. By autumn of 1983 he was homeless and disconsolate, staying wherever he fell asleep at night – at the homes of friends, at George Hormel's house, or with a new girl, Coleen 'Crystal' McGovern. He would go into bars, broke, and ask strangers to buy him drinks. 'I'm Dennis Wilson of the Beach Boys!' he would say, and more often than not, some stranger, remembering the music that had orchestrated his childhood, would buy him what he wanted.

All Dennis thought about was Gage, and – oddly enough – Murry. 'The last six months of his life Murry was dominant,' Bob Levine said, '. . . and he was totally enraptured by the child.' By late November, Dennis had hit rock bottom and on his thirty-ninth birthday, December 4, he discovered Shawn asleep in her room at the Bay Inn with two friends and went berserk. A final attempt to detoxify that began at St John's Hospital in Santa Monica on December 23, ended a day later when he was told that Shawn and Gage were going to be evicted from the Santa Monica Bay Inn for nonpayment of rent. Late Christmas night, one of Shawn's boyfriends beat Dennis up over a

427

disagreement about whether he could use the telephone in the hotel room.

Three days later, Dennis went diving from his friend Bill Oster's boat to find the lost treasures of better days.

4

Bill Oster stood on the deck waiting for Dennis to reemerge from the cold waters of Marina Del Rey. 'Pretty soon I saw him,' Oster said. 'He came up almost to the surface but he stayed about two feet underneath it and swam to near where my rowboat was tied up. He was up for maybe fifteen seconds and then he slipped straight down from there. I said, "I wonder where he's going? Is he going to come up the other side of the dock?" I had a few puffs on my cigarette and didn't see him or hear him, and I wondered where he was. I made some noise stomping on the deck, trying to flush him out, but I got no response. All that happened was the girls came up from the boat and said, "Where's Dennis?" I said, "I don't know where he is." At that point we started looking all around. I came around the other side of the boat and started looking under all the cocks in the air spaces. After a few minutes of this we started getting panicky.'

Oster spotted a Harbor Patrol boat nearby and flagged them in. 'We told them the story, and they said, "Well, are you sure he didn't get off the dock and go up to the bar or to somebody's house or sneak off?"' Oster said he didn't think so, and one of the harbor patrolmen took off his shirt and jumped in the water to look around. Oster and the girls started calling all over the marina, to the local bars and Aggie's Chris Craft. They enlisted the help of anyone they could find to search all the bars of the marina, hoping to find Dennis there.

They found Dennis forty-five minutes later. A four-man dragoon located his body on the muddy floor of the marina, directly underneath the spot where the *Harmony* had been berthed. Oster, his girlfriend Brenda, and Crystal stood on the dock and wept.

One by one the phone calls were made. Carl, Mike Love, Alan Jardine, Audree, the ex-wives, Shawn. But before everyone could be informed personally, the news media descended on Marina Del Rey, and the photographs of Dennis in a bodybag being carried away to the city morgue were flashed all around the nation on the eleven o'clock news.

At Brian's house in Malibu one of Landy's assistants told Brian there was a message for him on his answering machine. It was Jerry Schilling. When Brian called Schilling back, he said, 'I'm sorry to have to tell you that Dennis drowned.'

'I felt real *strange*,' Brian said. 'It's a weird feeling when you hear about a death in the family, a weird trip. It's not something you can really talk about or describe. I got tears after about a half-hour. Then I saw it on the news and thought, Oh God, there he is, lying there dead. I was blown out by the whole idea that he *drowned*, although I just let it lay; I didn't fuck with it. I didn't think too much about it. I let it lay . . . It pissed me off when he drowned because I felt I wasn't just losing a brother. I was losing a friend, and that compounded it even more.'

A meeting was called at Audree's house, attended by Dennis's three former wives – Carol, Barbara, and Karen – and his teenage widow, Shawn, for whom Carl had arranged a limousine. The group had only conversed for

429

a few minutes when it became clear that only one person had any say over what would happen at this point – Shawn. Shawn was legally Dennis's widow, because their divorce had not yet been final at the time of his death, and hers was the ultimate word.

Carl Wilson at first thought Dennis would be buried in a crypt next to Murry, but Shawn had decided that Dennis was to be buried at sea. When Dennis's sons Michael and Carl heard this, they were aghast. 'Do you mean Daddy's going to be thrown in the ocean?' they asked their mother. All of Dennis's former wives disagreed with the idea of a burial at sea, but legally there could be no dispute. Carl told Karen Lamm, 'It's Shawn's duty now, Karen, and I have to stand behind Shawn.'

The family decided on a small, quiet memorial service to be held at Inglewood Cemetery. Karen asked Shawn's permission to read from I Corinthians 13, and after some consideration Shawn acquiesced. But a half-hour before the service, Karen received a phone call from Shawn saying that she and Dennis's daughter Jennifer would read the Bible segment instead: 'Somebody closer to Dennis should read it.' Next, the question was raised as to what kind of music should be played. Someone suggested religious music, but Shawn objected, saying that the Police song 'Every Breath You Take' was Dennis's favorite song. The rest were dismayed at the idea of playing this current popular favorite at the funeral of a man to whom music meant so much. Karen suggested that 'Farewell My Friend' from Dennis's solo album would be more appropriate, and Shawn decided to consider the suggestion. Someone asked that Shawn listen to it right then, and the album was put on the stereo at Audree's house. Up until that moment everyone had remained composed, but when Dennis's voice came over the speakers, they all burst into tears.

That night, unable to sleep, Karen prayed for guidance, seeking to understand why Dennis's life had to end as it had. After she finally fell asleep, she had a dream. She and Dennis were sailing on the *Harmony* out in the open sea, and he turned to her and said, 'If I ever die, I want to be buried right here, because when you look out at the ocean I want you to think of me.' Karen called Barbara early the next morning and told her. Together, they encouraged Shawn to go ahead with her plan. However, it turned out that there was a federal law prohibiting burial at sea. A personal plea was made to President Reagan for special permission, which was granted. Said Karen Lamm disgustedly, 'He was put in a bodybag and dumped in the ocean.'

When the coroner's report on Dennis's death was made public, it was disclosed that the alcohol level in Dennis's blood was .26, twice that of legal impairment for driving. His liver was enlarged, there was a narrowing of the coronary artery, and there were traces of Valium and cocaine in his tissues. Deputy Medical Examiner J. Lawrence Cogan reported that the drugs and alcohol 'may have . . . bearing [on his death because] these drugs are associated with impairment of judgment of physical activity.' Even Dennis's doctor at St John's Hospital told a reporter, 'I'm not an expert on drowning . . . but sixty-five per cent to seventy-five per cent of drownings are drug-related . . . when you've had a couple of drinks and go in the water, your judgment's altered.'

Less than a year before, Bob Levine had obtained a new, $1 million insurance policy for Dennis, which named his four children and Shawn as beneficiaries. Previously, Dennis had a policy for only $250,000, which was in danger of cancellation because of erratic payments. Levine had wisely abandoned that policy and obtained the new one – Dennis passed the examination in Bob Levine's office. But when the results of the coroner's report were made public, the Transamerica Occidental Insurance Company refused to pay for Dennis's life-insurance policy, claiming his death was not an accident but attributable to his misuse of alcohol and drugs.

Barbara and Carol decided to settle with the insurance company for a reported forty cents on the dollar, but Shawn lodged a $20 million suit against the company for refusing to pay her and Gage full benefits. The suit asked for $400,000, which Shawn felt she was owed under the life-insurance policy; $50,000 in general damages; and $20 million in punitive damages. To complicate matters for them, Dennis's last will, written in March 1977 after the dissolution of his first marriage to Karen, stated that while no future wives would share in his estate, 'any other child of mine who may hereafter be born' would become a beneficiary. Shawn started a separate suit to share in Dennis's estate. Eventually, Los Angeles Superior Court Judge Billy Mills ruled that two-year-old Gage should be an heir to Dennis's estimated $2 million estate. Attorney Allan Cutrow, representing Dennis's estate, did not object to having Gage added as an heir, but pointed out that Dennis's will specifically excluded future spouses.

In the interim, Shawn was hospitalized in the summer of 1984 for what her lawyer termed 'inoperable stomach cancer.' After exploratory surgery and extensive radiation therapy she has apparently recovered. She told the press at the time, 'My life has been the pits since Dennis died. It's a real tragedy.'

5

In November 1982 Mike became engaged to Sharon Lee, a pretty seventeen-year-old Chinese girl. In 1985 his charitable organization, the Love Foundation, donated $5,000 to the committee to have rock lyrics rated for listener acceptability. He recently moved to Beverly Hills. He remains a devout practitioner of Transcendental Meditation, the premier spokesman and showman of the Beach Boys.

Carl Wilson, divorced from Annie, lives in Colorado with his fiancée, Gina Martin, daughter of singer Dean Martin.

Alan Jardine divorced his wife Lynda and married fellow horse breeder Mary Ann. He lives in Big Sur, California.

Marilyn Wilson and her two daughters live in a large home in Encino, California. Along with her cousin Ginger and sister Diane, they are pursuing singing careers as the Honeys. Carnie and Wendy had recently been allowed to meet with their father in an attempt to reunite them under Gene Landy's auspices.

Stephen Love lives in Hawaii, where he surfs every day.

Stanley Love lives on the Pacific Palisades and is still close friends with Rocky Pamplin.

Karen Lamm lives alone on the Marina peninsula and is pursuing a successful acting career.

Carol Wilson is remarried to movie producer Jeffrey Bloome.

Barbara Wilson is raising Dennis's sons Carl and

Michael, and is studying to be a psychologist.

Audree Wilson lives with her grandson, Jonah, Carl's son, in a house in the Hollywood Hills.

Brian Wilson lives in a six-bedroom beach house in the Malibu colony along with a full-time staff working for Gene Landy. He is relatively slim and considerably happier than ever before in his life. He jogs five miles a day, cooks some of his own meals, and eschews drugs. Although the *Los Angeles Times* reported he calls Landy 'Napoleon,' the treatment seems to be working for him. 'Dr Landy taught me things that I didn't know,' he said recently. 'He taught me that a glass or two of wine every other night is just as good as actually taking drugs. You can carry on a good conversation and appreciate the conversation. And he taught me things like manners. I never realized that I used to rush through my meals. He's taught me to eat slower and enjoy them! God, I could never mention all the things he's taught me.' Brian and the entire staff wear telephone beepers around their waists to remain in constant contact with Gene Landy, who lives in a house several miles down the coast.

The Beach Boys' most recent album for CBS was released in summer of 1985. Called simply *The Beach Boys*, it was produced by Culture Club producer Steve Levine. While the album was in production, Gene Landy was interviewed for *California* magazine. When asked if he would consider contributing lyrics to the album, Landy replied, 'Listen, all the Beach Boys make some contribution, and I'm practically a member of the band . . . Brian's got the talent to make the music . . . He's the creator. The other band members are just performers. So I'm the one who's making the album.'[3]

---

[3] Gene Landy is credited with contributing the lyrics to three songs on the album.

In 1985, the group was dropped by CBS Records when their contract ran out.

The Beach Boys continue as a number-one concert attraction, maintaining a $50,000-a-night guarantee. They are one of the most popular live entertainment acts in the world. For millions of fans, they are, and will always be, the essence of the California dream.

Index

436

441